T0319576

AMERICAN RHÔNE

THE PUBLISHER GRATEFULLY ACKNOWLEDGES THE GENEROUS
SUPPORT OF THE AHMANSON FOUNDATION HUMANITIES
ENDOWMENT FUND OF THE UNIVERSITY OF CALIFORNIA PRESS
FOUNDATION.

AMERICAN RHÔNE

*How Maverick Winemakers Changed
the Way Americans Drink*

Patrick J. Comiskey

UNIVERSITY OF CALIFORNIA PRESS

University of California Press, one of the most distinguished university presses in the United States, enriches lives around the world by advancing scholarship in the humanities, social sciences, and natural sciences. Its activities are supported by the UC Press Foundation and by philanthropic contributions from individuals and institutions. For more information, visit www.ucpress.edu.

University of California Press
Oakland, California

© 2016 by Patrick J. Comiskey

Library of Congress Cataloging-in-Publication Data
Names: Comiskey, Patrick J., 1960– author.
Title: American Rhône : how maverick winemakers changed the way
     Americans drink / Patrick J. Comiskey.
Description: Oakland, California : University of California Press, [2016] |
     Includes index.
Identifiers: LCCN 2016009427 (print) | LCCN 2016011006 (ebook)
ISBN 978-0-520-25666-8 (book/cloth : alk. paper)
ISBN 978-0-520-96514-0 (ebook)
Subjects: LCSH: Wine and wine making—History. | Wine and wine
     making—California. | Syrah (Wine) | Wine and wine making—Rhône
     River Valley (Switzerland and France) Classification: LCC TP548 .C646
     2016 (print) | LCC TP548 (ebook) | DDC 338.4/7663209794—dc23
LC record available at http://lccn.loc.gov/2016009427

Manufactured in the United States of America

25 24 23 22 21 20 19 18 17 16
10 9 8 7 6 5 4 3 2 1

For Laura

CONTENTS

Figures gathered after page 138.

ACKNOWLEDGMENTS

This book could not have been written without the generosity and patience of the staff at the University of California Press, especially Blake Edgar. I was greatly aided by several important wine professionals, outside of those who inhabit these pages. To Charles Sullivan, the California wine industry's most treasured historian, I owe a great debt, as well as research librarian Axel Borg at the University of California, Davis. John Gay, Stan Hock, Leon Sobon, John Livingstone-Learmonth, John Buechsenstein, Deborah Golino, Tom Hill, Carole Meredith, Andrew Walker, and Darrell Corti were all careful readers and advisors, steering me straight when I got too far afield. I also want to thank the editorial staff of *Wine & Spirits Magazine,* especially Josh Greene, Tara Q. Thomas, Wolfgang Weber, and Luke Sykora, who supported me in the years it took to complete this book; I became a better writer in their company.

INTRODUCTION

I came to wine by accident, by way of my writing and not my palate, with as much an ear for stories as any innate talent with the stuff. But the more attention I paid to it, the more I was attracted not just to the stories but to the flavors and the soft intoxication of this beverage, its allure, its elusive qualities, and the rich metaphorical terrain it could inspire.

My wine education begins on Martha's Vineyard in 1993, at a restaurant in one of the five towns that prohibits the sale of alcohol. There well-heeled denizens of nearby West Chop, including Mike Wallace, Arthur Liman, Art Buchwald, and William and Rose Styron, could uncork their vast stocks of older Bordeaux and Burgundy for a tiny corkage fee, and there they offered me tastes of their Lafons, Latours, and LaFlaives—a gesture repeated just enough times to discombobulate me. Something about this stuff was clearly and uncommonly rare, complex, and disorienting.

The following year I moved to San Francisco, where I took a job at a new restaurant called Forty-Two Degrees, owned by chef Jim Moffat. The name referred to the Mediterranean latitude, with the kitchen taking its inspiration from Marseille and Bandol, Siena and Pisa, Rome, the Greek Islands, Barcelona, the Costa Brava, and Portugal. It quickly became one of San Francisco's most popular restaurants.

The dining scene was already becoming a central part of the city's cultural zeitgeist, a sport and a pastime, a stand-in for theater, for nightlife, for sex—and wine often provided the lubrication, especially with the state's burgeoning wine regions just an hour away. Almost from the start our wine focus was southern France, especially Provence, Languedoc, and the southern Rhône, as well as a small well-chosen group of Californians emulating the flavors from those places.

It turns out I had a modest palate. I could distinguish the flavors in a wine and take an honest stab at describing its texture and its lift, and I could unfailingly wax poetic about its deliciousness. I had enthusiasm mostly, but as a writer I had an additional gift that my fellow servers didn't: a vocabulary, a facility with metaphor, and more than anything, an ability to describe how the wines made me feel.

Pretty soon wine became a new and thrilling metaphorical terrain, a chance for me to rehearse the story lines and contours of this newfound passion. Before long, every time a bottle was opened at the lineup preceding service, the staff would look to me for the words for what they were tasting. Eventually, I was hired to direct the wine program.

Forty-Two Degrees received glowing reviews from local critics and quickly vaulted to the national stage. In 1996, Chef Moffat was named one of the country's Top Ten New American Chefs by *Food & Wine Magazine,* and suddenly the world was descending upon us. Not least, in the wine trade ours became an A-list account, which meant I could get nearly anything I wanted from wine sellers.

Mostly this meant adhering to the latitudinal constraint implied by the restaurant's name. The forty-second parallel put us in line with Roussillon, Rioja, Priorat, Barolo, Montalcino, and the Piedmont, but the heart of the list remained the Rhône Valley and its American adherents: Bonny Doon, Sean Thackrey, Alban, Qupé, Edmunds St. John, Jade Mountain, Tablas Creek, Beckmen, and Sine Qua Non. We poured John Alban's Central Coast Viognier by the glass across nine vintages without a break, longer at the time than any other restaurant in the country.

In 1997, we reached out to this pool of winemaking talent to help with a tasting series I curated. John Alban, Randall Grahm, Sean Thackrey, Steve Edmunds, and Bob and Louisa Sawyer Lindquist all poured their wines in the restaurant's quiet, secluded patio, paired with tapas from the kitchen.

One such evening I'm sitting on the patio. It's moments before I'm to introduce Sean Thackrey, an American Rhône-affiliate who lives in a small Marin beach community called Bolinas, where he makes wine in a gimcrack winery near the vast lagoon. I'm pre-tasting Thackrey's wines, Pleiades, Taurus, Andromeda, and the red wine he calls Orion, the wine that made his reputation. Orion is where I lose my bearings entirely.

Orion is ostensibly Syrah, made from an old vineyard in Yountville. The wine smells of licorice and smoke and eucalyptus and bay laurel, pepper and earth. There's fruit I'm sure, but I don't remember the sort. Instead I remember a vinousness that borders on the otherworldly, as if you could identify the veins of earth that the vines' roots had deciphered and delivered to the cluster, pots of herbs, dried flowers, strange tinctures, fragrances so exotic I start thinking of it more as a potion than a wine. Tasked with introducing the winemaker, my mind is crammed with so many muddled associations and thoughts that I find I have absolutely nothing to say.

Thackrey tells the story of finding the vineyard and working with its remarkable grower, Arthur Schmidt. Schmidt received Syrah budwood some time in the sixties (it's not clear when) from Napa's winemaker monk Brother Timothy, who made the wines at Christian Brothers during their heyday. Brother Timothy had planted Syrah on a bad patch of ground near the Napa River, where it grew poorly; with the fruit from this same vineyard Joseph Phelps made the country's first modern Syrah in 1974.

Timothy never liked the variety, so it's a mystery as to why he'd sell cuttings. Schmidt grafted them onto old, established roots, interplanted among other vines; each Syrah vine was tied off with a red ribbon so that Schmidt and Thackrey could identify which plant to pick. Something about this expressive variety, given the chance to tap deeply into Napa's alluvial secrets, gives the fruit an enigmatic depth of flavor, which Thackrey merely channels for five memorable vintages, getting out of its way as best he can. Schmidt eventually sold the property to the Swanson family, creators of the American TV Dinner, who tore up the vines to plant Merlot. Says Thackrey, without vines to tend Schmidt was dead within months.

When we taste it, there is this awkward silence that seems to go on for several minutes, as everyone tries to make sense of what they're tasting, but like many a great wine, this one simply keeps eluding us, slipping through the safety net of what we've come to expect from American wine. It's my job to break the silence, and so partly to give us something to hold onto, I stand up and look at the group of tasters before me, turn back to stare in my glass and say, "Not only is this a great wine, this is a *weird* wine."

I suspect many of you reading this have had similar epiphanies, but there's something about your first sip of great Syrah that stands out, when you first encounter its wild, febrile magnetism, the heady disorientation in its inky, murky, smoky depths—it is a moment, in other words, when you realize that your love of wine need not be a chocolate-and-vanilla experience. For this very reason, the American Rhône wine movement is more than just a movement; it's the moment when many of us realized that American wine did not have to be defined by Chardonnay, Cabernet, and Merlot, that it could have breadth, dimensionality, an expanse of styles, and that it could be as quirky and singular and subversive as Orion.

For those who love American wine, American Rhônes are the first avenue out of the ordinary and into the realm of the odd and the extracurricular. This is the cultural landscape producers of the American Rhône occupied for a critical period of American wine history, roughly 1988 to 2005, when greatness and weirdness were routinely conjoined, where wine's capacity for seriousness and snobbery was once and for all disrupted.

For myself, this curious commingling of great and weird in Thackrey's Orion seemed like a lens through which I could see my future as a writer on this subject, that wine's capacity to inspire and confound would be a topic in its own right, that like any other art form, it could take you out of yourself into another altogether unfamiliar realm. When I became a wine writer, I felt duty-bound to bring people closer to these experiences. A half-dozen years later, when I was approached to write this book, I was reminded that the American Rhône had taken me there.

The market for these wines is massive now, and multifarious, and while some are great, most are no longer weird. Like many commercial products, their production volume has resulted in a "great middle" of wines that please but don't challenge. Still, the wines of the American Rhône overdeliver pleasure in a way that few categories can match. They remain prized for their charm, their hedonism, their wildness: this is their story.

PART I

PRELUDES AND ANTECEDENTS

1

THE SIXTIES, HEADWATERS OF THE AMERICAN RHÔNE

In a sense, it all begins with the sixties. The sixties give us all permission.

Before the decade of the sixties, American culture is narrowly defined, restricted by social convention, a fairly rigid Judeo-Christian moral framework, a troubled economic history. Personal expression has been underdeveloped or effectively suppressed for close to forty years, laid low by the Great Depression and by the obligations of the Second World War, after which the country clings to safe cultural models for a decade—notwithstanding incursions of fear brought on by a new nuclear reality. Americans do nurse a Bohemian culture, but it is largely a nocturnal phenomenon, limited to coffeehouses and basement stages.

In the sixties, the doors are pried open, American culture embraces possibility. Conformist models are debunked and devalued. Young people get restless, and demands for freedom of expression push into the mainstream, spurred on by student activism, opposition to the Vietnam War, the Civil Rights movement, the environmental movement, the human potential movement, feminism, and free love sentiments—all contributing to a new spirit of permissiveness, the sense that anything is possible. Psychedelic drugs and marijuana send shock waves through the population, and whether or not you partake of such substances, you can hardly avoid their influence on the culture at large. Indeed much of what was once considered deviant, subversive, or dangerous is now actively embraced.

With the seventies, alternative lifestyles beget alternative livelihoods. By the end of the decade an entire subeconomy supporting the counterculture has emerged, and as the counterculture expands, so do businesses to support it. A generation of young laborers questions the wisdom of following their fathers into conventional commerce. They have no interest in a professional life that involves suits and ties or stultifying commutes to drab suburban centers. They want something else.

It is the era where college professors walk away from tenured positions to start organic farms, where careers in medicine are abandoned to pursue vineyard planting, where big fortunes are made selling high fidelity stereo equipment, and small ones selling hand-made purses—parlayed into the business of importing wine.

As American culture opens up to new possibilities, so do the things one can do in it. In California, one of those things is to make wine.

If there ever was a hotbed for American counterculture, it was California, particularly the communities of San Francisco and Berkeley. San Francisco might be seen as the source of many of the social changes in the state, but Berkeley provided the intellectual frame-work. Berkeley was home to a flagship university, home to the brightest young people in the country's most progressive state. If the sixties fomented change in this country, California was its engine, and Berkeley was its brain trust.

Visit Berkeley today, and past and present mingle on practically every block. Many of the city's more iconic institutions got their start in the sixties, whose spirit still permeates the culture. It is a place where revolution took root, settled, institutionalized, and morphed into manageable expressions—where radicalism was transformed into more personal revolutions, where the impetus for changing the world found creative, entrepreneurial, and commercial expression. And of all of these transformations, few were more enduring and vital than those which involved eating and drinking. These changes too had roots in revolutionary fervor. During the early sixties the food industry had become industrialized to such an extent that conventional food was no longer recognizable as food. It was the era that gave rise to the TV dinner, to Tater Tots and Tang, to frozen pizza and Space Food Sticks. Industrial farming techniques allowed the country's productivity to skyrocket through the use of herbicides, pesticides, and fungicides, touted as "better living" through chemicals. Activists rallied people against these practices, and they got practical them-selves: coops sprung up in and around campuses, supermarkets were disdained in favor of local produce markets emphasizing the fresh, wholesome, and natural. The word "organic" entered the lexicon; though as a marketing device the term suffered in the early years, with less than pristine application, the notion itself came of age in this era.

Revolutions in food and wine culture lagged slightly behind the cultural revolution, but not by much. Part of the hippie ethos included an active mythologizing of country living, a back-to-the-land appreciation at once romantic and liberating. Communes were commonplace, and many attempted to become sustainable by growing crops—organically of course. Back-to-the-land movements changed the way we looked at food.

With an expansion of cultural consciousness came an expansion of the possibilities in food and wine, so that by the time the seventies arrive, the climate is right for a series of seminal events that, taken together, become the antecedents of the American Rhône wine movement.

With protests and activism come community, and communities need to eat. One of the students on hand to feed and support the protesters in Berkeley was Alice Waters, a student of French culture who grew up in Chatham, New Jersey, and moved to Van Nuys, California with her family in 1961.[1] After studying at the University of California, Santa Barbara, Waters completed her degree at Berkeley and immediately fell in with student activists, following or supporting protests throughout the Bay Area. In 1966 Waters moved in with a young intellectual and artist named David Goines, who was actively involved in the free-speech movement. Waters couldn't help but notice with some alarm that the revolution was being fueled on peanut butter sandwiches and canned soup—institutional, industrial, non-nutritional foods.

Alice Waters believed in food. Just after arriving in Berkeley in 1965, Waters had taken a trip to France, eating her way across the country and tasting food harvested or collected just hours, or moments, before being delivered to the table. There were several seminal meals during this trip, but Waters has consistently referred to a meal in Brittany as her epiphany. It began simply enough, a plate of melon with cured ham, followed by a course of trout amandine, and finished with a dessert of fresh raspberries. But those raspberries had come from the property, and the trout had been caught in a stream she could see from the table. "It was this immediacy," she recalled, "that made these dishes so special."[2]

Upon her return Waters started to cook communal meals that to her were simple reflections of the lesson she'd received in France; to those eating them, they were elaborate, stunning, and evocative, worlds from even the most wholesome hippie food of the street and far simpler than the continental French style of meals enjoyed by bourgeois diners and promoted by establishment restaurants, but no less stirring or satisfying. These became the culinary starting ground for Chez Panisse.

Waters founded the restaurant in August 1971, with mismatched plates and saucers, flatware rescued from thrift stores, and an aesthetic loosely tethered to ideals of community, immediacy, and creativity; what it possessed in spirit it may have lacked in focus at the outset. But Waters immersed herself in French cuisine and culture, reading influential authors like the English food journalist Elizabeth David and the American Richard Olney; she acquainted herself with the culinary advances coming from the northern Rhône restaurant La Pyramide, in Vienne, owned by the legendary chef Fernand Point. Point's kitchen was a proving ground for some of the greatest chefs in postwar France, including Paul Bocuse, Alain Chapel, and the Troisgros brothers. Inevitably a culinary bent that had been more broadly French took a distinct turn south.

Still other factors linked Waters to the south of France. One of her lovers, Thomas Luddy, was a film scholar and promoter (he eventually founded the Pacific Film Archive) who introduced Waters to a series of films authored by Marcel Pagnol known as the Fanny Trilogy. Three films, *Marius, Fanny,* and *César,* were produced in the early to mid-thirties, set on the Vieux Port of Marseilles in the heart of Provence, with stories that followed several interlinking characters from youth to middle age whose lives are centered around a café owned by César. Waters wound up naming her new restaurant Chez Panisse, after the genial, kindhearted sailmaker in the film; her only child she named Fanny.

As Waters was founding Chez Panisse, another Berkeley figure, an acknowledged ex-hippie, was developing a business that would complement Waters's culinary break-through.

Kermit Lynch was born into a teetotaling family in 1941, in San Luis Obispo, California. At the time this was a region better known for pastures than vineyards, and was still decades way from becoming the wine region it is today. He attended the University of California, Berkeley, and as a student, musician, and blues aficionado, Lynch developed a taste for wine that he casually cultivated as he pursued a career in music, all the while operating a small crafts business called The Berkeley Bag, wherein he transformed Asian rug scraps and bolts of fabric into women's purses. It was hardly something he saw himself doing forever, however, and in 1971, when an entrepreneur offered to buy the business, he cashed out and booked a trip to Europe to find out more about his avocation, wine.

The following year Lynch borrowed a small sum from his girlfriend and opened a wine shop in Albany, just north of Berkeley. Kermit Lynch Wine Merchant kept patrician hours, so as not to interfere with his music career. It was simple, crowded, fusty, and unkempt, "cool and dark inside," wrote Ruth Reichl in her memoir, *Tender at the Bone*, "and smelled like spilled wine. Cartons were stacked on the floor, hundreds of them, and way in the back a slight man with curly brown hair and a scruffy beard stood by a make-shift desk, watching me. I could feel his eyes on my back as I went up and down the aisles looking at the wine in the cartons and repeating the names to myself. The words were beautiful. I reached for a bottle, picked it up, and stroked the label.

"'It's not fruit,' said the man. 'You can't tell anything by squeezing it.'"[3]

In the beginning, Lynch sold whatever was available to him—and at that moment, this was a lot. A recession had made a great many great wines available on the cheap, including the portfolio of Frank Schoonmaker, whose extraordinary stock of Grand Cru Burgundy and First Growth Bordeaux Lynch was able to purchase for as little as 20 cents on the dollar. Soon after he started making trips to France, hardly knowing the language, with only the vaguest sense of what he was after, and where to get it. Lynch's clientele grew rapidly, and within a few short years he was selling to many of the best restaurants of the day, including Narsai David's eponymous restaurant in Kensington, founded the same year (it would soon be known for having one of the finest wine lists in the country), Michael Wild's Bay Wolf, and not least, Alice Waters's Chez Panisse.

Since the inception of his business, Lynch has imported wine from all over France—he continues to carry superb Burgundies and fine-boutique Champagnes, iconic Beaujolais, as well as a stellar collection of producers he's brought to fame from the Loire, Alsace, and Languedoc.

But within a few short years of opening Lynch's reputation rested on wines from the south of France. The wines of the Rhône Valley and Provence have remained the soul of his portfolio; it was in these regions that he was able to find producers that no one had tapped; he imported wines from domaines like Gentaz, Chave, Vieux Télégraphe, Simone, Trinquevedel, Gripa, Clape, Tardieu-Laurent, Jasmin, Chateau Grillet, and Verset, brands which had never been in the U.S. market or only spottily. By the end of his first decade as an importer, Lynch had adopted no less than two dozen producers from the south of France, including many from the Rhône Valley, Provence, and the Languedoc, importing more than a hundred wines from these regions and effectively exploding a heretofore underappreciated category.

As fledgling businesses in Berkeley's nascent food scene in the seventies, Kermit Lynch and Alice Waters were destined to meet, of course, and to do a brisk business together; Waters needed good wine for her restaurant, and Lynch needed a customer who could appreciate his unique palate.

But the synergies between Chez Panisse and Kermit Lynch Wine Merchants go well beyond a commercial relationship, even a friendly one. It's rare for two innovators of such intense conviction to find each other in the same place at the same time and have so much in common politically, philosophically, and aesthetically. Waters's ebullient menus and Lynch's ebullient wines seemed so ideally suited to one another that the connection almost bordered on myth—and that myth linked them and Berkeley to the south of France. No one who dined at Chez Panisse could fail to be influenced, not least a would-be winemaker or two.

The figure that fused their aesthetic vision was Richard Olney, the expatriate American writer living in the south of France, with whom both Lynch and Waters would develop an intimate relationship.

Olney was a painter and writer who emigrated to France as a young man, where he got to know several of the country's most talented winemakers and chefs. In the early sixties he landed a job writing about French food and wine for the influential magazine *Cuisine et Vins de France*. By 1970 he was living full time in Provence, where he'd purchased an old house in Solliès-Toucas, which he slowly refurbished, planting an elaborate garden and resurrecting a simple yet functional kitchen. Increasingly his daily life there informed his writings, and his home became a pilgrimage spot for American cooks, journalists, and restaurateurs, all of whom came away with an indelible image of a simple life, lived well, punctuated by memorable meals.

Olney published several books on French cooking, many devoted to simple country fare. His first, *The French Menu Cookbook*, was published by Simon & Schuster in 1970, just prior to the opening of Chez Panisse in 1971. Most likely Waters was familiar with the book at the time; certainly his second book, *Simple French Food*, she regarded as a bible.

Olney's books were a departure from the haute cuisine espoused by such leading resources in French culinary arts as *Larousse Gastronomique* or the writings of Georges

Auguste Escoffier. Olney's preparations were simple, his measurements inexact, his methods ad hoc, the results invariably delicious.

Waters and Olney met in California during Olney's American book tour for *Simple French Food,* in 1974; the following year Waters visited Olney in Solliès-Toucas and was introduced to the Peyraud family, who produced Provencal wines from Bandol under the name Domaine Tempier. Waters knew these wines, especially the robust, vivid rosé; the domaine had been imported to the Bay Area in minute quantities by the importer and wine writer Gerald Asher, and in fact Waters carried the wine on early wine lists. But wine tasted in the context of where it's grown and made is often transformative, and there's little doubt that Alice Waters was duly transformed.

"It is impossible for me not to love the wines of Domaine Tempier," wrote Alice Waters in Kermit Lynch's newsletter in 1978. "Once you have visited the Peyrauds in their 17th-century house surrounded by perfectly tended vines, eaten Lulu's garlicky food cooked over the coals, and drunk the wines with Lucien in his cellar, it is clear that they love wine and they love people drinking wine."

More than this, however, Waters was taken with the Peyraud family and with their way of life: "I felt as if I had walked into a Marcel Pagnol film come to life," she wrote in the foreword to Olney's book *Lulu's Provencal Table* some fifteen years later. "Lucien and Lulu's warmhearted enthusiasm for life, their love for the pleasures of the table, their deep connection to the beautiful earth of the South of France—these were things I had seen at the movies. But this was for real. I felt immediately as if I had come home to a second family."[4]

Kermit Lynch, meanwhile, was making more frequent trips to Europe, and as his own tastes and philosophy started to take shape, the trips became longer, devoted to small independent French growers who had broken from négociants and were trying their hand at making wine on their own. A new word was being used to describe them—artisans—and the results were revolutionary. But they were not easy to find without help. Lynch required the talents of guides who knew the lay of the land and could introduce him to producers who weren't being imported in California.

In 1976 he was about to embark on one such trip to France when at the last minute his guide and translator, Wayne Marshall, had to back out. Marshall suggested Richard Olney as a suitable replacement. Lynch was told that Olney was American, spoke French fluently, and that he knew a lot of winemakers; perhaps he might be able to help with a few discoveries.

When Lynch mentioned the prospect of traveling with Olney to Alice Waters, her eyes lit up. "Pack your bags," she said, "and get on that plane!"[5] Lynch did what he was told; it was one of the most momentous decisions of his career.

Meeting Olney changed entirely the nature and focus of Lynch's business. Olney's connections in the French wine industry were completely in sync with Lynch's developing aesthetic, and probably had a strong hand in shaping it. Says Lynch, for Olney drinking wine was like breathing. "Richard had a way of tasting—there was absolutely no pomposity at all. I can hear him saying in my mind, 'what does this wine have to say to us?' He tried not to impose anything on the wine; he just wanted to see what it had to give."[6] The wines he loved were not ceremonious, they weren't meant to be revered, they were meant to be shared and enjoyed in a social setting.

On that first trip Olney introduced his charge to many producers in France who were not yet on the radar, and important, seminal partnerships were cemented during this trip for Lynch, including his first contact with legendary Rhône producers Gerard Chave and August Clape. But by far the most powerful and far-reaching was the kinship Lynch struck with Lucien and Lucie (Lulu) Peyraud of Domaine Tempier.

According to Olney, Bandol was their very first stop, and it was momentous. "A visit to the Peyrauds at Domaine Tempier was inevitable," wrote Olney in his introduction to Kermit Lynch's travelogue, *Adventures on the Wine Route*. "The instant spark of sympathy kindled between Kermit and the ebullient family of Peyrauds could be likened to spontaneous combustion."[7] Just as with Waters, meeting the Peyrauds struck a deep chord with the young importer. "This was not Kermit's first wine-tasting trip to France," writes Olney, "but I think it may have been the real beginning of his Adventures on the Wine Route."

Lynch believes he didn't really have a chance. "It is my experience," he writes, "that when anybody makes the acquaintance of the Peyrauds and Domaine Tempier, he or she tends to mythologize them. Everything seems so down-to-earth and wonderful and perfect. Even the names: Lucie and Lucien. And the setting contributes, too; the rugged hillsides, the sea, and the enormous blue sky create a landscape of divine dimension. And one's glass is never empty; reverie is natural."[8] To this day, Domaine Tempier is one of Lynch's most iconic estates; in the U.S., the wines and the importer are practically synonymous.

What is it about the wines of Tempier? For one thing, they're made from the extraordinary ancient Mourvèdre, a red grape that basks in the sun of the south and produces powerful, earthy, massive wines with a rustic power that few can match. "When young the red is not exactly a delicate wine," writes Lynch in one of his early newsletters, introducing his customers to the variety. "It has the harshness and vigor and sunny ripeness of the south. With age it softens and develops nuances of flavor unimaginable in its youth. However, it makes good drinking youthful—rough-edged, lively, a bit *sauvage*."

Vigorous, rough-edged, earthy, rustic, openhearted—is it any wonder that these wines were the perfect complement to the cuisine at Chez Panisse? To this day, Tempier's Mourvèdre-based rosés and earthy reds are a fixture on the wine list, where they have been served, more or less without interruption, every vintage since. In fact, the restaurant poured Tempier Rosé by the glass for the first *thirty years* of its existence.

For an incredible decade, 1974 to 1984, the axis of Olney, Tempier, Lynch, and Waters (aided by Chez Panisse's gifted chef Jeremiah Tower) were routinely conjoined upon the pinewood tables of Chez Panisse, both in meals and in spirit. Not only did the restaurant go through cases and cases of rosé and red wine (they still do), but many of the restaurant's specially themed dinners featured Domaine Tempier on the menu; for M.F.K. Fisher in 1976 on the occasion of her seventieth birthday, for Julia Child, Diana Kennedy, Judy Rodgers, and Patricia Wells. Olney himself made several visits, as chef and honored guest, culminating in a series of dinners in 1984 in honor of Lulu and Lucien Peyraud, with menus designed by Olney and executed by Tower in the Chez Panisse kitchen.

Within a few years Chez Panisse had made Berkeley a culinary destination, and people started referring to the blocks in and around Shattuck Avenue as the Gourmet Ghetto. The world's cheeses could be found at the Cheese Board across the street; exquisite artisanal chocolates were being made at Cocolat by Alice Medrich, a former patissier at Chez Panisse; a stern Dutchman with ties to the European coffee and tea markets founded an eponymous coffee shop called Peet's where, somewhat obsessively, the beans were roasted fresh daily; and you could buy charcuterie at Pig-by-the-Tail.

Other restaurants riffed on the Chez Panisse aesthetic; these included Bay Wolf in Oakland, Zuni Café in San Francisco, Lalime's in Albany. Kitchen alumni Mark Miller, Suzanne Goin, and Mark Peel opened restaurants across the American West, initiating a diaspora which, with Wolfgang Puck and Thomas Keller, virtually defines the California food movement to this day—a movement that emphasizes immediacy, generous flavors, a life-giving aesthetic in need of wines as generous and robust to complete it.

After all, what was a Gourmet Ghetto without wine? The heightened cultural environment proved to be a very fertile one for its appreciation. Curious, learned, and well-traveled college professors and other professionals affiliated with the university amounted to a built-in consumer base for good wine—faculty and campus parties were famously lubricated with wine (you couldn't very well have a wine and cheese party without it).

Wine got an immeasurable boost in the American public consciousness in 1976, when a young British wine merchant named Steven Spurrier decided to throw a tasting of American and French wines in Paris, placed together and tasted blind by a number of French critics. In a stunning victory, the American wines trounced their French counterparts, in what came be known as the "Judgment of Paris." That result, and the chance attendance by *Time* magazine reporter George Taber, resulted in an explosion of interest in American viticulture. Berkeley and San Francisco, with its proximity to the wine regions in Sonoma, Napa, Santa Cruz, and elsewhere, amounted to an instant market.

Outside of Kermit Lynch's wine shop a number of important wine retailers catered to this new aesthetic in wine as well, selling the "little wines" of Kermit Lynch as well as American Zinfandel and Rhône-variety producers.

One of these was Trumpetvine, which Stan Hock and partners opened in 1979 on Shattuck Avenue, just a few blocks from the campus gates. It quickly became a favorite source of wine for college professors and students alike; eventually would-be winemakers flocked to the place to stock up on domestic Zinfandel and Cabernet. By the early eighties, Rhône winemakers like Randall Grahm and Bob Lindquist were coming through the door, and Hock started to promote the wines in his newsletters, espousing his share of

Berkeley's countercultural zeitgeist in his enthusiasm for newly minted Syrahs from Bonny Doon and Joseph Phelps:

> Our total grasp of reality leads to the inevitable conclusion that there is a world wide conspiracy to deny the noble Syrah of its rightful place on the grape pantheon with Cabernet and Pinot Noir ... mention Bordeaux and Burgundy, and the common wine buff thinks of first growths, elegant meals, and nobility. Mention a Rhône, and the association is with rustic, crude, alcoholic wines, swilled by peasants in the company of their livestock.[9]

Another was Solano Cellars, founded in March 1978 by Bill Easton, in Albany just west of Berkeley. From the beginning, Easton had in mind "a people's store," selling inexpensive wines for the community. But the industry was changing dramatically, and Solano Cellars, like Trumpetvine, became a haven for off-the-beaten-path wines and winemakers, and for alternative wines, including Rhône-variety wines, which clearly had an influence on the owner. Less than a decade later Easton sold his shop, left the retail business, and moved to the Sierra foothills to found his own Rhône-variety winery, Domaine de la Terre Rouge.

Several of the early Rhône-variety wine producers report on the powerful draw of Chez Panisse, Kermit Lynch's retail shop, and the whole of Berkeley's food and wine scene. John Buechsenstein, Randall Grahm, Bob Lindquist (and his non-Rhône oriented colleague Jim Clendenen), Steve Edmunds, Adam Tolmach, and Bill Easton, all spent formative years living in or visiting Berkeley, making regular visits to Waters's restaurant and Lynch's wine shop, collecting mixed cases of southern French wines, dreaming of making their own wines one day.

As the Rhône movement started to take shape, Chez Panisse and Chez Panisse Café were eager and generous supporters of its early efforts. Panisse was one of the first restaurants to sell the wines of Joseph Phelps, including its Syrah, and was an early supporter of the wines of Qupé. In fact Steve Edmunds, by now a friend of Kermit Lynch, had his first taste of an American Rhône wine, Qupé's Central Coast Syrah, at Chez Panisse—it was this very wine that proved to him that Rhône varieties were worth a taking a chance on in California—he founded his winery the following year.

Lynch meanwhile, became a sideline cheerleader for domestic versions of the varieties and blends he'd introduced into the American market. Bob Lindquist recalls an early encounter with Lynch and his friend and drinking buddy, the winemaker Joseph Swan, who was waiting for Lynch to close up shop so they could go to dinner at Chez Panisse. Lindquist remembers Lynch practically cornering him, fervently holding forth on the virtues of these as yet untested Rhône varieties. Lynch regularly set up meetings with his producers and these fledgling winemakers during the formative years, either in France on their home turf or when his producers made sales visits to the states.

As for Mourvèdre, it got its star turn at table at Chez Panisse as well. Old Mourvèdre vineyards were revived in Oakley, on the San Joaquin river delta east of San Francisco, on the strength of demand from new producers, which saved them from being ripped out. Waters noted this in her foreword to Olney's 1994 cookbook, chronicle, and memoir, *Lulu's Provencal Table:*

> Because of his enthusiastic promotion of Bandol and the influence of its flavors, a new generation of talented wine makers in California has planted many new vineyards of Mourvèdre (the grape that is the essence of Bandol) and are also happily harvesting fruit from recently rediscovered venerably plantings of Mataro (the state's legal name for Mourvèdre). I think this is as exciting a change in direction for California wine making as the shift to Cabernet and Chardonnay was a generation ago, and not only because these wines go so well with the kind of simple, garlicky food I love to cook at Chez Panisse.[10]

In 1987, Kermit Lynch arranged a meeting between newly bonded Rhône-variety producer (and Berkeley resident) Steve Edmunds, of Edmunds St. John Winery, and Francois Peyraud, son of Lucien and Lulu and winemaker at Domaine Tempier. Edmunds had made some older-vine Mourvèdre from Brandlin Ranch that he was really happy with and wanted Peyraud to try. Peyraud tasted a number of wines before the Mourvèdre and Edmunds remembers him politely tasting his wines but not betraying much excitement—until he was poured the Mourvèdre.

"When he got to the Mourvèdre," says Edmunds, "he stuck his nose in the glass, and he absolutely just stopped and stood there, for about two minutes. And then very slowly he lowered the glass and his head came up and his eyes rolled back and he took this deep breath and he said, "La terre parle."[11]

One could hardly imagine a more heartfelt or meaningful validation for an American producer. And it meant that the Rhône movement, guided by broader influences that reached across oceans to France and traced back decades, was on an unstoppable path.

2

A PLACE AND ITS PROGENY
A Guide to the Varieties of the Rhône Valley

In a little over 500 miles, the Rhône River goes through more transitional zones than rivers four times its length. Starting among the glacial tailings of the Swiss Alps, the river gathers strength in the mountains before draining into Lake Geneva, resuming on its western shore. It meanders westward through the Rhône Alps and their foothills until Lyon, in the country's eastern middle quadrant, where it turns abruptly south, passes beside the ancient towns of Vienne, Orange, and Avignon. In the ancient Roman city of Arles a branch of the river known as the Petite Rhône peels west, contributing to the Camargue, the great salt marshes of southern France, home to wild horses and flamingoes. The Grande Rhône reaches the Mediterranean at Port-Saint-Louis-du-Rhône about thirty-five miles west of Marseille.

However picturesque, this is a working river, like many in Europe—transporting barges laden with ores and minerals, home to as many factories and foundries as touristic endeavors. From the A7, the highway that runs from Lyon to Marseille, it isn't difficult to catch a glimpse of the three fully operating nuclear power plants on its banks, their conical towers furiously billowing steam—and most notoriously, the ecologically themed mural on one of the reactor towers in Cruas, near Montélimar.[1] In the spring you can see fruit trees flowering on its banks at certain stretches; just as often, the view is unattractive, industrial and charmless. There is an enduring sense, particularly in the north, that the battle between commerce and agriculture has been pitched for a very long time—certainly the vines of Condrieu and Côte-Rôtie seem encroached upon by industrial parks and transport hubs, while on less hallowed slopes, such as those leading out of Vienne on the highway north to Lyon, derelict vineyards cling to crumbling terraces as civilization roars past.

The Rhône consists of more than twenty-five appellations or AOCs (appellation d'origine contrôlée), many of which are still being defined, haggled over, named, and renamed. Many of the villages of the southern Rhône had just had some minor surgery on their appellation names: for example, Côtes du Luberon is now known as "Luberon." The Coteaux du Tricastin received a similar truncation and was referred to as Tricastin until an accident in 2008 at the nearby power plant made for a grim association, and so the name was changed altogether to the rather unwieldy Grignan-Les-Adhémar. Other southern Rhône villages, most of which have made wine in relative obscurity, are being debuted or revived. Only a few, however, have achieved cru status; Rasteau, Lirac, Cairanne, and Vinsobres recently joined Chateauneuf-du-Pape, Gigondas, Tavel, and Vacqueyras.

Just like the river, which in the north travels through narrow, vertiginous hillside vineyards on its banks, the northern Rhône has eight orderly appellations. North to south, they include Côte-Rôtie, Condrieu, Chateau-Grillet, Saint-Joseph, Crozes-Hermitage, Hermitage, Cornas, and Saint-Péray. Each are poised rather perilously on some of the steepest vineyard land in Europe, on hills that, outside of the vintage growing season, are a drab monolithic gray, adorned with tens of thousands of stakes that seem for all the world like they're holding the hill up against the sky.

The climate is cold and continental here—it has much more in common with Burgundy than with Provence. The region seems defined by mountains, by Alpine extremes of temperature and the Mistral winds, which are icier and more violent than in the rest of France. It is a region still in the thrall of butter, of warm continental dishes, of the defining cuisines of Lyon, one of the great gastronomical capitals of Europe.

These northern appellations form the geographical heart and origin of four of the most important Rhône varieties: Syrah, the sole red of the region, and the whites Viognier, Marsanne, and Roussanne. About these varieties and their history, more will be said later in this chapter, but the northern Rhône represents some of the most northern extremes of climate where they can grow. For this reason the wines here are for the most part single varietal wines and represent some of the finest examples of varietal wines in the world.[2]

At Montélimar the granite cliffs recede into an alluvial plain, and in the wider stretches of the valley, to the east, you can catch a good view of the Alps. Here fruit trees line the banks and channels of the river, and one drives through small farming villages overseeing the orchards. The river and its valleys become warmer at this point, with multiple crops, and culturally more broad, as Waverly Root in his *Food of France* explains: "The cuisines of Provence to the southeast and Languedoc to the west," he writes, "have been sucked into the valley of the Rhône by the constant stream of travel which has followed this great north-south artery for as far back as history goes. It has been modified, too, by the greater fertility of the river-washed lowlands, which have given the valley richer resources than the mountains. It is only east of the valley that we are in the region of mountain cooking."[3]

That greater fertility may account for the number of grape varieties in use in the southern Rhône, with its warmer climates, more diverse soils, and broader range of options. The climate favors heat- and drought-tolerant reds, which do not, on their own, necessarily produce the best wines, as Robert Mayberry asserts in his *Wines of the Rhône Valley*: "southern Rhônes made from a single *cépage* [variety] are characteristically 'extreme climate'; that is, boldly fruity and exaggerated in some dimension adverse to balance."[4] Mayberry is speaking indirectly here of Grenache, the dominant variety in the south, which on its own tends to be low in acidity as well as "blurred in outline by being both heady and astringent."[5] Thus, says Mayberry, "it is to achieve balance that traditional wines from the southern Rhône valley are in principle and in intent *vins d'assemblage* (generics) and not *vins de cépage* (varietals), 13 different *cépages* being permitted by law in Chateauneuf-du-Pape, 23 in regional Côtes du Rhône."[6]

The south, then, has always been prone to blending, with the express purpose of creating more harmonious wines, all of which stand in the service of Grenache, whose power and alcoholic strength is privileged but must also be mitigated, while its oxidative tendencies are suppressed with more reductive varieties like Mourvèdre and Syrah. Other varieties—the durable Carignane, the high-acid Cinsaut, may be called upon to play complementary roles and bring a wine more into balance. Mayberry suggests that in France these varieties are referred to as the "ameliorative," correcting the excesses of Grenache and lending complexity to the blend. The end result is wines that are more of a mosaic than a monochromatic picture.[7]

Here, then, are some of the more important role-players in the Rhône Valley. Not all of the French Rhône varieties are listed, but all that are described below are grown now in the United States.

THE RED VARIETIES

SYRAH

American Syrah remains the tent pole of the Rhône pantheon; it is the most ubiquitous Rhône variety in bottles and in vineyard acres, red or white. At more than 20,000 acres; it is the fifth most planted red variety in California (and at nearly 3,000 acres, it is the third most planted red variety in Washington State). Its acreage is slowly on the rise in Oregon, especially in the southern Oregon appellations of the Umpqua, Applegate, and Rogue valleys, but as interest grows in cool-climate iterations of the grape, it's being explored in the Willamette Valley as well.

Contrary to several alternate theories over the years, Syrah is a variety indigenous to the Rhône Valley, in France. Many have postulated about its origins outside of the Rhône—expounding on notions that either Syracuse, in Sicily, or Shiraz, in Iran, was its original home; that it was transported by the Phocaeans from Greece and the Romans from Italy; how it was tucked into the tunic of medieval knight and crusader Gaspard de Stérimberg, who dispersed cuttings on the same rugged slopes where he'd built the small refuge above Tain, a place that became known as Hermitage Hill.

But about a decade ago groundbreaking DNA research on the variety by Carole Meredith traced Syrah's lineage and that of its parents, Dureza and Mondeuse Blanche. In a masterful display of detective skills, Meredith proved conclusively that the pollens of the parent varieties would have had to have met up here in the Rhône and crossed.

For millennia, it thrived, its dark plush fruit and weighty structure used to fortify the feebler vintages in Bordeaux and Burgundy; wherever color and body was needed, Syrah was called upon, so much so that its use became a verb: an "hermitaged" wine had Syrah added to it, and was all the better for it. Indeed the Syrah-based wines of the Rhône were considered among the most stalwart wines in the world; their reputation and their imposing nature was captured beautifully by George Saintsbury in 1920 in his classic *Notes on a Cellar-book,* in which his famous maxim about Syrah's manliness is captured.

Saintsbury is commenting on a forty-year-old Hermitage wine he opened for his fortieth birthday, and is impressed with how well the wine has kept up with him: most red wines, he says, "are either past their best, or have no best to come to at that age." His wine, he said, wasn't like that.

> My Hermitage showed not the slightest mark or presage of enfeeblement. It was, no doubt, not a delicate wine; if you want delicacy you don't go to the Rhône or anywhere in France below Gascony. But it was the *manliest* French wine I ever drank; and age had softened and polished all that might have been rough in the manliness of its youth.

After a long diversion on aging bottles, he comes back to the experience of tasting the wine itself:

> the shade of its colour was browner . . . than most of the Hermitages I have seen; but the brown was flooded with such a sanguine as altogether transfigured it. The bouquet was rather like that of a less sweet wall-flower. As to the flavour one might easily go into dithyrambs. Wine-slang talks of the "finish" in such cases, but this was so full and so complicated it never seemed to come to a finish. You could meditate on it; and it kept up with your meditations.[8]

In France, in Australia, and in the United States, Syrah is still considered the most emblematic of all Rhône variety wines. And with good reason: cluster for cluster, there's probably not a grape variety that is easier to grow, or is so qualitatively superior in more appellations, than Syrah. It has adapted to California terroirs like few varieties have. "Not only is Syrah good in a lot of places," says John Alban, "it's great in places where fruit is otherwise mediocre."[9]

Syrah may well have the most body of all of the Rhône reds—some, like Mourvèdre and Petite Sirah, may possess more tannin, but none has the amplitude or breadth—it frequently translates to a plump midsection and an expansive palate weight, with a satisfying, supple richness that few red varieties can match. The tannins tend to be finer grained and more giving than those from Bordeaux varieties, which is not to say they go unnoticed, they're just more pliant.

At its best, it is among the most characterful varieties planted in California soil. That character, it must be said, is inconstant, shifty, at times strange. For some of course, that is the draw: Syrah's mesmerizing sensuality frequently stems from an indefinable quality, its flirtation with the exotic and the seductive in the glass even as it eludes description or understanding.

It is so exotic in some iterations that it sometimes seems out of place in the American pantheon, and for those who want a little more consistency in their wines, its exoticism might be a deal breaker—"weirdness" is cited as one of the reasons for the variety's mysterious decline in popularity in the last decade. Indeed, in the sunny panoply of fruit-driven reds from California and Washington, Syrah can seem like an outlier. It's possible to ripen or burn the exotic elements out of the wine, but such practices may be some sort of Faustian bargain: without that exotic element, Syrah would seem to be missing its soul. Along with Pinot Noir, Syrah is arguably the most soulful red wine in American soil.

Syrah frequently has impressive fruit, but to judge Syrah on fruit alone is to sell its merits short. It is the variety's most consistent feature: a dark, plummy, deep core of blue-black fruits, currant, cassis, blueberry, mulberry, plum, or the darkest of black cherry—on the spectrum, it is rare for a wine to brighten much past black cherry. Those flavors are bolstered by a texturally tight weave with a powerful center of gravity; like a black hole, very little light escapes.

That said, if Syrah were merely fruit-driven it would be no better than other ample reds—a dark-fruited Zinfandel, say. In fact, a Syrah that is merely fruity is frequently a disappointment. In the best bottles, the fruit serves in support of other complex attributes, and it is on those attributes which Syrah's reputation rests.

And what attributes! Blue flowers, violets, rose petals, garrigue herbs like thyme and lavender, rosemary, fennel fronds, pine fronds, black olive, green olive, eucalypt, bay laurel, sorrel, parsley, a medley of peppercorns (black, green, pink, Szechuan, and Longan), wood smoke, leaf smoke, peat and peat smoke, mocha, cocoa, tobacco, tar, rust, mushroom, game, smoked meat, bacon, dried beef, dried sausage, blood, bone and fur, horsehide, pigskin, organ meats, soil, brick, tanbark, wet hair, rubber, wet rubber, burnt rubber, latex, leather, oil, ink, and grease—the latter end of the list reads like the inventory of a sadist's pantry. On their own, of course, some of these aromas and flavors would be a little off-putting, but in a well-made Syrah, the fruit counterbalances the more savory elements and ameliorates what might otherwise come off as merely kinky or eccentric.

For years American producers, captivated by the exotic aromatics they found in French Syrah, despaired at finding just scant aromatic character in their own wines. But as the variety expanded in acreage, Syrah seemed to find climatic niches in California and elsewhere—places that were warm but not scorching, which brought the grape to full ripeness without burning off those more complex anthocyanins; at sufficient ripeness the wines would turn bloody and gamey, spicy elements held in a rich suspension of powerfully ripe fruit. These are the wines that made the reputation of Manfred Krankl and John Alban, of the Pax and Saxum wines.

Still others took the opposite approach, dialing back the excess ripeness, either by choice or in seeking out increasingly cool sites. From Santa Maria in California to the Eola Hills of Oregon, it is more and more common to see Syrah planted alongside Pinot Noir, a practice that would have been unthinkable just twenty years ago—with an end result of lightweight, aromatic Syrahs with alcohols in the neighborhood of 13%—a radical shift in approach and philosophy. Both, it seems, are very serviceable expressions of the variety.

GRENACHE

In the mid-nineties, as the American Rhône wine movement kicked into high gear, producers scoured the state for bona fide Rhône varieties already planted in California. They were somewhat surprised to learn that Grenache was everywhere around them. At more than 10,000 vineyard acres, the variety's numbers positively dwarfed that of any other Rhône grape. (Carignane, the next contender, fell some 3,000 acres shy of that mark.) Fifteen years later, that acreage has dwindled, but it remains one of the most ubiquitous Rhône varieties in California soil.

Grenache is believed to be the first Rhône variety planted in California, and it is, in some senses, the most enduring—while old vine Grenache is rare outside of a few pockets in Mendocino County, it has been a fixture in California soils for more than 150 years. Long before there was a Rhône consciousness, there were Grenache bottlings. You would just never know it.

That is because Grenache, in California, has lived a double life. Of 6,500 planted acres, all but a fifth are found in the Central Valley counties of San Joaquin, Fresno, and Madera. In vineyards from Modesto to Visalia, Grenache is the raw material for oceans of plonk; high-yielding vines producing light cheap fruity red juice, filling the boxes and jugs that have, since Prohibition, constituted the bottom rung of wine consumption in the United States. Grenache has long been one of California's great workhorse varieties, prized for its sugar development and easy fruitiness, valued most for its drought resistance and prodigious yields (as high as 14 tons an acre). All of it is anonymous, of course; varietal labeling on box and jug wines is still a relatively rare occurrence; instead, Grenache's identity is lost behind monikers like Hearty Burgundy, Paisano, Mountain Berry, and Sangria from California's jug wineries such as Franzia, Gallo, Constellation, and Bronco.

Grenache's character is hard to find in these wines. Partly this is the steamroller effect of industrial winemaking. But the vine itself has been watered down by generations of winegrowers propagating high-yielding plants, resulting in decades of natural selection that favored quantity over quality. For all but the last two decades, mediocrity was more than an outcome from Grenache vines in California; it was a goal.

Growers did plant the variety in more viticulturally challenging areas such coastal climates or in porous soils with poor water retention: it was planted in the fractured sandstone hills of the Santa Clara Valley in the forties and fifties, not far from where it had been introduced by Charles LeFranc a century before. There it matured in modest family plots; as the age of the vines grew the yields fell, with better fruit the result.

That is where nouvelle Rhônists, first David Bruce and then Randall Grahm, found forty-year-old plantings which had developed more balanced, complex fruit character. Bruce made Grenache for just two vintages, while he waited for his Pinot Noir vines to mature. Grahm tasted these wines, and at once saw Bonny Doon's future in what they presented to him. Bonny Doon's early success with Clos du Gilroy and the Grenache blend Le Cigare Volant were especially helpful in bringing attention to the vine's strengths—in giving Grenache a meaningful varietal platform for perhaps the first time in the twentieth century in California.

Grenache is so closely identified with the Rhône Valley that it is thought of as French, but its origins are Spanish, in Aragon, a mountainous province backed into the Pyrenees on the border with France. Historically, the kingdom of Aragon included parts of France as well as Corsica and Sardinia, where it is known as Cannonau. (There is some specula-tion, among Sardinians especially, that Cannonau is in fact the variety's progenitor, and it was transported to the rest of the kingdom of Aragon beginning roughly in the four-teenth century.) The kingdom's reach certainly had a hand in expanding Grenache's habitat: by the eighteenth century, when Aragon was annexed into Spain, the variety was commonplace in meridional France and was soon the lead variety in several French AOCs, including Roussillon, Languedoc, Gigondas, Vacqueyras, Tavel, Lirac, and not least, Chateauneuf-du-Pape. In the latter half of the nineteenth century, post-phylloxera, its acreage increased dramatically in both countries.

Grenache was among the cuttings brought by James Busby to Australia in 1832, where it thrived in South Australia vineyards and served for decades as a functional variety for that country's sweet red and tawny wines. It is still grown in Spain, of course, where it plays a vital role in the wines of Rioja, Navarra, Priorat, Tarragona, La Mancha, and Penedes and a minor role in several other DOs (denominaciònes de origen). It's grown in Italy, Sicily, Corsica, Sardinia, Morocco, Algeria, Israel, Cyprus, and Greece; it's grown, in short, wherever there is abundant sunshine, and remains the fourth most common grape planted in the world.

The double life Grenache presents in California is in fact a global phenomenon. Grenache is the base for much Spanish, French, and Australian plonk—by the same token, it inhabits some of those countries' most profound bottlings, whether from Hen-schke, Chateau Rayas, or Clos Mogador. The difference is largely yield: squelching Grenache's natural tendency to throw a huge crop is the secret to quality (vine age is certainly another). Grenache needs to struggle in poor, well-drained soils, high in sand

and rock content—in Chateauneuf-du-Pape, of course, the famously cobbled terrain is impoverished indeed, but what lies beneath the rocks—well-draining strata of limestone, sand, and sandstone—keeps those vines in balance, with indescribable concentration and a heady depth that's unparalleled in the world.

In the states two new sources of French clonal material revived the variety's fortunes somewhat. John Alban returned from France in the early nineties with cuttings, which he propagated and distributed throughout the Central Coast. And in 1990, Tablas Creek exported cuttings from Chateauneuf-du-Pape under the imprimatur of Chateau de Beaucastel. Both sources were available in commercial quantities by the late nineties; both dramatically improved the stock of the variety in the United States, offering a more attractive morphology than what had been available—smaller berries and looser clusters are their main advantage—providing depth to a variety that usually left wanting in that department.

American Grenache exhibits a classic profile of fruit upon fruit—mostly red, usually ripe, at its best, a vivid red and black raspberry mélange, falling to cherry and crushed strawberry in lighter iterations. In the best Grenache bottlings, there is always energy in the middle palate: they give the impression that that red fruit has a locomotive power, a drive that can sometimes seem to crowd out the savory elements—soil, spice, minerals—that would otherwise ground the wines or provide additional complexity.

American Grenache is usually bright, vibrant, fresh, and inviting; but it is rarely something to contemplate much beyond its high pitch of exuberance. There are notable exceptions, but most American Grenache cannot exceed beyond a wine of cheery simplicity; it is rare for American bottlings to approach the depth, the gumption, the profundity of a well-made Chateauneuf-du-Pape or Gigondas. Tasted side by side, American versions seem forward, energetic, a bit confected and daft, like a large-pawed puppy that won't stop jumping up and down. While you appreciate the exuberance you may, in the end, long for a little gravitas.

There are some who say why bother to look for something that's not going to be there? That's Steve Beckmen's position at any rate; for his eponymous winery he farms 30 acres of Grenache biodynamically at Purisima Mountain Vineyard in Ballard Canyon. Beckmen prefers to focus on the variety's hedonistic potential. "Maybe it's a little simpler and more forward," he says, "but in all honesty what's wrong with that?" Beckmen observes that structurally Grenache can feel front-loaded in its texture, a bit premature in its fruit-driven delivery. That is the best argument for blending it with other varieties, and in California the go-to complement is Syrah—indeed, Syrah is yang to Grenache's yin in California; Syrah brings color, structure, depth, and length; Grenache brings acid and of course, fruit.

Still others, like John Alban, Manfred Krankl, and Justin Smith of Saxum, have sought to push Grenache into heady, hedonistic realms. The best of these, like Sine Qua Non's Into the Dark, Saxum's James Berry's Rocket Block, and Alban's estate bottling, hit the palate with a swooning, intoxicating blast of fruit that feels unbridled and intense, bordering on excess. The ripest of these push well past any perception that the wine's delivery is front-loaded; these are wines that finish like a freight train.

Only powerfully ripe fruit achieves this sensation. Going over the top like this can be a risky venture—even in its best bottlings, Grenache can be very high in alcohol—but Grenache's exuberant fruit can often support high alcohol in the glass. Some winemakers, like Craig Jaffurs at Jaffurs Winery, Sashi Moorman at Stolpman and Piedrasassi, and Greg Harrington at Gramercy Cellars, tether this natural amplitude fermenting with a percentage of whole clusters—grapes and stems, together. The addition of stems actually gives these heady, powerful wines some ballast, a freshness and suppleness of texture: "They bring the wine back to the center," says Moorman.

In the cellar, Grenache is famously oxidative. Too much oxygen, and the wine becomes flat and shrill at once. The flavors dampen, but a gassy volatility can distort the wine's aromatics with an acrid, alcoholic top note and the aromatics and the flavors turn it an unattractive brown, like bruised fruit.

For this reason Grenache must be handled minimally and kept in a mostly anaerobic environment. It's common for producers to keep the wine in older barrels. A long *élevage*, according to Sashi Moorman, is crucial to its development. "When Grenache goes into barrel it's very two dimensional," says Moorman, "all fruit and not much else. It takes time for those secondary fruit aromatics to take on a third dimension." For Moorman, that's often a spice element, brown spices like cinnamon and allspice, and the fruit takes on a kirschlike note.

MOURVÈDRE

Mourvèdre remains one of the great component parts for American Rhône red-variety wines. It is rare for a Rhône blend not to include some Mourvèdre, bringing ballast, balance, tannic strength, and a bit of the funk. It has in fact played that role in California for well over a century, where it has been long known also as Mataro. At one time more than 7,000 acres of the variety was planted here; that figure shrunk to less than 500 acres by the mid-eighties.

U.S. plantings exceed 1,000 acres but not by much, that number reflecting modest and unremarkable growth from the early nineties. After enjoying some popularity in the early days of the Rhône revival, Mourvèdre has settled into its supplemental role, with acreage holding steady or creeping up slightly over the years. Mourvèdre gets plenty of lip service, but most growers would probably tell you it's not a worthy investment for precious vineyard land, short of modest supplemental increments. The amount of 100% varietal bottlings remains correspondingly small as well.

Still, when the movement was gathering momentum in the mid-eighties, it was greatly aided by the existing stocks of old vine Mataro in the sandy San Joaquin Delta flats of Oakley and Antioch. The fruit from these vines informed the wines of Bonny Doon and Ridge; eventually Cline, which had a commanding control over Oakley vineyard stocks, was able to produce Mourvèdre bottlings on a scale that others could appreciate. And Mourvèdre composed the wine that established the reputation of Steve Edmunds in just his second vintage, an old vine bottling from the Brandlin Ranch on Mt. Veeder, its distinctiveness confirmed by none other than Francois Peyraud from the venerable Bandol producer Domaine Tempier, perhaps the most important Mourvèdre producer in the world, to whom, it was said, the earth spoke when he took up his first glass of Edmunds's old vine Mourvèdre.

For the earth does speak in California Mourvèdre, if it's grown well and planted in the right place. Few American varietal wines are more grounded, more earthbound, more true to place. Left to its own devices, it can express a kind of robust, autochthonous disposition, rough-hewn, all thick skin and rawhide, a gamey, earthy variety that feels like it belongs in these soils.

Like Grenache, Mourvèdre's ancestry is from Spain and its reputation, from France; it was among the vines transported to Australia by James Busby from his Perpignan (Roussillon) selections; the variety still has a strong presence in south Australia, Barossa in particular, the "M" in GSM (Grenache, Syrah, Mourvèdre) bottlings.

In the vineyard, Mourvèdre has a narrow window: it is a wine that achieves grace and greatness only in unique places that allow it peak ripeness. The variety is so late to bloom and so late to ripen that it requires exceptionally warm sunny places with long growing seasons.

Traditionally, that has meant near the ocean, though not any ocean view will do. Much of the cool, fogbound outer Pacific Coast of California isn't suitable. For clues to its ideal locale you merely have to seek out the places from which its names are derived. Morvedre, in Valencia, Spain, has an unparalleled view of the Mediterranean, as does another village about 225 miles north, up the coast in Catalonia, called Mataro—the town that lent its name to the variety as its most popular synonym. Neither name is much in use in Spain—in its home country, it's known as Monastrell. Its most famous stronghold of course is Provence, where it informs the fiercely expressive rosés and powerfully sanguine, long-aging reds of Bandol, Palette, and the Coteaux Varois.

Mourvèdre, in short, likes an ocean view, and even in California that holds true in a sense: Mt. Veeder, where Brandlin Ranch is located, overlooks Los Carneros on the San Pablo Bay, just east of the Golden Gate; not far inland from this, the last great stock of old vine Mourvèdre in California remains in a coastal locale of sorts, amid chemical factories and oil refineries upon the San Joaquin Delta flats of Antioch and Oakley— as un-Mediterranean as any "coastal" locale in California. Mataro is thought to have arrived in California in the 1860s, through the efforts of two Santa Clara nurserymen, Pierre and Louis Pellier. It thrived in Santa Clara, it thrived in inland valleys from Anaheim to Mendocino, expanding dramatically to 7,000 acres for more than half a century until Prohibition. Charles Wetmore, Eugene Hilgard, and Frederic Bioletti all praised its complementary nature, with Zinfandel, Grenache, Carignane, and Petite Sirah. Even during Prohibition it fared well, prized by California home winemakers, who kept it for themselves, leaving sturdier varieties of lesser quality to be hauled east.

Unlike Grenache, which is drought tolerant, Mourvèdre vines need moisture—that is another reason it has adapted close to the sea. Yields must be closely monitored so that the grapes can ripen fully, in relation to the climate, though it can handle a decent-sized crop in a warm vintage. Its thick skins lead to a powerful tannic structure and antioxidant grip, which makes it well-suited to oak aging.

The adjective most often applied to Mourvèdre is "stalwart," which the dictionary defines as "strong, steadfast, stoutly built." The word is apt. If Mourvèdre were an animal, it would be an ox; if it were part of a building, it would be a strut. It is supportive and supporting, a grunt, a right guard, its haunches firmly planted in the service of more definitive, uplifting vinous elements. One of its great strengths is its ballast: like one of those childhood punching toys, its weighty posterior makes it seem like it will never fall.

On its own, and especially in youth, Mourvèdre can be somewhat gruff; one of its more colorful synonyms, *etrangle-chien* or "dog strangler," certainly reflects this trait.[10] Today, just as in France, Mourvèdre mostly plays a supplementary role in American Rhône wines. It is bottled on its own but perhaps it is more valuable as a component part, providing some depth and structure to brighter, more fruit-driven counterparts, namely Syrah and Grenache, grounding the former while complementing its savory aspects, providing ballast and length for the latter. Also, where Grenache is oxidative, Mourvèdre is reductive, and so contributes some longevity in blends that employ Grenache.

In Spain the vine is common in the central and southeast portions of the country where it originated, in such DOs as Alicante, Jumilla, Yecla, Castillia-La Mancha, and Valencia. Spain remains the country with the most Mourvèdre (Monastrell) acreage in the world.

At its best, Mourvèdre presents a meaty fruit component, somewhat charming, bright and peppery; though the wines can occasionally have a dark and plummy aspect, there always seems to be a beam of red fruit showing through the wine, taking the form of strawberry or black cherry. Frequently this runs hand in hand with a feral animal quality, scents of leather, horsehide, sweat, and fur are common, with gamey white pepper accents, as well as a soil-like foundation.

Some of these descriptors it shares with Syrah. Mourvèdre's savory elements are typically more animal than vegetable. Well-made Mourvèdre can still have scents of blood and iron, of animal hide and oxidized spice mixes, clove, mace, anise.

Of course, the set of flavors defers to structure in every case; to focus on the flavors would be like staring at the girders of the Golden Gate Bridge and being impressed with the paint. Structure is Mourvèdre's prevailing feature, its lasting impression, and the reason it is found in nearly every domestic red Rhône blend.

CARIGNANE

Carignane remains one of the lesser Rhône varieties, mostly overlooked while the rest of the Rhône pantheon caught fire in the nineties and aughts, only to be appreciated anew by the tiny minority trolling among old vineyards—in Lodi and in Mendocino County an impressive number of ably performing old vines were revived and reclaimed. Here was an old vine pedigree on a vine that typically still produced copious yields, or found a kind of effortless balance for more than fifty years, resulting in wines of a unique character for a modest price tag.

Traditionally in California Carignane was a workhorse variety, just as it was in the rest of the world, planted largely without regard to site, with an eye to quantity and not quality, and with little hope for greatness, or even goodness. So it is with workhorses; Carignane is a filler wine, occupying space in a bottle and waiting for other varieties—Mourvèdre, Grenache, and Cinsaut in other countries, Petite Sirah, Zinfandel, and Mataro in this one—to provide what it most often lacks, which is character.

It grew like a weed in Algeria, and became the engine of plonk in that country and in the country it supplied, France, which was obliged to plant its own Carignane in the lower Midi once Algeria achieved independence.

Its ubiquity frequently led to derision: indeed the first sentence in the entry for Carignane in Jancis Robinson's *Oxford Companion to Wine* called it "the bane of the European wine industry," damning it in no uncertain terms.[11] She is somewhat kinder in her new work, *Wine Grapes*, where she states that in the best of circumstances, it "can provoke mixed responses in wine drinkers."[12] And yet to this day almost 300,000 acres are planted to it. It may be a bane, but the industry still has it under its yoke.

Carignane originates in the Spanish province of Aragon, where it is known as Cariñena, though that country's best and longest-lived Carignane vines are probably in the Priorat, with significant plantings in Penedes, Tarragona, Terra Alta, and Costers del Segre as well. In France the variety still makes up great swaths of the Languedoc, in particular Hérault and Gard, but achieves perhaps its most noble expression in the high-elevation vineyards of Roussillon, in the mountain plains of the Pyrenees overlooking Banyuls and Perpignan.

In this country it arrived in the late 1850s, possibly with the same collection that Charles LeFranc deposed in the Santa Clara Valley. Its high yields and relative durability made it popular among immigrants in ensuing decades, though it rarely if ever delivered an exceptional product, as Hilgard and his cohorts conveyed in their 1885 report. "The results obtained with this grape in different localities of California are somewhat discordant," he writes. "In a few specially suitable localities it has produced a good wine, while in most other the wine is only fair to poor . . . it makes a good, neutral wine, lacking in color and tannin."[13]

This is all, it seems, that Carignane can aspire to—its best effort is only good, its pinnacle of expression is usually found wanting: depth, grip, and character. Concludes the *Oxford Companion*, "Its wine is high in everything—acidity, tannins, colour, bitterness—but finesse and charm."[14]

Nevertheless Carignane was an inevitable component in multiple-variety "mixed black" vineyards, the grape providing a weighty base to field blends, structural ballast and flesh to the middle palate, and a center around which more complex elements could adorn themselves.

It is in these mixed black vineyards that Carignane survives, while lesser plantings are being pulled with the alacrity of an eradication program: in 1991, there were 10,200 acres statewide; in 2000, that number had shrunk to a little over 7,000, and by 2005, the number was a little less than 4,000. In 2011 statewide acreage sits at 3,400, with only 100 acres planted in a decade. In 1936 Harold Olmo, at the University of California, Davis, crossed Carignane with Cabernet Sauvignon to create Ruby Cabernet, a variety he hoped would possess the grandeur of Cabernet with the heat tolerance of Carignane; it has become a bulk wine staple in the San Joaquin Valley.

Like Grenache, Carignane naturally throws a large crop, and can by and large support it; but like Grenache one must be relentless in dropping fruit several times during the season; large yields come at the expense of acid and color.

Nevertheless, there are old vine bottlings whose simple charm and attractive price have given the category a modest boost. Ridge Vineyards, with its long-established commitment to and resources in old vineyards, have been making a varietal Carignane on and off since the seventies, and a vineyard designate from Buchignani Ranch since 1999. Others, like Wild Hog, have been making it for nearly that long. Bonny Doon is currently making a charming little bottling it calls Contra, while Broc Cellars, having discovered a 120-year-old head-trained untrellised vineyard in the Alexander Valley, are making a wine using carbonic maceration which pushes the wine into more amiable territory. Other young wineries making Carignane include Lioco, Roshambo, Porter Creek, and Donkey and Goat.

A well-made varietal Carignane will be subtle. It will smell blue—blue fruit, a hint of blue flowers, a hint of dark earth at times. The flavors are often dark and briary, the flavors of blue fruit—mulberry, blueberry, a bit of cassis, carrying the wine through its dark middle palate. If the vines are old—and if the wine has been bottled as a mono-varietal that is a safe assumption—there will be a pleasingly earthy grip to gird that purple and blue fruit flavor, a texture driven by tannins and not by acid. It leaves a broad impression in the mouth, a certain textural flatness that can seem pleasing to some, boring to others.

COUNOISE

Counoise is something of a rarity in the southern Rhône, and yet is apt to turn up in the blended wines of the Languedoc and in Chateauneuf-du-Pape, providing at once a dark core of fruit, lift, and a whiff of pepper to southern blends. This large-berried, late-ripening variety needs plenty of late-season heat to reach peak expression. In 2013 only 58 acres of the variety were planted in California, with a smattering in Washington State and elsewhere. Only four acres have been planted in the last five years.

There is scant documentation as to its origin in southern France, though according to Jancis Robinson's *Wine Grapes* the variety receives mention in texts that originate in

Avignon around the time of Pope Urban V, in the middle of the fourteenth century. Despite marginal status and limited use, wineries like Chateau de Beaucastel and Chateau la Nerthe routinely employ the variety in their Chateauneuf-du-Pape blends.

Tablas Creek exported the variety from Chateauneuf-du-Pape in 1990 but hasn't made a monovarietal bottling since 2006. In Washington, Doug McCrea has made several, as has Bill Frick in the Dry Creek Valley (he also makes a blend of the three C's—Carignane, Counoise, and Cinsaut—called C3). Chris Brockway of Broc Cellars is making a highly regarded modern bottling, from which this tasting note is largely derived: on its own it is a darkly purple drink, offering hints of anise and blueberry in a dense core of rather simple fruit, adorned by a peppery bite, with a lifted tone that can offset the reductive tendencies of the more stalwart Rhône varieties Syrah and Mourvèdre.

CINSAUT

Cinsaut is a light-bodied component variety used in support of those more stalwart in the pantheon. It's used mostly for blending in the southern Rhône, contributing flavor and texture the way a spritz of lemon can brighten a monochromatic dish.

Prized for its ability to retain nerve in warm, dry climates, Cinsaut is a soft-fruited, high-acid, and low tannin variety that is believed to have originated in the south of France, in Provence or the Languedoc, where it's mentioned as early as 1600. It's been known variously as Cinsaut and Cinsault (silent 'l'), though the shorter spelling version is more common. Outside of France its heat tolerance makes it prized in Algeria, Morocco, and especially Lebanon, where the variety has always been an important component in the wines of the legendary Bekaa Valley winery, Chateau Musar.

In South Africa it received the aspirational name of Hermitage, and was crossed with Pinot Noir in Stellenbosch in 1925 by Abraham Perold to create Pinotage, that country's most popular red variety, and possibly its most reviled. In the U.S. it was commonly known as Black Prince, and as early as 1867 it was recommended as "deserving of planting" in Thomas Hyatt's handbook on viticulture.

It's not hard to see why. Drought-tolerant, heat- and cold-resistant, exceedingly amiable through multiple style and ripeness iterations, it was appreciated as a reliable grape of mild, pleasant character and modest rusticity—qualities that helped earn it the nickname Dago Red among Italian immigrant families in California and the Pacific Northwest.

In immigrant communities, Cinsaut is still preserved in places like Lodi, where it thrives in some of that delta region's most prized old vineyards such as Bechthold, planted in 1886 and dry farmed to this day, its fruit prized by such producers as Turley, Bonny Doon, and Birichino.

Cinsaut's freshness and lift make it ideal for rosé production, and this is still a practice for some producers, like Frick and Chateau Potelle. But carefully made red wines will have all of the freshness and charm of a good Beaujolais, a bright briary red with flavors that walk the line between blue and red fruit, simple and charming, driven by the most mouthwatering acidity of any red Rhône variety, which makes it a very serviceable component in blends.

The one red variety we haven't yet addressed is the category's most mettlesome, Petite Sirah. It deserves a lengthy exegesis, and is explored in Chapter 4.

THE WHITE VARIETIES
VIOGNIER

Despite being passed over in recent years in favor of other white varieties, and despite being repeatedly, systematically misunderstood by growers and producers, by sellers and consumers, Viognier remains the emblematic white variety in the Rhône pantheon. It is an unequivocal success story, a part of the American Rhône movement that, more than any other part, may represent the most dramatic, lasting impact: Syrah may have established the movement, but Viognier put it over the top.

Not only is it the most planted white Rhône variety in the U.S., but in no uncertain terms Viognier owes its global success to American interest and cultivation. And despite a considerable slowdown of plantings in this country, Viognier is still going into the ground.

Currently there are about 3,000 acres of Viognier vines in California, another 400 in Washington, Oregon, Virginia, and elsewhere: essentially up from nothing one generation ago, from almost nothing two decades ago. The Viognier revolution begins in 1981 but remains essentially shapeless until the mid-nineties, when, suddenly, it explodes. In 1991 nurseryman Rich Kunde of Sonoma Grapevines sold no Viognier cuttings; three years later in 1994, he sold 250,000. In that same year Mat Garretson took a census of plantings for the second Viognier Guild gathering at Alban Vineyard; incredibly, it was in the ground in eighteen states.

All of this suggests there was a kind of Viognier bubble, akin to the Dutch tulip craze, in the mid-nineties. Consumers, tasting it for the first time, were dumbstruck. Never before had an American white wine seemed as exotic, as arresting. Compared with the butterball stylings of full-blown American chardonnay, Viognier seemed like a breath of fresh fruit. Growers, responding to an anything-but-chardonnay mood in the market, planted hundreds of thousands of vines, far exceeding any potential demand, resulting in an ill-considered range of styles and occasionally, levels of bombast which probably should have been avoided.

But such was the allure of this grape variety. Taken together, its surface prettiness, its seductive florality, its voluptuous fruitiness, and the sheer mass of its texture were like a siren's call to producers and consumers alike: in the anthology of vinous anthropomorphisms, Viognier was our first "it" girl, a temptress, a seductress, in possession of ample charms and dangerous curves, captivating wine lovers with its full-figured, buxom sensuousness. At its best, few white wines are more alluring.

That allure, however, is built on a precarious balance—if the fruit isn't sufficiently ripe, the wine feels faint and inexpressive; too ripe, it has a kind of swooning, heady intensity that feels artificially endowed—like the cartoon décolletage of Jessica Rabbit—a hot, thick reminder that too much of a good thing is rarely a good thing.

Viognier's origins are fairly obscure. The Dalmatian coast, in Croatia, is frequently mentioned as a source location; Oz Clarke, in his *Grapes and Wines,* relates an odd tale of the variety making its debut in the Rhône. After emissaries of Emperor Probus, in 281 A.D. on their way to Beaujolais, were hijacked in Vienne, near Lyon, their cargo pilfered and subsequently planted. More recent research on the variety's parentage casts doubt on the transport theories: Dr. Anna Schneider from the Consilio Naturale delle Ricerche in Turin and Dr. Jose Vouillamoz of University of California, Davis and the Istituto Agrario di San Michele all'Adige have posited that at least one of its parents is Freisa, an indigenous Piemontese variety, suggesting that its migration was considerably more modest.[15]

It seems likely that Vienne might have lent a few of its syllables in the service of the variety's name, though there also exists a grim fable that its name is derived from *Gehennae,* Latin for "the Road to Hell"—a reference, possibly, to the hell one is put through in growing the stuff. Prone to shatter, poor sets, rambling vegetative growth, various ignoble rots including oidium (powdery mildew), and peripatetic ripening patterns, it is a notoriously difficult grape to grow.[16]

Indeed, early varietal bottlings in California frequently suffered from high alcohols, a threat to this day under the warm California sun. Come harvest, Viognier presents a dauntingly narrow window of peak ripeness; harvested at low sugars, it renders a nervy white with little character, a wan imitation of Sauvignon Blanc. But if you veer past the ripeness window the wines are desultory, blowsy, and fat, the vinous equivalent of a fruit-flavored marshmallow.

Not so in Condrieu and Chateau-Grillet, in the northern Rhône where the variety found its permanent home and where it has thrived for millennia. Planted on dramatically steep east-facing slopes the variety baked in the feeble sun of midi-France. The difficulty of growing the variety naturally limited its expansion, and yet those who loved the wine believed it to be one of the great white wines of the world. Viognier is grown in Côte-Rôtie as well, where it is used in small quantities to brighten and lift the aromatics of their dark, brooding Syrah-based reds.

Like Muscat or Gewurztraminer, Viognier has a distinctive flavor profile. In blind tastings it is so easy to detect that exams for master sommelier certification rarely bother.

Aromatically few white wines are more jarring, an inimitable amalgamation of floral and fruit. Those floral notes can run from honeysuckle, acacia, and violet to more in the realm of fruit blossom—orange, peach, pear blossom, even white cherries. Occasionally one can detect a faint herbal note, suggesting garrigue herbs.

As for fruit, it is nearly always sultry and tropical, inhabiting the realm of peaches, apricots, mangoes, pineapple. Frequently floral and fruity jostle on the surface of the glass—neither one or the other, both creating their own tension. Sometimes they're allied; sometimes they're at odds in interesting ways.

There are wines of exceptional fruit-richness, and another set for which there seems to exist a kind of Maginot Line between pear and peach flavors, where pear is a kind of base broadness, and peach the sunny adornment. There is a particular pleasure in a Viognier which has both, such that with each sip, you're not sure which it is you're tasting.

For all this it is the delivery of these fruit flavors that makes Viognier special. The best wines have a textural, phenolic richness, a mouth-filling amplitude like few other white wines possess—certainly in France, where the climate is generally cool and the wines relatively lean, such richness amounts to an almost indescribable exoticism, an impression that may have been enhanced by the wine's scarcity.

Sometimes these disparate elements simply don't mesh, or the sweetness of one element clashes with the sweetness of another, an unpleasant, cloying mélange of flavors that resembles some sort of horrible pileup in an English candy dish.

ROUSSANNE

The runner-up white variety in the American pantheon of white Rhône varieties is Roussanne, a distant second to plantings of Viognier but growing slowly each year. Despite enthusiasm among winemakers, Roussanne remains a difficult vine to grow, harder still than Viognier. And compared with the flamboyance of Viognier, Roussanne's charms are much more circumspect.

In fact of all the white varieties in California, I don't believe there is a variety more mysterious, peripatetic, haunting, and strange. Roussanne is astoundingly inconstant: it can seem obvious one moment, complex the next, fruity one moment, savory the next; it can seem deft and lifted, then cumbrous and large-limbed; when you open a bottle, you're never altogether sure what you're going to get. And yet that variability, so mistrusted in other wines (Riesling comes to mind) is in part what attracts winemakers to it, and may account for the fact that, at 360 acres, there is three times as much Roussanne in the ground as Marsanne—in 1997, they were neck and neck, at 44 acres each.

Comparing acreage isn't necessarily fair, of course. But Marsanne and Roussanne have been cultivated side by side for centuries, and presumably compared for as long; it is almost impossible to speak of one without the other lurking. In the northern Rhone Valley they've alternated in the occupation of Hermitage hillsides and Saint-Joseph slopes, where a centuries-old cycle of sorts can be imagined: Roussanne's routinely poor vintages oblige farmers to throw up their hands in frustration and turn to Marsanne for a few decades of sturdy reliability, only to grow impatient with that variety's servile blandness, and return to the more elusive thrills of its peripatetic complement.

Their similarities in weight and temperament, and in the spectrum of their flavors, make them seem like blood relatives, and perhaps contribute to these routine tradeoffs.[17]

Strip Roussanne of its curious phenolic tics—honeycomb, Karo syrup, elderflower water, white tea, dried flower petals—and you have left something remarkably Marsanne-like as a kind of vinous base. They are comparable in body and in breadth, they both typically come into the winery with high pHs, a glyceric abundance of amplitude and richness.

But where Roussanne is unpredictable and animated, Marsanne is relatively deadpan. Where Roussanne is hard to pin down, Marsanne is merely backward until many years have passed, when the full range of its complexity finally comes into view. It may be the most enigmatic of all of the white varieties associated with the Rhône.

Roussanne is believed to have originated in the Isere Valley, near the Rhône, and in its traditional habitat had not strayed much further than Switzerland (it is found in the Savoie, where it is known as Bergeron). Even so, it has not spread around the world with the same rapidity or interest as has Viognier. Outside of California it can be found in small quantities in Australia, Italy, and Spain.

In the northern Rhône it is found in Hermitage, Crozes-Hermitage, Saint-Joseph, and Saint-Péray. In the south it is more rare, except for important holdings in Chateauneuf-du-Pape, where it is vinified unblended in wines like Domaine de 3 Cellier's l'Insolente, Domaine Raymond Usseglio's Cuvee Pur, and not least, Chateau de Beaucastel's majestic Vieilles Vignes, perhaps the first Roussanne to grace the U.S. market with any regularity, the wine that revealed to American consumers and producers alike just how profound the variety can be, a wine that John Livingstone-Learmonth, author of several important books on the Rhône, described as "one of life's eminent joys, far off the superhighway in an age of homogenization."[18]

There has never been much of it, though it was never threatened with oblivion the way Viognier was. Just like Viognier in Côte-Rôtie, Roussanne is employed in red wines in Hermitage, though less and less of it is planted on Hermitage Hill—it has been replaced with Marsanne. Marsanne, in the end, is easier to grow: Roussanne is a spindly plant, susceptible to wind, to rot, mildew, and oidium. Uneven ripeness, as well as botrytis, is common, and multiple passes are frequently required for a proper harvest. In the vineyard it is so fickle, in fact, that a grower at Novavine, a Sonoma nurseryman, gave it the nickname "the Princess."

Its name is derived from the russet color of the grapes at harvest, a coppery pink, a coloration that no doubt lends to the complex phenolics that the wine imparts in the glass. (Marsanne, by contrast, has no such coloration).

Roussanne, with Marsanne, garners infrequent mention in nineteenth-century U.S. texts on viticulture. Those growers with an interest in Rhône-variety wines learned about the symbiosis between red and white grapes in the northern Rhône Valley—namely, that aromatic white grapes could be depended on to lift the aromatics of the more dour Syrah wines. So it is believed that Hiram Crabb and J. H. Drummond both planted Roussanne and Marsanne, and it was grown at the Natoma Vineyard, in Folsom.

It's not clear that any of it was vinified with any regularity on its own, though there are tantalizing comments in the *Pacific Wine and Spirit Review* by Federico Pohndorff suggesting he had tasted single varietals with interest. In what is now known as the Pohndorff Evaluation, he refers to them both as "excellent types of Hermitage white wines, of fine bouquet and mellow frank taste; acids graceful." He pronounced them "opportune for blending with certain red grapes for red wines as well as for direct white wines, are recommendable for adoption in our vineyards."[19]

John Alban was the first to plant Roussanne in California in the modern age, with cuttings believed to have come from the southern Rhône. His initial propagations were snatched up by a large number of nascent Rhône producers, including Zaca Mesa and Andrew Murray. His efforts were followed by those of Tablas Creek, with their vine material associated with Chateau de Beaucastel, one of the most revered sources for the variety in the world.[20] As we'll note elsewhere (see Chapter 14) initial claims by Randall Grahm of bringing in Roussanne from the southern Rhône proved to be false, or at least mistaken.

Roussanne, like Viognier, must be cropped to a level where it can achieve full ripeness; anything less yields a wine faint of expression. In California, in warm sites, it can hang a reasonably large crop, as much as three tons an acre. In cooler sites, that number shrinks by as much as a ton. Typically it hangs late into the harvest season, well into October depending on the site; in some vineyards, like Stolpman, in Ballard Canyon, the vineyard manager Ruben Solorzano strips the vine of much of its canopy in the fall and rotates each cluster toward the sun so that more of the grapes can achieve that characteristic pink, russet color. Fermentation may occur in stainless steel tanks or large puncheon barrels, and it is extremely rare for the variety not to undergo malolactic fermentation.

In the glass, Roussanne delivers contradictions. It's a rich wine, but it can possess good acidity; it is savory, but with fruity overtones. The well-made Roussanne boasts phenolic flourishes that few white varieties can match, possessing flavors and sensations that seem at once exotic and indeterminate. The flavor set is diffuse, even unfocused, so divergent at times that the descriptors used to illuminate the wine's character can be oddly vague or contradictory. The normally exacting Oz Clarke, for example, musters the not altogether helpful adjective "herby" to describe Roussannes of the Rhône. In his book on Chateauneuf-du-Pape, author Harry Karis denotes characteristic aromas of coffee; in the *Oxford Companion to Wine*, writer Jancis Robinson denotes aromas of tea.

Much of the confusion, I think, stems from the fact that Roussanne can be both savory and fruit driven, often at the same time. Neither element holds the pole position—on the contrary, their even weight and lack of assertiveness probably contributes to a kind of vagueness of expression, which some read as complexity and others simply dismiss as beneath scrutiny.

We can however devote a little attention to those elements. In the fruit spectrum tropical and citrus notes vie for attention, with elements of peach and apricot in the mix. In this they are similar to some Viogniers. But they're usually rendered as darker and richer than comparable attributes in an American Viognier, bearing a depth of caramelly, oxidative flavor. Mango and pineapple occasionally make a contribution, but so do grapefruit, pomelo, even a kind of Creamsicle orange. To this add pear and apple flavors in less than assertive versions.

The savory elements are an even more exotic bunch. Many describe the wine's complex savory character using words like "'beeswax,'" or "honeycomb," words which encompass a panoply of flavors within it—honey, royal jelly, bee pollen, white flowers, and an elusive fruit character that might be described as fruit processed by the hive. Often there is a very pronounced scent of white flowers –from chamomile, paperwhite, almond blossom—with a hint at times of bitter almond. This unique aroma set seems to stay bright and lifted—while there are sometimes mineral accents. And yet they are heavy wines—they possess a weighty, almost oily texture, an emollient thickness that is frequently thrilling. For this reason they nearly always possess more gravitas and compacted, channeled depth than Viognier.

In the best wines, all of these features seem slightly untethered, texturally, a loosely gathered set of attributes whose clarity of expression seems destined for some future point in time. Put another way: in the glass, Roussanne is the opposite of immediate; rather, it projects its promises toward a peak experience in the future. Indeed, the variety is famously long-lived, an anomalous attribute in a wine often short on acidity.

The secret to Roussanne's longevity may lie in its curious oxidative tendencies. It can go through a myriad of phases in its life—even in the course of an evening—when the wine can seem madeirized and flat, only to rebound with a bright seductive florality. That elasticity, that chameleonic knack keeps wine collectors and winemakers on their toes.

But caveat emptor. The wines famously go through a dumb phase in which the flavors seem to shut down inside the wine and there is a period—usually lasting years—when the flavors seem shrouded by a thick blanket. They can seem so fragile and delicate in this phase that most winemakers use very little sulphur in finishing the wines, so Roussanne wines are in many ways as pure and as weird as they seem to be.

MARSANNE

Marsanne is arguably the sturdiest of the whites of the Rhône; it may be one of the sturdiest white varieties on earth, a three-legged stool with a low center of gravity whose weight and texture are its most abiding features, coming well ahead of flavor and aroma—indeed, Jancis Robinson, writing about the variety in the *Oxford Companion*, speaks of an aroma of glue—not inaccurate, and probably not its best feature. Its best feature might be its texture, plump, emollient, and satisfyingly weighty, of the sort that only grows more complex and compelling with age.

Marsanne originates in the Rhône Valley, most likely in or near the commune of Marsanne northeast of Montélimar, the town that roughly serves as the midline between the northern and southern Rhône. It is, indisputably, a northern Rhône variety—while it's found in the southern Rhône, and bottled in Côtes du Rhône blends, it is not one of the white grapes sanctioned in Chateauneuf-du-Pape.[21] Instead, it's an inhabitant of the Hermitage, of Saint-Joseph, of Crozes-Hermitage and Saint-Péray communes, where presumably the longer, cooler growing seasons afford the variety a longer growing season and more languorous harvest. I suggested in the Roussanne section that its fate seems forever associated with that variety, and its genetic heritage suggests a link between the two, though the exact relationship is not yet established.

Both received praise from the country's first Wine-Geek-in-Chief Thomas Jefferson, an avid collector of French white wines. James Gabler, in his book on Jefferson's wine journeys, writes that "Jefferson considered white Hermitage and Champagne the two best white wines of France. He held the former in such high esteem that he called it 'the first wine in the world without a single exception.'"

In the present day the Marsanne-based wines of Hermitage are arguably the world's finest, notably those of Domaine M. Chapoutier and Domaine Jean-Louis Chave, whose wines inspired American producers to plant it in California, notably Randall Grahm and Bob Lindquist, who planted in 1985 and 1987 respectively. Qupé was the first to bottle 100% Marsanne in the modern era, and its bottlings remain definitive for this country; in fact, in 2011 Bob Lindquist shared a memorable vertical tasting of Qupé's Marsannes going back to his first vintage: the wines proved to be dramatically long-lived, growing more subtle and concentrated with the years.

In California a surprising number of wineries have given Marsanne a shot, both Rhône-oriented producers like Phelps, Cline, Preston, and Beckmen, and less likely practitioners like Beaulieu, Inglenook, and Ma(i)sonry.

Nevertheless, plantings in California remain minimal; only 125 acres. About twice this number is found in Victoria, Australia, home to the world's largest concentration of Marsanne vines. There, in a region known as the Nagambie Lakes, Chateau Tahbilk maintains the oldest Marsanne vines in the world, planted in 1927, and makes a fabulous long-lived rendition that remains one of the great values of the wine world.

Marsanne's flavors hint at Roussanne's, but ultimately lack the finesse, the complexity, and the allure, though its true character may not appear before the vines—or the wine—are sufficiently mature. It too can give off a scent of honey and white flowers, but the flavors are more neutral, falling to melon, golden apple, pear. Texturally it is rich and broad, and despite its "tendency to flab"[22] (as Jancis Robinson puts it) it is prized for its weight and sturdy breadth, making it ideal for blending, with Roussanne in particular, but also with Grenache Blanc. It remains a grape of impressive ambiguity, not as elusive as Roussanne, but still alluring all the same.

GRENACHE BLANC

Grenache Blanc is the white variant of Grenache Rouge, and is one of the great workhorse varieties of southern France (and the country's fourth-most planted white variety). It plays an important role in its home country, in Priorat, Rioja, Tarragona, and Catalonia, and elsewhere. Like its red counterpart, it is a stalwart presence in the southern Rhône Languedoc-Roussillon, where it performs a vital role in blending.

Like red Grenache, the blanc version is vigorous, high-yielding, and requires diligence to keep yields low. Also like red Grenache, judicious blending with more reductive varieties, like Roussanne and Marsanne, will result in wines with better balance.

In the Old World—Priorat, in Roussillon, and in the Rhône Valley—the variety is broad and mouth-filling, with a character that's similar to Marsanne in its heft and richness, with a slightly honeyed, slightly citrusy scent and golden fruit flavors, though this is another white variety where flavor neutrality, or ambiguity, is the hallmark, with its lush, weighty texture leaving the most lasting impression.

In this country, Grenache Blanc is noted in nineteenth-century plantings, but barely acknowledged, and disappears well before Prohibition. It is overlooked entirely in early plantings by the Rhône white pioneers, Lindquist, Alban, Grahm, and the Phelps team, until Tablas Creek introduces the variety to California soil in 1992. From there its ascent is rapid, as Rhône-oriented producers in all the western states take to the grape with great enthusiasm. And when you taste a New World bottling, it's easy to see why: they are wildly different than the *blancs* of France and Spain.

For starters, there's fruit: a citrusy note akin to yuzu or Meyer lemon, with a bit of pink grapefruit and lemon zest. Its flavors aren't so much rich as racy, with a lean edge of saline acidity supporting fine if vague citrus flavors. Where Old World bottlings impress with their weight, New World Grenache Blanc has movement, and lift, and a sunny disposition that one clever critic referred to as "a sneaky brightness." It lends that sneaky brightness to blends and to varietal bottlings; while it's far from being a household name, acreage for the variety is already nearing 340 acres, triple that of Marsanne and closing in on Roussanne, which has been in California far longer.

3

HOW RHÔNE VARIETIES
GOT TO AMERICAN SOIL

We think of Rhône varietal wines in the New World as a new development, the product of modern effort and modern hands. They are not. Rhône varieties in one form or another have been in California soil for more than 180 years, since before the Civil War.

One could argue that by the middle the nineteenth century most of the state of California served as a great playground of wine commerce. Grapes thrived then where they thrive now, in Napa, in Sonoma, in Paso Robles and the Santa Clara Valley, in the foothills of the Sierras, not far from the gold sources and other mineral riches that drew tens of thousands to these lands. Sometimes those efforts proceeded willy-nilly, and sometimes with tremendous forethought. In the end the Rhône varieties would fail to survive categorically, but their vestigial remains were there if you knew where to look.

The grapes we now take as the great alternatives to those of Bordeaux and Burgundy weren't alternative in the eyes of early viticulturists. Indeed, they were much admired, for their yields, for their hardiness in the cellar and bottle, for their durability under the duress of nineteenth- and early twentieth-century transport. Most of the vines we now associate with the Rhône Valley were rejected at one time or another as being too difficult to grow or too odd to perpetuate. But that's not to say they weren't explored in depth, alongside hundreds of other prospects as early Californians tried to determine which were going to be the legacy grapes of the country, which were going to compete with the Old World.

Of course all of this exploratory fervor would be curtailed by Prohibition, which ravaged vineyards and wineries and storage vessels and livelihoods, as well as tradition and the transmission of knowledge and experience. The vines that stayed in the ground stayed where family traditions were strongest and most binding, where Italian and Portuguese immigrants were slower to assimilate. They were stubborn in their ways, and Mataro, to take one example, was the beneficiary of their stubbornness. In truth each variety in the California pantheon clung to a similarly tenuous history, its future bobbing dangerously close to the shoals of Prohibition; in 1936, when Prohibition ended, there was much to unlearn and relearn.

The current viticultural era might seem like one of limitless possibilities, but we could have hardly fathomed the limitlessness of the nineteenth century, with would-be wine and vine entrepreneurs careening across Europe with dampened sticks in their trousers or their trunks, returning to California to engage in ambitious viticultural enterprises, with little sense and maybe little regard for what would take and what would not. Even then viticulture represented the opposite of a get-rich-quick scheme, ironical when you consider that gold, and the potential for overnight riches, is what drew so many immigrants to California in the first place. Hundreds of varieties were put in the ground here, but in a system as painstaking and slow as viticulture, it was impossible to say for sure what would taste good and what would not, what would make great wine and what would not, what would take, and what would have to be abandoned. The trial-and-error period was fraught mostly with errors, so many in fact that in most instances hardiness was prized above all other considerations, at the expense of everything we value in wine today, whether complexity, lusciousness, or abundance.

So the Rhône varieties that survived from their initial plantings—Grenache, Mataro, Carignane, Petite Sirah, and Syrah, possibly Cinsaut—outlasting not only man's fickle tastes and profit motive, but also politics, Prohibition, and science, pseudo and otherwise—did so not only from chance or indifference or isolation. Perhaps there was, as some have argued, a broader perspective with which to interpret this survival, that these varieties survived owing to a grander evolutionary scheme, drawing from the notion that "the ancient marriage of plants and people is far stronger and more marvelous then we realize," as Michael Pollan posits in *The Botany of Desire*.[1] Whatever the case, these varieties endured long enough to directly inspire one of the most fertile periods of viticultural exploration ever conducted in California—a survivalist tale if there ever was one, and exactly the sort of serendipity that this movement would rely upon time and time again.

Already by the middle of the 1850s, the newly established California State had become a wine growing state. Vineyards dotted hillsides and valleys from San Diego to Santa Clara. In Los Angeles, sprawl was defined by vast tracts of vineyard land—by 1860 Charles Kohler and John Frohling had planted much of Anaheim to vineyards (where the parking lots of Disneyland now take up dozens of acres).

Most early plantings in California were given to the Mission grape, a variety that traveled up the state with the expansion of the Mission communities in the eighteenth and early nineteenth centuries. High-yielding, heat-resistant, and often drought-resistant, Mission was a heavy and reliable bearer, a sensible choice for settlers looking to make a living on the homesteads surrounding Spanish settlements.

For years, it was assumed that the Mission had been exported from Spain, though there was little evidence that the variety had a home there. A more likely explanation is that missionaries found the grape in the New World and took it with them into California. The variety was thought to be a relative or offshoot of Criollo and may have originated with the Spanish Conquistadors; it was widely planted in Central and South America. Some believe it is related to the Sardinian variety Monica.

Jancis Robinson's most recent book on grape varieties, called *Wine Grapes,* makes the definitive claim that the Mission is none other than Listan Prieto, an antique variety that originated in the Castilla La Mancha region of Spain. In that country the variety was almost completely eradicated by phylloxera and disuse, but had been transported to at least four locations beyond Europe in the fifteenth and sixteenth centuries—to Chile, to Argentina, to the Canary Islands, and to Baja Mexico. In each locale it thrived, in each locale it assumed a different name. The cuttings that made it to Mexico were transported to California with the missionaries, which accounts for its name.[2]

Most agree that the variety is inferior: dark-skinned, dully flavored, low in acid, the Mission was plainly a grape of convenience to the missionaries, who might have done better by exporting some of the existing options already well established in Spain. Evaluating the variety in 1884 in his seminal *Ampelography of California,* California's chief viticultural officer Charles Wetmore expressed puzzlement by the choice of the Mission grape to propagate, when Spain had so many other desirable Mediterranean varieties, including some associated with the Rhône Valley. "That the Fathers," he writes, "considering their great resources at that time, would have neglected, if they made their selections in Spain, such noble vines as the Pedro Ximines, Grenache, Carignan, and Moscatel Gordo Blanco, is not to be supposed."[3]

For two centuries, the Mission variety proliferated. Better vinifera varieties were being imported to California by as early as 1833 by the aptly named Jean-Louis Vignes, and by the middle of the 1850s other varieties replaced the Mission with increasing regularity. Immigrants, drawn initially to the state by the great Gold Rush, acquired cuttings and planted them as they settled. Others found a prosperous business in the selling of vines to future California winemakers. As vineyards expanded so did the number of varieties for planting, as entrepreneurial growers made special trips to the wine regions of Europe to secure cuttings and plant material, to propagate and sell in America's glorious new wine territory.

California's agricultural industry in the 1850s stands out as a period of searching and experimentation, as entrepreneurs and farmers alike endeavored to find the right crop for the right site. The effort extended to vinifera vines, too, led by a small number of vine growers who were devoting much of their business to importing and propagating European varieties. "So far as wine-growing was concerned," writes wine historian Charles

Sullivan in *Like Modern Edens*, "it was not a question of 'whether?' but 'where?' and 'with what?'"[4]

Some of the most enterprising settlers were French: a substantial French population had gathered in San Jose and Santa Clara County, after the Gold Rush. Among them, Antoine Delmas, who is considered the first to import French wine-grapes to California, exhibiting sixty-seven varieties by 1854; Charles LeFranc, who took over New Almaden Vineyards in Santa Clara County in 1857 and began to import French cuttings; the brothers Pierre and Louis Pellier, who founded a nursery called City Gardens in San Jose; and Louis Prevost, who was said to have 35,000 vines planted in Santa Clara County. It's quite possible that any one of these growers may have been imported a small number of Rhône varieties, but the first known planting was Grenache at LeFranc's new vinifera vineyards.[5]

Meanwhile in Sonoma County, one of the most colorful characters in California's wine history, the Hungarian immigrant Agoston Haraszthy, was getting his start in the wine business. An adventurer, entrepreneur, agronomist, viticulturalist, distiller, mint administrator, con artist, and possible thief, Haraszthy harbored ambitious plans to lead California's commercial wine production, and his promotion of these efforts, as well as his promotion of himself, changed the California wine industry.[6]

Considered one of the fathers of modern viticulture in California, Haraszthy was one of many entrepreneurs who established businesses to capitalize on the new demand for better viticultural material. After first immigrating with his family to Wisconsin in 1840, Haraszthy arrived in San Diego in 1849, where he was elected sheriff. But the lure of gold attracted him to the Bay Area; there he set up a nursery near Mission Dolores, which included grapevines, but most of his professional concern at the time involved gold smelting and processing; in fact, from 1854 to 1857 he served as assayer of the U.S. Mint, until he was accused of skimming gold from the coffers (he was acquitted). He resigned and moved north to Sonoma, where he purchased a small existing vineyard just southeast of the town square called the Buena Vista Ranch, which he expanded to more than 250 acres by 1860.

The following year, Haraszthy arranged a voyage to Europe to visit wine regions and collect cuttings. (He managed to get the state of California to sponsor his trip, but they refused his requests for them to pay for it.) He returned in December 1861 with nearly 500 cuttings.

His trip was chronicled in a book entitled *Grape Culture, Wines and Wine-making*, published by Harper & Brothers in 1862 (before departing, Haraszthy had made a stop in New York to secure a publisher). This somewhat hastily written account is odd for how little it in fact illuminates his visits and his trip in general—it does almost nothing to document the vines he procured—ostensibly the reason for the voyage. But a list of 496 cuttings appears in a supplementary report by the state's viticultural commissioners in 1881 (it appears many were duplicated or mislabeled; the actual number is believed to be closer to 400). At least some of these bear a resemblance in name to Rhône varieties, including three varieties of Clairette, Mataro, Crignane [*sic*], a Petit Roussanne, a Grosse de Roussanne, Vigney [sic], Picpoule in three shades, something called Sirac Noir, and another named Grosse de Serine, both of which were approximate synonyms of Syrah at one time or another.[7]

Despite persistent and mistaken rumors that Haraszthy was responsible for importing what is now known as American Zinfandel (rumors mostly perpetrated by his son), there's little evidence that any of Haraszthy's vine cuttings did much to advance California's viticulture in that decade. His ventures started losing money soon after they began—by 1867, most of the varieties were employed in the production of brandy; eventually the vineyard succumbed to phylloxera. By then Haraszthy was long gone from California, leaving in 1869 to supervise a sugar plantation for the production of rum in Nicaragua, where it's believed he was devoured by an alligator while trying to cross an infested river in 1869.

Few figures in the California wine movement are as colorful or as controversial. Most agree that Haraszthy's drive and his ambition, while meant for personal gain, advanced the California wine industry in important ways, especially in his tireless advocacy for better European vine stock for use in California. It's easy to see Haraszthy as a misguided figure, a man whose ambitions and appetites far exceeded his practical ability. Nonetheless, his energy and single-mindedness were instrumental in giving shape and impetus to the fledgling winegrowing industry.

More systematic (and less dramatic) plantations followed Haraszthy's efforts, spurred in part by the outbreak of oidium or powdery mildew abroad, a vine disease that afflicted many of the wine regions of Europe in the mid-1850s. That setback had American vine growers seeking to fill the void: "Bacchus would be compelled to emigrate," writes Thomas Pinney in *A History of Wine in America,* "and would become an American citizen with all those Frenchmen and Germans that preceded him. After 1855, under the rallying cry of 'California, the vineyard of the world,' plantings increased by leaps and bounds."[8]

Several enterprising vine importers added to the state's experimental and commercial plantings. The historical record for the imports themselves is minimal, the collectors' travels undocumented and the vineyards and nurseries they visited in Europe unrecorded. Many, however, put up cuttings for sale, which were regularly featured in trade journals of the era that specialized in agriculture and viticulture. From Gilroy to Geyserville, that meant a trade publication that went by several names in its forty-year history; the one that stuck was the *Pacific Wine and Spirit Review.* Established in 1879 as the *San Francisco Merchant,* the *Review* was a trade journal that by 1890 had become the leading voice for the wine and spirits trade and remained a tremendous source of information until its demise in 1919.

The *Review* was a reliable source of information on the drama of early American viticulture. It reported on the latest findings of scholars, the results of exhaustive evaluative tastings, the proceedings of the latest viticultural convention, new inventions, pest remedies, reports from wine-growing regions abroad and, not least, the chronicling the ravages of the phylloxera epidemic. Produced biweekly the *Review* was supported in part by advertisements for cuttings, and at least some of the varieties were associated with the Rhône Valley.

"Important Vine Stocks For Sale" proclaimed J. H. Drummond's advertisement in the *San Francisco Merchant* on January 1, 1886. Drummond was a Scotsman, a retired ship's captain who bought 1,000 acres in Glen Ellen, in Sonoma County, naming it Dunfillian Vineyard. His brother, Hamilton Drummond, had obtained cuttings from France, specializing in "Medoc" vines but hardly limited to these. In all, twenty-four grape varieties were featured in the advertisement, just a fraction of what they had on offer, including Saint-Macaire and Gros Mancin [most likely, Gros Manseng], Tannat, Franc Cabernet, Franc Pinot, Pinot de Pernand, Gamai Teinturier, Verdot Colon, as well as Cabernet Sauvignon, Malbec, and Alicante Bouschet. Included among these were two vine selections from the Rhône, Marsanne and Petite Sirrah, both "Imported from the Hermitage," the Syrah "giving a wine of intense color and great quality."[9]

Drummond's Petite Sirrah plantings are thought to be the first in California, and he was also among the earliest to make a 100% varietal Syrah, labeled aspirationally as Hermitage. Drummond was also the first to blend Syrah with a fraction of juice from the white grape Marsanne, as was done in Hermitage.

Soon others had planted and were advertising the Syrah (known variously as Petite Sirrah, Petite Sirah, Petite Syrah, Sirah, Serine, Syrac, and other synonyms—a seed of confusion that would be amplified considerably in years to come). The principal producers and propagators were John T. Doyle (Cupertino), J. H. Drummond (Glen Ellen, Sonoma Valley), Charles McIver (Linda Vista Vineyard in San Jose), Charles Wetmore (Livermore Valley), Charles Krug and Hiram Crabb in the Napa Valley, and the Natoma Vineyard, in the foothills of the Sierra.

On Charles McIver's 400-acre vineyard south of Mission San Jose, Linda Vista, were planted a wide array of varieties, known to include Syrah as well as the southeastern French varieties Durif and Beclan.[10]

At Hermosa Vineyard in Oakville, in the Napa Valley, Hiram Crabb compiled one of the most exhaustive collections of vines in California, a collection which included Marsanne and Syrah, as well as Mataro, Carignane, and Grenache.

One of the most ambitious plantations grew out of a mining operation in Folsom, not far from the original gold strike. The Natoma Vineyard Company was begun in 1883 as an outgrowth of the Natoma Land and Water Company, owned by one of the better known nineteenth-century California landowners, Charles Webb Howard. Howard entrusted a considerable vineyard project to Horatio Livermore, who established more than 3,000 acres of vineyards, an area so vast that four work teams on four separate work camps were employed to manage it.

At its height the Natoma Wine Company was one of the most ambitious vineyard projects of its era. In 1888 viticulturalist George Husmann declared, in his book *Grape Culture and Wine-Making in California*, that the Natoma Vineyard was one of the state's most exciting viticultural developments, "a most striking illustration of the rapid advance of the viticultural interests in the state."[11]

The vineyard was planted to a dizzying array of varieties. Husmann, in his enthusiastic review of the property, lists no less than a hundred varieties planted, the largest selection of Rhône varieties that California had yet seen, including Mataro, Petite Syrah, Roussanne, Marsanne, Grenache, Clairette Blanc, Clairette Rouge, Carignane, and Cinsaut, as well as a number of vines believed to be of southern French origin including Serine, Beclan, Chauche Gris, Frontignane, and Piquepoule Gris. There's no question that, should anyone have cared, the Natoma Company had cornered the market in Rhône variety wines.

The story doesn't end happily, however. Shortly after Husmann's glowing report, Horatio Livermore left the project, and it fell quickly into decline; less than ten years later, only half the vineyard acreage remained, and most of the crop was used in the making of brandy. By 1927, all the Natoma vines, one of the largest vineyards ever developed in California, had been ripped out.

In its first quarter-century, the California wine industry seemed robust, productive, and woefully disorganized. Vineyards were expanding rapidly, inhabiting the hillsides of virtually every arable valley in California, but many of the plantings were haphazard, composed of literally hundreds of ill-considered varieties, planted in a scattershot array, with little notion of what was best planted where, or even what was best for the many climates in the state. In many cases, quantity was often privileged over quality, and there seemed to be little regard for what was finally making it into the bottle.

Around 1880 that started to change, however. Two organizations took on a greater role in the improvement of wine quality for the benefit of the industry and the state. They were, in effect, America's first critics, a group of powerful arbiters of quality and taste whose analysis and findings were vastly influential on the nascent wine scene in California: they determined what would and would not be planted in California soils.

The first was the University of California, Berkeley, where the state's viticultural studies were located, under the direction of Eugene Woldemar Hilgard, with Frederic Bioletti.[12]

Hilgard came to the university after an already distinguished career as a geologist and mineralogist—his early studies on the soil makeup of the muds of the Mississippi Delta were considered seminal for that state, and in fact a mineral compound found in that region, Hilgardite, is named for him.

Hilgard was named a professor of agriculture at Berkeley in 1875, having almost no experience in viticulture or enology, but he thrust himself into varietal studies during his first decade at the university. He quickly became one of the leading advocates of quality for the state, believing that dependable, high quality wine was California's best chance of success. He commenced, in the early 1880s, with a systematic sampling of wine and fruit from the state's best growers, including Charles Krug, J. T. Doyle, Hiram Crabb, and

Isaac DeTurk. The Rhône varietal wines he evaluated included Marsanne, Roussanne, Clairette, Syrah, Grenache, Mataro, and Carignane.

In his report of 1883–84, Hilgard grouped varieties into various regional European "types," such as Bordeaux Type, Burgundy Type, Rhenish Type, and so on. These he refined in the ensuing decade, so that by 1890 his reports depicted Jura Type wines, which comprised the northern Rhône varieties of Syrah, Roussanne, and Marsanne, and Southern French Type, which included varieties like Mataro, Carignane, Grenache, and Clairette Blanche. Most of these were favorably reported on.

In 1880, right around the time that Hilgard was finding his voice within the university, a state-sanctioned industry advocacy group known as the California Board of State Viticultural Commissioners, was founded, led through most of its fifteen-year existence by the estimable Charles A. Wetmore. Wetmore came with his family to California from New England in 1856 and embarked upon a career as a journalist in the Bay Area, turning his interests to wine in 1874. By the end of that decade he was lobbying the state legislature on the need for a viticultural commission, and was appointed its chief viticultural officer.

The commission took on many tasks: they collected and disseminated information on pruning and grafting, on pest management and the prevention of phylloxera. Wetmore himself tirelessly wrote reports, vintage summaries, pamphlets, and speeches to advance the industry. In 1884 he created the comprehensive *Ampelography of California*— an evaluation of most of the varieties then in the ground in the state. Perhaps the commission's most consuming task was to determine which grape varieties were best suited for plantation in California. Rhône varieties were among those recommended.

Like the university, the viticultural commission devoted tremendous energy and resources toward evaluating and assessing California vineyards, winemaking, and production. Unlike the university, the commission was less interested in quality than fashioning an industry devoted to mass production. Hilgard believed that wine quality rose above all other concerns and was the only way in which the industry could excel in the world market, while Wetmore was content with producing wines that would satisfy a thirsty if undiscriminating public. The two men wrangled for many years over their differences, with Hilgard's point of view prevailing, more or less, at least until Prohibition laid waste to the entire effort. Both men, however, are remembered for their painstaking evaluation of dozens if not hundreds of grape varieties in California soil, and those would include Rhône varieties. Their evaluations are an important record of what was grown and what succeeded critically among a huge statewide proliferation.

For Rhône varieties, here are some of their findings.

SYRAH

Hilgard makes an initial assessment of Syrah in 1883, referring to the variety by several names, including Sirah, Petite Sirah, or Sirac. It is, he writes, a grape of southeastern

France, "a large ingredient of the high grade red wines of Hermitage, Côte-Rôtie, and other localities."[13] His assessment of the wine, from J. H. Drummond, is generally positive, calling it "a very useful wine, of splendid color, fine fragrance, and a frank, clean, vinous taste." He notes as well that Drummond blended the wine with one-fifth Marsanne, in the manner of the Hermitage, "and this blend was a very good one."

Within two years, his assessment of Syrah has improved modestly; in his *Report of the Viticultural Work* of 1885–86, he says "Its high qualities have attracted much attention, and it has been planted or grafted, although not very extensively, at numerous points in the State. It certainly deserves to be widely grown, the more as its productiveness is quite equal to that of many other widely spread varieties."[14]

In 1887, Hilgard begins expressing reservations about the variety and its placement in warmer regions, owing to the residual sugars the wines retained at bottling.[15] It has been observed, he writes, "that its wine, particularly when grown in a warm climate, contains some undecomposed sugar, which is quickly transformed into lactic acid, and we therefore think that the Sirah should mostly be used in small quantity for blending."[16] His tastings from that year are not particularly favorable, ranging from "a good, bright, well-developed wine of full vinosity and marked and characteristic bouquet" to a less than favorable assessment from a different bottling, "a bright, very heavy-bodied, deep-tinted wine, with perhaps a trace of sugar; a bitterish taste, not strikingly developed bouquet and rather backward vinosity."[17]

Wetmore praises the variety in his *Ampelography*. He writes, "this noble variety is the same that forms the foundation for the grand wine of the Hermitage and Côte-Rôtie in the valley of the Rhône, France. A small quantity of wine made in 1882 by Mr. Drummond and sufficiently proved its fidelity to its reputation. None are yet planted in practical quantities."[18]

Wetmore concluded, "I believe that the sirrah would succeed well at San Gabriel, although a small crop could only be expected. It would set its berries well also in San Diego County, probably. In a few years we shall know something of this interesting variety."[19]

Two other Syrah advocates are worth noting. An evaluation published in the *San Francisco Merchant* in March 1885 authored by J. H. Drummond, Eugene Hilgard, and Federico Pohndorff (and known today as the Pohndorff Evaluation) was an important assessment of wines of the period. Of Syrah Hilgard's words are repeated regarding its "frank, clean, vinous taste"; Syrah is included in their final recommendations.[20]

But because Syrah was considered a "shy bearer," despite generally positive reviews by critics, the vine was rarely planted, nor much referred to, after 1895. Phylloxera, and then Prohibition, all but finished off the variety in the modern age. However, a small number of vines, planted on resistant rootstock around the beginning of the twentieth century, survived phylloxera and were rediscovered during Syrah's second coming in the 1970s and early 1980s.

GRENACHE

At the time of the great period of assessment in the 1880s, Grenache was already prolific, had already found a home in the Santa Clara Valley, and already had a somewhat middling reputation as a grape of great bearing capability but less than stellar quality, prone to thinness, to premature aging, and to faults mostly likely associated with its oxidative properties. Hilgard assesses the variety with characteristic frankness: "Its wines are rather heavy-bodied and rich in alcohol," he writes, "of a moderately deep-red color, which tends to become brownish or yellowish with advancing maturity. This tendency to lose its color has been prominently noted in California, as also the strongly pronounced 'caramel' taste of its more mature wines, that, while much liked by some, is objectionable to others."[21] Hilgard's evaluation is cautious, suggesting that when the wine is made in a proper manner,

> it has certain good qualities, but without such precaution it is of poor quality and a poor keeper.
>
> It may be blended with other wines, such as the Mataro, Cabernets, Gamay, and Malbeck; but never with the Carignane, this blend being very unsatisfactory. When used for blending purposes the Grenache should never exceed the proportion of one tenth or one fifth at most. . . .[22]

Wetmore has a more generous assessment, though he too has reservations. "The vine is so vigorous and fertile," he suggests in the *Ampelography*, "that there is danger that it may be planted too numerously. In France it does not go alone into the cellars. Its chief value is in adding finesse and delicacy to the Mataro, although it may be used to make a sweet red wine. It is destined to play an important part here, but should be kept out of the claret vineyards of the coast counties. For the interior and some parts of the south, it will probably find its true place, as in Europe. It will succeed and flourish in arid places, where a zinfandel would fail, and it will strike its roots into rebellious soil where a Mataro would perish."[23]

MATARO, OR MOURVÈDRE

Mourvèdre's late ripening, youthful potency, its tannic vigor, its blending affinities, and its durability in transport accounted for a wide range of opinion on the grape in the late nineteenth century.

"It comes to us from two parts of France," writes Wetmore, "under different names. Along the Mediterranean coast of France, it is called generally Mourvèdre, although it is sometimes dubbed etrangle-chien (dog strangler), probably on account of the roughness of the wine when young."[24]

In certain circles the variety was held in such high regard that it was recommended for planting in nearly every California vineyard. "I believe there are few red wine vineyards in California," writes Wetmore in the *Ampelography*, "wherein the introduction of a proportion of Mataro, varying from ten to seventy five percent, will not be a positive gain."[25] Wetmore places its importance alongside that of Zinfandel; "indeed," he says, "I believe that for the future it will have a wider range of usefulness." He notes as well their usefulness to each other: "The Zinfandel and Mataro," he writes, "each good bearers, will, I believe, become the basis of our red wine vineyards, and the foundation of our trade in dry red wines." The Mataro and Zinfandel, he said, were compatible in blends as well, "the Mataro correcting any excess of ripeness of the Zinfandel."

As to its forbidding youth, Wetmore is dismissive: "The apparent defect of this grape is the roughness of the new wine; but this is the defect of most noble varieties. Like the Cabernet Sauvignon of Bordeaux, it requires age to develop its quality."[26]

Bioletti, on the other hand, vigorously discourages its planting, calling it inferior and lumping the wine into a category with other lesser varieties, under the heading "A few suggestions as to what 'not to do.' Don't plant Mataro, Feher Szagos, Charbono, Lenoir, or"—he adds helpfully—"any variety that makes poor wine everywhere."[27]

Hilgard is notably more neutral, recognizing it to be a sound wine but in no way inspirational, as in this tepid entry: "The Mataro by itself gives in France a heavy-bodied, well-colored wine of good keeping qualities. It may be blended with the Grenache, the Carignane, and the Aramon, but at least in the proportion of one-half to two-thirds, whenever we desire choice wines."[28]

In his sampling of wines from cooler regions, Hilgard describes it as "a very harsh, low-bodied, common wine, often deficient in sugar, and seldom ripens before the autumn rains begin."[29] His assessment of the grape in warmer regions isn't much better, describing it as making "a sound, solid, somewhat coarse wine, good for blending purposes in the production of ordinary wines." He has his highest recommendation for the grape in Los Angeles and San Diego counties. His assessment of a Mataro from Amador County is typical: "The wine was rough, but bright and sound, and was racked for the second time. After this it lost a little of its roughness, but though sound and agreeable was far from delicate." After three years, Hilgard thinks, it is fit to drink, "found to be perfectly sound and in good order, clean-tasting and agreeable, but with little character."

Husmann, for his part, is half-hearted:

> I put this grape here, not because of its high quality, but because it forms a basis, and often a wholesome addition to many French clarets, and may become useful as a blend with zinfandel and others, as it ferments easily its wine is said to be very healthy and improves with age. Otherwise it rather produces *quantity* than *quality*.[30]

CARIGNANE

Carignane was one of the most prolific grapes in the world in the nineteenth century, a staple in France and Spain and the source of sturdy *vins ordinaires* in both countries. It was put to the same use in California, primarily in the service of blends, which were recommended regularly by the evaluators. "This variety has proved a fine grower and very abundant bearer here," writes Husmann in 1888; "its young wines rank with the finest reds I have tasted in the state, but it is said to deteriorate with age. If this should be so, and it seems to have the same record in France, there are certainly ways and means of counteracting this, by judicious blending with other varieties."[31]

Hilgard, in 1887, has a similarly middling assessment: "Its wine is deeply colored," he writes, "alcoholic, rather smooth, but coarse while young, and requires much care in finishing. It improves in quality when blended with the Mataro, the Pinots, and even the Aramon," going on to say that blends with Zinfandel are common and well regarded.[32]

Pohndorff gets at the essence of the grape in this frank assessment, from his evaluation in 1885: "a wine of full body, lacking a fine fruity expression."[33]

In his comments, Wetmore dissuaded those who thought it was better in California than in Spain and France. "I believe they are misled," he said, "by the delusions of new wines." He too cites the grape for its seemingly poor aging qualities, noting that a sample from Captain Niebaum's Inglenook estate, a favorite in the year it was made, had become "diseased and acid." Nevertheless, he calls it "a most valuable wine, used in conjunction with such grapes as the Mataro and Grenache. It is best suited to districts where the earlier-ripening noble vines are apt to become over-ripe."[34]

THE WHITES

Of the hundreds of white varieties in play in California in the nineteenth century, only five of them had any association with the Rhône Valley: Marsanne, Roussanne, Clairette, Grenache Blanc, and Picpoul Blanc—of these, only the first three are described with any regularity. None survived into the twentieth century.

As in the Rhône, Marsanne and Roussanne are often mentioned in tandem, grown alongside each other, compared frequently, and often associated with Syrah, with which they are blended in the northern Rhône, Hermitage in particular; comparable blends were attempted, with apparent success, as early as the 1870s.

"Marsanne and Roussanne are two excellent types of Hermitage white wines," writes Federico Pohndorff in his 1885 evaluation in the *Pacific Wine and Spirit Review*, "of fine bouquet and frank mellow taste; acids graceful. These varieties are opportune for blending with certain red grapes for red wines as well as for direct white wines, are recommendable for adoption in our vineyards."[35]

Perhaps because it is easier to grow, Marsanne is mentioned slightly more frequently. It was grown in Folsom at Natoma, and Crabb and Drummond both had plantings; both used the grape in blending in early efforts for Hermitage-style wines.

"The geographical distribution of the Marsanne is very nearly the same as that of the Roussanne, above given," writes Hilgard:

Its wines fall considerably below those of the Roussanne in quality, but as the vine is very vigorous, and at the same time a heavy bearer, even under short pruning, it is in favor with the vintners of the region, and serves, as before remarked, as a blend for the Roussanne, and also, in small proportions, with the red wines from the Sirah and other varieties.

The Marsanne bears large bunches, somewhat straggling; its berries are rather small, with a thin and rather delicate skin, which remains of a greenish-white color where not much exposed to the sun, but assumes a fine golden hue under good exposure. Flesh soft, juicy, sweet, and agreeable, without special aroma.[36]

Elsewhere, Hilgard quite accurately if inadvertently describes the variety's intrinsic neutrality. "The condition of the wine is not quite clear," he writes. "The bouquet has developed decidedly, and the flavor is vinous and agreeable, the acid is adequate, and the wine as a whole is agreeable, though not equal in quality to that of the Roussanne. The variety doubtless deserves more attention than it has thus far received, being both a prolific bearer and furnishing a wine of good medium quality, which is very desirable for blending."[37]

Hilgard's report on Roussanne is more favorable. "The Roussanne is not a grape of wide distribution," he writes in the 1884 *Report of the Viticultural Work*. "It is most extensively cultivated in Savoy, and more or less in the adjacent departments of the Isere and Drome, forming in the latter an essential ingredient of the noted vineyards of the Hermitage, in the wines of which its product is mostly blended with that of the Marsanne. The Roussanne vines of Savoy have a peculiar perfume similar to that of the Hermitage wines; they keep indefinitely, improve greatly with age, and acquire remarkable qualities."[38]

Bioletti, finally, in "The Best Wine Grapes for California," recommends Marsanne for plantings in California's inner valleys in 1907. That wasn't meant to be. If anyone followed his lead, the vines perished during the phylloxera epidemic.

Starting in the 1890s, the California grape industry endured a seesaw series of advances and declines that, taken together, did little to advance Rhône varieties meaningfully—the industry enjoyed modest commercial boom years only to be plagued by events that set back initial gains, starting with phylloxera, moving on to economic uncertainty, financial crises, production gluts, and of course, the advent of Prohibition, which very nearly finished it off for good.

However none of these indignities can quite explain the fate of Syrah in the early twentieth century. As it grew unknown and unregarded in vineyards up and down the California Coast, it would be obscured not only by neglect and by Prohibition's dark shadow, but by ampelographical and lexical confusion: for more than eight decades, another grape variety effectively usurped its name, its identity, and presumably, its popularity and momentum. This twisted tale deserves a chapter all to itself.

4

THE CURIOUS CASE
OF AMERICAN PETITE SIRAH

Recession, faint praise, a reputation for difficulty, and Prohibition all contributed to Syrah's unenthusiastic reputation after a hopeful early run in the latter half of the nineteenth century. But as if all that wasn't enough, the variety suffered a final indignity as it lurched into the twentieth: it became the victim of identity theft.

The Hermitage variety, as it had come to be known in California, had adopted several name variations in its twenty-odd years on American soil, some from the French, whose own nomenclatural aberrations had been imported with the vines. The modern current spelling, Syrah, was perhaps its least common variant in either country; other forms, like Sirrah, Sirah, Sirac, Serene, and Serine were used interchangeably in published reports, sometimes on the same page, by the same authors.

The most common variant, Petite Sirah, was French in origin. The modifier "Petite" delineated the vine of the northern Rhône from a strain of the grape then believed to be a different variety, Grosse Sirah, with higher yields and larger grapes and cluster weights. It's now believed that this was a clonal distinction, the Petite Syrah a superior clone with smaller grapes and greater concentration.

We know that the term "Petite Sirah" was in common parlance among vine growers in the latter half of the nineteenth century, and the variety was the base material for a small number of highly regarded bottlings usually labeled "Hermitage." So far as we can determine, these were mostly varietal wines, with a few blending in a small percentage of Marsanne, as was done in the Hermitage, or used in experimental blends which were subsequently evaluated by the likes of Hilgard, Husmann, Pohndorff, Wetmore, and others. Durif, the variety we know now as Petite Sirah, did not arrive on American soil until 1884. And from its very first appearance, a remarkably well-documented confusion is interplanted into Durif's identity on American soil—but the only real mystery here is the persistence of the mistake.[1]

The levels of confusion are intricate, contrary, and sometimes difficult to interpret, fraught with large patches of shadow on the timeline and perpetuated with bouts of collective amnesia that seem to extend decades. Upon emerging, Durif is known as Petite Sirah, and nearly all traces of the true Syrah, both in name and in the ground, have disappeared. Even when the error resurfaces in the years following Prohibition, when Petite Sirah's true identity is called attention to by writers and scholars, few go further than to express doubt, leaving the matter in a cloud state for another fifty years, until 1998, when DNA testing finally puts an end to the speculation, and the matter is laid to rest.

What's known as Petite Sirah in the United States is a relatively modern invention, isolated by a French nurseryman named Francois Durif around 1880. Durif was employed at the University of Montpellier, the source of a great deal of French viticultural research, where he isolated a seedling in a vineyard of Peloursin vines.[2] The vine yielded a deep-colored wine, of stalwart black fruit and sturdy, gripping tannins, and proved to be especially resistant to downy mildew, a perennial problem for the cooler, damper regions of France. These virtues, however, were not enough to make the vine popular in its home country, where to this day it is all but forgotten. As DNA testing more than a century later would confirm, that lucky Peloursin vine was the recipient of a few grains of Syrah pollen, creating a new cross which Durif alertly isolated, named after himself, and made available for sale and propagation shortly after its discovery.

Four years later, in 1884, Charles McIver of San Jose imported Durif cuttings and planted them at Linda Vista, the 400-acre vineyard near Mission San Jose he had purchased the year before. There he planted a number of progressive French varieties. Almost as soon as he had imported the variety, McIver started referring to the Durif as Petite Sirah, even though he already had Syrah vines bearing that name in his vineyards.

We don't know why McIver started calling his Durif Petite Sirah. Perhaps he was given the Durif with the wrong name, and so mixed up his cuttings before they were planted; or, after planting, perhaps he mistook his Durif for the true Syrah, since there are modest similarities in the wines produced. Perhaps, in his foraging, he thought that he had stumbled on a better, more vigorous Syrah strain and wanted to promote it thus, especially since true Syrah was regarded as a poor bearer.

What seems likely is that If McIver was keen on selling this new variety, he'd have promoted it as one—not as a variety that had seen only limited success in California to that point. No marketing advantage would be gained by promoting the Durif as Syrah.

Some researchers in France have suggested that confusion around the Durif may have originated there. In 1996, the French ampelographer Claude Valat published a paper, entitled "Syrah N[oir] (true Syrah), Grosse Syrah, Petite Sirah and Durif" in *Le Progrès agricole et viticole.*[3] It turns out there was plenty of uncertainty in the home country as well. In fact, Valat writes, Durif turns up in a surprising number of vineyard censuses throughout the Rhône Valley, from northern Rhône-Alps provinces to Gigondas and Vaucluse. No one knows how they got there; and Valat suggests that they wouldn't have been deliberate plantations.

"In the region of traditional cultivation," he writes, "a confusion has existed for a long time between the Syrah (or Serine) and the Durif, most of the time called the Petite Syrah (or Petite Serine). "One can imagine," he adds, "that mix ups and substitutions might have happened when filling orders for foreign vineyards. A request for Petite Syrah," he concludes, "could be filled by a shipment of Durif."[4] So perhaps McIver's mistake wasn't his. But there is no doubt he perpetuated it.

We know about McIver's name-swapping because of the apparent confusion it caused his friend and fellow vintner, Hiram Crabb, winemaker and proprietor in Oakville of one of Napa's largest and most prestigious properties, To-Kalon Vineyard, in the heart of the Napa Valley. Crabb is one of the most important early vintners in California and certainly in Napa, making many of its most significant early wines. But he was also a tireless experimenter, bringing in hundreds of varieties and planting them in test plots on his property that were used extensively in trials and in competitions alike. It's safe to assume that Crabb was an enthusiastic salesman of different varieties over the several decades he was making wine, and had the distinguished advantage of being a frequent contributor to various newspapers and professional journals.

Crabb made a number of published observations about McIver's new import. These are at times baffling and even contradictory accounts; nevertheless, Crabb addresses the Durif/Petite Sirah conundrum several times over the course of a decade. From these passages it's plain that Crabb knows he is dealing with two different varieties, and tries at length to distinguish them, first for the sake of McIver, then for himself. In the end, confusion gets the better of him; either that or he decides, simply, to go with the flow.

One thing that is plain is Crabb's enthusiasm for the new variety: "It is a very heavy bearer, excelling [McIver's] other varieties," he reports in the *Pacific Wine and Spirit Review,* "and makes a very fine wine, intensely dark and beautiful and retains its color for years."[5]

In the same publication, Crabb wrote a set of recommendations based on results from his experimental vineyards at To-Kalon, and Durif is among his recommendations. "From a collection of four hundred varieties," Crabb wrote confidently, "I would select the following varieties for red wine in the order named, viz. Serene, Mondeuse, Duriff, Beclan, Refosco, Alicante Bouschet, Mourastel Bouschet, and Petite Bouschet." These are all good bearers and strong growers except the Beclan and the Duriff."[6] Meanwhile, Crabb singles out a variety he calls the Serene, which he tries to differentiate—but in doing so, seems only to make things more bewildering.

"The Serene," he writes, "resembles the Petite Sirrah in every respect and fully equals it in quality, but has the additional advantage of being a good regular bearer." He goes on to say, "It is also called Marsanne Noir and Petite Sirrah, but is quite different in the quantity of its fruit."[7]

So to take him at his word: this so-called Serene resembles the Petite Sirrah, appears *not* to be the Petite Sirrah, and yet is also *called* Petite Sirrah. Confusion abounds.

The most sensible interpretation of this passage is that Crabb is describing Durif, which resembles Syrah but is more high-yielding. Except that in addition to the Serene, Crabb recommends a variety called Duriff. In fact it is among the first mentions of Durif in the English-speaking press—but it passes with scant further mention.

One year later, an unattributed passage in the *St. Helena Star,* which is almost certainly written by or supplied by Crabb, reports that McIver had imported a vine to Linda Vista Vineyard that was supposed to have been the true Syrah, but wasn't.[8] That same month, Crabb speaks of the Serene again, this time addressing directly the confusion surrounding this variety (or at least McIver's confusion) in this curious passage: "Serene," he writes, "called by C.C. McIver, Esq., of Linda Vista Vineyard, Mission San Jose, the 'Unknown,' was imported eight years ago for the Petite Sirrah, but it proved to be a different variety. It is a very heavy bearer, excelling his other varieties (of which he has a large number) and a short pruner; makes a very fine wine, intensely dark and beautiful and retains its color for years."[9]

Setting aside Crabb's misnomer Serene for Durif, it is strangely compelling that Crabb refers to McIver's persistent uncertainty on this matter: some thirteen years after importing it, it's still known only as Unknown. Clearly there is an underlying meaning to this passage; Crabb may even be poking some gentle fun at his fellow vine grower, as if the two vignerons spent more than a few afternoons on the veranda tasting wine from this plot of vines and vigorously debating the true nature of the wines in the glass, with McIver insisting that the wine was the Syrah of the Hermitage, and Crabb insisting otherwise. Perhaps they agreed to disagree.[10]

Of course while Crabb is writing about it, McIver is busy selling it. The power of the printed word may not come anywhere near that of a persuasive salesman telling people to put it in the ground, especially when those recipients are among the most influential in California.

Nevertheless, Crabb would get in his last word in 1897, in the pages of the *Pacific Wine and Spirit Review,* where he seems to have resolved the matter, at least to himself: "The Durif is the same as the McIver vine," he writes. "It is called Pinot la Drôme, and is extensively cultivated in that district."[11] "Pinot la Drôme" is a reference to the river in France's Isère department, where Peloursin was said to make its home. "The Petite Sirah," he goes on to say, "is a very different vine, and is cultivated there also, for finesse."

There can be no mistaking the meaning in this passage. Crabb had it right in 1897, and there appears to be no reason for any confusion to persist.

And yet it does. Despite Crabb's best efforts, the Petite Sirah moniker for Durif proved to be stubborn. Many producers, including McIver, Niebaum, J.T. Doyle, and others, put the Durif edition of Petite Sirah in the ground, seemingly without comment, inexplicably adopting for it the name they had once used for another variety. If they ever bothered to comment on the inconsistency, those comments never reached print. Crabb himself planted Durif on his property, presumably from cuttings given to him by McIver, which he was soon calling Petite Sirah as well.

You would think that the parade of experts who tasted their way across the latter decades of the nineteenth century and into the twentieth would have put an end to the confusion, but in their published reports, they seemed only to add to it. Bioletti, who in 1884 was part of the team which evaluated the Syrah of the Hermitage and other varieties, less than twenty years later writes a full and enthusiastic recommendation for Petite Sirah in his 1907 report, "The Best Wine Grapes for California," wherein he praises Petite Sirah for its high yields and excellent quality. But which Petite Sirah?

"Of the many scores of red varieties which have been widely grown in this region," Bioletti writes, "the Petite Sirah has undoubtedly given the most generally satisfactory results. Some growers are dissatisfied with its bearing, but most report that it produced as much as the Zinfandel. . . . Its wine is of excellent quality, but apt to be somewhat harsh."[12]

There can be no doubt Bioletti is referring to the Durif in his description. But it remains a puzzle that this scholar, who was part of Hilgard's viticultural team just twelve years before, as foreman of the cellar, and who with Hilgard tested, wrote about, and evaluated the true Syrah under the name Petite Sirah, now refers to Durif using the same name. He describes accurately the qualities of Petite Sirah—but why does its new name pass without comment?

Perhaps, says Sullivan, he didn't need to. The name was so firmly affixed just twenty years after its introduction that he felt that no distinction was necessary. "Or perhaps," writes Sullivan, "he didn't want to write anything that might cause confusion in the industry. Later, some UC Davis professors did take this tack in simplifying their explanations. And perhaps here and there some growers actually thought they were planting Syrah."[13]

In any event, the matter dies with the principal players. By the end of the century those who may have made or remembered true Syrah were dead, as were virtually all of the Syrah vineyards in California. "So, seemingly, was the memory of them," writes Sullivan, "at least during the next three decades. But the California Petite Sirah was by no means dead."[14]

In the period following the California phylloxera epidemic, a plague-like root-louse infestation which devastated the state's vineyards in the 1890s, California winegrowers rallied around two grape varieties, Zinfandel and Petite Sirah. Petite Sirah's good yields, powerfully deep color, and satisfying grip made it a favorite among new vine growers, and the variety experienced a kind of craze in planting.

Thousands of acres were planted in the decades leading up to Prohibition. Its range expanded into Lodi and the San Joaquin Delta, into the Central Valley, Santa Clara

County, and the Livermore Valley, where it was planted in 1911 by the Concannon family; fifty-four years later, that winery would become the first to bottle a varietal Petite Sirah.[15] Nowhere was it more common than in the Napa Valley, where it dominated vineyard acreage well into the 1960s, and was second only to Zinfandel in Sonoma County.

Despite its obvious popularity among growers, it remained more or less an anonymous workhorse in the service of blends. It was rare for a wine to be made as a single varietal, and even if it was, varietal labeling was still decades away from common use. Instead, wine labels tended to be aspirational, named for the Old World regions they were meant to emulate: wines made with Cabernet were Medoc;, Zinfandel-based wines, usually blended with Mataro and Carignane, were called Claret; wine made with Pinot Noir was called Chambertin; and what few wines employed true Syrah were called Hermitage.

Single varieties mattered so little that vineyards were rarely planted to one variety but rather to several—the so-called mixed black vineyards whose vestiges remain in California ground to this day. So into this fairly elastic system was dropped a sturdy but remarkably neutral grape variety, which seemed to gird the attributes and fill in the deficiencies of the fruit it was planted among, contributing depth and longevity to Zinfandel, breadth to Carignane, fruit and flesh to Mataro, putting stuffing and color into just about everything it touched, enhancing American "Burgundy" wines with its unassuming berry fruit, its muted depth and power, a variety possessing a Zelig-like capacity to fill out the whole but remain relatively impassive, especially when other varieties had more to express.

It became such a valued component to the field blends of the era that the moniker "Petite Sirah" became virtually synonymous for all the varieties found in mixed black vineyards. It not only assumed the identity of what was left of the Syrah in California soils, but became the adopted name for many other varieties, including Beclan, Serine, Lenoir, Mataro, Trousseau, Poulsard, Carignane, Mourastel, and Mondeuse, as well as Peloursin and of course itself—which is to say Durif. In this way Petite Sirah's true identity as Durif was obscured even further—its affinity with and connection to Syrah blurred still more into a murky lexical haze. Only Zinfandel, with which Durif fused so seamlessly, retained an identity for these styles of wine.

And it's here, in the haven of mixed black vineyards, that Syrah was preserved in California soil. It's safe to assume that more than a few of these producers had the true Syrah in the ground simultaneously, perhaps side by side with the new identity Petite. As Gerald Asher speculates in a 1997 article on Syrah for *Gourmet* magazine, not all Syrah vines would have been ripped out in the late 1890s; indeed, quality plots which either survived phylloxera or which were replanted on St. George rootstock would not have been so casually ripped out once this pretender came along. "For that to have happened," Asher writes, "every grower would have had to make a deliberate effort to avoid cutting Syrah/Sirah/Petite Sirah when he took wood from his vines in new plantings."[16]

In other words, Syrah would not have been eradicated: on the contrary, it survived.

The theory explains how old vineyards like Stags' Leap Winery's Ne Cede Malis block in the Napa Valley, the Buckman Ranch (now the McDowell Valley Vineyard) in Mendocino County, the exceptional vineyard plots in the Sonoma Valley like the one now called Bedrock Vineyard (formerly Madrone) used by Morgan Twain-Peterson, and countless other unmapped "Pets" (the common concatenated nickname for Petite Sirah) vineyards contain a fraction of true Syrah in their vine rows. It accounts for Joseph Phelps's winemaker Walter Schug, when he sourced fruit for the Gallo Brothers in the seventies, routinely hearing from growers that their Pets vineyards contained the French variety.

It accounts, too, for the quality of some Petite Sirah blocks as being richer, smoother, generally more appealing than others, wherein vines that yielded more expressive fruit were propagated more frequently.

And finally it accounts for University of California, Davis professor Carole Meredith's curious initial findings in the mid-nineties, when she tested for DNA in old Petite Sirah vineyards and typically found as many as a half-dozen distinct varieties, including Durif, Peloursin, Syrah, Carignane, Mondeuse, and others. Thus Syrah, having had its identity usurped, manages to survive the ravages of phylloxera and Prohibition and subsists alongside other mixed black varieties, further mixing the mixed blacks, a survivalist within the ranks of the vine that usurped its identity, anchoring itself upon the California firmament, where it hides in plain sight for decades.

By 1919, the year Prohibition became the law of the land, Petite Sirah plantings had climbed to more than 20,000 acres in California. Sturdy, concentrated, dark, and demonstrative in tannin, it was among the varieties whose demand skyrocketed among home winemakers, leading to a dramatic expansion of plantings even during Prohibitions deprivations.

According to government statistical reports, Petite Sirah was the fifth-most popular grape variety traveling to the eastern states during the earliest home-winemaking years of Prohibition; its transport numbers fell, however, as demand for the grape grew in California (the also-popular Zinfandel experienced a similar decline). "The San Francisco and Oakland markets were close at hand," writes Charles Sullivan in his book *Napa Wine: A History from Mission Days to Present,* "and here the Alicante was not so popular. In San Francisco the Zinfandel and Carignane were the champions of flavor, and Petite Sirah was desired for color."[17]

Its popularity provided Petite Sirah with a unique advantage enjoyed by few grape varieties of the era: name recognition. Discerning home winemakers learned quickly that certain varieties could be relied upon to make better wine, and would ask for them by name. Thus the Petite Sirah, a slippery varietal term to begin with, was conceptually established, renowned for its quality, and known more or less permanently by its adoptive sobriquet. As Americans gravitated toward varietal wines, they began to ask for Petite Sirah by name.

And yet the academics were getting wise to the switch. Just thirteen years after his significant omission, Bioletti makes the distinction in a 1921 California Agricultural

Experiment Station bulletin, wherein he states explicitly that Petite Sirah is identical to what the French call Durif. "The variety grown under the name Petite Sirah in California and to which the tests in Table XXIX refer appears not to be the real Petite Sirah of the Rhône Valley. It is the Duriff, a heavier bearing variety of the same region."[18] And just three years later in *California Grape Grower,* the magazine that would become *Wines & Vines,* his colleague Leon Bonnet lays out a fairly explicit description of Petite Sirah's identity, as well as a quite accurate accounting of the source of the Durif variety.

"The synonymy of this variety of grape is rather interesting," Bonnet begins, providing five alternate names for Durif, none of which is Petite Sirah. However, he writes, at Davis the vines "are grown under the names of Petite Sirah and Durif," adding, "no difference can be seen in these vines." He goes on to describe some indisputable morphological differences between true Syrah and Petite Sirah, concluding, without the slightest doubt, "the Petite Sirah is then in reality the Durif."[19]

The Volstead Act was repealed in 1933, but by this time the reputation of Petite Sirah, and certainly its name, was fixed. By the early forties Davis was hard at work assessing its virtues. "The Petite Sirah produces above average crops," wrote Maynard Amerine and Albert Winkler in their seminal 1943 assessment, *Grape Varieties for Wine Production.* "In regions II and III it produces standard, heavy-bodied, moderately distinctive red table wines except in the hottest years. It should have a permanent place here, but here alone."[20] The emphasis on varietal labeling in this report may have inspired Louis M. Martini and Larkmead wineries to label wines as "Durif" in the 1940s.[21]

By the time academics finally chose to tackle the problem of Petite Sirah, there was much to fix. In 1955, H.P. Olmo noted in the *American Journal of Enology* that "the Petite Sirah has suffered because of incorrect identification of the variety. No less than three distinct varieties have been intermixed in plantings and in order to properly evaluate these varieties of the Rhône Valley, further work will be necessary on the evaluation of the wines."[22] Olmo is mildly upbeat about its quality however, especially in blends, suggesting that "this general type of wine should continue to be useful in Burgundy type blends, adding excellent high color, tannin, and body so characteristic of these varieties."

After more than three decades of confusion on California soil, Petite Sirah was progressively outed in popular press, starting in the late thirties and early forties. The American wine writer Frank Schoonmaker was the first to have distinguished what was being grown in California as something distinct from the vines in Hermitage and Côte-Rôtie, and he was among the first to reestablish its connection to the Durif (which, in keeping with the tradition of lexical confusion, he spelled Duriff). "One does not have to be an ampelographer to know that it is not the Petite Sirah from which the great wine of the Hermitage is made," he wrote in the 1941 edition of *American Wines,* begrudging that the variety was useful in the better Burgundy blends: "Planted on upland vineyards and properly cared for, [it] can yield about as agreeable an undistinguished wine as the authors have ever drunk."[23] Schoonmaker's conviction on the matter grew ever more solid as the years passed; the 1951 edition of his *Dictionary of Wines* contained a passage on Petite-Sirah, or Syrah, "A red wine grape widely planted in California. It is not the Syrah grape of French Hermitage; it is probably the Duriff."[24]

But even as late as 1977, Schoonmaker's lengthy entry on Duriff maintains a level of doubt in its assertions: "It seems very probable," he writes, "that the so-called 'Petite Sirah' of California, which is one of the most widely planted of red wine grapes there, is in fact the Duriff, rather than the illustrious vine whose name it has assumed."[25]

One of the other practical guides for American wine consumers was Maynard Amerine and Vernon Singleton's *Wine: An Introduction for Americans*, published in 1965 by the University of California Press. Amerine and Singleton list among red wine types Petite Sirah with the caveat "(possibly Durif, Shiraz; more than one variety sold under this name; fruity, tannic)."[26] Elsewhere they distinguish the two by listing Petite Sirah and Durif separately in a chapter entitled "Classification of Wines." Petite Sirah is classified as a wine with a distinguishable varietal aroma; Durif, a wine without one.

Despite such attempts at clarity, still other attempts serve only to muddy the waters, as we find here from Robert Balzer in his book on California wines. "Frank Schoonmaker," he writes, "suggested that the California Petite Sirah, while presumed to be the Syrah of the Rhône, was probably a more vulgar vinifera called Duriff, a heavy-bearing variety that also grows in the Rhône Valley and that resembles the Petit Syrah of Hermitage. This is probably a partial truth, but I believe that some true Syrah clones, descendents of the ancient Syraz, give greatness to some California vinifications of Petite Sirah vines."[27] It's not at all clear how Balzer arrives at this conclusion, but in this passage he presages Gerald Asher's observations nearly twenty years later.

In 1984, in the massive book on California wine edited by Doris Muscatine, Maynard Amerine, and Bob Thompson, there remains plenty of room for doubt. In an entry on both varieties, Syrah and Petite Sirah, the authors admit that these two varieties represented "an ampelographical tangle that still has not been completely unraveled. What is widely grown in California is called Petite Sirah, or even Petite Syrah. It is probably not the same variety as that grown as Syrah in Hermitage on the Rhône, as Shiraz in Australia or, on very limited acreage, as Syrah in California."[28]

The net effect of these accounts is to link Petite Sirah not only to Syrah, but to associate the grape with the Rhône Valley itself, though no solid connection existed. In countless renditions the lesser variety is recognized as possessing qualities within striking distance of the more noble one. Of course Petite Sirah producers, in their quest for "honoring the lineage," didn't mind that their bottlings were ennobled by the association.

In the late sixties and early seventies Petite Sirah received some overdue acclaim as a stand-alone variety, and certain wineries cultivated reputations for well-made, balanced Petite wines, mostly from older vineyards, or from wineries with a traditional esthetic that knew how not to screw up a good Petite. Wines from older Italian family wineries like Parducci, Foppiano, Gemello, Fortino, and Teldeschi produced solid, workmanlike wines that were popular throughout California. Freemark Abbey was celebrated for its '69 Petite, a wine of uncommon depth and power. In 1971, Paul Draper produced his first Petite Sirah from York Creek Vineyard on Spring Mountain, and three years after that, Carl Doumani founded Stags' Leap Winery in the Napa Valley and aggressively promoted the Petite Sirah derived from his remarkable old mixed black vineyards in the shadow of the palisades in Stags Leap District.

The advances in modern winemaking in the seventies certainly benefited these normally gruff, tannic wines; gentler handling gave the wines better balance and an ungainly grace; certainly their ageability is without question. In the last few years I've been lucky enough to taste a number of older Petite Sirahs from this era, and most, now thirty-five years old and older, have been spectacular: long-lived, fruit vibrant and intact, the tannins gracefully polished, the textures lithe and elegant.

Those seeking to reestablish Zinfandel as the heritage variety in California had a similar pull toward Petite Sirah. Like Zin, Petite Sirah was a quintessentially American wine, and was recognized as such. That may have falsely elevated its status or assessments of its quality, but it hardly mattered. "We think we can make wine, and have made wines from Petite Sirah, equal or superior to some of the greatest Rhônes," asserted Paul Draper of Ridge Vineyards, in 1994. "I'm much more interested in working with a varietal like Petite Sirah that is uniquely Californian than something like Syrah that was virtually nonexistent here until recent years. It's a wonderful grape, but it's a French varietal. It produced its quality and it built its fame in France, not here, whereas Zinfandel and Petite Sirah have done what they have done in the world, as far as quality, in California. So they interest me."[29] Of course, true Syrah could claim the same quintessential history in American soil. It just didn't stick.

In the mid-seventies, the French ampelographer Paul Truel examined specimens of Petite Sirah in the vine collections at Davis, and concluded that at least some of them were Durif. But just as Petite Sirah was establishing itself as a varietal wine and an American classic, true Syrah reentered the market, giving its former namesake something to bump up against.

In the ensuing years Petite Sirah producers tried to make more explicit its connection to the Rhône Valley, especially as interest in Rhône varieties and in Rhône Ranger events started to heat up the market. According to Dennis Fife, who made both Rhône variety wines and impressive Petite Sirahs and blends, there were few Petite producers who did not refer to the Rhône Valley in their promotional material, usually taking the form of this conditional clause found in a 1992 newsletter: "The bottom line is that regardless of what grape is in the Foppiano's and others' fields, there is no doubt that it does produce outstanding wine."[30] In an article Fife wrote about the subject in the journal *Wines & Vines*, he quoted Remington Norman from Norman's book, *Rhône Renaissance:*

"Whatever the truth, and however vocal the dissenters, the variety can make excellent wine and is often indistinguishable from true Syrah."[31]

By the middle of the 1980s, rising interest in Rhône varieties in California was calling attention with increasing frequency to the conundrum that was Petite Sirah. New pressure from the media and confusion in the marketplace had brought the issue to the forefront yet again. Was it indeed from the Rhône? Was it still in use there? If it wasn't Syrah, how did it relate to Syrah? Most importantly, was it meant to join the pantheon of Rhône varieties now being assembled and collectively marketed? Was it legitimate, and if it wasn't, what was to be done about it?

Fortunately, as these questions were reformulated, the academic community finally acquired the means to get to the bottom of them, with tools of detection that hadn't existed before. The longstanding ambiguity of Petite Sirah's identity was to meet its match in the person of Carole Meredith, Ph.D.

Carole Meredith was born in Wales but raised in Northern California, in Orinda, not far from Berkeley. She took to science an early age: from her first *Golden Book of Astronomy,* she knew her fate was sealed. Eventually she focused on biology, embracing plant biology before her matriculation at University of California, Davis—her father wouldn't allow her to attend Berkeley in the sixties, she says, because it was Berkeley, in the sixties.

After graduate study in genetics at Davis, a postdoctoral stint at Michigan State University, and distinguished research on corn, tomatoes, tobacco, and cotton, Meredith learned of a vacancy in the viticulture and enology department at Davis and was offered the chair once occupied by Harold Olmo, the legendary viticulturalist, without ever having worked with grapes before. But the field of plant genetics was much the same no matter what the plant, and technological advances in the field put Meredith in a position to conduct research that would change the way we look at grape varieties forever.

With her graduate student John Bowers, Meredith became interested in DNA markers, specifically in the way they were being used to identify individual humans and their familial relationships to one another. The technology used to study the human genome could be used on all living things, including grape varieties, each of which carried a unique genetic blueprint.

Initially, the plan was to fingerprint grape varieties in order to have a permanent identification system—objective, unambiguous, and irrefutable. But as new kinds of DNA markers were discovered in humans, it occurred to Meredith and Bowers that these tools could be used to answer some of the nagging genetic questions in California viticulture. "We started to think we could resolve some of the identity issues that had plagued certain varieties in California," she says, "like 'What is Petite Sirah? Or is this Pinot Blanc really Pinot Blanc? How is this variety related to that variety? They kind of look alike, and they probably come from the same region of France, are they possibly genetically related? Do they have a common origin?'"[32]

To get a baseline, the team tested a wide array of varieties in the Davis collection, and that initial selection that included a Petite Sirah vine and a Durif vine. They expected to confirm that Petite was Durif, but to their surprise, the vines were not the same. Finding this odd, Meredith sampled seven other Petite Sirah vines from the collection, and found four distinct varietal types. At this point, she contacted her colleague Jean-Michel Boursiquot, who directed the enormous vine repository at Domaine de Vassal in Montpellier, France. Boursiquot sent DNA samples of Durif, Peloursin, and other varieties close in phenotype to the various iterations of Petite Sirah in California soil. In the second finding, four of the initial seven vines were identical to Durif, but the remaining three matched Peloursin, Syrah, and of all things, Pinot Noir. In a much more comprehensive experiment, drawing from so-called Petite Sirah vineyards all over California, the samples yielded multiple varieties in almost every place. Most were Durif; many were not.

The finding confirmed a common practice both in France and California. "In many parts of the world you had vineyards that were mixtures of varieties," says Meredith. "Vineyards were often planted with budwood obtained from neighboring vineyards that were themselves variety mixtures or with mixed plant material sold by nurseries as 'mixed blacks' or 'mixed whites.'"

In March 1996, Meredith published "What is Petite Sirah?" in *Practical Winery & Vineyard*. The paper did not directly connect Petite Sirah to Durif—there were still too many variants in each vineyard for a scientist like Meredith to draw such conclusions. "While winemakers may be content to live with the genetic heterogeneity that is Petite Sirah today," she wrote, "varietal labeling regulations may eventually force the issue. One day the winemakers may be asked to agree upon a single variety that can bear the name Petite Sirah. Which one will they choose?"[33] But her research confirmed, beyond doubt, that much of what was being called Petite Sirah in California mixed black vineyards was Durif. Hiram Crabb was vindicated at last.

Soon after publication Meredith and her team shifted their focus toward vine parentage. The same powerful technology that identified grape varieties could help tell the story of how each variety originated, and Meredith and her team confirmed what had long been suspected, that each of the varieties we now bottle and enjoy came from a cross of two other varieties. This was natural cross-pollination that had somehow been isolated by a farmer or eventually an estate, with the sort of serendipitous good fortune that makes one believe in the existence of God. Meredith and her team had found a way to map that serendipity.

From among the thousands of grape varieties that exist, they chose to study about 300 on the basis of relationships already postulated, morphological similarities, varieties that looked similar, and varieties that had a long history in the same place, like the Pinots: Blanc, Gris, Meunier, and Noir. "We ended up focusing a lot on northeastern France just because it seemed like kind of a cohesive group," explains Meredith, "and involved relationships that people had suggested in the past." Keeping close to Burgundy directed her to the Ardeche, the Isere, Jura, and Drome departments, as well as the Rhône, in particular the geographically constricted valleys of the northern Rhône. In her array she included a number of obscure varieties, many of which were all but extinct in the regions themselves but were potential parent material.

In the course of that study, a number of mixed black varieties were analyzed, and in that initial set, Petite Sirah's parentage was discovered: Durif was a cross between Peloursin and true Syrah.

The parentage of twenty-seven varieties was determined in that initial foray, including Syrah's, which turned out to be a cross between two obscure varieties, Dureza and Mondeuse Blanche. Dureza was commonly found in the Ardeche, while Mondeuse Blanche had its home in the Savoie. The geographical overlap for those two varieties—the area where it's most likely pollen from one variety would have encountered the plant of another—is in the northern Rhône Valley: Crozes-Hermitage and Hermitage fall within that area. That outcome suggested with a fair degree of certainty that Syrah's origins were in the northern Rhône, and not, as some have suggested, in Syracuse, Shiraz, and elsewhere.

The discovery of Petite Sirah's parentage was just the second mapped variety after Cabernet Sauvignon, and it seemed to present Petite Sirah producers with good news and bad news. The good news was that their claim to Rhône roots wasn't entirely unfounded; Syrah, after all, was a parent. But at the same time, suggestions that Petite belonged in the pantheon of Rhône varieties, grew more tenuous.

They have rightfully sought to create their own separate identity, aided by the small but very vocal organization PS I Love You, a group established in 2002 "to promote, educate, and legitimize Petite Sirah as a noble varietal, with a special emphasis on its terroir uniqueness."[34]

It's safe to say that none of these objectives were meaningfully pursued before 2000, in large part because it was commonly believed that Petite was in fact several varieties. There have been almost no clonal studies of the variety, for example.

You would think that, on the basis of all of this conclusive evidence, the lexical slipperiness between "Petite Sirah" and "Durif" would have come to an end. It has not. The TTB, the acronym used for the Alcohol, Tobacco Tax and Trade Bureau, was petitioned once to create an official status of synonymity between the two varietal names. But that effort was bundled with another such effort, to link Zinfandel and Primitivo, which Zinfandel advocates successfully thwarted, jettisoning both efforts.[35] Now that status remains in a curious limbo, as Petite Sirah producers currently exceed 700 wineries in the United States.

5

RHÔNE VARIETIES THROUGH PROHIBITION AND AFTER

On January 16, 1919, Nebraska became the thirty-second state to prohibit the sale of alcohol in the country.[1] Nine months later the Volstead Act prohibited the sale, manufacture, and transport of intoxicating beverages in the United States, stating that "no person shall manufacture, sell, barter, transport, import, export, deliver, or furnish any intoxicating liquor except as authorized by this act." Any beverage with an alcohol by volume higher than 0.5% was prohibited, a limit which of course included wine in its snare, though by and large the temperance movement had its sights set more on hard liquor and beer.

The industry withered: in 1922, according to Department of Treasury statistics, there were nearly 700 bonded wineries in California; by 1933 that number had shrunk to 268. Wine production declined accordingly, from 20 million gallons in 1921 to 3 million in 1930. Those who struggled to stay afloat watched their vineyards decline, their equipment fall into decrepitude, their barrels and storage tanks warp and crumble from disuse.

But wine was not abandoned completely: significant loopholes in the Volstead Act not only kept California winegrowers alive, it saved the industry from failing altogether. For starters, under the act sacramental wine was allowed; produced for consumption in religious rites and celebrations, such libations were made for mass or temple, and also could be stored in small quantities in the home. Venerable wineries like Beringer and Beaulieu Vineyard were among the largest suppliers and were able to survive by the grace of God and the clergy's sacramental requirements.

The Volstead Act prohibited the sale of sacramental wine to anyone but "rabbis, ministers of the gospel, or any officer duly authorized for the purpose by any church or congregation," write Ruth Teiser and Catharine Harroun in *The Book of California Wine*.[2] Such a loophole would not go unexploited. On the contrary, it led to the establishment of sects with entirely new religious rites, write Teiser and Harroun, "performed by self-styled clergymen who did not appear particularly holy."[3]

Medicinal wines and spirits were also restricted, though winemakers found ways to inflate the health-giving properties of certain concoctions, the "medicinal champagnes" produced by Paul Masson, for example.[4] But by far the most actively exploited loophole in the Volstead Act was contained in an ambiguously worded article in the bill, less than forty words long, which changed the complexion of enforcement, and the California wine industry, to its core: "The penalties provided in this Act against the manufacture of liquor without a permit shall not apply to a person for manufacturing nonintoxicating cider and fruit juices exclusively for use in his home."[5] The word "nonintoxicating," Teiser and Harroun point out, was never defined, opening the way for an unprecedented interest in home winemaking, which kept the wine business in California on life support for years.

It remains one of the most astounding statistics in California's wine history: during the first half-decade of Prohibition, acreage and production of wine grapes nearly doubled. "Bearing vineyard acreage in California in 1920 was about 300,000 acres," says Thomas Pinney, citing USDA reports. "By 1927, the peak year, it touched 577,000. The figures of grape production doubled in six years, from 1.25 million tons in 1920 to 2.5 million in 1927."[6]

Entire freight trains were loaded with lugs of grapes and transported to Chicago, St. Louis, Philadelphia, and New York, the fruit distributed to families in urban areas.

Of course, only the sturdiest of varieties could make the journey across country without succumbing to rot or spoilage. As a result, the Volstead loophole skewed usable plantings away from quality and toward durability. "The great explosion of grape planting that took place under Prohibition," writes Pinney, "was not of grapes suited to making good wine but of grapes fit to be transported long distances and capable of attracting an uninstructed buyer—'shipping grapes' rather than true wine grapes. Home winemakers a continent away from the major source of grapes naturally wanted fruit that stood up well to the rigors of a long transport over deserts and mountains and broiling prairies. No wine grape of high quality could withstand such an ordeal."[7]

As Charles Sullivan writes in his *Napa Wine*, "The criteria for keeping a vine in your vineyard now were: thick skin, heavy color, and heavy yield. Other varieties approached the Alicante in these characteristics. Zinfandel qualified for yield and flavor. So did Carignane and Mourvèdre (Mataro). Petite Sirah (Durif) made it, particularly for color. If one were really interested in flavor, all these latter varieties beat the coarse Alicante. Among San Francisco's North Beach connoisseurs it was considered little more than a junk grape."[8]

California vineyards would suffer a second decline in the middle of the Prohibition years, after a wave of planting to meet home winemaking demands resulted in oversupply. By the mid-1920s, the grape market had collapsed again; then after repeal in 1933, vineyards once again were threatened with decline, as the Great Depression killed demand.

The end result is one of devastation and preservation for the wine industry: wineries hung on by a thread; growers that kept their vineyards alive did so at their own financial peril. A decade or more of modest demand by immigrants to California from Spain, Italy, Portugal, and Greece—consumers with the experience to be more discerning—rejected varieties of such coarse durability as Alicante. They wanted quality, and chose not only Zinfandel, but Carignane, Mataro, Grenache, and Petite Sirah, often in the same vineyard, a mélange which came to be known as mixed blacks.

In this way thousands of acres were spared, among them a modest rampart of Rhône varieties. Their preservation and their heritage, their subsequent rediscovery later in the twentieth century, was vital to the early momentum of the Rhône movement; when interest kindled for these grapes, winemakers were thrilled to find a trove, poorly identified but full of character and history. Eighty years and more after their planting, having endured an ill-conceived law-of-the-land, their modest popularity spiked like it never had before.

The California wine industry limped out of the Great Depression with few resources, an ill-fitting patchwork of vineyards, decrepit and outmoded equipment, and perhaps worst, an intellectual deficit. Prohibition had amounted to an untimely disruption of intellectual and cultural practices that set the art of winemaking back significantly, curtailing research, obliterating vine stocks, disrupting the lineage of countless strains of heritage vines—and with the exception of Grenache, Carignane, and Mataro, vines with ties to the Rhône Valley were all but destroyed.

The job of rebuilding the state's beleaguered wine industry fell to the viticulture and enology staff of the University of California, Davis—Harold P. Olmo, Maynard Amerine, Albert (A.J.) Winkler, Maynard Joslyn, Harold Berg, Vernon Singleton, Cornelius Ough, and others.

The university at Davis was founded in 1905, and viticulture and enology studies, established by Eugene Hilgard, were moved there from Berkeley. Prohibition forced the department's closure in 1919, and it was reopened following repeal in 1935.

For the first eight years of their reanimated existence, the Davis staff collected huge amounts of data not only on what the regions of California were capable of. Their duties were manifold: they cleaned up existing vine stocks that were exhibiting viruses, they set about correcting rampant misidentification and systematically taking stock of what remained; they replenished the raw materials—vines and rootstocks—that would reestablish California as a viable wine region.

They evaluated the state's agricultural land, and set about a laborious period of study and analysis to recommend specific varieties to suit the state's many subregions. Climate took on a vital, defining role like never before: The concept of degree days, a summation of the degrees of heat above 50 (on the Fahrenheit scale) from the beginning of April to the end of October as a tool to help analyze the climatic range of a given site, was developed during this period. In California five indisputable zones were employed to encompass the range of climates, and grape varieties best suited for each were lined up to fill these zones.

In 1943 and 1944, Amerine and Winkler published a series of instructive articles which quickly became the standard for what to plant where. The most influential of these, "Composition and Quality of Musts and Wines of California Grapes," appeared in the journal *Hilgardia* in 1944 (it was revised extensively and distributed across the state for the next twenty years); the report evaluated more than fifty varieties for use in California soils, each given a number on a 100-point scale as to its relative value as a table wine or dessert wine.

Rhône varieties are part of the discussion but are not highly regarded, and as the lists were revised in ensuing years, they slip even further down. Marsanne, for example, guardedly recommended in 1944, is discouraged twenty years later. Praise for Mataro, though common and admired during and after Prohibition, is suppressed in the decades that follow. Grenache is also frowned upon for table wines, though the authors acknowledge that the grape can produce some serviceable dessert wines. Oddly, the authors acknowledge that Grenache is the principal variety behind well-regarded rosés from the Rhône Valley and Languedoc, and then stop short of recommending it for this purpose in California.

Petite Sirah (Durif) gets an earnest recommendation in 1943; by 1963, the reception is more tepid, and by the early sixties another variety under consideration is acknowledged, the Petite Sirah (French) or the French Syrah. The praise for it is faint—it does not mature early, the report says, and requires considerable barrel aging to reach high quality. "It is not a particularly distinctive kind of wine," the authors conclude, "and would therefore need a period of familiarization before being accepted by the public."[9] An addendum, however, is hopeful, and somewhat prescient: "A dedicated grower, willing to age the wine properly, both in the wood and in the bottle, might produce a high-quality wine that would bring a price sufficient to compensate for the time spent." This optimistic assessment may have come from colleague Harold P. Olmo, who had persuaded growers in the Napa Valley four years earlier to plant a small amount for evaluation.

Olmo, one of the most influential grape researchers ever to work and study in California, was born in San Francisco in 1909 and raised in that city's Mission District.[10] Olmo went to Mission High School where he excelled in the sciences (tall, with enormous hands, Olmo excelled in high school basketball too, evidently). His early interest in the study of plants is remarkably easy to pinpoint: when he was quite young, his mother's gave him several books based on the studies of Luther Burbank.

"There were I think seven volumes, and they gave me a lot of inspiration," says Olmo in his oral history. "I read some sections so many times I think I memorized some of them."[11]

Olmo attended Berkeley, where he focused on plant genetics. He was hired by Frederic Bioletti at Davis in 1934, and the emphasis of his studies shifted from tobacco to grape-growing and viticulture. Bioletti was working on an ampelography of California wine grapes; Olmo became his research assistant.

So began a career as omnivorous as any plant scientist's in the twentieth century, astonishing for its breadth and reach. It is hard to put a finger on Olmo's most important contribution, but certainly his study of and emphasis on clonal selection with respect to grape varieties was critical to the success of many varieties in the state. He made ground-breaking research on vinifera clones, establishing some of the selections best suited to California—his work on Chardonnay in particular may partly account for its success and ubiquity here. His early advocacy led to what is now known as the FPS, or Foundation Plant Services, an institution devoted to providing clean and healthy vine stocks to American nurseries for propagation all over the country.

Olmo is also responsible for creating more than two dozen grape varieties, hybrids established to improve their base material.[12] His pursuit of vinifera led him, during one Guggenheim-funded year, to the ancestral home of the species, Afghanistan, where he traveled remote regions under enormous hardship, scrambling up rock cliffs and steep hillsides to track down vinifera plants in their native state.

He made seminal trips to Europe, Australia, Africa, Iran, Pakistan, India, and Brazil, to procure and study different types of grape varieties, arranging for the transport of several of these to California soil, where they were developed and propagated. Many are in use today, including an important strain of Syrah which Olmo imported to this country from Hermitage in 1936. In 1959, Olmo persuaded Brother Timothy of the Christian Brothers Winery to plant Syrah on the Napa Valley floor in Oakville, an initial planting that led to the country's first modern bottling of that variety nearly two decades later.

In his preface to the Olmo Oral History transcript, Davis enology professor J.F. Guymon called Olmo "a rugged energetic person, fiercely independent in many respects but equally open, friendly and congenial. He tends to live to the hilt, is completely dedicated to his work, but at the same time enjoys parties and social occasions to the fullest. Playing practical jokes to invoke hearty laughs runs in his veins."[13]

It would be years, however, before the raw material waiting in the wings would be recognized for its potential, and longer still for the American public to become familiar with varieties now thought to be commonplace.

In the American marketplace, wines from the Rhône Valley were still an unknown quantity. After the ravages of Prohibition and the Second World War, French wine imports didn't recover until well into the fifties, and the revival, at first, was largely reserved for three areas: Bordeaux, Burgundy, and Champagne.

Rhône wines were not among the imports. There were a number of reasons for this. The Rhône was smaller, produced far less in volume, and had fewer wineries. Transportation and tourist routes limited the exposure of visiting Americans to the region and its wines. The finer restaurants of Paris had wine lists dominated by Burgundy, Bordeaux, and Champagne—less so Côte-Rôtie or Chateauneuf-du-Pape.

Meanwhile much of what made it to the U.S. market was bottled by négociants, who purchased Rhône Valley grapes and finished wines to blend and bottle themselves. Chapoutier, Jaboulet, and Guigal in the northern Rhône got their start this way after the war. Négociants from Burgundy and Beaujolais like Georges DuBoeuf also brought in Rhône wines, mostly from the south, to round out their portfolio. In American sales catalogs these usually appeared beneath the Burgundy offerings, often without any explanation as to where they came from and the fact that they were sourced hundreds of kilometers from the Côte d'Or. Even the finest of these were a bargain compared to Burgundy.[14]

Even if California producers knew enough about Syrah to make a go of it, the market price for these wines would have been discouraging. "If we only paid two dollars a bottle for imported Rhône wines," says retailer Darrell Corti, quite sensibly, "why would anyone use Rhône varieties to make $2 bottles in California?"[15]

Nevertheless, by the mid-sixties one could find a handful of bona fide Rhône wines in the American market. Jaboulet, Chapoutier, and Guigal were imported, and in the south, wines from Mont Redon, Chateau de Beaucastel, and Chateau de la Gardine were imported by forward-thinking importers like Winebow, Bercut Vandervoort, Classic Wines, and not least Vineyard Brands, founded by the enterprising importer Robert Haas.[16]

It's fair to say that the wines imported in the period from the middle of the 1950s to the mid-1960s bore no resemblance to the wines of today, or even of the wines from thirty years ago. By most accounts, *élevage* for these wines would have been at the expense of any youthful energy, and in the wine's settling its early exuberance would have been lost to the barrel and the cellar.

Darrell Corti, an early California proponent of Rhône variety wines, recalls that on his first trip to France in 1967, he visited the cellars of Chapoutier in Tain l'Hermitage. When he asked if he could sample the finished white Hermitage wines from the 1966 vintage from barrel, he was politely rebuffed: the wines weren't ready, he was told. Nor could he taste the wine from the 1964 vintage. He could, if he liked, taste the 1962, but they didn't consider that one finished either. Such lengthy time in barrel would have significantly muted the wine's youthful life, as it transformed toward a secondary, more oxidative state, rendering them less attractive, at least by modern standards.

These were early times, but Darrell Corti represents a new sort of retailer whose discernment, curiosity, knowledge, and interest in the unusual and the delicious made him one of the great tastemakers for California and for the rest of the country. Corti imported or inspired the importation of products that seem today like things we've never lived without, specialty items like truffles, brie cheese, balsamic vinegar, even extra virgin olive oil. He had the same discerning taste for wine—in fact the first wine purchase he made for his father's store, several cases of nineteenth-century Madeira worth $1,000, nearly broke the company.

But the American Rhône movement needed agents like Corti—messengers, teachers, gadflies, guides. Corti would inspire many students of viticulture at Davis to try new things, as well as embrace old things—meaning the Rhône Valley, Languedoc, and the Piedmont, and meaning heritage California varieties such as Zinfandel, Mataro, and Petite Sirah, varieties with marginal identities prior to Corti's taking notice. He took in Davis students as interns and stock boys and never failed to pass up a teaching moment.

PART II

PIONEERS AND PLAYERS

6

THE PATH TO THE FIRST
AMERICAN RHÔNE

It's difficult to isolate the first Rhône bottling of the modern era, especially when Rhône varieties already inhabited American blends of questionable quality in jug wines long before even Côtes du Rhône blends emerged as a viable category. Anomalous varietal bottlings of Carignane, Grenache (rosé), and Petite Sirah surfaced occasionally after Prohibition—such efforts were usually short-lived. But if you wanted to pinpoint the first varietal bottling, David Bruce's inaugural Grenache, a detour on his sojourn toward Burgundy, would count as the first.

Dr. David Bruce recorded his first wine epiphany in the early 1960s, when he was knocked back on his heels by a bottle of Richebourg from Domaine de la Romanée Conti in Portland, the town of his medical residency. "I popped the cork and the whole room was pervaded by this haunting spice," he says. "As I was drinking that wine, I was imagining walking on a mountaintop, making Pinot Noir."[1]

Ten years later he was doing exactly that in the Santa Cruz Mountains, following the footsteps of pioneer Martin Ray, whom Bruce believed had made the finest California Pinot Noir to that point. David Bruce Winery was bonded in 1964, with the express purpose of producing Pinot Noir. There was, however, little to be had, and so Bruce made whatever was at hand, from the vineyards in and around Gilroy and Morgan Hill, south of San Jose, varieties that included Petite Sirah, Aleatico, Palomino, Mataro, Carignane.

This is how, in 1969, Bruce bottled the first dry varietal Grenache table wine in the modern era, from a single vineyard of older vine fruit owned by Mary Carter in the Santa Clara Valley, planted by her father, and at least thirty years old.

Bruce made three vintages of varietal Grenache; the first, 1969, was a dry rosé; in 1970 and 1971, Bruce made red wines, in the manner of Pinot Noir—supple reds with succulent fruit and a fine, lacy structure. They were, in the end, like a dry run for Bruce, who always felt he made the wines as a stopgap measure for something to practice on and sell as his Pinot Noir vines matured. In hindsight he's grateful for his trial runs. "I think the fact that I was forced to deal with all of these other varietals is extraordinarily important," he says. "I had to learn the personalities of all of these different varieties. If I was forced to just stick with making pure Pinot Noir, I'm not sure I'd have been successful."

Around the time Bruce was releasing his first varietal Grenache, Joseph Phelps was encountering his first Rhône wine at the home of a business acquaintance in San Francisco.

Joseph Phelps was born in Missouri in 1927 and raised in Greeley, Colorado. Within a few weeks of his honorable discharge from the Navy he joined his father, Hensel Phelps, at the family's construction business. Hensel Phelps Construction was soon on its way to becoming one of the nation's most successful general contractors, a multibillion-dollar company specializing in large civil and private projects, from airport terminals to convention centers. The firm opened a satellite office in Burlingame, California, in 1967; by this time Joseph Phelps was the company president, and he helped to build one of its largest public works projects to that point, the Bay Area Rapid Transit system.

Through the firm's banking connections he met and became friends with Adolph "Bud" Mueller, a vice president of Wells Fargo Bank in San Francisco, who in 1966 poured for Phelps a Côte-Rôtie. "I was very much impressed," says Phelps with characteristic understatement, "and it was interesting to learn that this was a variety that was much overlooked in France and everywhere else, except Australia perhaps. My interest grew from there."[2]

In 1972, Bud Mueller was issuing a loan for a new winery project in the Napa Valley called Souverain Cellars, and asked Phelps if he might be interested in bidding on the construction. Phelps won the contract and began building his first Napa Valley winery. Within a year he would be planning one of his own.

Phelps was not unacquainted with fine wine; in college he bought many California wines, especially Zinfandels; within a few short years he was collecting Bordeaux. But the memory of that Syrah from Côte-Rôtie was never far from his mind; he was particularly struck to learn that the very same wines from Bordeaux that he loved so much had been, through the years, routinely beefed up with the addition of Syrah wine from the Rhône.

"I thought that if these Chateaux went through the process of 'Hermitaging' their wines," he said, "and if those wines were used to 'improve' the wines from Bordeaux— well then, Syrah must be something worth looking at." He began to add what Rhône wines he could find to his burgeoning collection; when Kermit Lynch Wine Merchants opened in 1971, Phelps was one of the first through the door.

Phelps's love of Rhône wines eventually compelled him to take several trips to the region to taste and tour, often staying in a village called Villefranche sur Mer, outside of Nice. Phelps immersed himself in the language and in the irresistible ambiance of the French Mediterranean culture. In 1989, he would purchase a house in the shadow of Mont Ventoux, in the southern Rhône.

Joseph Phelps Vineyards was founded in 1973, part of a large incoming class of wineries in the early seventies that included some of Napa's icon brands such as Cakebread, Domaine Chandon, Stag's Leap Wine Cellars, Caymus, Diamond Creek, Silver Oak, and Franciscan. It is now best known as a Napa Valley winery that excels in red wines, in particular Bordeaux variety wines. Most famously, in 1974 Phelps crafted a wine called Insignia (the name came to him one morning while shaving), California's first proprietary red blend, a wine that predated all of the iconic red wines that the Napa Valley has come to be famous for, including Opus One, Dominus, Rubicon, and Quintessa.

But from the winery's inception, Phelps intended to pursue Syrah and instructed his winemaker, Walter Schug, to find some. If anyone could ferret out a nearly nonexistent variety in the North Coast, it was Schug, the former director of Growing Relations for E & J Gallo, who had firsthand knowledge of the vineyard holdings for more than 500 growers statewide. It was a network he put to good use.

Grower relations in the 1960s consisted of purchasing quality grapes at a tonnage rate. Fruit was then combined into generic blends stamped with names like Hearty Burgundy (which contained no Burgundy of course, and little if any Pinot Noir) and sold cheaply across the country. Then as now, the Gallos purchased fruit from a vast network of growers who brought in field blends from Prohibition-era plantings.

These were family operations, with vineyard plots handed from father to son, propagated, often as not, by cuttings from within the vineyard itself. Their composition, then, was always a bit of a mystery: grape varieties went largely undocumented, but were usually a complementary tangle of dark-fruited grapes, usually dominated by Zinfandel, but supplemented by Petite Sirah, Mataro, and Carignane, Cinsaut, Grenache, Alicante Bouschet, Lenoir—and at least some Syrah. Growers tended to harvest the varieties together, throw it into the same bins; producers purchased it in bulk and never bothered to separate it.

In all of the thousands of tons he had processed over the vintages, Walter Schug was certain he'd seen his share of Syrah. He recalled, for example, the contributions of a man named Sattimo del Porto, owner of a small vineyard on Mee Lane in St. Helena in the Napa Valley, a typical vineyard of the time. This vineyard, recalls Schug, wasn't just mixed; it was interplanted with prune and walnut trees; when the grapes didn't bring in money, the grower could fall back on another crop. Del Porto brought his grapes in every harvest and Schug was always struck by how different they looked; they were lighter, dustier, slightly more oblong, the clusters larger, bearing a heady fragrance.

"He'd say 'what do you think of my Pets?'" says Schug, "and I'd say 'It looks great.'"

"'I know,' said del Porto, "'because it's the French kind.' It didn't dawn on me until later that what this guy had was actually Syrah."[3] Now he was tasked with finding the very thing he'd been buying in hidden quantities for many years. Schug called Harold Olmo at Davis first.

"Gee, Walter," Olmo replied, "you have some right under your nose." Olmo told him about the experimental plot at Wheeler Ranch, owned by the Christian Brothers Winery on Zinfandel Lane in St. Helena. It was a homely site, situated near the Napa River. With its heavy clay soils, the vineyard was compromised from the start; the vines took up so much moisture that the berries typically came in with very high water content, which limited their concentration and never really allowed them to ripen fully. "The vines were very close to the river," explains Bruce Neyers, the winery's first sales director, "so when the fruit started to ripen they would gobble up water; they never really ripened effectively."

Moreover, according to Schug, the vines were virused, and yields were notoriously uneven. "It was one of those calendar pictures in the fall," said Schug, "with beautiful bright red leaves"—pretty, but a sure sign of disease.

Christian Brothers threw a modest amount of the vineyard's fruit into a blend they called Napa Gamay, or sold off the occasional lot in bulk where it got incorporated in other similarly prosaic blends. Brother Timothy, the winemaker for Christian Brothers, never thought much of the fruit there, so when someone came along to buy it, he was happy to sell. In 1974, the Phelps winery took ten tons.

Schug remembers the 1974 Syrah harvest as drawn out and slow. The vines, in their diseased condition, dropped most of their leaves long before the fruit had matured, basically bringing to an end the ripening process—they were left to sugar up as they desiccated on the vines. "We'd already picked all of our other grapes," he said, "and it was coming on to November." Schug went back to Phelps and laid out the situation, and Phelps asked what they should do. Schug said, "Well, let's give it a try. I kind of have a feeling that the long hang time might give us enough color and the flavor; we won't worry about the alcohol."

The percentage of alcohol came to 11.2%, about that of a German Riesling. They bottled this wine as the first varietal Syrah in California history, and did so for the next forty-two years. Bruce Neyers, whose stint as sales director for the brand commenced in 1975, was less than optimistic about these first efforts.

"It did *smell* like Syrah," says Neyers of the first vintage, "it smelled like the northern Rhône. But it tasted kind of flat, it had a very high pH, and as such the color wasn't stable, and there were tartrates. We had a lot of people bring it back or complain about it."[4]

While the first Syrah reposed in barrel, the Phelps team started to actively seek other sources of grapes, as well as plant material for their Rhône/Syrah project. This would prove to be both ambitious and, at times, wildly quixotic.

They learned that FPMS (Foundation Plant Materials Service) and its caretaker, Austin Goheen, possessed three Syrah clones, starting with the one they were already using, brought in by Harold Olmo in 1936—the one planted at Wheeler Ranch, known as Syrah Noir. A second had been procured in 1970 by Goheen from a Victoria, Australia, plant research facility, and was said to have originated from a mixed black vineyard at Seppelt Winery in the Great Western. (This would become known as the Shiraz clone.)

Then in 1973 Goheen visited the vine repository facility in France, ENTAV (Etablissement National Technique pour l'Amélioration de la Viticulture), and asked its esteemed director, Claude Valat to supply him with the "best" Syrah clone he had available. This Valat did; the clone would come to be known as the Espiguette clone, after the nursery it came from.

Additionally, small amounts of a clone derived from a small old vine selection of Syrah in the McDowell Valley were collected, as well as what became known as the Estrella River clone, developed by Gary Eberle; these were employed by Phelps as they became available. A sixth, said to have been brought in by a Davis graduate student in 1974, was eventually acknowledged as well.

FPMS stipulated that since none of their stock had yet been officially released, that the team would be required to keep the selections separate and clearly marked, as well as available to testing once they were established. These promises the Phelps team abandoned almost immediately, in their haste to fill hillsides with vines. In some cases the vine rows contained two or more clones as the team propagated as fast as they could.[5]

In 1975 Phelps persuaded a couple of students at Davis, John Kongsgaard and W.M. Hin, to conduct research on the variety. In a brief 1976 report on the subject, Kongsgaard and Hin traced its origins in France, documented its relative rarity in that country even as its reputation as a quality wine grape remained high, and began to sort out the confusion in California between Petite Sirah and Syrah. The researchers concluded that "the Syrah appears to offer unique and unrealized potential under certain California viticultural conditions, and deserves evaluation as a premium varietal wine grape."[6] But no one yet knew what those conditions were.

Even as they were trying to improve a wine that none of the Phelps team was particularly happy with, they still had to sell it. That herculean task was left to Neyers, the sales manager and eventual president of the winery.

Neyers came into the wine business through a venerable wine shop in San Francisco called Connoisseur Wine Imports, whose selection of imported wines from the Rhône was derived from the portfolio of Frank Schoonmaker and were as good as any in the city at the time—Chave Hermitage, a centuries-old benchmark for the world's Syrah, was sold at the store in small quantities.

Neyers was still in the Army at the time, and worked in the shop on weekends for a pittance. He abused his employee discount, ending up with a wine collection and indebted to the shop. It was in those aisles that Neyers met a man named Kermit Lynch who said he was going to get into the wine business—they went to coffee together and chatted about wine. One afternoon Bob Travers, then winemaker at Mayacamas Winery, delivered twenty cases of wine to the shop and invited Neyers to help out at harvest, which Neyers did. "It was the most exciting thing I had ever done in my life to that point," he says.

The following year Neyers was assisting Travers at Mayacamas, still putting in time at the store, and casting about for winemaking positions in Germany (reasoning, he knew German, he loved German wines) when he attended a dinner in Napa and happened to be seated next to Joseph Phelps. The two men hit it off, and Neyers was impressed with the young entrepreneur. "He was clearly a man of substance," says Neyers, "and the winery itself sounded extravagant. No one had spent that kind of money on a winery in the Napa Valley." Neyers evidently made an impression himself. "'When you get back from Germany,'" said Phelps, "'if you're looking for something, give a call, we'll give you a job.'" Neyers did, and became sales manager for the winery in March 1975.

The first Syrah was released in 1977, to almost universal disregard. Phelps was mystified. "I thought it was a pretty good wine," he says, "but people didn't know what it was. I came into the wine business with the misconception that there would be an advantage to being the only one, to be a pioneer and be able to say, 'We're the only house that makes it.' So we sort of broke our pick on Syrah in the early years."[7]

A varietal Syrah certainly could trade on its novelty, to an extent. Neyers recalled a private gathering for the Society of the Medical Friends of Wine of Northern California. A group of about sixty doctors came to the winery and were served the wine at a luncheon. Every single one of the doctors bought at least one bottle. It was his single biggest sales success to date, and it was rarely repeated.

This continued for more than a decade, after which Neyers resorted to desperate measures. "We finally hit upon a program that really worked," he says. "Buy one case, you get two cases free." All of their best efforts had not made the wine good enough to sell. "It was probably a little embarrassing to all of us," says Neyers. "Here we are a leader in this category and the wine we're making is among the least attractive."

Phelps was not the only winery to have taken on this burden. In 1975, Caymus Vineyards produced a single barrel of Syrah from the same vineyard as the Phelps source. Caymus, of course, is best known as a Cabernet house, but in 1975, according to Chuck Wagner, nothing was cut and dried. They made white wines, Zinfandel, Pinot Noir, Petite Sirah, and a half-dozen other varieties, as they hedged their bets against a shifting market. It would be another decade before Cabernet became predominant in the Napa Valley.

So in 1975 Chuck Wagner purchased a small amount of Syrah from Christian Brothers, enough to fill one barrel, which Steve Wallace stumbled on in a visit the following year. His son Charlie, who would become winemaker but who was just old enough to drink at the time, had no idea what Syrah was. "I doubt I'd ever had a bottle of Rhône wine," he says.[8]

He remembers this wine, though. "It was so dark," he says, "and it didn't behave like Petite Sirah, it didn't have that aggressive dry tannin. It was softer, more yielding."

Those qualities were certainly what appealed to Steve Wallace as he dipped his nose into the barrel in 1976, and came away impressed. Wallace bought the barrel's contents outright, and had it bottled with his own label, designed by the abstract artist and print-maker Sam Francis, who was a friend and customer of Wallace's; the label was a worked, blue painterly square beneath which a single word, "Syrah," was etched in a faintly Gaelic script. The production was credited to Caymus—Chuck Wagner's wife hand-labeled each bottle in her kitchen. According to Wallace, it went almost unsold. "I think I still have some in my warehouse," says Wallace sadly. The word Syrah, placed boldly on the label, had absolutely no impact on the American public at the time.

In winemaking, they say, you only get one chance a year to get it right. With planting, those already long odds get much longer, and the Phelps team devoted much of the first decade of their Syrah program planting or contracting for the planting of new Syrah plots.[9] But each of the clones possessed flaws—either viral impediments or other genetic short-comings, like stem-pitting—that kept their academic sources from wholesale endorse-ment. The Phelps team meanwhile, eager to get vines in the ground, chose to work with them all in the absence of consensus of which was the best. "Nobody was around," says Schug, "who knew enough to praise one [clone] over the other."

For the next twelve years, Phelps and his winemaking team, consisting of Schug, winemaker Craig Williams, who joined the winery in 1976, as well as a host of other players drawn to the project—including Damian Parker, John Buechsenstein, Bruce Ney-ers, and eventually, Markus Bokisch and Ehren Jordan—all toiled together to make Syrah against long odds, purposely, according to Williams, "to elevate the specificity of the varietal nature." For more than a decade, a successful bottling remained elusive. "The first few releases," he says, "were interesting, but I don't think we'd achieved a likeness to the French model, and that was definitely our focus, Côte-Rôtie in particular, Guigal being the reference point."[10]

Williams by then was tasting northern Rhône Syrahs regularly with Phelps and Neyers, both of whom had cellars filled with French wines. There was a wildness that all three loved in good northern Rhône Syrah that went missing in the wines they were producing. "Joe was driving the search for this pepper thing," says Williams. "It was something that he thought California could do because it had these granitic soils, the same as Côte-Rôtie."

In their fifth vintage, 1979, Williams believes they produced an excellent wine, one that showed off some of the pepper and the spice found in good northern Rhône wine. Williams changed things up slightly that year, he remembers, with a bit of whole cluster fermentation. But the efforts in 1980 fell short again.

Williams made his first visit to the Rhône in May of 1982. Williams and his wife had spent some time in Burgundy with Kermit Lynch, and were driving down to the Rhône through Beaujolais. "I was thinking it's called Côte-Rôtie, Roasted Slope, it's got to be hot, right? I'm going to be in swim trunks, a t-shirt and flip-flops. But it's cold there, really cold! It's more close to the Côte d'Or than the rest of the Rhône Valley."

So Williams went further south to Hermitage, and met with Gerard Chave, and asked him when he typically picked Syrah. "Ideally, we like to pick it before it snows," was the reply.

Chave informed him that in Hermitage Syrah didn't even get fully ripe until October, and they usually started picking in the middle of that month. "Here, if I'm thinking if I pick past September 10th I've got raisins," says Williams. "Something was amiss. I guess you could say the light bulb finally went off."

During the next several years Williams started moving all of Phelps's Syrah plantings progressively south to cooler areas, and the wines steadily improved. By the end of the eighties, none of Phelps's Syrah was coming from the Napa Valley.[11]

Twelve years after the first vintage, the 1986 Syrah convinced Bruce Neyers that they were onto something, with a compelling aromatic complexity that had attracted Phelps to the variety in the first place. By this time the team had also begun experimenting with Viognier, a variety they were keen on developing alongside Bill Smith, Pete Minor, and Josh Jensen, both as a stand-alone variety and to blend with their Syrah. "We needed to get some grace into our Syrah," said Phelps, "which was a very forward brute."

By this time Phelps had purchased land in Luberon, in the south of France, and a more southern French aesthetic started to creep into the team's mindset. "Mourvèdre and Grenache didn't find their way into our repertoire until the late eighties," says Phelps.

To blend, you need more fruit, of course, and that effort was led by Markus Bokisch, who served as team forager, pursuing older vine and mixed black fruit from Mendocino to Cucamonga. "I spent my time running around the state, going to the major old viticultural areas," he says, where he would visit Agricultural Commission offices and get a list of older plantings in each county, track down the owners, and make them offers.[12]

On more quixotic excursions they would take to the air. "Joe and I would fly up and down the North Coast," says Bokisch, "scouring the mountainsides, looking for old vine patches in Sonoma, or Mendocino, or inland areas. If we found one we're circle around and fly over the nearest road, trying to determine which driveway took you over to the vines we just located." Bokisch would take pictures from the air of identifying landmarks which he could rediscover first by consulting geological survey maps. Then he would cold call them, and if they agreed to meet he'd follow up by car, walk the vineyards, map their varietal content. If it fit the program, Bokisch would offer the grower a better price for their fruit.

Mostly, he says, he was turned down. "Much of it was tied up by Gallo," says Bokisch, "we'd be offering $1,000 a ton for Carignane, and no one would bite." By the early nineties, with increasing regularity, Bokisch would make a call and realize he'd been scooped, that another winemaker had rediscovered his discovery some weeks or months before.

Eventually they'd had enough fruit to develop a number of bottlings—a Syrah, a Viognier, a Grenache Rosé, and a blend—to merit the establishment of a separate brand line for the effort, which they called Vin du Mistral, an effort marked by a vivid back-label text written by Gerald Asher:

> Only the sturdiest of temperaments, it is said, can live with this wind that scours the Rhône Valley from the Alps to the Mediterranean. The vines of that valley, too, need vigor and tenacity to resist it—the reason, perhaps, why the wines made from them are prized for their boldly individual character. When grown in California, these Rhône varieties display that same distinctive character, thus our choice of the term Vin du Mistral to describe them.[13]

The Mistral line caught the momentum begun with Rhône varieties and finally Phelps's long-term efforts gained traction. "I'm not going to sit here and say that Joe was genius for wanting to do Syrah," says Neyers, "but the fact that he put so much time and energy and money into it, and made us do it, and made us get better, and solved the problems, when times were tough, when we were failing that much, vintage after vintage, for more than a decade—I don't think anybody else would have done that, would have put so much into that variety except for him."[14]

7

SYRAH'S PROUD FATHER
Gary Eberle and the Making of Modern Syrah

Joseph Phelps may have been the first to bottle a varietal Syrah in the twentieth century but his planting efforts were actually preceded by another producer some 300 miles south, unbeknown to Phelps, with a similar taste for the quixotic. Gary Eberle's early plantings beat Phelps out by about a year, and his expectations were immense, which made him as naïve and unrealistic as Phelps. But Eberle's folly would become a great catalyst for Syrah's rise as a viable category: without his outsized interest, Syrah might never have gotten off the ground.

In 1972, Gary Eberle enrolled as a graduate student at the University of California, Davis, having first attended Penn State on a football scholarship and excelled as a tackle for Joe Paterno's storied team. He excelled academically as well, moving on to a course of study in cell biology and zoology at Louisiana State University, where at a faculty social event a professor poured him a glass of Bordeaux, a 1966 Saint-Julien from Ducru-Beaucaillou. "I realized," he joked, "I didn't want to be a geneticist anymore; I just wanted to drink."[1]

Eberle's academic record and strong science background got him on the short track at Davis the following year. Still a wine neophyte, and eager to catch up, he surrounded himself with a core of fellow students and together they set about tasting as many wines as they could find. It was, in retrospect, a remarkable group of students—many of them now hold important positions in the California wine industry, including David Stare, founder of Dry Creek Winery, longtime winery executive Tom Selfridge, and future California fortified wine producer Andrew Quady.

Also attending that year was a young winemaker from Australia named Brian Croser. Croser is now one of the eminences on the Australian wine industry; in 1971, he was a young recent hire at the venerable South Australia winery Thomas Hardy and Sons. Upon hiring, Croser was promptly shipped off to Davis for intensive technical training. He was there just three months, after which he went to Europe for more training. He represented a winemaking culture and tradition that was thoroughly unfamiliar to his fellow students, and the bottles he shared from the home winery in Adelaide were vivid to all, and life-changing to some.

Croser admits to having been something of a proselyte for his home country at the time. Americans, even enology students, were only barely acquainted with the country's venerable history in winemaking and grape growing. They knew even less about one of its signature grapes, Shiraz.

It was an especially good time to be sharing, according to Croser. Australia was just beginning to shake off a fairly moribund period of its winemaking history, where much of its red fruits were typically sacrificed to make dull, oxidized, fortified wines, which were then sold cheaply in a market that barely existed beyond the country's inhabitants. The country had acres of old vine Shiraz vines which no one thought much of. Indeed in a staggering display of shortsightedness, the Australian government would establish an eradication program in the 1980s meant to rid the countryside of old vineyards, replacing some of the world's oldest Rhône variety vineyards with Cabernet Sauvignon.

But a small group of young winemakers had begun moonlighting in wineries across the country to create stirring red wines from the Barossa, Coonawara, and McLaren Vale— made, says Croser, "from the wonderful vestigial vineyards of the nineteenth century." This modest revolt from current practices ignited new interest in these old vineyards.

The wines were also very good. Croser remembers this period as particularly energized and significant, indicative of the great potential that consumers around the world soon embraced. "Those wines," writes Croser, "were probably the greatest Australia has ever known, stunning and unique examples of Australian Shiraz-dominant wines from an era that probably will never be repeated."[2] These were the wines Croser received from his colleagues at Hardy's, which he shared in tastings for Davis students and staff, and were deeply formative for Eberle and his fellow students.

For the continental portion of his extracurricular education, Eberle had food and wine merchant Darrell Corti to thank. Eberle and his classmates would make regular pilgrimages to Corti Brothers, a grocery and specialty store in nearby Sacramento that even then was well known for its broad assortment of wines from all over the world, a selection that was probably without parallel at the time in California. Eberle still refers to the store as UC-Davis East. Corti took over the wine selection at the store when he joined the family business in 1962 and was soon making regular trips to Europe to procure, often directly, shipments of hard-to-find wines from all over the continent.[3]

Already by the early seventies, Corti was one of the most articulate modern champions of California's wine heritage, seeking out and selling new bottlings of California

Cabernet—he was a customer of Ridge Vineyards six years before Paul Draper was hired—as well as newfangled varieties like Chardonnay and Riesling. He also had an abiding enthusiasm for mixed black vineyard bottlings, wherein older Rhône variety vines lay in repose.

Eberle loved Bordeaux, but Corti tirelessly redirected him and other students out of their comfort zone, and introduced Eberle to the wines of Hermitage, Côte-Rôtie, and Saint-Joseph, Chateauneuf-du-Pape, rosés from Tavel, wines that back then even students could afford.

"There was a big table in the store," says Eberle, "with all these wines. Darrell was not above pulling a cork if he thought it was a wine we might be interested in." Corti kept abreast of the new wines coming in from the Rhône Valley, still in a relative trickle, but at any given time, recalls Eberle, the store stocked about a half-dozen Syrah-based bottlings, which he frequently sampled and resampled in the years he studied at Davis.

A year before graduation, Eberle attended a family reunion in Southern California and met up with his half-brothers, Clifford and James Giacobine. Eberle told Cliff about his plans to become a winemaker. "Cliff was into real estate in Southern California for years, and a bit of a hustler," says Eberle. "Jim was a surgeon with a lot of money and no time to do anything with it." Cliff often found building and real estate projects in which he could invest Jim's capital. All the while, says Eberle, Cliff harbored a somewhat misguided desire to own a ranch, and live life like a cowboy.

Seeing his chance, Eberle suggested that perhaps Cliff could combine his interest in cattle with a small vineyard. "Once he started down the path with the grapes the cattle thing went by the wayside," says Eberle. With the Giacobines as partners, Eberle laid plans for a new venture, Estrella River Winery, named for a small Paso Robles tributary that drained into the Salinas River. The vineyard site was just east of Paso Robles, in a warm grape-growing region that had remained largely unplanted after Prohibition.

Eberle completed his degree and set about planning his new venture. His intention all along was to focus on Cabernet Sauvignon, but his experience with Syrah weighed on him, and he started to consider working with the varietal.

He asked Darrell Corti what he thought about planting Syrah in Paso Robles. Corti didn't know much about Paso Robles, but about Syrah his enthusiasm was wholehearted. "He checked his ampelography books and said to me, 'I don't know why it's not planted; it's a natural for California. You should do it.'"

His professors urged him in the same direction. "I had looked at my charts," he said, "and I thought it would be a perfect grape for the region, and so I went to Harold [Olmo] and said 'hey, what do you think?'" Olmo, whose original cuttings from Montpellier had been planted in Napa and which had led to the first Phelps bottling, was supportive, as was Austin Goheen, a plant scientist for the USDA with an interest in Syrah. So was

Curtis "Doc" Alley, a viticulture specialist who told Eberle, "We don't know why it's not being grown in the state, but it should. It would do beautifully. Do it!"

Now the question was, where to get Syrah vines?

By this time there was plenty of evidence that the vineyard which Christian Brothers had planted on Zinfandel Lane from Harold Olmo's original Montpellier cuttings was badly virused, and Eberle's professors discouraged him from using it. FPMS possessed another clone from the collection that Austin Goheen had procured from Australia, but neither Goheen nor the university staff were ever convinced it was free of virus sufficient to merit release.

One spring afternoon Eberle ran into his friend and viticulture mentor Doc Alley, who asked him how things were going. Eberle told Alley of the difficulties he'd been having getting Syrah; what little was available was compromised. Alley thought a moment and said "Come with me."

They climbed into Alley's old Toyota pickup and drove across campus, to a small triangular vineyard plot that had once been part of the university's vineyard, but which some years before had been separated from the rest of the campus by the construction of Interstate 80, the main road from Sacramento to San Francisco. Eberle had been to the site plenty of times before; as a student he and others would come and practice their pruning on the vines that remained there, and while the vineyard wasn't formally maintained, it was still very much in use.

Alley took him to a corner of the vineyard to a plot of vines, to which he pointed: "I have no documentation," he said, "but this is Syrah. It's from Tain, it's Chapoutier, and it's clean."[4] Alley instructed him to take as much budwood as he wanted, and get it propagated.

Eberle took cuttings to December Pacific Nursery in 1973, where it was propagated by Doug Meader. Eberle started planting in 1975. When he was finished, he had put in 18 acres.

To this day, the selection that Eberle planted is known as the Estrella River clone, not the Chapoutier clone. It has been disseminated all over California and other western states. For more than thirty years, Eberle kept the actual source of these cuttings private; if the subject ever came up, he insisted that he himself had suitcased the cuttings—usually the matter would end there.

Eberle decided it was necessary to protect the reputation of the Davis faculty members who taught him, whom he considered close friends and mentors.[5] He made a decision early on that while Professors Alley and Olmo were alive, he would keep their role secret. After all, the true source of the Syrah cuttings that Doc Alley pointed out to his student in 1972 remains unknown; Alley may have insisted they came from Chapoutier, but it's impossible to document this fact, and even if his claim is true, it remains a mystery how it found its way into the Davis experimental plot. So rather than cast aspersions upon the reputations of his teachers, Eberle decided to weather by himself whatever blame might arise with this material.

Estrella River's plans for Syrah were ambitious, not to say foolhardy. Having laid down one 18-acre parcel, they followed with another 20 acres, for a potential yield of nearly 200 tons of fruit, and 5,000 cases of wine—for a largely unknown, mostly untested variety. None of this daunted Eberle. He was certain that people would come to Syrah because it was new and different; they would come back, he thought, because they would find Syrah as irresistible as the Hermitages and Australian Shirazes that had so moved him and his colleagues at Davis.[6] Instead, things unfolded quite differently.

In its first vintage, 1978, the Estrella River Syrah sold well, on minimal, young-vine yields. Eberle placed his 1979 Syrah into three wine contests—the Los Angeles County Fair, the Orange County, and the London International Wine Competition, and the wine took a gold medal in each—owing as much to its novelty, perhaps, as its quality—but the good showing was encouraging to the young winemaker, and also made that vintage relatively easy to sell.

As Eberle headed out to sell the 1980 vintage wine, he'd walk into accounts he'd been to the year before, accounts that had enthusiastically taken a case or two of the 1979. When he got there, Eberle often found six bottles of last year's vintage still on the shelf. The novelty sales phase was over; few committed to the 1980 vintage. By the time of the next vintage Eberle clearly had some choices to make. He had to get creative.

Estrella River's Syrah crop in 1981 was its largest ever. Faced with a surplus he knew he couldn't sell, Eberle took note of the fact that the market still showed high demand for white wines, and made a fateful harvest-time decision—he would take half of his Syrah crop and make a white Syrah.

It is hard to imagine today a decision to make a colorless wine from a grape variety whose pigmentary gifts are celebrated, a variety known for some of the inkiest wines on the planet. But that is the position Eberle found himself in. They called it Syrah Blanc, bottled it in an attractive, "smoked" Burgundy bottle; in flavor, says Eberle, it came off not unlike a Semillon and accounted, in 1981, for almost half of his Syrah production. In an era where white wines still dominated the market, the Syrah Blanc was considerably easier to sell than Syrah Rouge. "Our plan was to sell 5,000 cases of Syrah a year," he says. "By 1981 it was very obvious we couldn't sell 5,000 cases."

An extended run of Syrah Blanc, of course, was not an attractive option. Eberle's next alternative was to sell fruit; by this time a few Rhône variety producers were beginning winery projects, and they came knocking, drawn in by a low price and as yet nonexistent demand. Ultimately, Plan B was a modest boon for the category—as bottlings proliferated, so did visibility, and with each new vintage, the word started to spread. Eberle's memory of his fruit customers is a little fuzzy, but he believes that Bob Lindquist was his first, followed by Randall Grahm and Steve Edmunds, Adam Tolmach, Zaca Mesa, and others.

From his vantage point, Eberle watched as Bob Lindquist and Randall Grahm became the true accelerators for Syrah in those early vintages. "It was definitely Lindquist," says

Eberle. "Syrah was his baby." No one could mistake the seriousness of Lindquist's bottlings: they were stylish, aromatically arresting, nuanced affairs that caught the attention of virtually anyone who tasted them. Lindquist's early efforts taught more than a few winemakers that Syrah wasn't just a lark, it was a definite possibility in California.

It was Grahm, however, who brought the style. "I think it would have taken much longer for Syrah to really move into the kind of prominence that it has today without Randall Grahm," says Eberle. "There were Rhône producers, but there really wasn't a movement until Randall came along. I could have been making Syrah down here for twenty years and not done what he did in three or four years."

Eberle's third option was to sell cuttings of his own. Thousands of sticks were collected each winter during pruning and were propagated. The response was enthusiastic, and surprising. Eberle believes that he sold more budwood than fruit in bulk at the time. "There was no negative connotation for Syrah," says Eberle, "there was no connotation at all, unlike the reputations of Grenache and Carignane, which were considered 'valley grapes.' Syrah was a virgin," says Eberle, "it was new and different."

Already by 1980 the Estrella River production model was burdensome for Eberle, with hundreds of thousands of cases in the pipeline. Two years later Eberle asked to be bought out, and the Giacobines did so, with Eberle taking much of his payout in wine, which he sold and parlayed the proceeds into the winery that bears his name, just a short drive from his original property. The Giacobines sold Estrella River in 1987 to Meridian Winery, which ripped out the Syrah vines in 1996.

The first beneficiary of Gary Eberle's third option was Zaca Mesa Winery, in Santa Barbara County. Having traveled the Central Coast helping other wineries get going, consulting, selling his services and his grapes, Eberle looked to sell cuttings to other wineries. His offers of Syrah typically went unheeded, until he came to Zaca Mesa, where he could not have found a more receptive team.

Zaca Mesa is set on the northern reaches of the Santa Ynez Valley on Foxen Canyon Road.[7] As the name implies, the vineyard is set on a mesa, stretching 1,700 acres at 1,500 feet of elevation, inland from the Pacific by about twenty-five miles. It is a fairly desolate place, surrounded by pastureland and canyons filled with oak scrub that set one mesa apart from another. It is probably the warmest place for viticulture in the Santa Ynez Valley; from a promontory on the mesa's eastern edge, you can actually make out some of the structures that once composed Neverland Ranch, the remote, extended fantasy of the late Michael Jackson.

That, of course, was not the draw of the property in 1973. But it's hard to say what was. Certainly the founders, when they started planting, demonstrated only a rudimentary knowledge of the area and its potential. There was little if any vineyard development in the area, few experienced enough to offer advice—not much to draw from at all if you weren't a cattle rancher. Nevertheless, the partners set about planting a scattershot array of varieties, from Riesling to Cabernet Sauvignon, with significant plantings of Sauvignon Blanc, Chenin Blanc, and Chardonnay.

Zaca Mesa was founded by one of the more high-powered partnerships ever assembled in the domestic wine industry, a consortium that included the president of Standard Oil, the chairman of Amoco, the CEO of defense contractor TRW, and the future real estate tycoon John Cushman (who remains the current owner, with his wife). The day-to-day operations of the winery fell to another oilman, the heir apparent to the chair of the Atlantic Richfield Oil Company (ARCO), Marshall Ream. It was, in some ways, an ideal situation—a group of investors who knew how to work with land and knew it took long-term investment to bring its full potential to fruition. Ream—a young, ambitious, and ebullient captain, spared no expense, and handpicked some of the most compelling winemaking talent assembled in California to that point.

Ream hired Fresno State graduate Byron "Ken" Brown to head up the winemaking. Brown in turn gathered a gifted group of winemakers, assistants, enologists, and hands that would form the core of artisanal wine production in the Central Coast through the 1980s, a trend that would continue long after these individuals had moved onto their own projects. In fact, it was not an exaggeration to say that most of the winemakers in the region's new wineries were alumni of Zaca's cellars. But at the core of that first group were three men: Jim Clendenen, Adam Tolmach, and Bob Lindquist. Their friendship, partnership, and early adventures in Rhône wine-tasting and winemaking became a driving force in the early American Rhône movement.

Jim Clendenen was born in Ohio, moving west to study pre-law at the University of California, Santa Barbara. Now considered among the most verbally gifted, articulate winemakers in California, Clendenen seemed practically hard-wired for the law. However as a junior he took a year abroad in France, was introduced to the glories of French wine, and was transformed. Two years later he returned for a month of study, this time in Burgundy and Champagne, and realized that the law was not his calling. After a formative stage under the wing of Burgundy merchant Becky Wasserman, he returned to the states and did a helpful stage with Fred Brander at Brander's new winery in 1976. Two years later, Zaca Mesa promised him training in winemaking under Brown.

Clendenen was joined one year later by Adam Tolmach, a young recent Davis graduate whose winemaking ambitions originated with his father, a medical doctor who for years carried on a busy practice in Ventura, California—busy enough, says Tolmach, to convince his son to choose another profession. His father did love wine, however, and shared a number of bottlings with his son when he was of age; Tolmach remembers his father's love for Burgundy and Beaujolais, as well as the occasional American Cabernet and Zinfandel.

Tolmach went to Davis for a general course of study, but eventually the enology program lured him in, and he got a degree in enology. He returned to the area and found one of the few winemaking jobs available in the as-yet undeveloped Santa Barbara County. As the company's youngest hire, Tolmach was perhaps its most resilient; he lived on the Zaca Mesa property for a winter in an unheated trailer.

The third member of this team was Bob Lindquist, who had been hired to help run a small wine shop that Marshall Ream had opened in the nearby town of Los Olivos. Ream appointed his son to run it; Lindquist was taken on as his assistant.

Lindquist was born in Missouri in 1953. At a young age he moved with his family to Orange County in Southern California, where his father was a civil engineer in the aerospace industry. Lindquist quickly and effortlessly became a quintessential South Coast boy: from surfing to music to baseball, the region became a source of inspiration to him, shaping his career in countless and unexpected ways.[8] He spent a few years at the University of California, Irvine, got married, had his first child.[9] To support his family he worked a number of thankless jobs, including a stint at an advertising agency. There, in the mid-1970s, one of his clients offered to pay him with bottles of wine, and Lindquist obliged.

One bottle in the lot, the 1970 Simi Sonoma County Cabernet, left him stunned. "That was the watershed moment for me," he says. "I couldn't believe what I was tasting. I thought 'I've got to find out more about this stuff.'"[10] The next day he went to Hi-Time Wine Cellars in Costa Mesa, and bought all he could for $100, wines from Ridge, David Bruce, Heitz Martha's Vineyard. Within a year he'd packed up and moved his family to Santa Clara County, where he had an uncle—not exactly wine country, but more of one than Orange County. He took on various wine-related jobs in the area—in tasting rooms, cellars, helping out at harvest—before a winery in San Martin asked Lindquist to manage a tasting room in Ventura County. One year later he met Marshall Ream, who hired him for the shop.

Despite his father's investment, or perhaps because of it, Ream's son John seemed to have little interest in wine—or in working, evidently—and it fell to Lindquist to all but run the place. The clientele was sparse—no one yet thought of the Central Coast as a wine destination—but a sparse assortment of tourists and area wine professionals frequented the place; mostly it was a chance for Lindquist to taste a lot of wine, and learn as much as he could.

Then as now, Lindquist was a huge music fan, and early into his tenure at the wine shop he learned that the Kinks were due in town on a Sunday for a concert at the Santa Barbara Bowl. He bought his tickets and told John Ream that he wouldn't be able to work on that day. A week before the concert he reminded Rehm that he'd be away that day, and Ream, who'd had his heart set on dove hunting that day, refused to grant him the day off. An argument ensued, ending without resolution; Lindquist went to the concert, and when he returned to the shop the following Monday, he learned he was out of a job. A few days later Marshall Ream called Lindquist, apologized for his son's behavior, and offered him a job at the winery.

Lindquist was hired in the tasting room, giving tours and performing administrative tasks, with the odd sales or delivery trip thrown in for good measure. In fact most of his time was spent in the cellar, learning winemaking shoulder to shoulder with Clendenen and Tolmach. Clendenen and Lindquist became close friends, and Clendenen, with just one vintage under his belt, became Lindquist's mentor. Lindquist says he's never learned so much in so little time. "One year with Jim is like ten years with someone else," he says.

When they weren't making it, the three spent nearly all of their spare time trying, tasting, drinking, and dissecting every wine they could get their hands on. They pored over wine shops for obscure bottles and made regular excursions to Los Angeles and the Bay Area to forage.

"We had a lot of energy," says Tolmach. "And those passions led to some pretty dramatic decisions on that property. And we certainly knew how to drink back then—your liver works a lot better when you're twenty." But in that excess, a remarkably uniform set of aesthetics was taking shape among the three would-be winemakers, guided by the mysteries of Burgundy, and increasingly by the earthy pleasures of the Rhône Valley.

As their interest shifted toward the Rhône, they learned of an importer in Berkeley named Kermit Lynch who was starting to import some of the wines from the region to California, many for the first time, many others for the first time with any consistency.

As tour guide and occasional salesman, Lindquist had the fewest winery entanglements, and could make regular trips to the Bay Area to sell and of course to buy wine: invariably he'd make stops at Lynch's store. On one of his first visits, he had a formative encounter with Lynch, receiving some memorable advice in the process.

It was late in the day, and the store was about to close. Lindquist asked for some help in selecting a mixed case of wine. Lynch turned out to be the one helping him. Right after Lindquist arrived Joe Swan walked in—Lynch and Swan were going to dinner at Chez Panisse. Lindquist introduced himself as an employee of Zaca Mesa.

Lynch immediately went into a fairly warm-tempered diatribe. "'You know,' said Lynch, "'you shouldn't be making Chardonnay, or Pinot Noir in California! You should be growing and making Marsanne, Syrah, Mourvèdre!'" Lindquist nodded; he wasn't even sure what grape varieties Lynch was talking about. "I knew about Syrah, but I had never tasted a Marsanne by that point; I didn't know what a Condrieu was."

Lindquist stocked up, and in subsequent trips he made sure to pick up on whatever was latest and greatest, a rapidly expanding universe of wines from southern France and elsewhere, Mourvèdre-based Bandols of Domaine Tempier, Viognier from Andre Perret and Chateau-Grillet, Saint-Joseph Blancs and Rouges from Jean-Louis Grippat, Cornas from Clape, Côte-Rôtie from Robert Jasmin, and not least, the great Hermitage whites and reds from Domaine Jean-Louis Chave.

By the time Gary Eberle came knocking with Syrah cuttings, there was an energized and vociferous fan club for the variety. Clendenen, Tolmach, and Lindquist convinced their superiors to graft over an underperforming block of Petite Sirah. That original Syrah, now called Black Bear Block, was planted in 1980, is producing to this day, and remains the oldest modern Syrah planting in the Central Coast, and is one of the oldest in California.

After just two years at Zaca Mesa, Clendenen and Tolmach started talking about their own venture, and founded Au Bon Climat in 1982. Tolmach followed with his own parallel winery venture a year later, Ojai Vineyard, planting Syrah cuttings from Estrella River outside of Ojai, in the hills south of Santa Barbara. Inspired by Chateauneuf-du-Pape, Tolmach intended to push hard down the Rhône pathway—in fact he had the initial high-minded notion to produce just a red and white blend, the best the vineyard had to offer in that vintage. He became a bit more pragmatic after that, making highly regarded Pinot Noir and Chardonnay wines. His Rhône focus has been almost exclusively devoted to Syrah, about which he is one of the country's most devout practitioners and among the first to explore the vicissitudes of regional expression with vineyard designates.

He and Clendenen meanwhile forged a joint effort with fruit derived exclusively from the south Central Coast, with just Pinot Noir and Chardonnay in their arsenal at first, though Clendenen's ambitions and intellectual appetites could hardly be constrained to just these for long. Within a few short years they had outgrown every winemaking operation they had leased and were making wine in the tens of thousands of cases—too much for Tolmach in the end, who opted out in 1992.

Lindquist, meanwhile, with no formal training, thought long and hard about striking out on his own. It wasn't his first inclination. "I wasn't really planning on being a wine-maker," he says. But he was inspired by Clendenen and Tolmach's efforts, and was encouraged by Clendenen especially, who told him repeatedly that most people making wine in the south Central Coast knew less about winemaking than him. So Lindquist pulled together a loose group of investors, bought some barrels, and founded his own winery late in 1982, taking the name of Qupé from the Chumash Indian word for the California poppy which would adorn the first label.

Lindquist, along with Tolmach and Clendenen, were itinerant for the first several years of their existence, renting out space in existing wineries or custom crush facilities, often at the same facilities, where they still influenced each other.

For the next six vintages Lindquist scrambled to find Rhône varieties, sourcing from Estrella River, Phelps's Napa properties, and other places, without being entirely satisfied with the results. He sought to make other Rhône-inspired bottlings and wanted, eventually, to make a white wine inspired by his tastings of Chave's majestic Hermitage Blanc—if he could find the grapes.

As a hedge against the untested market for Rhône varieties, Lindquist made Chardonnay as well, a grape variety that was a lot easier to come by, even in the Central Coast. One of the region's most cherished sources was Bien Nacido Vineyard in the Santa Maria Valley, set on sprawling slopes in a gloomy, fogbound transverse valley with an unobstructed pathway to the ocean—cool climate in the extreme. Bob Miller owned and managed Bien Nacido Vineyard, an ambitious grower whose benchland had been planted to a scattershot array of varieties—a trial and error process led Miller one day in 1986 to ask his client Bob Lindquist whether he thought Bien Nacido might ever be a good place to grow Syrah.

Initially, Lindquist was flabbergasted. "No way," he said. "It's too cool."

"Well," said Miller, "we ripen Cabernet there."

"Yeah, but have you tasted it?" asked Lindquist.

"I know," admitted Miller, "it's never been that good, but it does get ripe. I think Syrah would too."

Lindquist pondered the notion a few days longer. The truth was, despite the fact that he'd made a few good wines from his Estrella River fruit, it never had the balance he was looking for; not a vintage had gone by without him adding acid to bring the wine some harmony. Cooler sites made sense, and yet . . .

Lindquist had dinner with his old boss, Ken Brown, and told him he was thinking about planting some Syrah at Bien Nacido. "And he thought I was crazy. 'Syrah?' he said. 'You can't ripen tomatoes in Santa Maria Valley—what makes you think Syrah is going to get ripe?'"

Lindquist felt the same: Estrella River may be too warm, but Bien Nacido was definitely too cool. Nevertheless, Lindquist agreed to come out and take a look, and they found a few blocks that might get enough sun and grafted over some vines. Thus began a successful partnership that has established Bien Nacido as the first true cool-climate Syrah site in California. The wines were spectacular right out of the gate—cool, meaty, low in alcohol, fine-boned, but with an impassioned depth of flavor that felt natural, unforced. Clearly Syrah's range in California was much broader than anyone had imagined.

Just after settling with Bien Nacido, Lindquist found a vineyard site near Los Olivos owned by a woman named Charlotte Young, whose vineyard had a track record for trends in the Central Coast. Young had planted Cabernet vines in 1973, which she had a difficult time ripening; by the eighties she'd grafted her vines over to Chenin and Sauvignon Blanc, neither of which excelled. Just before she was going to give up and rip out the vineyard, Lindquist convinced her to let him take it over; in 1986 he grafted over four acres, to Syrah, Mourvèdre, and the state's first Marsanne in ninety years. They got a crop the following year. Qupé becomes the first winery venture to immerse itself in Rhône varietal wines.

Within five years, Syrah bottlings had begun to surface across the state, and acreage actually crept into discernible figures. By 1985 more than 130 acres were in the ground; that number would skyrocket in the decade that followed.

Much of this growth was in the Central Coast, the result of the Estrella River vine and cuttings diaspora, through Eberle's tireless and at times desperate efforts. Here, in this Mediterranean milieu, Rhône varieties demonstrated their versatility. They were among the best suited to many of the climates that the Central Coast offered, and thrived in both warm and cool zones. Syrah in particular, with Pinot Noir, gave the region its first iconic variety, something that many new wineries could find success with, and the pool of talented winemakers willing to try them out grew with each vintage.

8

OTHER PIONEERS
From the North Coast to Gold Country

Just as Syrah plantings and bottlings were getting underway in the Napa Valley and the Central Coast, a small, virtually hidden vineyard in Mendocino County was rediscovering it anew.

McDowell Valley Vineyards was established in 1970 by William and Karen Crawford, who purchased 450 acres of vineyard land in a gorgeous, remote valley a few miles east of Hopland in the southeast corner of Mendocino County. It was a remarkable property, a sloping valley hemmed in by the foothills of the Mayacamas Mountains, with low hills framing three sides. A single road led into the valley from Hopland, that same road trailing east into the mountains toward Lake County, making it not only isolated, but practically secret.[1] Best of all, it came with old plantings, about which the new owners knew almost nothing, but were eager to learn.

The valley had been settled by pioneer Paxton McDowell, and descendents of that family, the Buckmans, still lived there when Karen and Bill Crawford purchased parcels in 1970. On one occasion when the Crawfords and Fred Buckman, then more than eighty years old, walked the vineyard together, Buckman told Karen that he had planted those original vineyards with his father, somewhat against the son's will, in 1919. Fred told her that just as he was ready to strike out on his own, his father asked him to stay and help plant the vineyard.

William Crawford installed a short airstrip at the farm, from which he could fly a single-engine Cessna in and out of the valley. Less than one year after the Crawfords had purchased their land, Crawford took off and didn't return. For several months he went unaccounted for; his wreck was eventually discovered in remote, densely forested wood-land near Laytonville, about sixty miles away. The investigator hired to pursue the matter was Richard Keehn, whom Karen Crawford subsequently married, and together they carried on the business of the vineyard estate.

The vineyard, with 350 acres planted, was composed of four parcels, each thought to have been planted by different homesteaders. The oldest block, planted in 1919 on its own roots in the southeast corner of the property, practically abutting the rise of the foothills that composed the eastern end of the valley, was about 40 acres in all, set on the flake and alluvium from the surrounding hills. A second block, believed to have been from material derived from that original block, on rootstock, was planted in 1948. According to old records, the vineyards had been planted at the turn of the century to Grenache, Syrah, Mission, Alicante, Golden Chasselas, and Carignane. To this the Keehns added Petite Sirah and Zinfandel.

In their first decade, the Keehns sold fruit to a number of A-list winemakers of the day, including Robert Mondavi, Rodney Strong, John Parducci, Barney Fetzer, the team at Simi Winery, and Julio Gallo. It was Robert Mondavi who encouraged and eventually convinced the family to make wine on their own, which they did, founding their winery in 1978. They hired a young recent Davis graduate named George Bursick to make their wine.

Barely out of college, Bursick found himself in a tenuous position, making wines in a region that he knew little about, from an older vineyard about whose provenance he knew nothing. He was able to recognize the Zinfandel, the Petite Sirah, the Carignane. Some of the blocks, however, didn't correspond with anything he'd seen before; they weren't covered in his coursework or his textbooks. The vines were robust, distinctive, shooting out fruit that seemed markedly different from the known varieties in the vine-yard. And the fruit was amazing. "I realized I was handed something special," he says. "I just didn't know what it was."[2]

In order not to screw anything up, he decided to ferment every distinguishable variety separately. "I didn't have any experience differentiating between Syrah and Durif," he says, "but there were differences—in cluster morphology, and especially in leaf morphol-ogy." The finished wines, too, were different from the blocks he knew about, and in his tastings, he focused in on one block in particular that was especially distinctive, even majestic. "The wine was silky, it was powerful, it had elegance. It was almost like the anti-Petite Sirah; it had everything good that Petite Sirah had bad. But I couldn't have known it was Syrah; I had never seen Syrah before."

After consulting his ampelography books, Bursick determined that at least some of the vines he'd kept separate might be Rhône varieties. He contacted Lucie Morton, a noted ampelographer who had worked on editing and translating Pierre Galet's famous tome on ampelography; Morton flew out from Virginia and walked the vineyard with him. Morton was able to identify true Syrah among the vines. "We took samples," says Bursick, "and she said 'I think you're onto something here.'"

The vines weren't about to wait for harvest however, and in 1979 the Syrah went into a Petite Sirah bottling. But the following year McDowell Valley Vineyards debuted a varietal Syrah, as well as a Grenache Rosé.[3] By this time it was clear that this was one of the oldest surviving plantings of Syrah in California.

The discovery of Rhône varieties on their property energized and focused the vineyard enterprise of Karen and Richard Keehn. Like most early eighties wineries, in their plantings they had placed emphasis on white varieties—in addition to the old vine reds, their property had French Colombard and Chenin Blanc, to which they added Sauvignon Blanc. But their exotic new offerings attracted attention. "The people who came to our tasting table," says Karen Keehn, "at tastings and trade lunches, they all wanted to taste our Syrah; it was the wine that we started to get some word of mouth, a reputation for."[4]

Before long they were making trips to the Rhône Valley to learn more about the region, its winemaking, and its traditions, befriending the Chapoutier, Guigal, Chave, and Vernay families along the way. Richard Keehn dove into vine growing with impressive zeal; within five years he served as director of the California Association of Wine Grape Growers, which led to stints with the California State Board of Food and Agriculture, the board of the Wine Institute, the California World Trade Commission, and the American Vineyard Association.

Karen, meanwhile, spearheaded an effort to apply for AVA status for the McDowell Valley, whose physical boundaries and natural isolation made for an easy argument; it became an AVA in 1982. And as Rhône varietal wines in California started to gain prominence, Karen Keehn became one of the movement's earliest, most vocal, and impassioned spokespersons for Rhône varieties' facility for food pairing, producing pamphlets and leading seminars on the subject at Rhône Ranger and similar gatherings.

McDowell Valley Vineyard's embrace of Rhône varieties attracted the attention of a young winemaker named John Buechsenstein. Buechsenstein was born in San Francisco and raised just south of the city in San Mateo, where his father managed what was then called a liquor store, though he loved wine and made frequent trips with his family to wine country in Napa and Sonoma, as well as to the Bay Area wine regions of Livermore Valley and Santa Clara Valley. Buechsenstein can still recall the sweet smell of the old wooden fermenters in the cellar room at Concannon Winery in the Livermore Valley, and the sensation of his first sip of wine, at age eight, a Charles Krug Chenin Blanc, then one of the most successful in California.

In 1967 Buechsenstein attended University of California, Berkeley, where he studied music composition and had a number of side professions that somewhat inadvertently inched him closer to the wine business. He worked for a company, for example, which printed the early menus and wine lists at Chez Panisse; he had friends and instructors who shared wine with him, including one professor who, when he learned of Buechsenstein's interest in California wine, made a point of opening French wines with him, hoping to prove the point that the French were better. One such bottle, a 1955 Chateauneuf-du-Pape from Alfred de Montigny, he'd kept unopened for several years.

One evening in 1972 he brought the Chateauneuf to the home of his friend and fellow wine lover who was intending to open a bar that served only wine—a wine bar.[5] All that Buechsenstein remembers about the evening, however, is that wine. "It was so beautiful, so layered, so many different flavors," he says. "That was it, it completely sent me over the top."[6] His allegiance to Rhône wines was sealed in that evening.

Buechsenstein transferred to Davis, where his fascination with Rhône varieties went unabated, fanned by judiciously chosen bottlings from Darrell Corti and by his friendship with the as-yet-unconverted Rhône aficionado, Randall Grahm. When Buechsenstein left Davis in 1980, he put in an application at just one winery, at the only place he knew where Syrah was being made—Joseph Phelps Vineyards—and was hired.

He spent two years at Joseph Phelps, learning as much as he could about Syrah, though he was just as dissatisfied with the wine's lack of typicity as they were. "We made a fairly smooth-tasting wine," says Buechsenstein, "but we couldn't bring into it the things I was tasting in the Rhône, the exotic flavors, the spice." In 1985, Buechsenstein was given the opportunity to succeed George Bursick at McDowell Valley Vineyards and try his hand at some of the oldest vine material in California.

McDowell became Buechsenstein's own experiment station. He bartered Rhône variety cuttings to obtain Mourvèdre from the Brandlin Ranch, Syrah from Estrella River, and eventually Viognier from Pete Minor at Ritchie Creek, in many cases using McDowell cuttings as trade and disseminating Syrah in the process. He made many pilgrimages to Berkeley and Kermit Lynch—a three-hour trip from Mendocino—and would call his neighboring winemaking buddies in Mendocino County if only to deliver one of the most abused groaners in the American Rhône joke repertoire: "I'm heading down to Kermit Lynch," he'd say into the phone, "who wants to go in on a case of the Clape?"

Upon completing his first vintage at McDowell, it occurred to Buechsenstein that the valley was warmer than most coastal vineyards, including the Napa Valley. Despite having some of the oldest Syrah in California, it started to dawn on him that it may not be planted in the most ideal place. "It was patently obvious that we did not have Côte-Rôtie," he said.

Instead, Buechsenstein found many similarities between McDowell Valley and the southern Rhône, where his epiphany wine, the de Montigny Chateauneuf-du-Pape, was from. There, Syrah was a bit player and the producers would mitigate its ripeness tendencies by blending—leading with the bright red cherry flavors of Grenache, which needed lots of heat to achieve maximum ripeness. Mourvèdre added depth to the Grenache; Cinsaut added acidity. McDowell had analogous conditions—might not blending be the answer?

McDowell Valley's first blended wine, Les Vieux Cépages, debuted in 1986, years before Buechsenstein had traveled to the Rhône and become intimate with the blending traditions of the region. Indeed, blending was still something of a mystery to the handful of American Rhône producers who cared. Few had traveled to France, and communication lines between French and American winemakers were still in their early stages. Shortly thereafter he would discover a book that put an end to much of the mystery, which methodically explicated southern Rhône winemaking and blending for Buechsenstein and other American producers.

Elsewhere in California, epiphanies drew would-be producers ever closer to the Rhône. In 1969, Lou Preston was sitting in an office at Beaulieu Vineyard in Rutherford, in the Napa Valley. A recent graduate in business at Stanford, on that day Preston was serving as the winery's auditor, and it didn't feel right. In another room he could hear the sound of glasses clinking on a table and bottles being uncorked, the low murmur and slurps of wine tasting. "Here I was sitting at the desk with a stack of papers," he says, "ticking off invoices and things like that and looking across the desk to all this commotion, all this excitement, and all these goings on, and all of the aromas wafting in from the cellar and I'm thinking 'Shit, I don't want to do this; I want to do *that*.'" So Preston went back to the office of the CPA firm and asked for a leave of absence. "I was thinking I might go back," he says, "but I never went back."[7] Preston enrolled in Davis the following semester.

This was not altogether a reversed course. Preston was raised in Sonoma County on his family's farm in the Russian River watershed, where his father ran a dairy and kept a small vineyard. His idea was to return to the family farm and revive what his father had planted. His siblings, however, planned to sell, so Preston went in search of another piece of land.

He had the good fortune to have Americo Rafanelli as his land broker, father of Dave Rafanelli and part of the farming family that has had long roots in the Dry Creek Valley. Longtime growers in the valley, the Rafanellis had just established their brand, and Americo Rafanelli directed Preston to nearby benchland property and urged him to get to know other Italian grape-growing families.

"I had become enamored of the traditions of the neighborhood, which were conditioned to a large extent by the Italian farmers who lived here when we came. And they all had their zinfandel lore, it's what they fussed over and what they drank at home and sold to Gallo down the road. It was the grape of the Dry Creek Valley, going back as far as anyone knew. I fell in love with the whole thing," he explains, "with farming, with old timers, with the lore and being Italian, and with Zinfandel. I just thought, 'I gotta do this.'"

On Preston's original property he'd acquired a small mixed black vineyard, a collection of varieties he knew little about and for which he had little interest. It included some Petite Sirah, Grande Noir, Alicante Bouschet, and Napa Gamay. He decided to keep the Zinfandel and sell the rest to his neighbor David Stare of Dry Creek Vineyards.

A few months later, Preston realized he didn't have enough wine to top off his tanks, and asked Stare for it back. In that short period, the wine had blossomed; it was an object lesson on the power of field blends from mixed black vineyards. Not long after, Preston acquired some new land to plant. He consulted his fellow farmers in the valley about the best vines to plant; many recommended their Pets. "'It'll get real sweet' they told me. If it was good enough for old timers, it was good enough for me."

As Preston looked for a clean clonal selection of the recommended Petite Sirahs, he started to hear about the other Syrah, the French Syrah. Preston's only experience with Syrah was on trips to France with his wife, Susan. "I wasn't a Rhône-ophile in any sense of the word," he says, "but my thinking was—and this was the goofy part—if Pets grows well here, then probably Syrah does too. It was just the alliteration of the names that convinced me."

Meanwhile down valley, Preston's neighbors Andy and Deborah Cutter had founded Duxoup Winery in 1977, and were also looking to plant. They'd heard from a friend in Davis named Dan Baron about an opportunity. Baron worked with Austin Goheen, the USDA plant scientist, who was going to have to rip out the vineyard in Davis to make way for a new gymnasium. That plot contained Goheen's mildly compromised Syrah, and Baron asked Cutter if he'd be interested in some Syrah cuttings to plant. Cutter knew little about Syrah, but he was intrigued enough to say yes. He reached out to Lou Preston to see if Lou might be able to plant some on his property, and Preston agreed.

A half-acre planting commenced the same year, and a small workable crop in 1979 was enough for Duxoup to produce a small bottling, the first from Sonoma County since the Hermitages of J. H. Drummond in the late 1890s.

Preston soon became enamored of the fruit he was growing for Cutter and the following year retained a bit to make for himself, as well as expanding his acreage for the variety. The vine seemed like a natural fit for the heritage varieties that he was already pursuing. As early as 1980 Preston had the name Syrah Sirah copyrighted, and by 1983 was producing a blend to match.[8]

Within the decade Preston had committed wholesale to Rhône varietal wines, accounting for roughly a third of his production, as well as other varieties that may be said to fall within the old timer pantheon, like Barbera, Petite Sirah, Carignane, Mataro. and of course Zinfandel. Preston's experiments with blended wines went beyond the Syrah Sirah blend. In 1993 Preston debuted a blend of Grenache, Mourvèdre, Carignane, and Syrah which he called Fauxcastel, a play on the name of Chateauneuf-du-Pape producer Beaucastel, who, after two vintages, politely asked them to desist. Preston shortened the name to Faux the following vintage.

That wine, now called L. Preston, was a mainstay of the Preston line for many vintages, and perhaps the winery's best expression of its philosophy and traditions, recalling the blending traditions of his Italian neighbors while updating slightly the components.

Andy Cutter continued to make small quantities of Syrah for Duxoup, which saw limited distribution in Northern California restaurants and wine shops. They were joined in the Rhône varietal explorations by Bill Frick and Judith Gannon, who founded Frick Winery in Geyserville and who specialized in the three C's of Rhône varieties, Carignane, Cinsaut, and Counoise, as well as Syrah and Grenache.

Also by 1990 the venerable Ridge Vineyards in Cupertino had acquired the Lytton Estate in the Dry Creek Valley, after using the fruit from those vines for many vintages. They planted Syrah there to complement the older vines of Lytton East, a famed mixed black vineyard which included Carignane, Mataro, and some of the oldest Grenache in the state.[9]

In the Sierra foothills, 150 miles to the east, another small Rhône-focused enclave took shape. Like the Dry Creek Valley, the small towns of Murphys and Placerville in El Dorado County had served as repositories for mixed black Zinfandel vineyards, and these treasures drew would-be winemakers toward the area. One of them, John McCready, set a decidedly empirical path toward the establishment of Syrah in the area in 1976.

John McCready was an electrical engineer, who served in the Navy before settling in Ohio with his wife, Barbara, where he worked for National Cash Register. He and his wife made modest investments before deciding that the most practical investment might be in land, preferably where he could grow something if he wished. Grapes were one of the crops that McCready looked into, though the wines from the Ohio Valley he found somewhat discouraging.

In the mid-seventies, McCready was informed he would soon be transferred to facilities in Wichita, Kansas. "Nothing against the good people of Kansas," he says, "but I didn't want to live there." He started looking for work in California, and took a job in Sacramento working for a small computer firm. When land became available near his sister's property near Placerville, in the Sierra foothills, he put down a deposit. A farm adviser pronounced it suitable for grape growing; there wasn't another winery for miles that could verify that assertion.

Nearly a century before, in Folsom, twenty-five miles to the east, Horatio Gates Livermore had planted a 2,000-acre vineyard for the Natoma Vineyard which was, for a brief time, the world's largest vineyard, and included some of the most substantial Rhône varietal plantings in California. None of this heritage concerned McCready, however, who had about 30 acres to work with. He approached the project with an engineer's pragmatism: "We were looking to plant something besides Zinfandel and Cabernet," he says, "and I didn't think we could do Pinot Noir."

Looking at a vineyard map of France, McCready noticed a region just south of Burgundy called Côte-Rôtie. "I looked that up, and it meant "roasted hill," and I figured that it might be a little warmer than Burgundy. We didn't know what grapes were planted there, but we went out and bought a bottle or two of this Côte-Rôtie and liked it." McCready went back to his books, to find out what grapes were planted on this roasted hill, and those grapes turned out to be Syrah.

Gary Eberle supplied him with enough Estrella River cuttings to plant an acre in 1979. Sierra Vista's first commercial release of Syrah was in 1982. What he did not expect was to find so many similarities between the western Sierra foothills and various subregions of the Rhône Valley—in the north, the slopes on Côte Blonde in Côte-Rôtie were granitic in origin, as they were in part in California.

McCready's lead brought others in contact with Syrah, and in contact with Gary Eberle as well. A group of aerospace scientists had founded a small winery project called, appropriately, Argonaut Winery, and had been persuaded to plant Syrah in the early eighties. The winery was short lived, but the plant material supported the plantings of Leon Sobon, yet another aerospace researcher in the early eighties.

Winemaking was Leon Sobon's second career; his first, as lead researcher for Lockheed's Research Lab in Los Altos, allowed him to pursue home winemaking with a tinkerer's curiosity and more than his share of natural skill. In 1977 he decided to explore winemaking as a full-time endeavor and moved to the Sierra foothills, near Plymouth, founding Shenandoah Vineyards with his wife, Shirley.

Like a lot of home winemakers Sobon's love of wine went through Zinfandel, which he planted in the late seventies and remains a staple of the brands he makes wine for, Sobon and Shenandoah Vineyards. But in the early eighties his son Paul took a pair of winemaking trips to Australia and came back extolling the virtues of a wine they made there from Shiraz. Soon after Sobon found the source of his cuttings, Argonaut, and planted, in volcanic soils on a high elevation ridgetop site near Plymouth. Shenandoah Vineyards became one of the early proponents of American Syrah, and Sobon played an enduring role not only in its establishment in the Sierra foothills, but statewide, participating in several Rhône Rangers events in the late 1980s.

But if there is a name synonymous with Rhône varietals in the Sierra foothills, it's Bill Easton. His dedication to the varietal focus led him to create an offshoot winery from Easton Winery which he called Domaine de la Terre Rouge (French for red earth). It remains one of the region's most important practitioners, and certainly its most prolific.

Bill Easton was raised in Sacramento, by wine-loving parents, who partook of the fare of local family wineries like d'Agostini and Frasinetti east of the capital, some of which were among the oldest in the state. Easton remembers fondly the trips to the country to collect bottles of bulk wine, which his parents drank nightly with their evening meal. He spent summers and school vacations with his grandparents in Berkeley. It was foregone that he'd go there for college, which he did in 1972, just as the seeds of the gourmet ghetto were bearing fruit.

When he graduated Easton was hired by the former newspaperman Davis Bynum to help with a wine shop that Bynum had started in Albany, just west of Berkeley, on Solano Avenue. Bynum sold his own wines as well as a few others, but the venture lasted only a couple of years. When he decided to close, Easton took over the lease.

Solano Cellars, founded in March of 1978, was designed to be a people's wine store as Easton describes it, an open-armed, utopian gathering place for wine lovers offering well-made back-to-the-land wines. "We used to love offering a good jug wine," he says, "because jug wines were good then."[10] Often as not it would be Easton, in his own truck, picking up the wines at the old wineries his parents used to frequent in his youth.

Eventually Solano Cellars came to be known for its robust selection of Italian red wines, a reputation that soon carried over to Côtes du Rhône and other artisan offerings. Easton was one of the first in the Bay Area to carry the wines of Ravenswood, Saintsbury, Caymus, Joseph Phelps, and Benziger, and, as they came into production, those of Bonny Doon, Qupé, and Ojai.

As a retail establishment it was small, new, and nimble, its owner curious and hungry, with more influence than the square footage would suggest. "It felt like we were all surfing the same wave at the same time, just as it was cresting," says Easton. "A lot of the people selling these artisanal wines to us were also selling them to restaurants like Chez Panisse and Bay Wolf and Mark Miller's restaurants.[11] Customers would have them at the cutting-edge restaurants and want to buy them. It was a great time. I think we were all on a learning curve, not just the customers but us, too, everybody was kind of growing together, we were all learning together."

It wasn't much of a stretch for a guy like Easton to want to make wine, and when he did, he had a lifetime of lessons available to him. He wanted his wines to be "for the people," drawing from alternative varieties, starting with Zinfandel. He did some research and learned that the volcanic soils of the Sierra foothills bore similarities to the Old World terroirs he championed in his store. It also had a climate that compared favorably with that of St. Helena and the warmer parts of the Rhône Valley.

Like so many of the early pioneers of the Rhône movement, Bill Easton gained entry to the Rhône pantheon because of Zinfandel, but where Zinfandel led him, he found tradition, authenticity, an established and attractive history into which he could slip without effort. At the time, Rhône varieties seemed like an inevitable expansion of a Zinfandel-inspired portfolio.

In 1983 he convinced a grower to graft his vines over to Mourvèdre, Grenache, and Syrah, drawing cuttings from Brandlin Ranch (Mourvèdre), Syrah from local sources, and Grenache from the Besson and Marston Vineyards. Viognier, Marsanne, and Roussanne plantings would soon follow.[12]

PART III

ARTISTS AND ICONOCLASTS

9

RANDALL GRAHM, THE MOVEMENT'S COSMIC IMPRESARIO

The American wine industry has had its share of colorful characters, but prior to 1980, winemaking had traditionally been a behind-the-scenes position. Most were farmers, with their hands in the dirt and their butts in a tractor seat—or scientists, with backgrounds in chemistry, biology, agricultural sciences—fields that do not typically attract large personalities. Indeed, most winemakers were drawn into the business of making wine from tasting it, from discovering a life-changing bottle a thrilling, head-turning sip. But a transformative moment is rarely enough to inspire one to chase the spotlight. Wine may make a person voluble, but it rarely makes one articulate, or theatrical. Wine can do many things, but it cannot transform a technician into an impresario.

In the early eighties the wine industry wasn't looking for an impresario, but they created one in Randall Grahm, founder of Bonny Doon Winery. In every respect, the industry was ready. Table wine consumption exploded in the eighties, shooting from 228 million gallons in 1976 to 487 million gallons in 1986—more than doubling in a single ten-year period. Per capita consumption increased just as dramatically. For the first time in history the wine drinking public was expanding, leaving behind the extended fantasy of snooty upper class and upper middle class collectors—wine became for Americans what it always was meant to be: an agent of pleasure.

The burgeoning market would foster countless changes in the industry, but one of the most revolutionary was the addition of labor; with higher sales and increased bottle prices, wineries could hire more winemaking staff, freeing up the owner/winemaker (usually one and the same) to visit the market and put a face before the bottle like never before. Winemakers took on a public role with increasing regularity, appearing at auctions, events, special dinners, satisfying an interest in personality that hadn't really existed before.[1] Wine's new cachet in the marketplace and the culture created a need for marketing, just as Randall Grahm was unknowingly walking onto the biggest stage of his life; indeed, before he ascended to the glare of the klieg lights, no one was really aware of the stage.

Even now, long past the gaudy heyday of his showmanship, Grahm is still thought of as a jester, whose outsized personality has routinely eclipsed the wines he promoted. Over the last thirty years he has taken the lead on a staggering array of issues facing the wine industry—he championed Pinot Noir, terroir, blends, Syrah, Grenache, white Rhône varieties. He is essentially the first winemaker in history to employ humor on wine labels, though the government's "truth in advertising" campaign, which lists the full range of ingredients in a bottle as if it were a can of soup, might be more lasting. He advocated screw caps in this country years before they became commonplace. He endorsed and pursued nascent Italian varieties in American soil almost as soon as he had begun to champion the Rhône, and had they taken off in the market, we would be celebrating him as the Pope of the American Cal-Ital movement. But he didn't limit himself to Italian: he supported countless other outré varieties and bottlings, infusions, fruit wines, cryogenically induced ice wines. He made wine in three states and on two continents: he was among the first artisanal California winemaker to sample the fruit of Washington and Oregon, and made wine in France and Spain years before American winemakers would do this as a practical matter.

He pursued the organoleptic mysteries of micro-oxygenation, reverse osmosis, "visualized" minerality, crystals, ionic polarization, and biodynamics with the zeal of an alchemist; he pursued abstruse and lofty conceptual paradigms so complex and aspirational it seemed farfetched that wine, a mere beverage, could embody all of the things he saw in it.

He explored the arcane and the outlandish in conversation with journalists, fellow winemakers, and of course, consumers. He marketed himself and his wines with a peripatetic, joyous, manic energy, made outrageous claims, embraced questionable practices, placed his own intellectual restlessness and verbal gifts on display on back labels, front labels, promotional material. He revolutionized the newsletter. He sent opuses, parodies, detective novels, epic poems, songs, cartoons, novels, and novellas in the mail; he parroted his literary heroes and rewrote their masterworks to accommodate his message. He caught the attention and occasionally the ire of critics whose patience he exceeded in his antics.

For a critical period, roughly the years between 1987 and 1995, Randall Grahm embodied the zeitgeist of American wine. He lurched his company and his brand in a half-dozen different directions, often at once, that herky-jerky movement a product of the rapid expansion of the wine business and of his own manic imagination. For each restless pursuit he became an articulate, on-the-fly, off-the-cuff frontman, a barker, a vaudeville showman, an emcee devoted not just promoting his new ideas but assimilating them in some dramatic framework. He didn't simply promote screw caps, he announced the death of the cork, and gave it a funeral; he didn't just proclaim his love for Rhône varieties, he produced a musical, "Born to Rhône," employing a San Francisco circus theatre and inviting nearly 300 guests. He was, without question, the showiest winemaking talent in the history of American winemaking. He made Robert Mondavi look like a monk.

Marketing was not something Grahm initially believed was a personal forté. He had never done much of it in his youthful life, and aside from brief periods in retail wine and food shops, stints for which Grahm probably had more selfish aims, he hadn't really sold much of anything at all—not himself, certainly nothing he had ever made. Indeed, he hadn't yet made anything. And in fact there may have been a compensatory element in his marketing efforts. As he writes in an anthology of his writings, *Been Doon So Long,* most of which first appeared in one promotional form or another: "You could say that much of the writing in this collection emerged from the fact that the wines were not as brilliant as I wanted them to be."[2]

Nevertheless, it's easy to see that he had showmanship in his genes.

Randall Grahm was born in Los Angeles in 1953 and raised in Cheviot Hills, just south of Beverly Hills, the oldest of three children. His father, Alan, was an accomplished musician who played saxophone and clarinet, but as his family grew he went into sales, eventually opening a small chain of vacuum cleaner shops, which in turn morphed into a successful wholesale and retail business that sold a variety of dry goods, from hand tools to ladies' purses.

Grahm's mother, Ruth, was born in Philadelphia and lived there until she was five, when her father, Lou Herscher, a vaudeville musician and composer, decided to move his family to Los Angeles so he could break into show business. The family settled in Hollywood on Delongpre Avenue, not far from Sunset and Vine, the epicenter of Hollywood's music industry at the time. In the family living room on a rented upright piano, Ruthie's father banged out hundreds of songs for the movies and the era's performers—love songs, sentimental ballads, novelty ditties, incidental music, Western themes, and Jazz Age standards, with names like "The Scarlet Lady," "Hot Rhythm," "Hot Money," and "The Fighting Texans." He scored dozens of films—westerns, adventures, romances, from "Dream Daddy" to "Elmer: The Knock-Kneed Cowboy."

It was, for Ruth, a milieu of constant creative excitement, a house filled with actors, writers, and performers most hours of the day and night, with impromptu rehearsals and all-night jam sessions a regular occurrence. By the time she was fifteen, Ruth started secretly writing lyrics to her father's compositions; when he saw her talent, he took her on as a writing partner. Together they collaborated on hundreds of songs for stage and screen, a partnership that lasted more than three decades.

As the eldest, Randall had a special relationship with his grandparents, and spent many weekends at their Beverly Hills home (the Grahm family moved to Beverly Hills when Randall was a teenager). Grahm says that his grandfather would rarely leave his bench at the piano; speaking with him, Grahm says, you were just as likely to get a tuneful reply. "It was a little like being in a musical," says Grahm. "If you asked him a question, he would respond in song. The difference between being in real life and being in a movie was pretty tenuous."[3]

Ruth Grahm describes her firstborn as a consummate book nerd, spending most of his waking hours reading. He read everything he could get his hands on.[4] When called to dinner, she says, Randall would walk into the dining room with his nose buried in a book, propping whatever he was reading next to his plate, read his way through the meal, read on his way back to his bedroom, closing the door to read some more. According to Ruth, Randall had a small close core group of friends who were fiercely individual, theatrical, and flamboyant, prone to elaborate pranks and theatrical costumes.

In 1970, somewhat in defiance of his father's wishes for Randall to attend an Ivy League school, Grahm enrolled in the University of California, Santa Cruz, pursuing a degree in philosophy. Early in his academic career, he fell under the spell of two professors, Gregory Bateson and Norman O. Brown, who both taught in the History of Consciousness and Literature program, a fiercely interdisciplinary "department" of their own design whose pedagogy encompassed an array of disciplines, including classics, philology, mythology, literary theory, cybernetics, psychoanalysis, systems theory, history, and cultural anthropology. For four years, Grahm nurtured his prodigious verbal skills and exercised a literary dexterity that would serve him prolifically in his eventual career.

Grahm returned to Southern California in 1974, having completed his course work (though he never finished his thesis) and took a job with the Beverly Hills Wine Merchant. This was where his wine education began. He made friends with legendary Los Angeles collectors Ed Lazarus and John Tilson, and they explored old Bordeaux and Burgundy together, with the two collectors often supplementing the education of this future winemaker by canny auction purchases and raiding their parents' cellars. As a result, says Grahm, there was not just one life-changing wine, but several.[5]

One of the most important events in Grahm's wine upbringing took the form of a case of old Burgundy and Rhône wines from vintages in the twenties and thirties which he managed to procure at an auction. "It was a total lowball bid," says Grahm, "not great bottles, village wines with smudged labels, not a premium lot." The wines got held up in transit for the better part of a year, and by the time he was able to retrieve them there were some additional fees. So he brought in some friends to help pay off the bill, and they decided to open them all at once. "Every one of them," says Grahm, "was great."

Grahm came away with an abiding love for Burgundy, and for the first time started to consider making wine as a living. So he took a home winemaking course and soon after, wrote to fifty California wineries that he had either heard about or knew slightly, asking them if he could work there for free and help him determine whether he should pursue this business. Not a single winery responded. So, after tucking some science classes at UCLA into his résumé, Grahm applied to Davis.

By his own admission, Grahm's years at Davis were marked by enological rebellion; his brush with Burgundy had rapidly transformed him into a fierce terroirist, a believer in terroir above all else, which rendered as anathema nearly everything he was being taught in school. "I was largely insufferable," he writes in his anthology,

at least to my professors, who had a tendency to duck into empty janitorial closets when they saw me coming down the hallway. I imagined that I was somehow the loyal (or not so loyal) opposition to standing up for the alternative, that is to say French wine-worldview, where terroir was absolutely sacred, and hubristically interventionist winemaking and grape growing was not so routinely accepted, if not discouraged.[6]

Grahm found a more sympathetic environment in Berkeley, and he made frequent trips to take advantage of its bookstores, cafes, wine shops, and attractive coeds. He spent time in Kermit Lynch's store and got his first taste of wines from the Rhône. "It was tiny, disorganized, kind of vaguely beatnik-ish," says Grahm, "and very very hip. The wines were a little hit and miss in those days, but I was really into this stuff, and so when I met him I told him I was a student at Davis he started turning me on to one thing after another."

Stan Hock, the owner of Trumpetvine wineshop not far from the Berkeley campus, remembers Grahm spending lots of time in his store as well, tasting wines and trying to pick up girls. Back in Davis, Grahm moonlighted for a brief time at Corti Brothers in nearby Sacramento, establishing a friendship with Darrell Corti that would become very useful in his first years as a winemaker. But his formative years as a student of the vine seem to be marked by restlessness and a capricious streak. There was no telling where he would land.

Grahm left the Davis program with a degree in plant science in 1979. After a brief winemaking stint at a winery project owned by comedian Dick Smothers, Grahm purchased vineyard property with the help of his parents in a small hamlet north of Santa Cruz called Bonny Doon. Settled by Scots in the 1850s, the place was given its cheery name by area founder John Burns, who took it from an ode by his countryman, the poet Robert Burns (no relation) about the bonny Doon River.

Bonny Doon is situated less than five miles from the coast, set among redwood forests and horse farms, and probably more than a few clandestine marijuana plantations. Like many such hamlets in the Santa Cruz Mountains, it is rustic and remote, seemingly lost in time and well off the grid, but its proximity to the town of Santa Cruz was vital. For Grahm, Santa Cruz was and is a touchstone of cultural inspiration, a city whose laid-back surfer culture, its alternative-education university system still firmly rooted in a sixties ethos, a town that has always had a flair for the dramatic and the theatrical.[7] The city would remain a strong influence on Grahm, his winery, and the branding it would come to be famous for.[8]

Grahm planted 28 acres, mostly Chardonnay and Pinot Noir, with some Bordeaux varieties. The vineyard started bearing in 1982, and Grahm was able to produce a passable Chardonnay—he would make Chardonnay for the next eight vintages—but he felt that the Pinot Noir from the property was lackluster, a fact that was confirmed in 1983 when he purchased fruit from Bethel Heights Vineyard in Oregon's Willamette Valley, only to find that the Oregon fruit was, in his estimation, better "by several orders of magnitude" than his own. Grahm concluded that Bonny Doon was too warm for Pinot to achieve the sort of complexity he strived for. He thought perhaps he should replant. But to what?

Noting how France and Spain's Mediterranean regions might be closer in character to California than Burgundy, he started to explore the possibilities of making the sort of wines to which he had been directed by Lynch and Corti.[9] "I had this very simple intuition," he says, "it's warm and dry in California, and it's warm and dry in southern France. I didn't study weather charts," he says, "at least not with any rigor, but anecdotally it all seemed to make sense."

Then he recalled that his proximal vineyard neighbor David Bruce had produced some varietal Grenache in the early seventies. Grahm managed to locate a few bottles in two vintages, 1971 and 1972, languishing on the shelf of a wine store in Orange County called Hi-Time, and tasted them.[10]

The '71, he says, had turned, but the '72, to Grahm's great surprise, was quite good: "It was high in alcohol, it was purple, it was fruity, tasted like raspberries, I thought, 'it's pretty darn good.' And I thought, 'if he can do it, I can do it,' you know? 'If he can do it, it can be done.'"

By this time Syrah too was trickling into the market from Phelps, Estrella River, and McDowell. Grahm tracked them down and tasted them in one sitting. "None of them were really all that swift," he says. "I mean there was Phelps beating their brains against Syrah, to not much effect; there was Estrella River, which seemed like a difficult place to be growing the stuff since you usually had to add a lot of acid to get it balanced, so that didn't seem right."

Grahm located a Grenache vineyard not far from Bruce's original source farmed by George Besson, a 10-acre old vine site with head-trained vines planted in the forties. Grahm blended the fruit with North Coast Cabernet to produce what he called Vin Rouge in 1982, a wine that pleased him and a few critics.

In 1983, reflecting what would become a common theme for Bonny Doon, Grahm overextended himself, growing Chardonnay and Cabernet, making Pinot Noir from Oregon and other California fruit sources. Spread thin, he couldn't afford to buy both Grenache and Syrah, so he bought just Estrella River Syrah. Grahm showed the finished wine to Fred Ek in Boston, who was taken enough with the Syrah that he placed an order for it, which Grahm says froze in its entirety during shipment. Still, Ek's endorsement was encouraging.

Around this time Grahm contacted Darrell Corti to ask him what he thought. Corti not only encouraged him to throw his hat in with Rhône varieties, he reminded Grahm to include Mataro in his calculations.

"I'd love to," responded Grahm. "What's Mataro?"

Corti informed him of the variety the French called Mourvèdre, grown in the southern Rhône and Provence. Grahm was able to locate a plot in San Martin, a tiny vineyard not far from his source for Grenache, the Besson Vineyard. In ensuing years Grahm would employ the old vine Mourvèdre from the San Joaquin Delta towns of Oakley and Bridge-port, where there remained Mataro vineyards planted at the beginning of the twentieth century.

That year was 1984. Grahm had Syrah, Grenache, and Mourvèdre aging, and still not a clear idea of what he was going do with them. To this point he'd had three years of winemaking experience under his belt. Plan A, a Great American Burgundy, had been compromised; Plan B would have to involve changing varietal focus, at least at the home vineyard in Bonny Doon, something better suited to the Santa Cruz Mountains. Plan B would also have to include changing the name Vin Rouge, whose smug ambiguity was a liability in the market, serving only to gratify the francophilic notions its maker.

If Plan B was to take the route of the Rhône, it occurred to Grahm that no one had yet taken the *southern* Rhône as a suitable model.[11] He had the varieties *en repose,* and none was entirely satisfactory on its own. Working with Estrella River fruit convinced Grahm that Syrah wasn't meant to be a stand-alone variety. "Syrah needed too much interven-tion," he says. "It needed to be acidulated for one thing, and Mourvèdre from Oakley needed help, it needed acid too, it was just too darn hot.

"So the one insight that I had was that maybe if you took the Grenache, which already had wonderful natural acidity, if you blended these together you didn't have to mess with these so much." It dawned on him that he had the raw material for "something vaguely Chateauneufian."

"I thought, 'Why not try to make a California version of Chateauneuf-du-Pape? This will create some sort of conceptual framework for people to understand the wine.'" He blended Santa Clara Grenache, Paso Robles Syrah, and San Martin Mourvèdre for his "vaguely Chateauneufian" Rhône blend, the first American version of the modern era. Now all he needed was a hook.

Blends, in fact, were all around him. Blends were by far the most common wines produced in California by volume, since most or all of the stalwart jug wines of Carlo Rossi and Almaden and E & J Gallo made after Prohibition were blended wines, employ-ing the fruit of mixed black vineyards or mixing the fruit themselves as harvest approached, drawing together the viticultural efforts from old growers tending plots from Windsor to Merced. Blends fit into the broader marketing framework established by this category, which borrowed heavily from French regional tradition without resembling it in the least, and entered the market with marvelously vague brand names like Hearty

Burgundy, Mountain Chablis, Rhine, Claret, and Port. Blends even had an historical tradition, documented in great detail by Eugene Hilgard and Federico Pohndorff in their early trials.

Furthermore, a modern history of blends was just starting to be written, based on the exploration set forth by Joseph Phelps in the Napa Valley for his iconic blend Insignia; blends which would soon be known as Meritage were being accelerated by the new projects underway at Opus One and Dominus. The American Rhône blend, however, did not yet exist.

Armed with a liberal arts education and an especially deep literary background, Grahm approached the problem of selling a blended Rhône varietal wine with a philosopher's pragmatism: "Everyone comes to a wine they've never had," he says, "and they wonder 'How do I know if it's any good? How do I know if I'll like it? What will it taste like?' It occurred to me that I needed to give people a sort of conceptual hook to understand the category.

"I thought maybe if I could begin with the Rhône as a pickup point, and use those grapes as a template, maybe I could create some dialogue along the lines of 'Oh, I've had Chateauneuf-du-Pape, I wonder what the California version tastes like.'"

Grahm's original idea was to call the wine Old Telegram, in homage to the great Chateauneuf-du-Pape producer and Kermit Lynch import Domaine de Vieux Télégraphe.[12] "And then I thought 'you know what? before I start down the path of making a faux Chateauneuf-du-Pape, I should probably try to learn something about it.'" He started doing research, which meant consulting virtually the only guidebook on the Rhône in English to that point, *Wines of the Rhône* by John Livingstone-Learmonth and Melvyn C. H. Master, whose second edition had fortuitously appeared in 1983.

The first thing Grahm learned was that more than forty producers were listed for the region; Vieux Télégraphe, great as it was, was but one of them. "Obviously," says Grahm, "'Old Telegram' presupposes that you've heard of Vieux Télégraphe, and at the time there were about like four people who knew what that was. Then I read this funny thing about the flying saucers."

Wines of the Rhône author Livingstone-Learmonth had spent months in the Avignon library researching his chapter on Chateauneuf-du-Pape as a wine region. In the second edition he delivered a thorough rendering of the making of the appellation in 1923, the first region in France to set down laws defining how its wines could be grown, blended, and made, resulting in the first *appellation d'origine contrôlée* (AOC) laws in Europe. "For their time," writes Livingstone-Learmonth, "these laws were monumental," noting that they remained largely unchanged sixty years later.

The region's penchant for bureaucratic thoroughness extended well into the fifties, apparently: Livingstone-Learmonth goes on to relate one of the weirder bits of Chateauneuf trivia he was able to unearth, a document decreed by the governing viticultural body seeking to address a potentially vexing problem involving interlopers.

The village decree definitively stated:

Article 1. The flying overhead, landing and taking off of aeronautical machines called "flying saucers" or "flying cigars," of whatever nationality they may be, is strictly forbidden on the territory of the commune of Chateauneuf-du-Pape.

Article 2. Any aeronautical machine—"flying saucer" or "flying cigar"—that lands on the territory of the commune will be immediately taken off to the pound.[13]

Inspired by this passage, Grahm decided to call his blend "Le Cigare Volant" ("flying cigar," the French term for a flying saucer), a New World spoof of an Old World tradition, with the requisite level of ironic distance.[14]

To this point in history, no wine label had ever spoofed anything; none had invoked humor, even remotely. Wine labels, indeed, wine itself, had been a pretty serious business, mostly occupying a very snooty niche in the culture, lurking in academic enclaves and special occasion restaurants, enjoyed in otherwise painful dinners with parents. Wine might be enjoyed, but it was not a thing to have fun with.[15]

Labels were limited to strictly utilitarian functions, to convey factual and legal information. Any messaging involved tradition, legacy, and times gone by. Grahm thought, quite sensibly, that this was restricting, that once the legal requirements were met, the design need not be limited at all.[16] "I realized that people would rather be intrigued," Grahm says. "Labels didn't need to be dull and boring. Plus, it was an opportunity to get in the last word on what you were doing."

He tracked down Chuck House, a graphic designer who had shown tremendous prowess with his first wine label design, for Frogs Leap in the Napa Valley. House and Grahm quickly came up with an idea, of an antique-looking collage (the illustration came from a book on Bordeaux, from 1855), employing equal parts vineyard pastoral and Jules Verne fantasy: a landscape featuring a small vineyard and chateau, with a tall tree in the foreground, behind which a large flying saucer hovers, casting an ominous ray of rosé-tinted light upon the scene: a vineyard, and a sensibility, under threat.

On the wine's back label, Grahm wrote:

No woofer this wine, we feel rather that it is quite a stellar accomplishment. The composition of our Flying Cigar is based on the traditional encépagement of Châteauneuf-du-Pape. It contains 72% Grenache, 25% Syrah, and 3% Mourvèdre. The wine possesses a rich, soft velvety mouthfeel, true to type, with a powerful, haunting bouquet of raspberry, pepper, anise and earth.

In subsequent editions, the reference to the decree was more explicitly stated:

In 1954 the village council of Châteauneuf-du-Pape was quite perturbed and apprehensive that flying saucers or "flying cigars" might do damage to their vineyards were they to land within. So right-thinking men all, they adopted an ordinance prohibiting the landing of flying saucers or flying cigars in their vineyards. (This ordinance has worked well in discouraging such landings.) The ordinance states further that any flying saucers or flying cigars that did land would be taken immediately to the pound.

What makes the Cigare label so effective is its subtlety: its subversive elements aren't immediately clear. The classical French design is at once bucolic and mollifying. While the flying saucer isn't actually hidden, it seems to quietly intrude upon the scene, lurking like a floating predator. Only after you're in on the joke, perhaps, would you notice that the neck label is designed to resemble the paper cigar ring. Detection of these elements tended to dawn on the viewer, creating small frissons of discovery, as if solving a puzzle.

Once unfurled, the Bonny Doon brand, its labels and back labels, its myriad bottlings and eventually its newsletters told some of the most elaborate stories the industry had ever seen, that diverted potential buyers away from the usual information about an American wine—appellation, variety, place—and into the realm of the wonderful.[17]

Did he answer the questions he set out to answer? Many might argue he hadn't at all, but it didn't matter. Cigare told a story, at once comical and weird, rich in reverberant meaning. It evoked the source of the wine's inspiration while remaining sufficiently distant so as not to appear stuffy or stuck up. It was, in current parlance, an updated meme, and thoroughly transporting.

No one was more surprised than John Livingstone-Learmonth, who stumbled upon a display of Le Cigare Volant in a London Oddbins wineshop in 1986. He studied its label carefully, and he says it took him just a few moments to decipher its mysterious iconography, and when he did he muttered, under his breath, "cheeky monkey." He bought a bottle, took it home, opened it, and while he felt it lacked slightly the concentration of a typical Chateauneuf, he was struck at how authentic the wine seemed "a fair stab at the real thing."[18]

The early reputation for Le Cigare Volant rests squarely on the quality of fruit Grahm found in the decades-old vineyards of the Santa Clara Valley. Indeed Grahm refers to the period from 1984 to 1989, the years which established the Cigare Volant as one of the most identifiable bottlings in California, as "The Hecker Pass Years," referring to a roadway through the Santa Cruz Mountains linking Watsonville to inland valleys. There were situated many older vineyards which still contained Grenache.

The Besson Vineyard was owned by George Besson, Sr., whom Grahm describes as warm and garrulous, prone to malaprops and, in his later years, resembling an aged Walter Brennan. From 10 acres Grahm would harvest anywhere from 20 to 35 tons, not enough to sustain the expanding production of Cigare. He supplemented this with Grenache from the vineyards across the street from Besson, a slightly rockier site which produced smaller clusters, lower yields, and more expressive fruit. Focused, nervy, concentrated, and vibrant, it served as the spine of the blend and enlivened the Estrella River Syrah and the Mourvèdre from San Martin.

Girded by encouraging words from wine distributors and inspired by his newfound meridional direction, Grahm became more concerted in his efforts to source fruit and to plant Rhône varietal material. There wasn't much available, but he took what he could, occasionally crowding out some of his fellow producers in the process.

In 1984, Bob Lindquist wanted to expand his Syrah production, and so he called Estrella River and asked for twice what he was getting. They said they didn't have it. How could they be out of it? Lindquist asked. Then he learned that all of it was going to Randall Grahm. "He started edging me out," says Lindquist. "It wasn't mean-spirited in any way, it was just his competitive zeal, and his ambition."

In the fall of 1984 postharvest Grahm made his first trip as a winemaker to France with the express purpose of collecting plant material for white varieties. He visited with a number of producers, procuring cuttings from Hermitage, Condrieu, and Chateauneuf-du-Pape. With his family and a small number of employees, including viticulturalist Merrilark Padgett, he replanted portions of his vineyard to Rhône varieties, grafting his Pinot Noir over to Syrah, planting a bit of Cinsaut and Mourvèdre as well. His newly acquired white varieties, Roussanne and Viognier, were propagated and planted as well, alongside Marsanne acquired from Foundation Plant Service in the early eighties.

Bonny Doon proved to be an exceptional place for growing white Rhône varieties, producing wines of nerve and character, exceptional purity of fruit, and elegance. In 1988 Grahm developed a wine to accompany Cigare, which he called Le Sophiste, a blend of what he thought was Roussanne with Marsanne and a touch of Viognier. It featured on its label a jaunty dancing man dressed in tux and tails and sported a cumbersome plastic "top hat" that fitted over the cork and added nearly two inches to the bottle's height, to the annoyance of retailers and restaurant wine directors everywhere.

The wine, however, was a sound evocation of white Rhône blends, and was very well received; Grahm felt it was among the most distinctive white wines he'd ever made.

As the years passed Grahm hardly limited himself to Rhône varieties. As Italian varieties were reintroduced to California soils, Grahm was among the first to plant them and market them. He made Zinfandel, Riesling, Muscat, Nebbiolo; he made whatever might set him apart from the mainstream wine world. As dessert wines found their way back into the California pantheon, Grahm plunged into their production, including berry-fruit infusions and a charming Rhône-inspired Muscat ice wine, the bottle dressed in lingerie decals to mirror its "seductive" qualities.

He developed new brands and labels to accommodate his new ideas, like the Ca' del Solo line which included the successful "Big House" series of red and white blends, as well as an array of Italian varietal wines, from Freisa to Trebbiano. As his vineyards succumbed to disease and fruit sources became increasingly limited or expensive, he embarked upon a costly and complicated project to make and import Malbec from Cahors, Syrah from southern France, and Grenache from Spain. He also developed

Pacific Rim, a brand devoted to American Riesling and other aromatic whites, eventually composed entirely of Washington State fruit. (He sold the brand in 2010.)

In his early efforts to distinguish himself from the pack, he had seized upon a persona and brand identity that could do little else but insist on difference, often for its own sake. Indeed, brand identity for the Bonny Doon pantheon was like trying to pin down a multiple personality. Each brand received a campaign like no other in the history of California wine marketing. Each bore the stamp of Grahm's peculiar, high-minded, pun-infused, irreverent, energetic humor, with colorful images from famous artists like Ralph Steadman and Gary Taxali, with texts that were challenging, highly verbal, intensely literary, and nearly always excessive. For his newsletter, Grahm wrote parodies of Edmund Spenser, James Joyce, Dante Alighieri, Basho, Samuel Taylor Coleridge, Philip Roth, J.D. Salinger, Miguel de Cervantes, T.S. Eliot, and Allen Ginsberg, he wrote send-ups of Bruce Springsteen songs, of Wolfgang Amadeus Mozart's *Don Giovanni,* full-length parodies of Dante's *Inferno,* operas of his own design.[19]

"I sometimes say this, and it's not said disingenuously, looking back I was incredibly lucky. I could just as easily have been unlucky and gotten very discouraged. I lucked out that the first wine I made didn't suck. And I did it again the next year and it was actually better, and so I did it again. Really lucky to have gotten this positive reinforcement. Because if I had gotten this negative reinforcement, I'd have thought nah, let somebody else do it."

Perhaps the best way to judge the efficacy of Grahm's efforts is to look closely at the only wine he has made for all but the first two years of his twenty-five-year history, the wine that brought him to fame and which is in every way his flagship, Le Cigare Volant.[20]

In early 2010 Grahm gathered journalists, sommeliers, and guests at the Los Gatos restaurant Manresa, to partake in an epic vertical tasting covering the lifespan of his flagship red wine, Cigare Volant. He presented twenty-five vintages of Cigare, most in large format bottles, from 1984 to 2008 inclusive. It was an opportunity to take measure of one of the most influential, controversial, and peripatetic winemakers to have worked in California in the last quarter century.

A Cigare vertical tasting is an entirely different experience than your average vertical. In the Old World, vertical tastings are used to show the consistency of a given domaine; to demonstrate adherence to tradition, delivered as a testament to steadfastness and consistency of expression from a particular patch of earth.

In California, of course, tradition comes in a more liquid form. A robust vertical of California wine will certainly capture consistencies of place if they exist, as well as variations in vintage. But just as often a vertical will reveal whatever was *en mode* in a given winemaking or viticultural epoch, the trends and fashions that held sway, and not least, the emerging tastes of the consumer.

In California, that means the austere eighties, for example, when red wines were built to age, rendering them fairly ungiving upon release. These give way to the Parker era and the inexorable escalation of ripeness levels in the middle nineties, which in turn spawns the era of the Frankenwine, where wines exhibited the effects of remedial manipulation, additives, enzymes, coloring agents, tannin, removing alcohol.

But this applies only peripherally to the wines of Bonny Doon, especially Le Cigare Volant. Over the years fruit sources have come and gone, which has led Grahm to call Cigare his *vin d'effort,* a "composed" wine, rather than a *vin de terroir.* For Grahm, Cigare has always been aspirational, serving the passions, curiosities and occasionally, the obsessions of a man who believes in terroir but who has rarely been able to possess it.

For this reason, perhaps more than any other wine in California, a bottle of Cigare Volant amounts to an epistemological snapshot of its winemaker. In his pursuit of the unique in his flagship wine, Randall Grahm is guilty of a sustained, willful inconsistency, and like a palimpsest, each wine allows a glimpse the peripatetic nature of its maker.

In this sense, the earliest wines were the most pristine, the least impinged upon by Grahm's coercions, and they were among the most beautiful. The '85, probably from a riper vintage, retained more sensuality and seductive power, and revealed, to me at least, the wine of a winemaker who'd made the best wine of his life the year before and who had discovered what he was capable of.

Grahm increased his production of Cigare thereafter, going from 3,200 cases in 1989 to 7,300 cases in 1996. Such a dramatic increase, of scarce Rhône varietal sources, certainly compromised quality in certain years. The wines from the first half of the nineties reflected these inconsistencies; however, the '90 and the '94 both showed beautiful, demonstrative Grenache character (composing about 40% of the blend in each) with a sleek, integrated set of fruit and savory flavors that were deeply reminiscent of the southern Rhône palette.

In the latter half of the nineties, the wines received an exceptional level of tinkering, with blends, sources, closures, and additives from one vintage to the next. This resulted in the least consistent flight of the evening.

Despite their failings, they reflected an age where technological innovations—some promising, some manipulative, some disastrous—inevitably changed the winemaker's craft; it makes sense that such an inquisitive winemaker should attempt a few, if only to learn from his mistakes.

Grahm brought us home with wines from the last decade, a distinctly Burgundian phase of winemaking in which he experimented with extended lees contact, reduction, stem inclusion, large format barrels. These were very un-Californian in some senses: they were "fruit backward" almost, flying in the face of the most obvious advantage given to grape growing in the California: sunshine. These latter-era wines can suffer from what I'd call a faintness of expression. But there was no question that Grahm was still on his game, even as he's been changing the rules on himself, sometimes radically, for more than a quarter century.

Of the many firsts the American Rhône movement could boast about—first commercial bottlings in several varietal categories, first plantings and resuscitations of long-lost varieties, milestones in marketing and in overall tomfoolery—there is one achievement that probably surpasses them all: it was the first wine category to be recognized with its own celestial body.

In July 1992, asteroid #4934 was give the name "Rhôneranger" by its discoverer, Edward Bowell, an astronomer with the Lowell Observatory in the hills above Flagstaff, Arizona. Bowell had found the asteroid in its solar orbit in 1985, just as Randall Grahm's winemaking prowess was reaching a celestial height of its own. Bowell, already a long-time wine lover, was a fan of these wines from their earliest vintages.

Sometime during the seven-year period when the asteroid's particulars were gathered and verified for posterity, it occurred to Bowell that he might name the object for the talented winemaker who'd invoked the heavens with Le Cigare Volant. "I just thought, 'this wine connects very well to asteroids,'" says Bowell, "why not name it after Grahm?"[21] In the end Bowell settled on Rhôneranger, but insists "it was a distinction meant for Grahm. I regarded him as the head of this so-called band of winemakers called the Rhône Rangers."

Once the name was approved, Bowell conspired with an Arizona wine distributor and Grahm's mother, Ruth, to lure Grahm to Arizona for a dinner and naming ceremony.

"I remember complaining mildly about having to go," admits Grahm. "I mean it was yet another sales trip to yet another place, and to Arizona, in July." But his mother insisted, so he agreed.

Lowell Observatory is a private astronomical research institution founded in 1894 by Percival Lowell, housing the telescopic equipment that led to countless celestial discoveries, including planets and evidence of the expanding universe. More recently Bowell was tasked with mapping the objects within the solar system; he is of one of the most prolific asteroid discoverers in the world, responsible for discovering more than 300 celestial objects. He also directs LONEOS, the Lowell Observatory Near-Earth Object Search.[22]

The event was held at Lowell Observatory in the hills above town, at the end of a steep winding road leading away from the Northern Arizona University campus. The facility housed a 24-inch telescope which was used to conduct interplanetary research of great historical significance; in fact researchers at Lowell were the first to discover Pluto, then thought of as the solar system's most remote planet, in 1930.

A dinner at an observatory was a bit unusual, but not outrageously so, explains Grahm—"They hold dinners at a lot of funny places," he shrugs, "and this was just one of those funny places." So Grahm did attend, with his mother and his girlfriend at the time, Martha Dyer. There they met Bowell for the first time. At the end of the meal, during which plenty of Cigare Volant was consumed, Bowell rose to speak.

"I put a slide up on the wall," he says, "of an asteroid known as 1629 Geographos—which is surprisingly flying saucer shaped." Then he raised his glass and announced that one of his more recent findings, #4934, first isolated in 1985, he was going to name "Rhôneranger," in honor of Grahm, the "eclectic and irrepressible owner and winemaker of Bonny Doon Vineyard, near Santa Cruz, California. Often referred to as the Rhône

Ranger, Grahm is best known as the creator of Le Cigare Volant, a Rhône-style wine that in some vintages has reached celestial heights."[23]

Ruth Grahm remembers a long exposition on asteroids, what they are, where they come from, how they name them, and so on. Her son, she says, was visibly bored. "Randall was kind of fiddling around," remembers Ruth, "looking like he really wanted a crossword puzzle to work on." Then Bowell made his announcement, and Grahm sat up in his seat before deflating slightly. "I'd never seen such an expression on his face," says Ruth, "just the shock, the surprise, and certainly the interest."[24]

"It took a moment for the information to sink in," says Grahm, "I was profoundly, profoundly surprised. This seemed like a deeper kind of accomplishment. This was the universe tipping its hat in a pretty significant way– everything else seemed sort of ephemeral."

Grahm burst into tears and in the moments it took for him to gather himself his mother, Ruth, the old vaudevillian, thought "this has to be commemorated with a song." So she ran to the kitchen, tracked down a pencil and paper and rapidly scribbled a ditty, rushed back into the hall, having collared a local radio announcer with some musical talent, to sing, a capella, these words (to the tune of "Thanks for the Memories"):

Thanks for the asteroid
We'll never be the same
Ted Bowell was to blame
For putting Randall Grahm's name
In Heaven's Hall of Fame
We thank you so much.

Asteroid Rhôneranger is between 7 and 15 miles in diameter, quite large for a recently named asteroid, according to Bowell. "Its surface area," Bowell added helpfully, "is about one-third that of all the vineyards in California." Only two other asteroids had ever been given wine-related names to that point, #739 (Vinifera), discovered in 1913, and #2063 (Bacchus), discovered in 1977.[25]

After the announcement, the dinner guests were escorted up to the observatory's historic 24-inch telescope, where they gazed at Saturn's rings and took in this new domain that the Rhône Rangers now inhabited. To this day Grahm seems overcome by the gesture. "While I desperately crave approval," he says, "when people actually come up and tell me favorable things, I tend to get very uncomfortable. Normally this sort of occasion would be impossibly painful for me, but for some reason this particular evening was so cosmically aligned that I just thought, 'okay, the universe wants me to have this, so I'm just going to chill out and accept it.' I mean, this was the universe speaking, after all."

10

STEVE EDMUNDS,
THE QUIET ICONOCLAST

If Randall Grahm brought the flash to the Rhône movement, Steve Edmunds brought the soul, a framework for authenticity that faithfully served the movement through its early years and provided a kind of moral compass. His sensitivity translated effortlessly to his wines, in blends which reflected an authentic Côtes du Rhône charm, and in meditative Syrahs. The combination got to the heart of what the movement was about.

Steve Edmunds came to winemaking through home brewing in the seventies. In 1972, a shop for home brewing and winemaking supplies hired him, on the condition that he learn about wine as well. He said sure. "I used to just drink wine, never think about it," he says. "You'd put it in your mouth and swallow it and if it wasn't bad you'd do it again. And at a certain point in the evening you'd decide either 'It's time to stop' or 'It's time to get up on the table and dance.'"[1] That is until one evening when he sat down with a friend to taste a few California wines in a serious manner. All was revealed then.

"Just in the act of slowing down and paying attention to the aromatics, how they played in the mouth and in the back of the palate," Edmunds says he discovered "that wine had texture, and complex flavors I'd never noticed before. It was as though someone had installed a whole set of circuitry I didn't even know I had and flipped the switch; everything just lit up. Some part of me that I had no acquaintance with emerged, and I was just on fire."

Edmunds began tasting as many wines as he could get his hands on. He met with California producers, read voraciously, and when a new wine shop opened in Sausalito in 1973, he was hired as their wine buyer. Within a few years he had begun to make basement wines from concentrate, and eventually found inexpensive mixed black grapes to crush. By the end of the decade he was out of the retail business—he was a mailman for a brief, dispiriting period—but his interest in wine had not abated. In a soul-searching moment with his wife, Cornelia St. John, they decided against formidable odds to start a winery—a decision, he says, involving "a tremendous amount of naïveté and impulsiveness." Just how to employ such passionate new circuitry, though, was not impulsive. As he is with most things, Edmunds was deliberate and empirical about what kind of winery to create.

There was no doubt as to which wines moved him: "I kept going back to wines from the Rhône and Italy," he says. "I knew I wouldn't be able to get much in the way of Italian varieties, but with a little searching I could find some Grenache and Mourvèdre, and I knew that there was Syrah around." Indeed, the first Rhône varietal wines were just making their appearance in shops and the press was taking notice. Not that he thought much of them. Early efforts, to Edmunds, seemed pretty discouraging: "That first group of domestic Syrahs was pretty boring stuff," he says, "not very Syrah-like at all. They didn't remind me in the slightest of wines from the northern Rhône."

People started to drop things into his lap—wines, press clippings, phone numbers—in one such instance, a letter to the editor written by Robert Mayberry in *Practical Winery and Vineyard,* suggesting that somebody in California ought to find some old Carignane, and old Mourvèdre and Grenache, and make a California Côtes du Rhône, because the climate was so much more Mediterranean.

Then one evening Edmunds and his wife were waiting for a table at Chez Panisse and asked for the by-the-glass list. One of the wines was the 1983 Qupé Syrah, Bob Lindquist's first vintage. "I remember thinking 'well this is Chez Panisse; maybe it won't be that bad,'" says Edmunds. "So they brought me a glass and I stuck my nose in it and smelled violets and bacon fat and smoke, all these interesting Rhône markers, and I said 'My god this guy's onto something. Maybe you really *can* do this here.' That was a little tipping point."[2]

The following year Edmunds purchased Syrah grapes from Estrella River Winery in Paso Robles. On the phone he made some specifications about what sort of picking numbers he wanted to hit, and had his brand new half-ton bins shipped directly to the vineyard. He asked them for a low Brix count; he'd been warned by Bob Lindquist that the site was warm and the grapes always came in ripe. The farming was absentee in the years after Gary Eberle's departure, however, and the crop load on these young vines was very high.

Edmunds rented two trucks which he and his stepson Ben drove down, and on the way back, grapes in tow, both trucks broke down at different times. It took him twenty hours to get the fruit back to the winery. He crushed all nine tons by foot, and had bought used, well-seasoned barrels from Joseph Phelps. "Which was a good thing," he says, "because this wine was so light. The aromas were really pretty, it had a nice fruity floral, violet scent. But it never colored up. I measured the alcohol and I think it was like 10.5%."

The high crop load had led to a fairly dilute crop, with Brix levels under 20. Edmunds bottled the wine and released it under the name Petit Rouge.

Like any regular patron of Chez Panisse, Edmunds had consumed his share of Domaine Tempier Bandol, both the rosé and the red, and naturally wanted to try his hand at Mourvèdre, if he could find it. After scaring down a few dead ends he found a small notice in a home winemaking shop in Berkeley, written on the scrap of a paper bag, about a ranch on Mt. Veeder selling Sauvignon Vert. Edmunds called the number, and Richard Brandlin answered the phone. Edmunds asked him if he had any other grapes to sell.

"You mean you don't want the Sauvignon Vert?" said Brandlin. "I got Palomino."

"How about red grapes?" asked Edmunds.

"'Well we had some Zinfandel, but we sold it.'"

"I was looking for Mataro," said Edmunds.

"Oh, we've got some of that," said Brandlin. There was a pause; then Brandlin asked, "What do you want with Mataro?"

Only then did Edmunds think to ask where this Brandlin Ranch was located. On Mt. Veeder, Brandlin told him. Edmunds was stunned. Mountain fruit was some of the most prized in California's North Coast, and Edmunds realized at once that he had chanced upon not just any Mataro, but a hidden treasure. "To me, it was like someone saying we've got a few extra tons of Lafite left, would you like some?"

When Edmunds finally got to the property, it seemed practically mythic. Acres of old head-pruned vines were spread out before him in a mountain aerie, farmed by two middle-aged farmers, Richard and Chester Brandlin, who had been raised on this land, and with their father farmed it through Prohibition. The sixty-year-old property was planted to mixed blacks and the odd Palomino and Sauvignon Vert, and had been dry farmed for decades with an almost nineteenth-century-era simplicity; the Brandlins even grew willow trees so they had striplings to tie off their vines.

Edmunds purchased the fruit and brought it to his rented winery space. In the 1985 vintage, he made just a hundred cases. The wine was met with early enthusiasm by friends and colleagues in Berkeley. He shared a bottle with his friend Kermit Lynch—Edmunds was a regular at Lynch's store—who shared it with Alice Waters. When they were introduced, Alice's eyes lit up and she exclaimed, "Oh, you're the one who's doing that!"

In 1986 some rain and cool weather had extended the growing season, ideal conditions for Mourvèdre. The response to the wine by advocates like Lynch and Waters suggested to Edmunds that this wine might serve as his hallmark. With the following vintage, he took extra care with its *élevage*, tasting it frequently in barrel, maintaining its energy and freshness. It became clear that this wine was developing into something special.

This was the wine for which Francois Peyraud was moved to say "La terre parle" (the earth speaks.) Those words have served as a touchstone experience for Edmunds over the last twenty-five years, validating a winemaking aesthetic that would become more refined and artistic as the years progressed. Steve Edmunds has always possessed a touch of the poet, but few winemakers to this day are as committed to what amounts to an artistic vision of winemaking.

By 1986 Edmunds had three reliable sources for Rhône red grapes, all of them from mountain vineyards: the Brandlin Mourvèdre on Mt. Veeder, Grenache from Michael Marston's vineyard on Spring Mountain, and Syrah from Durell Vineyard, on Sonoma Mountain, a site planted to Syrah in 1979 on behalf of Kenwood Winery, who relinquished their interest six years later—each mountain property providing stellar fruit of impressive drive and intensity, set on granitic, volcanic soils that resemble those of the northern Rhône.

In just two years, Edmunds foraged his way into the top echelon of Rhône selections. He soon added Viognier and varietal Syrah bottlings, but his production was always, for better or worse, a bit of a moving target as he moved from fruit source to fruit source, trying in vain to get producers in Napa and Sonoma to plant Rhône varieties for him—he was obliged to head east, concentrating his efforts on El Dorado County, which possessed more land, higher elevations, and comparable growing seasons to the vineyards of the coastal ranges. It also had growers still open to handshake deals.

In Placerville, Edmunds bought a bag of peaches that were so delicious he thought, "with tree fruit this good, what if this guy was growing grapes?" That's how Edmunds was introduced to the talents of Ron Mansfield, a tree fruit farmer who had dabbled in grape growing. After meeting Edmunds, he agreed to graft over his modest vineyard to Syrah for Edmunds. Before long Mansfield was managing two vineyards for Edmunds, Wylie and Fenaughty; Wylie, located at a hilltop just shy of 2,800 feet near the American River, is grown in thin soils of quartzite and clay. Fenaughty Vineyard, at about the same elevation on the opposite side of the river, possessed more volcanic soils, interspersed with clay loam.

Edmunds would eventually make a blend from these two sites called Wylie-Fenaughty that was among the most successful wines in his career, the two parcels performing a complex yin and yang, with Wylie bringing a dark core of structure and spine, and Fenaughty a more feminine, filigreed adornment. They were in every way complementary, in every way they served each other.

11

SEAN THACKREY,
THE THINKING MAN'S RHÔNIST

In an illuminating 2001 interview, the writer Alan Bree introduced his rather complicated subject with a particularly well-phrased understatement: "If you want to understand Sean Thackrey, you need to reset your reference points."[1] With respect to winemaking and its heritage, improvisation, notions of terroir, fruit selection, synthesis, and *cépage*, no one operates quite like Sean Thackrey.

Thackrey personifies the spirit of independence that came to characterize the Rhône movement, but he is not part of the Rhône movement. Thackrey is emphatically not a joiner. As the Rhône movement took shape its early adherents welcomed him into the fold, and he attended a few early Rhône Ranger meetings, including the dinner at Lalime's in 1987, which he enjoyed immensely, and he was delighted to taste his fellow winemaker's efforts. But when the discussion turned toward banding together to form a group he politely excused himself, wishing them luck. He preferred to go his own way.

Thackrey has worked with Rhône varieties (and many other varieties) almost since he started taking winemaking seriously. His affinity for Rhône varieties was happenstance; he took to them, he says, because they were different.[2]

Thackrey was never interested in chasing trends, and had no interest in leading them. More than most, his winemaking career is less a vocation than the product of a sophisticated intellectual and sensual appetite, the sort of curiosity that had him veering from the conventional path and onto less trammeled ones, whether unusual varieties or the chance symmetries of field blends. His peregrinations had little to do with commercial success and even less to do with inspiration—he is emphatic on this point. There were no conversion experiences in front of a glass of great Burgundy—while he is moved by wine, there is no one wine beyond his own that moved him into winemaking. He has never been interested in owning a vineyard or nurturing a piece of ground into the acme of its expression, preferring to find vineyards, often of great age, where that has already been done; his job being to take such fruit and transform it into the most delicious wine possible. He is, above all, guided by a well-honed, steadfast sense of his own taste.

"The perfect analogy," he says of his aesthetic, "would be a chef like Daniel Patterson.[3] Daniel is impossible to 'type' as a chef. He just looks at what he's got and comes up with what he thinks would be the most interesting thing to make. He's very intrigued by the *process*. And what would lead me down that path would be deliciousness, something that I thought could be absolutely delicious."

Sean Thackrey was born in 1942 in Los Angeles, the son of Eugene and Winfrid Kay Thackrey. Both Eugene and Kay had careers in Hollywood. Eugene started out as a journalist writing for the *New York World* in its heyday in the late twenties. In the 1930s he turned to screenwriting, where he wrote a number of light romantic comedies for the director Gregory La Cava, including the movies *Unfinished Business*, *Artists and Models*, and *Lady in a Jam*.

Eugene Thackrey's greatest triumph, however, was one for which he received only partial credit: according to his son, Thackrey was the uncredited author of *Both Your Houses*, a Pulitzer Prize winning play that eventually was adapted into the Hollywood movie *Mr. Smith Goes to Washington*. Eugene Thackrey wrote the play in collaboration with Maxwell Anderson; it was first performed in 1933. The play went on to win the Pulitzer Prize for drama in that year, but through a complicated series of circumstances, Thackrey relinquished his credit rights despite receiving royalties for the play after its release.

Thackrey's mother, meanwhile, came to Hollywood in 1921, intent on becoming a set designer, but for years was barred from the career because of her gender. She persisted, becoming instead a script supervisor and special projects assistant on many movies of Hollywood's Golden Age. She chronicled her success story in a memoir called *Member of the Crew*, published in 2001 when she was 102; at the time of its publishing, she was the oldest first-time author in history.

In 1959 Thackrey entered Reed College, the famous Portland breeding ground for independent thinkers, to study art history. He studied under a professor named Lloyd Reynolds, whose radicalized lectures on art history—positing that art's inception, with cave paintings, rendered its creation then and now as a life and death proposition—deeply affected Thackrey. In his sophomore year he moved to Vienna to continue his studies, returning to Reed for a brief time but left in 1962 without completing a degree, settling in the coastal town of Bolinas, north and west of San Francisco, in 1964.

Bolinas, too, fits the trope of iconoclasm. Set off by a large inlet from the rest of Marin County, the town's isolation is augmented by its residents, who routinely remove the town sign at the entrance road so that visitors miss the turn, preserving the surf waves for themselves. If you do find it, there is little to see beyond a hamlet of eerie quietude, lined by eucalyptus groves, with waterfowl circling overhead or landing in the quiet waters of the lagoon, which Thackrey's winery abuts.

In 1970 Thackrey and a partner started an art gallery on Union Street in San Francisco initially called The Poster, which seized on a growing interest in poster art, from Art Deco Paris and Secessionist Berlin to the images of insurgency from the Russian Revolution. Eventually the gallery name was changed to Thackrey & Robertson, and broadened its scope to include another relatively unexplored art market, photography. It became one of the first galleries in the country to focus solely on that market, and had Thackrey traveling all over the world to unearth collections or bid on pieces at auction.

In San Francisco Thackrey frequently visited Singer and Foy, a Washington Square wine bar and retail shop run by Dennis Lapuyade and Stephen Singer. While Thackrey says he'd long been interested in wine as a pleasant beverage with which to pass the time, here was a cadre of wine people with whom he shared artistic sentiments as well as an adventurous palate. They brought him up to speed on what was new in California wines, and sourced French and Italian wines for him as well. The shop also became a trusted source of refreshments for his monthly gallery openings.

Thackrey started making small amounts of wine at home in the late seventies, frequenting Peter Brehm's Berkeley shop Wine and the People to root around for fruit sources. It was there that Thackrey chanced upon some Cabernet in the Napa Valley from Fay Vineyard, already a prized source for Stag's Leap Wine Cellars (the Stag's Leap Cabernet that took first prize at the Judgment of Paris tasting in 1976 contained Fay fruit). Thackrey's first wine in 1979, a Cabernet from Fay, was very good then, and is, he says, still very good. His success with the wine certainly reinforced his interest in winemaking as a sideline, even a career. "I felt like it was my first time sitting down at a piano and realizing I could play," he says.[4]

His experience with Fay, combined with lackluster results from lesser vineyards, proved to Thackrey that the vineyard was carrying the tune, not him. As winemaker, it was his job merely to be attentive, to defer to the ingredients: "You look around the vineyard and you sniff and you smell," he says. "It's almost like a chef at a restaurant, where you actually just go to the market, have a look around and see what's there—you don't have a bunch of preconceptions in your head. You just look at a melon, for example, and you say 'now that looks really good. With a melon like that I could do something that I wouldn't have thought of with a melon before.' My approach to winemaking is exactly the same, it's *cuisine du marché* in the best sense."

It's how he discovered the Yountville vineyard of Arthur Schmidt, who advertised Syrah on the bulletin board at the Wine and the People shop. Syrah was a variety Thackrey had little experience with, beyond the dollop or two found in Chateauneuf-du-Pape blends, a wine he enjoyed a great deal.

But when he got to the Schmidt Vineyard, he knew he'd hit upon the right place. Arthur Schmidt lived in a small clapboard house built by his grandparents in the middle of an old, 20-acre vineyard pruned in a California sprawl of head-trained vines.

"Going into his vineyard was like wandering into a Walker Evans photograph from about 1936," says Thackrey. "Nothing had changed, the worn linoleum on his kitchen counter, the single bare light-bulb over his bare bedstead; I mean, this is the Napa Valley, and he's right in back of [the Napa restaurant] Mustard's Grill, with all of the BMWs racing by. You just never see that anymore."

At the time, Schmidt's fruit was being purchased for $300 a ton by Charles Krug Winery, who employed it in generic reds and whites. Thackrey offered him slightly more for the Syrah and shook hands. In the years that followed, after Thackrey's meteoric success with Schmidt's fruit, he insisted on paying Schmidt more, and Schmidt refused. "I said 'Look I'm selling the wine for a very good price, I love it, I'm going to keep on buying it.' He'd say 'No, if you raise your price and you go out of business, then I won't be able to sell the grapes to anyone.' And we'd go around and around half an hour, I had to arm-wrestle him into taking a little more money."

The wine Thackrey made from Schmidt Vineyard Syrah became known as Orion, a Syrah first bottled in 1986, one which quickly vaulted to the head of the existing Syrahs in the market, particularly in California, where Thackrey's résumé and biography as a reclusive Bolinas nonconformist resonated most fully. Thackrey's winemaking was notoriously improvisational, determined by practice and experience, but also by whimsy and chance. There is an often-repeated harvest story of an exhausted Thackrey crushing a delivery of grapes late in the day, and instead of disposing of the leftover stems, he left them on the crush pad overnight.

When he arrived the next morning he picked up a few stems in his mouth to smell. "They were absolutely wonderful," he says. "They gave off this beautiful aromatic of warm olives. It was a taste you get fairly frequently in Hermitage, and I thought 'what, you're going to throw that away?' So I kept them in."[5]

Stems, old vines, perhaps a stray frond or two of eucalyptus, and countless other tiny inventive maneuvers made Orion distinct from any other Syrah in California. It was so vinous, so savory, so alternative to California's strengths, that it wasn't for everyone. But it set Rhône-inspired wines along a distinct path from the rest of the wine firmament.

Thackrey continued to experiment; he made Mourvèdre from fruit purchased through the Cline brothers in Oakley, a short-lived experiment he has gone back and forth with. But his largest production, and his most successful, most accessible wine has proven to be Pleiades, a nonvintage blend of a dozen or more ingredients, including Barbera, Zinfandel, Syrah, Petite Sirah, Grenache, Alicante Bouschet, Mourvèdre, Carignane, and other odds and ends. It is the wine that follows most closely his dictum of deliciousness, of trying to assemble the most irresistible cépage based on the best most interesting ingredients he's been able to acquire—and while it doesn't fall strictly within the Rhône pantheon, it still feels emblematic of the cause.

"The goal was always to make a wine that was so much better than the sum of its parts," he explains. "I wanted to take wines that were incomplete and put them together in a way that one corrects the faults of the other. Take a variety with beautiful aromatics but a short finish, too acidic, put that together with something voluptuous but without much structure, and so forth, to make it complex and interesting and delicious."

Thackrey was able to make this edition of Orion for just five vintages, from 1986 to 1990, when Arthur Schmidt retired, selling the vineyard to the Swanson family (scions of the American TV Dinner). He was in despair over losing Schmidt, and didn't really know where to turn for a vineyard of similar character. Then one day, he was in the Oakville Grocery in the Napa Valley to pick up some Lucques olives, and ran into winemaker Tony Soter, then the winemaker for Spottswoode, in St. Helena. "He said 'You know, Sean, there's a guy in back of us who raises some of the weird grapes you like to make wine with,'" says Thackrey. "You ought to take a look."

Thackrey made a visit and immediately fell in love. "We tromped over there and I knew I wanted it. It looked like it had been nicely taken care of, it felt completely good, well pruned, clean but not uptight, a beautiful sense to it." He didn't have the slightest idea of what was planted there.

Strictly speaking, he still doesn't, though at this point it might be the result of selective attention.[6] He can say it was planted to mixed blacks in 1905, including Petite Sirah and at least some portion of Syrah. Thackrey wants to believe that the variety called Serine in the nineteenth century might be part of the makeup. That isn't something that can be proven currently. What's clear however is that it is a unique *cépage*, made even more unique by Thackrey's peculiar *élevage* habits. It is also, in a sense, finite—the vines are slowly dying, and the Rossi family has been reluctant to replace the vines that have met their demise. It seems that one day in the near future Thackrey will have to find another vineyard of character to call Orion—whether that includes any Rhône varieties remains to be seen.

Thackrey skirted the Rhône movement for much of its heyday in the nineties, though he continued to cross paths with several producers, with whom he sometimes shared fruit sources and, occasionally, affinities. He has always been very cordial with Randall Grahm, who shares his love for language and tendency to verbosity.

He has attended tastings with other producers as well, but often when there he tends to remain somewhat aloof. Others have tried to get him involved more formally in Rhône-related events, and he declines most offers. Not long ago, he says, John Alban approached him to participate in the Hospice du Rhône in Paso Robles (named after a charity auction in support of the Hospices de Beaune, a home for the terminally ill in Burgundy). Thackrey turned him down, but couldn't resist adding, "John, is that where Rhône varieties go to die?"

12

MANFRED KRANKL,
THE FIRST SUPERSTAR

In 1995, in something between an afterthought and an absentminded gesture, Sine Qua Non winemaker Manfred Krankl sent a bottle of his newly bottled Syrah, the 1994 Queen of Spades, to the offices of Robert M. Parker, Jr. in Parkton, Maryland. "I knew a little about him," Krankl told me one afternoon in his rustic winery on "the Avenue" in Ventura, an industrial sector of town that's about as homely a locale for a winery as any in California. "I knew about his publication, but I'd never met the guy.[1]

"So I sent him a bottle," says Krankl, "with a little note, telling him who I was and what it was and that was that." Two weeks later Parker called the Krankl household; Elaine took the call; moments later she called Manfred at the winery to tell him that Parker had loved the wine: not only was he going to give it a great score, he wanted to buy two cases." Parker gave the wine 95 points, and a first for an American Rhône variety wine.

As retold in Elin McCoy's book, *The Emperor of Wine,* when Parker realized he was calling the Krankl's home line, he counseled them to get a business line immediately. "Trust me," Parker told him, "I've been through this before. You're going to get a ton of calls after the next issue of the newsletter goes out. You don't want me to print your home number."[2]

Parker, of course, had some experience in kingmaking. He'd made stars of several producers in the Napa Valley, some already well-established, others just getting their start with super-premium bottlings, so scarce in some cases that a new term, "cult" wine, had been coined to describe their furtive presence and freakish demand in the market. Every one of these possessed a Napa Valley appellation; all were Bordeaux-style blends. Now Sine Qua Non's first wine was on the brink of being added to their ranks.

Installing a business line was sage advice. Calls were soon coming in from all over the world, most reaching an answering machine that quickly filled with requests. What few bottles of Sine Qua Non wine that the Krankls possessed were sold within days. Within weeks, Sine Qua Non, a winery that had been in existence for less than two years, had a waiting list with more than 500 names.[3]

In the weeks that followed, Krankl started to appreciate just how unlikely an achievement this was, and the extent to which Parker had gone out on a limb for him.

"Let's say I'm a food writer in Los Angeles, and I'm new and want to make my name," says Krankl. "Say I'm going to review Spago. If I say it's great, I make no impact because 60,000 other people have said the same thing. I can take the other route and try to really trash him to get attention, but it would probably discredit me more than Puck. Of course if you write a review that says 'it was ok,' then your impact is like Muzak, it's almost like saying nothing."

"So what I like about this story is, here's Parker. He is already well-established. When he comes out and reviews Mouton and Cheval Blanc and DRC and says they were all great, big deal, anybody can write that, there's no risk in that, there's only a risk in him saying less than that. But there's also a risk in having a complete newcomer like me and say 'that is great,' when the easy thing to do would be to say 'I tasted some wine by this new guy,' 90 points. He didn't have to take a stand, but he did. It takes some balls to do that."

Krankl, of course, can make a similar claim. At several critical points in the inception of his brand, Krankl made decisions for Sine Qua Non that many considered counterintuitive, brash, recalcitrant, foolhardy, even a bit crazy—and every one of these decisions are now thought of as acts of genius, from his outsized bottles to his outsized pricing, from his gorgeous handprinted labels, upon which were printed fanciful, cryptic, sometimes profane proprietary names which he insisted on changing with each vintage, breaking every established rule of wine branding; to the wine itself, among the most voluptuous, seductive, indulgent wines in California to that point. Many, many winemakers have tried to emulate the Sine Qua Non style, from its packaging to its Rabelaisian excess, but none has been as successful as the original.

Manfred Krankl was born in 1956 and raised in Enns, one of Austria's oldest towns, about a hundred miles west of Vienna. Like many European households, the Krankls family enjoyed wine every night with the evening meal, a factor that Manfred considers to be a vital first step on his eventual career path.

The town was small and provincial, and Krankl, having put in a stint with a hotel and restaurant management school, was eager to leave as he reached college age. In 1978, with a friend also named Manfred, Krankl left his hometown for Toronto, Canada. Only after they arrived, however, did they realize that they'd need work permits to stay. With limited funds and limited English, the two Manfreds had few options. They were able to get passage back to Europe on a freighter bound for Greece, where Krankl thought he could live cheaply and put off going back home. That is how he ended up on the island of Mykonos, staying in a small guesthouse also occupied by a couple of sisters from Southern California, Gail and Nancy Silverton.

The Silvertons were from Thousand Oaks, California; Nancy had been training at Le Cordon Bleu in Paris, and the two of them were spending a bit of time in Greece before they headed on to Israel for an additional stay—after they met Krankl, that leg of the trip didn't materialize. They spent an idyllic summer together—Krankl and Gail Silverton became romantically involved (they eventually married in 1980). Krankl stayed as long as his funds allowed; Gail paid for his train ticket back to Austria.

Krankl spent the next year as a waiter; Gail later joined him in Austria. Eventually they made their way back to Los Angeles, where Nancy was involved in the burgeoning LA dining scene, cooking at Michael's in Santa Monica, then Spago, where she met her future husband and business partner, Mark Peel. Krankl landed a position at the Cheese Store in Beverly Hills, owned by fellow Austrian Norbert Wabnig. He and Gail were married and had twin boys.

By 1988, Nancy, Mark Peel, Gail, and Krankl were all living under the same roof, when Peel and Silverton approached Krankl with the prospect of becoming a partner on a new Mediterranean restaurant venture on La Brea Avenue. The location was an older Italianate structure that had once housed Charlie Chaplin's offices; they called it Campanile, for the rustic bell tower that shot up behind the central courtyard. Peel would serve as chef, and Silverton as pastry chef; Krankl would head the front of the house and compose the wine list.

From the moment it opened its doors in 1989, Campanile was one of the most important and influential restaurants in Los Angeles, launching the careers of countless chefs and sommeliers.[4] Peel placed an Italian focus on the menu, adding French and neo-Californian accents with a unique fusion of each. Success bred important side projects: when the partners couldn't find good bread, they started a bakery next to the restaurant; they called it La Brea Bakery. Modeled after Acme Bread in Berkeley, within a few years there were not only lines out the door for fresh loaves, the outfit was shipping bread to hundreds of restaurants and retailers statewide, becoming one of the most successful artisanal bakeries in the state.

In its day, Manfred Krankl's front of the house staff was among the best trained, best managed in the city. His staff was among the most wine-savvy in Los Angeles (one server, Elaine Mills, became Krankl's second wife). They had to be. For your average Angeleno wine lover—a fairly unadventurous California Chardonnay and Cabernet crowd at the time—the list at Campanile was an affront, an excursion so far outside the usual suspects that most customers needed guidance. At first glance it seemed like a thicket of unknown regions and unpronounceable names, with peculiar Italian varieties, obscure southern French appellations, or from what might be called the new guard among California producers. Every few months Krankl would make excursions to Napa and Sonoma Counties in a La Brea Bakery delivery truck to collect wines personally from producers who weren't yet selling consistently in Los Angeles.

He was among the first in California to import wines, especially Gruner Veltliner, from his home country, Austria, and almost collaborated on an import venture with fellow Austrian Wolfgang Puck, but couldn't find an import partner in California. Of course, demand for Gruner Veltliner just a decade later proved that he was just ahead of his time.

Krankl would force diners into uncomfortable selections, Marsanne instead of Chardonnay, Côte-Rôtie rather than Cabernet. His love of Italian white wines led to deep selections of Vermentino, Vernaccia, Tocai Friulano, Pigato, and Arneis—indeed, there were extended periods when California Chardonnay simply disappeared from the list altogether. At one point he got onto a sustained Freisa kick—a brisk light, fruity northern Italian red variety that was just about as polar an opposite of California Cabernet as a red wine can be. He trained his staff relentlessly to make this assault on diners' comfort zone easier to manage, and the dining experience became a voyage of discovery.

"There were definitely customers saying 'What are you talking about Schioppettino for, I want Opus One!'" he says. If he did offer a California wine, it would tend to come from some of the most progressive, obscure artisanal producers that had little cachet or carriage in Los Angeles to that point. That didn't stop Krankl. He says he once dropped in on the Napa winemaker Philip Togni on Spring Mountain, negotiating a difficult road in his La Brea Bakery truck, and refused to leave until Togni sold him a few cases of his hard-to-find wine. "It made an impression on him," says Krankl.

These encounters were seldom repeated, but for Krankl, that wasn't the point. "I was never super concerned with continuity," he says. "In fact I was the opposite in many ways. I wanted the wine list to be constantly evolving, just like the menu." Just like the menu, at Campanile they reprinted the wine list every day—every day it was evolving. "We didn't do it just to be weird," he adds. "It's nice to be a little bit weird, but you have to have the right motivation for it. If you're doing it from the heart, you'll always encounter a little resistance."[5]

He also became known for patronizing emergent American winemakers like Helen Turley and David Abreu, Cabernets from Togni and Spottswoode, as well as the groundbreaking Pinot Noirs of Williams Selyem. Lastly, he was especially supportive of American Rhône variety producers. Often on the Campanile wine list, selections of California Viognier outnumbered that of Chardonnay—he listed Qupé, Ritchie Creek, La Jota, and Phelps, a fact that did not go unnoticed by an aspiring Viognier producer, John Alban.

Alban met Krankl at the restaurant in 1992. The winemaker had come to sell him his first vintage of Viognier, which Krankl bought enthusiastically. They became fast friends; Krankl was impressed with Alban's intensity and verbal wit, while Alban found Krankl's energy and iconoclasm hard to resist. Krankl became one of Alban Vineyard's biggest supporters, taking on his Syrah and Roussanne in their first release; eventually the two of them took trips to wine regions, including the Rhône Valley. Beyond the bottle they even hatched business plans together—on one trip to Austria they became so enamored of Styrian pumpkin seed oil that they explored the prospect of importing it, even conspiring to plant pumpkins and make the oil themselves. "I'm pretty sure that we knew more about pumpkin seed oil than anyone else in this the United States," says Krankl. They talked constantly about wine, opened bottle after bottle, trying to decipher its secrets. In the course of these conversations, Krankl's aesthetic started to take shape.

Almost from the first time the restaurant opened its doors, Krankl looked into developing special house wines for the restaurant; he was especially interested in avoiding something that tasted like most house wines, which is to say cheap and generic: on the contrary, he meant for them to be as good as or better than what he could buy elsewhere. In 1990 he collaborated with Bryan Babcock on a Chardonnay which he called The Thief and which became the restaurant's house Chardonnay, a popular, serviceable wine that would be remembered not for its flavors, but for its label design.

Krankl had long been interested in the artwork adorning wine labels. The most famous example, Chateau Mouton Rothschild in Paulliac, had been commissioning and employing art from some of the world's greatest artists on their labels since 1924.

Closer to home, Krankl was amused by the kerfuffle over Kenwood's Artist Series Reserve Cabernet, released under three labels in 1975. Kenwood had commissioned the artist David Goines to design a portion of the label much like Mouton, and Goines had obliged with an illustration of a naked woman reclining in the vines. The BATF (Bureau of Alcohol, Tobacco, Firearms [and Explosives]), keeping the world safe from human anatomy, rejected the label, and Goines responded with the same design, only this time, the woman's figure had been replaced by a skeleton. Unable to see the humor, the BATF rejected this one too, so Goines removed the human figure altogether, leaving a third design with neither flesh nor bone, just a denuded vineyard landscape.

Krankl was taken in by all of the cheekiness that went into the process, and the notoriety heaped on the winery for its efforts certainly wasn't lost on him. "The whole thing fascinated me," he says. "I'd always thought of the wine world as so stodgy and predictable, so serious. But with labels you could really be in your face if you felt like it."[6]

Campanile had many regular patrons, but one of its most devoted was Sid Felsen, who had cofounded a lithography service not ten blocks away from the restaurant's doors called Gemini G.E.L., where many of the country's greatest artists had their print work processed, including Roy Lichtenstein, Robert Rauschenberg, Jasper Johns, Richard Diebenkorn. When they were in town, Felsen frequently brought artists to dine with him. That is how Krankl met Jim Dine, the pop artist, who, Krankl quickly learned, had an abiding interest in wine. Krankl persuaded Dine to do the label work for The Thief in exchange for a few cases. The subject was a well-worked heart, one of Dine's most iconic images, drawn in charcoal; the bottling became a flashy, in-house hit in the restaurant.

That same year Krankl negotiated with the Coppo brothers in Piedmont, for an unlikely blend of barrique-aged Cabernet, Freisa, and Barbera, which he called Terzetto (for the triumvirate of Peel, Silverton, and himself). He collaborated on two wines the following year—a wine from Alban's fledgling Roussanne block, the label for which he attached a rather obstreperous design called Legs, featuring a female pair in a mildly salacious pose (anticipating a BATF reaction, Krankl designed a more chaste second label; both were approved.) The second wine, Black and Blue, a blend made with Napa's Michael Havens, was fashioned after a famous Provencal blend of Cabernet and Syrah called Le Trevillon.

These were project wines, as Krankl called them. He loved working with innovative winemakers and loved hashing out the blend toward what he wanted to achieve in the wine, tailoring it to the Campanile cuisine, and ultimately learning the keys to what made wine good. "They were fun on a small scale," he says, "but it was starting to occur to me it might be nice to make my own little brand." It was a long way from running a restaurant floor, he says, but in the end the restaurant figured into his plans considerably. "I thought 'we can always force *them* to sell it,'" he says. "Even if the wine sucks, we'll never be stuck with it; we'll pour it off by the glass."

One evening around this time, Krankl and Alban opened a bottle of Chardonnay from Marcassin, John Wetlaufer and Helen Turley's new brand. "It was better than any California Chardonnay we'd ever had," he says, "Better than anyone's. For a long time we kept saying that California wines weren't as impressive as French wines. But when you saw someone doing it this well—and if it was doable with Chardonnay, you could do it with anything, Syrah, Grenache, Viognier, whatever. I think we both felt we got strength from the skill exhibited in that wine. We both realized it was possible."

It was around this time that Krankl started to seriously consider becoming a winemaker. It would be on a small scale, and he intended to remain involved with the restaurant and bakery. To his friend John Alban he seemed tentative, however, and Alban would have none of it. "I remember him saying 'Of course I'll help you, but you've got to be serious about it.'" Krankl convinced Alban that he was ready to commit. (He also convinced Elaine, who is his partner and co-owner in the project.) With the help of Ojai's Adam Tolmach, Krankl was able to secure a contract for Syrah fruit from the Z Block at Bien Nacido Vineyard, some of the oldest in the Central Coast. He was able to farm it to his specifications, which were somewhat radical.

The Krankls chose the name Sine Qua Non, a Latin term with the literal meaning "without which nothing," and which referred to an essential action, condition, or element. "It was sort of a little wishful thinking on our part," says Krankl, "like we were going to make something that everybody will want to have."

For five years as a wine buyer, Manfred Krankl had had the benefit of touring and tasting in some of the most famous cellars in the world; he'd had scores of relatively unguarded conversations with great producers ("I wasn't a winemaker," says Krankl, "so they didn't hold anything back"). He asked a lot of questions, filled books with notes about barrel regimes, hang times, yields, yeasts, stem use, the techniques used to craft his favorite wines. "I thought, all I have to do is retro-engineer what I've learned," he says. "I was sure I'd find some common thread." In fact at first he found no thread at all. "Everybody used barrels, but no one used the same kind," he says. "Dujac loved to use stems in his fermentations, and Jayer hated them.[7] I thought 'Shit, now what do I do?' It's not going to be as simple as I thought."

But after more conversations, and much contemplation, Krankl felt he could discern a through-line—one that had little to do with winemaking or technique. Style, he realized, was a much broader concept than he had at first presumed, not just a sum of parts. There were components, yes, but the reason Chave was Chave had less to do with the barrels Gerard Chave used, or the maceration times, or the length of *élevage*, than with the commitment of the man himself.

He thought about the time he had spent with Jacques Reynaud, the proprietor at Chateau Rayas in Chateauneuf-du-Pape. "I realized," he says, "this guy is maniacal about his vineyard work in relation to everyone else. What does he do out there? Why does he do it? Well, it's not because he's a masochist, he doesn't do it just to torture himself every day or create more work for himself.

"The common thread with all these winemakers was that they were very passionate and deeply committed about their own style," he explains. "And that deep conviction manifested itself not in the specific things they did, but in how they executed, how meticulous they were and uncompromising in their pursuit. That's what made them great. They paid attention to things that other people did not.

"What I liked about Rayas is that it was lush, and full of flavor and aromatically complex, and still elegant and spritely, it had nuances and layers. I would never say 'I'm going to make a Grenache just like Rayas,' because if I think like that, inevitably I will fail. So at every point in the process I'd want to know, why was he doing what he was doing? And I wanted to take what he did and make a wine like that in California."

California vineyard practices in California, compared with Reynaud, were relatively laissez faire at the time. But a small number of winemakers and viticulturalists—Turley, Abreu, Beckstoffer among them—were getting dramatic results by making adjustments in canopy design, fruit exposure, and especially crop load. Krankl, on his own path, had drawn similar conclusions, and in his vineyard practices, was getting similar results.

In his first vintage at Bien Nacido Vineyard, Krankl stripped leaves from his Syrah canopies to expose the fruit to more sun. He dropped unripe clusters so that the remaining fruit could develop more fully. He picked fruit weeks later than all of his contemporaries. He became a compulsive sorter, removing detritus and less than ripe fruit, any clusters that seemed to him less than pristine. He used only new oak barrels—like Guigal, he felt that the quality of the fruit could support that approach. He made countless other small tweaks in winery practices to home in on purity of fruit expression; no detail in the process was too minute. It was his goal to make a wholly Californian *cépage*, one that reflected the sun and heat the state had to offer, to maximize that expression. Above all he wanted to distance himself from producers who insisted that French methods, technique, and styles were somehow best for California fruit. If Krankl had a stylistic agenda at all, it was to prove that this approach had been misguided from the start.

"I wanted to make my wine distinctly in the American spirit," he says. "If anything I was going to go out of my way to let everyone know in no bloody way was I going to ever emulate a French guy. Not to diss the French of course, but that's not what we are, and not what we were attempting to do. And just by the fact that we would want to do this, it would emphasize our own individuality." From its very first vintage, Sine Qua Non wines expressed that difference: it was as dramatic as it was inescapable.

The brand diverged in more ways than just the wine itself. In its execution, its exclusivity, and striking design, Sine Qua Non stood apart. Throughout its conception, Krankl applied some of the more important lessons he'd learned in his many careers as restaurateur, sommelier, project winemaker, artist, peripatetic traveler, and husband.

At Campanile Krankl had an opportunity to witness firsthand just what his customers were attracted to in the wines they drank with dinner; what moved them, what sorts of details transformed an okay experience into something vivid and memorable. It's worth noting that Campanile is just a stone's throw or two from Hollywood—its customers were sophisticated, creative, artistically inclined, well-heeled patrons of the arts and in many cases, creators of it. They were accustomed to fine things, and certainly weren't above falling victim to a little flash. Sine Qua Non delivered: a visual, tactile, and of course gustatory experience unique to all other wine experiences.

It began with the package. The label revolution that had begun with Randall Grahm was well underway in California, but not even Grahm made his own label. Krankl had the artistic skills to pull it off: at once high-minded, visually arresting, and deeply personal, Sine Qua Non's label design is still one of the most unique in the American wine market. Inspired by his old customer Sid Felsen, Krankl decided to employ lithography in the design; his interest had been given a boost one Christmas when Elaine presented him with carving tools for woodcutting. The woodcut would become his principle medium.

Like Mouton and Kenwood, Krankl's designs would change every year: the vintage was different from one year to the next, he reasoned, why shouldn't the label reflect that? "I just thought that if I had the same label every year I'd be bored," he says. That was never an issue with Sine Qua Non labels. The design reflected a bold, confident line and a feel for drama; in some cases the cropping gave the viewer a mildly disoriented, out-of-context feel, as if you were only seeing part of the picture.

Of course, Krankl didn't stop at the label design: each year the name of the wine would change as well—illustration and name were always deeply linked.

College semiotics seminars could be built around an extended discussion of the proprietary names of Sine Qua Non wines. Some (The Marauder, The Hussy, Red Handed, Imposter McCoy, Covert Fingers) wouldn't have been out of place adorning a noirish detective novel, while others (Into the Dark, Against the Wall, Twisted and Bent, Sublime Isolation) seemed like a stroll in an existential minefield. Still others (On Your Toes, Just For the Love of It, The 17th Nail in My Cranium) don't read like names at all, but seem closer to unfinished thoughts, as if the label had snatched a fragment of Krankl's latest daydream.

Clearly Krankl delights in stymieing those who wish to decode them, second-guess them, or anticipate them. Krankl's even been known to strike back at those who call them into question, as in 1998, the year he invited a journalist from a major wine publication to visit the winery. The visit went poorly; the writer was dismissive about the artistic flourishes in the project, and was especially flippant about the effort that went into the packaging. "He kept asking 'Why do you mess around with the label?'" says Krankl, "'Why don't you just concentrate on the wine?' I thought, 'What makes you think I *don't* concentrate on the wine?' It was just so weirdly condescending, and this person felt so soulless and unemotional." As a reaction to this encounter, Krankl scrapped the design for that year, presenting instead a murky brown blank label, beneath which were the words: "E-Raised." On the back label there was this very pointed, if cryptic explanation:

> This wine is dedicated to all the nay sayers, the squares, the antagonists. Those who tell us to "just concentrate on the wine," to "give up the gimmicks with those odd, those quirky labels; what's the deal with them anyway?" So here it is. We RAISED the wine with love and care and we E-raised the quirkiness, the label. Now it is plain and simple and as "traditional" as we know how to make it. We left the canvas (speak label) blank. Those of you who might have started to get the hang of our bottle adornments are invited to fill in the blank yourself . . . while you toast all those antagonists. We will. Now if you want us to continue with our more (un)usual bottle identities, drop us a note, give us a call, protest and complain. We'll hear you.

Krankl affixed those labels on hefty, heavy-gauge bottles; when you held a Sine Qua Non bottle in your hands, it felt substantial. The wines were packaged in wooden six-bottle cases, like fine Bordeaux, its surface also adorned with original Krankl designs. All of these things, taken together, reinforced the notion that, like the vintage, the blend, and the circumstances under which this wine came together, was one of a kind.

And you would pay handsomely for it. Krankl's conceptual coup de grace was a price tag; he entered the market with the most expensive Syrah in the country, at a suggested retail price of $31. Certainly this reflected the costs of his fanaticism in the vineyard. But it also signified that Sine Qua Non was not an afterthought, not a second-tier bottling from a Cabernet house, like Joseph Phelps, who sold his Viognier and Syrah at a fraction of the price he sold his flagship Bordeaux blend, Insignia. That, to Krankl, was a grave mistake. "If your Cabernet was $50, and your Syrah was $15, what did that tell the market about your Syrah? I wanted to take a stand; I wanted to make the statement that I was very serious about this."

It remained to be seen whether the market would accommodate such innovations. Krankl remembers first explaining these concepts to Rand Yazzolino, whose Bay Area distribution company, Estate Wines Ltd., who would be responsible for selling Sine Qua Non. "He looked at me and said 'Are you crazy? That's the strangest thing I've ever heard—you have a new brand, and just at the moment people can learn to recognize it you're going to change it?' I said 'Yeah, that's what I'm going to do.'"

Yazzolino was taken aback by Krankl's approach, but after years of collaboration at Campanile and seeing the ease with which many of his innovations took hold, he wasn't concerned. "It seemed like a complicated issue to overcome," he says, "from a marketing standpoint it's hard to build continuity without a label." Instead the label change became an annual event: customers looked forward to seeing what was coming. "He clearly proved me wrong," says Yazzolino. "I am continually surprised by Manfred. He's crazy: crazy in a good way."

Sine Qua Non's impact on the Rhône movement was immediate and powerful. Parker's imprimatur vaulted this unknown winemaker into the upper echelons of stardom overnight.

In Ventura there were ever more frantic attempts to secure bottles. Offers well beyond the asking price were left on the business line. At the restaurant Krankl was accosted on several occasions by studio executive assistants who begged him for a bottle for their powerful bosses: one told Krankl that if he didn't come back with a bottle, he would be fired.

The following year, 1995, Krankl returned to market with two wines, The Other Hand, a Syrah, and a white blend of Roussanne and Chardonnay from Alban Vineyard he called The Bride. That year he sourced fruit from Alban and Stolpman Vineyards, in addition to Bien Nacido: no less opulent than the Queen, the Bride earned 92 points in Parker's *Wine Advocate*.

Perhaps Krankl's greatest gift was for timing—here was an iconoclastic wine with an exotic story to tell, championed by Robert Parker, whose pulpit was just reaching the peak of its authority—an authority aided in no small measure by finds like Sine Qua Non, whose complete obscurity guaranteed a splash when its greatness was revealed.

With Helen Turley, Sine Qua Non wines represented the triumph of a California style, a style that glorified the abundance that the state's wine regions could offer, the bounty of sun and heat that winemakers for years had hedged against. Krankl embraced these conditions. He wasn't the first to the gate, but he was the first to have Syrah as his vehicle. He and his wines became a standard-bearer for a new style that gripped the country.

Quite apart from its synergies with Parker, Sine Qua Non performed two contradictory tasks simultaneously: it exalted American Syrah's position in the public eye, even as the wine itself transcended any varietal association. Because it was the first American Syrah to achieve commodity status, it became one of the variety's most iconic flagship wines; and yet, no one cared what was in the bottle.

Sine Qua Non also ended for a time the attempts by American winemakers to recreate French wines in California. So many of the early efforts in Syrah winemaking in California were defined by a desire to replicate the flavors and textures of inspirational Hermitages and Côte-Rôties. Sine Qua Non obliterated that model for the better part of two decades.

Inevitably Sine Qua Non's success led to imitators, none as discriminating or complex, none as deft in the glass. Most mimicked the ripeness levels, without building any other complexities in the wine. For better or worse, these too were lauded in the press. Krankl, who always maintained that his style stood between the poles of Australian ripeness and French austerity, likes to point out that when he started harvesting Syrah in leased vineyards, he was the latest to pick by a wide margin. Now his picking date falls more or less in the middle of those harvesting alongside him.

To this day Sine Qua Non wines are frequently spotted in auction catalogs—their resale value remains very spectacularly high in an era where Syrah's fortunes are wavering.

"This is a Horatio Alger tale," Parker writes, "of an immigrant (in this case, from Austria) who arrived with only a backpack to his name, and who in a few short years opened the finest artisanal bakery in Los Angeles (La Brea Bakery) as well as one of the area's pioneering Mediterranean-styled restaurants (Campania [*sic*]—still flourishing today). However, Krankl's fame rests on the strength of his wines—compelling, singular, and world-class wines that are like no others being produced on Planet Earth."[8]

Indeed perhaps more than with other cult phenomena, Parker and Krankl seemed closely linked in reputation, mutual respect, and of course, in the perpetuation of spectacular careers. Indeed, Parker seems to like being associated with Krankl and his wines. In conversations with Elin McCoy, Parker has intimated that he feels he has a lot in common with Krankl: both were small-town guys who achieved success in much larger arenas. They shared tastes for great wine and great food, and he believed, both were honest and direct. In fact Parker told McCoy that if he could become friendly with winemakers, Krankl would certainly be one of them.[9]

FIGURE 1
Alice Waters at the entrance of Chez Panisse, 1970s. *Courtesy of Chez Panisse.*

FIGURE 2
Kermit Lynch with Lulu Peyraud at Domaine Tempier,
Provence, 2005. *Copyright Gail Skoff.*

Demand for Grapes.

Another year's experince and observation in the vineyards and the markets has more fully convinced me that grape growing is among the best and most certain of fruit-growing interests. As vineyardists learn to care for the vines better, and better modes of packing and transporting the fruit are employed, and the prices get within the reach of the laboring people, the quantity grown can hardly equal the demand. Only a few years ago our foreign population were our grape eaters; now our grapes are found by our native population to be delicious and healthful, and already they have become on thousands of tabies an article of daily consumption. The quantity now received and consumed in any of our large cities would utterly astonish one whs has never seen the whole train loads and steamer loads daily unloaded, and all good grapes have sold at remunerative prices.—*Correspondence Rural New Yorker.*

Please notify this office of an irregularity in receiving the MERCHANT.

FOR SALE.

GRAPE CUTTINGS

—OF THE—

FOLLOWING VARIETIES,

Which are considered by the

MOST INTELLIGENT VIGNERONS

THE BEST IN THE STATE.

Grenache,   Carignane,

Folle Blanche,

Trousseau,   Berger.

PRICES ON APPLICATION.

J. DEBARTH SHORB;

OR   **J. M. TIERNAN,**

SAN GABRIEL, Los Angeles Co.

FOR SALE.

CUTTINGS OF

VALUABLE

IMPORTED VINES.

CABERNET-SAUVIGNON,   FRANC CABERNET,
SEMILLON,   PETITE SIRRAH (also rooted vines.)
FRANC PINOT,   PINOT DE PERNAND,
MALBEC (and roots),
PINOT GRIS,   GAMAI TEINTURIER.

All the Champagne Varieties.

— AND —

PETIT VERDOT,   VERDOT COLON,
MEUNIER,   MERLOT,
And a few cuttings of rare table varieties.

Also all Varieties of

RIESLINGS, CHAUCHE NOIR AND GRIS, FOLLE BLANCHE, SAUVIGNON VERTE, CHALOSSE, GROSSER BLAUER, TEINTURIER MALE, GUTEDEL, and all ordinary wine varieties.

J. H. DRUMMOND,

GLEN ELLEN, Sonoma Co.,

No orders can be taken after 1st March.

Cuttings!   Cuttings!

For Sale.

MOSELLE RIESLING,   CHASSELAS DE FAY,
MELON BLANC OR PINOT BLANC,
WHITE BURGUNDY,   SEEDLESS SLUTANA,
LISTAN OR GOLDEN CHASSELAS,
MARSANNE,   FRANKEN RIESLING,

——AND FOR——

Sauterne Wines.

WHITE SEMILLON AND SAUVIGNON VERTE.

——FOR——

Red Wines.

MALBEC,   BLACK BURGUNDY,   MATARO
CARIGNAN, GRENACHE,
ZINFANDEL,   GAMAY LOUTURA,
PIED DE PERDRIX, PETITE SIRRAH,
CABERNET SAUVIGNON,
KOLNER NOIR OR GROSS BLAUE.

AND MANY OTHER VARIETIES.

INQUIRE OF

H. W. CRABB,

OAKVILLE, Napa Co., Cal.

FIGURE 3

Advertisements for vine cuttings from J. H. Drummond, H. W. Crabb, and J. DeBarth Shorb in the *San Francisco Merchant,* an early wine trade publication, 1885. Note references to Carignane, Grenache, Marsanne, Petite Sirrah (Syrah), and Mataro (Mourvèdre). *Courtesy of archive.org and the San Francisco Public Library History Center.*

Important Vine Stocks
FOR SALE.

For sale a number of Cuttings from carefully selected Choice Wine Vines. The original stocks were imported from the most famous French Vineyards at great expense.

Malbec, Claret variety imported from Chateau Brown Cantenac, Bordeaux, $2.50

*Cabernet Sauvignon, imported from Margaux, Lafite and Chateau Brown —Cantenac. This vine produces the highest class Bordeaux wine (claret).

Price per M.......... $8.00   Price per 100........... $1.00

Cabernet Franc, from the above vineyard. A high grade claret variety.

Price per M........... $8.00   Price per 100........... $1.00

Verdot and Verdot Colon, also renowned for Clarets.

Price per M........... $6.00   Price per 100........... $ .75

*St. Macaire, from the Palus District, Medoc. A strong, thrifty vine with great bearing powers, yielding a wine of intense color and of a true claret type. Ripens early.

Price per M........... $20   Price per 100........... $2.50

*Gros Nancin, from the same locality. A great bearer; the wine is of great color and quality. Ripens later than the St. Macaire.

Price per M........... $20   Price per 100........... $2.50

*Franc Pinot, from Vougeot and Beaune in the Bourgogne. Is a fair bearer and yields the most famous wines of Burgundy.

Price per M........... $18   Price per 100........... $2.00

*Pinot de Pernand, from Beaune. A good bearer, giving a wine of a high class Burgundy character.

Price per M........... $18   Price per 100........... $2.00

Gamai Teinturier, from Beaune. A fine bearer, ripens as early as the Pinots; gives a wine of great color and of high value for blending.

Price per M........... $6.00   Price per 100........... $ .75

*Tannat, imported by Mr. Wetmore from Madiran. Is an extremely heavy bearer, producing a wine of fine color, great quality and tannin and possessing remarkable keeping powers.

Price per M........... $1   Price per 100........... $1.75

Petite Sirrah, giving a wine of intense color and great quality. Imported from the Hermitage.

Price per M........... $6.00   Price per 100........... $ .75

*Semillon, from Yquem. A good bearer, ripens early and produces the world renowned Chateau Yquem.

Price per M........... $8.00   Price per 100........... $100

Sauvignon, from Yquem. Enters into the best known wines of the Sauterne.

Price per M........... $8.00   Price per 100........... $1.00

Merlot, from Chateau Brown Cantenac.

Price per M........... $6.00   Price per 100 .... $ .75

Also a limited number of cuttings of the Champagne varieties—also Pinot Blanc, Clairette Blanche, Petit Bouschet, Alicante Bouschet, Marsanne, Grosser Blauer, Meunier, Teinturier Male, Folle Blanche, Kadarkas Noir, and many fancy table varieties.

Cuttings of ordinary wine varieties at from $2 to $3.50 per M. All cuttings from healthy vines and carefully packed. Length, 18 inches between terminal buds.

☞ For the more choice varieties only early orders can be filled, and prices for other than above can be obtained on application.

The greater portion of the wines made on this vineyard, season of 1885, from vines marked thus * realized $1.00 per gallon.

Slight charge made for packing.

J. H. DRUMMOND,
DUNFILLAN,

GLEN ELLEN,   SONOMA COUNTY, CAL.

FIGURE 4

Advertisement for cuttings from J. H. Drummond for Petite Sirrah, "imported from the Hermitage," 1888. *Courtesy of archive.org and the San Francisco Public Library History Center.*

grafted into upwards of twenty thousand old Mission vines ;
Carbernet Sauvignon, Carbernet Franc, Merlot, Verdot, Mal-
bec, Semillion Blanc, Sauvignon Blanc, Muscadelle de Bor-
delais, Aramon, Petit Bouschet, Mourastel, Cinsaut, Beclan,
Poulsard, Serine, Mondeuse, Clairette Rouge, Pécoui Touar,
Clairette Blanche, Ugni Blanc, Rousanne, Marsanne, Tannat,
Petite Syrah, Malmsey Madeira, Tinta Madeira, Verdellho,
Boal, Muscatel Madeira, Pedro Ximenes, Palomino, Mantuo
Castellano, Veba, Péruno, Mantuo de Pilas, Bastardo,
Mourisco Preto, Tinta Coa, Morete, Mourisco Blanco,
Tinta Amarella, Touriga, Bokador, Yellow Mosler, Pever-
ella, Rothgipler, Rhulander Grey, Slankamenka, Yellow
Silk Grape, Steinschiller, Green Sylvaner, Spicy Tramin-
er, Green Veltliner, White Vernaccio, Waelschriesling,
Zierfandler, Affenthaler, Kadarka, Lagrein, St. Laurent,
Marzemino, Portugieser, Refosco, Spanna, Barbera, Terol-
dego, Wildbacher, Malvasia Bianca, Moscato Rosa, Rosara,
Aleatico, San Giovetto, San Columbano, Trebbiano, Cana-
jola Nero, Canajola Bianco.

Satisfactory success was attained with the most of these
varieties, and thus was established a store house of viticultural wealth for the State, which subsequent vineyard planters
have largely and profitably availed themselves of.

It was fortunate for the State that this work could be
undertaken by a corporation wherein those interested were
few in number and had ample means, and whose property
was so favorable, in all respects, to such experimental test
work, and great benefits will undoubtedly result to the State
of California therefrom, though, since Mr. Livermore's retirement from the active managership of the Natoma property
(which took place in 1885) not all his wise and public spirited plans have been carried out by his successors.

Continuing the plantation in the years 1883-4, a decidedly
unfavorable season was encountered, owing to the protracted

FIGURE 5

Partial census of vines planted at Natoma Vineyard in Folsom, one of the most
comprehensive early plantings of Rhône varieties, from George Husmann, *Grape
Culture and Wine-Making in California,* 1888. *Courtesy of archive.org and University of
California Libraries.*

FIGURE 6

Darrell Corti, retailer, tasting in Hungary, 2011. Photo by
Rick Minderman. *Courtesy of Darrell Corti.*

FIGURE 7

Joseph Phelps (left) and Walter Schug with plans for new
winery, 1970s, Napa Valley. *Courtesy of Joseph Phelps
Vineyards.*

FIGURE 8

A young Gary Eberle about to embark on the first modern Syrah plantation in California, at Estrella River, Paso Robles, 1975. *Courtesy of Gary Eberle.*

FIGURE 9

Bob Lindquist (left) and Adam Tolmach, sampling the wares, 1984. *Courtesy of Bob Lindquist.*

FIGURE 10

John Buechsenstein (left) with Randall Grahm (right) looking on, 1979. *Courtesy of John Buechsenstein.*

FIGURE 11

Randall Grahm at Bonny Doon, 1984. *Courtesy of Randall Grahm.*

FIGURE 12

Ruthie Grahm, former sales director for Bonny Doon, showing maternal pride. *Courtesy of the author.*

FIGURE 13

Steve Edmunds (center) with growers Chester and Rich Brandlin, 1990. *Courtesy of Steve Edmunds.*

FIGURE 14

Sean Thackrey, among the vines, 1980s. *Courtesy of Sean Thackrey.*

FIGURE 15
Manfred Krankl in his cellar, 1994. *Courtesy of Elaine Krankl.*

FIGURE 16
John Alban on his way to Chateau Rayas in Chateauneuf-du-Pape, undated. *Courtesy of John Alban.*

FIGURE 17

John Alban in a room filled with cuttings he has propagated, undated. *Courtesy of John Alban.*

FIGURE 18

Robert Haas and Jean-Pierre Perrin planting the first vines at Tablas Creek in Paso Robles, 1992. *Courtesy of Tablas Creek.*

FIGURE 19
David Lake (left) and Mike Sauer (on one knee) with crew planting the first Syrah in the Columbia Valley at Red Willow Vineyard, 1985. *Courtesy of Mike Sauer.*

FIGURE 20
Christophe Baron, Cayuse Winery. *Courtesy of the author.*

FIGURE 21

Cailloux Vineyard, in The Rocks of Milton-Freewater, one of Syrah's most distinctive terroirs. *Courtesy of the author.*

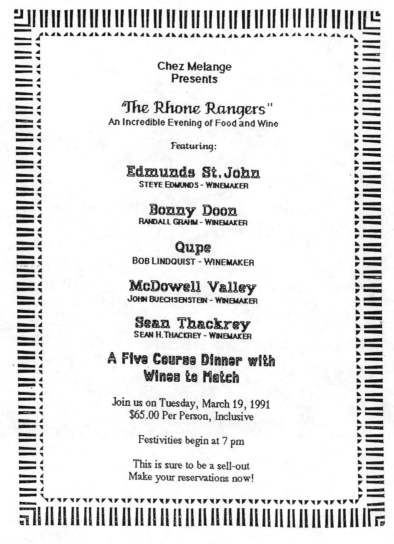

FIGURE 22

Advertisement for a star-studded wine dinner featuring the Rhône Rangers, Chez Melange, Marina del Rey, 1991. *Courtesy of John Buechsenstein.*

California Producers of Rhône Varietals

"The Rhône Rangers"

FIGURE 23
Promotional brochure featuring a variation on Pablo Haz's Rhône Ranger illustration,
early 1990s. *Courtesy of Bill Smith.*

FIGURE 24
Robert Mayberry and John Buechsenstein (left) on a visit with Jacques Reynaud (middle) at Chateau
Rayas, undated. *Courtesy of John Buechsenstein.*

FIGURE 25

American contingent, International Colloquium on Rhône Varietals, 1991. *Colloquium transcript, photographer unknown.*

FIGURE 26

French contingent, International Colloquium, 1991. Robert Haas is eighth from left. *Colloquium transcript, photographer unknown.*

FIGURE 27

John Alban, Mat Garretson, and Vicki Carroll, founders and organizers of Hospice du Rhône, 2007. *Copyright Mel Hill Photography.*

FIGURE 28

Yves Gangloff, one of the Four Amigos, bowling at Hospice du
Rhône, 2003. *Copyright Mel Hill Photography.*

FIGURE 29

Mat Garretson (in tights) and entourage, rosé lunch, Hospice du Rhône, 2000. *Copyright Mel Hill Photography.*

FIGURE 30

A recent Rhône Rangers tasting, San Francisco. *Courtesy of the Rhône Rangers organization.*

PART IV

THE MOVEMENT STARTS TO MOVE

13

VIOGNIER, THE RHÔNE MOVEMENT'S FLOWER CHILD

As Syrah was gaining its foothold on the American wine scene, another Rhône variety, Viognier, slowly crept into the consciousness of American winemakers. By the early seventies a smattering had had a chance encounter with Condrieu, or with Chateau-Grillet the tiny appellation in the northern Rhône controlled by a single estate; they'd tasted a Viognier at friends' dinner tables or on the wine lists of discerning restaurants. Many were overcome, finding the wines so otherworldly, so exotic, so profoundly different from any other wine they'd ever had that they speak of their first taste using the language of conversion and epiphany.

"My first taste of Condrieu was under ideal circumstances," says John Alban of his first time, in 1985. "I knew nothing about the wine, varietal composition, or region." The Condrieu was brought to a party by a friend, and Alban had brought a wine too; "I recall feeling foolishly pleased that the wine I had brought was going to be the wine of the night." With the swirl of a glass, he was proven wrong:

My first sniff of the Condrieu triggered momentary bewilderment as I held onto my silly prepossession just long enough for the wine's aromatics to completely engulf my olfactory lobe. Overwhelmed by the completely unexpected freshness of stone fruits, rich apricot, and vibrant honeysuckle, pleasure centers took charge and reason no longer got in my way. I couldn't wait to taste the damn thing. Long before any flavor component took hold, I was absolutely captivated by the weight and texture of the wine. Once the glycerol peeled away, the apricots, minerals, and golden cherry notes penetrated; I remember feeling like I was drinking crème brulee, a descriptor I still use today. It was that effect, as much as anything else, that went on to change my life.[1]

Viognier was the only significant Rhône variety not to have been exported to California in the nineteenth century—in the thousands of pages of viticultural reports and varietal assessments from that era, Viognier is mentioned only in passing as a blending grape for Syrah in Côte-Rôtie.[2]

Post-Prohibition, tasting Viognier would have been exceedingly rare because of its scarcity: for all practical purposes it was grown in just two places on earth, in Condrieu and at Chateau-Grillet, constituting an area of just 500 acres, of which just a tiny fraction had survived the deprivations of the Second World War.

Because of this, there simply wasn't much imported. Chateau-Grillet was coveted, but it was the tiniest appellation in France, at 3.8 hectares, from which barely 1,000 cases were produced for the world. Meanwhile by the 1960s the area under vine in Condrieu had shrunk to 10 hectares. Many of its estates were approaching ruin, laid low by inferior clone selection, high labor costs, and neglect; worse, the prices fetched for bottles of Condrieu weren't nearly enough to offset the cost of growing grapes in such a challenging growing region.

Slowly, however, the climate for imported wines from the northern Rhône Valley villages of Condrieu and Ampuis started to change. Much of the credit must go to two proprietors, Marcel Guigal, who at seventeen took control of the estate from his father, who had been temporarily stricken blind by illness; and Georges Vernay, whose tireless efforts to resurrect the region eventually earned him the nickname "Mr. Condrieu." Both men invested time and energy in reviving the vine stock, repairing derelict vineyards, investing in the infrastructure of the crumbling slopes, securing fruit sources along the way. Guigal wines were imported on a handshake deal between the family and Fred Ek of Classic Wine Imports in Boston in 1968; their first Condrieu debuted in this country in 1973; the wines of Vernay were introduced not long after.

Meanwhile in California, Kermit Lynch acquired forty cases of the 1970 Chateau-Grillet in 1974, a virtually unknown wine that he now had to sell. "It occurred to me," Lynch writes in the introduction to his anthology of newsletters, *Inspiring Thirst*, "that my clientele might not know what a Chateau-Grillet is, so I decided to put a short explanation about each wine into my price list, to try and let my clients know what to expect when they uncorked a bottle."[3] The now famous Kermit Lynch newsletters were borne of this moment.

Four winemakers—Pete Minor of Ritchie Creek, Josh Jensen of Calera, Bill Smith of La Jota, and Joseph Phelps—debuted Viognier between 1985 and 1987. The early efforts were so coincident with one another that they resemble a concerted effort—and close observers came away with the impression that it was a race.[4] Remarkably, each gathered plant material independently of each other, without knowledge of each other's efforts, from completely different sources.

The first of these four winemakers to act upon their epiphany was Josh Jensen, founder, proprietor, and winemaker for Calera Vineyards outside Hollister.

In the late sixties, Jensen was a student at Oxford who upon his graduation traveled to France on a postgraduate fellowship, driving around the countryside in an old Citroen Deux Chevaux and making frequent trips from Paris to the Riviera and back, with stops in Burgundy and the Rhône Valley along the way. He got his first taste of Viognier in 1969 in Condrieu, at the Hotel Beau Rivage, charmingly situated on an otherwise prosaic stretch of the Rhône. There, over a plate of *quenelles de brochet*, Jensen had his first sip, and was transported.

"It just knocked me out," he says. "I had become familiar with German wines, which like Condrieu are very aromatic and floral, but when you put it in your mouth those wines are very elegant, delicate, even elusive. But Condrieu was like this blockbuster. It wasn't small and elegant and delicate, it was huge and explosive and rich, a powerhouse. I used to think of the wines as almost schizophrenic, because the aromas lead you to expect one thing and then when it hits your mouth, kapow!"

Jensen returned to Ampuis the following year, just prior to a harvest stint at Domaine de la Romanée-Conti. Once again, Jensen dined at the Beau Rivage and sampled Viogniers from its prodigious wine list. He was able to arrange a tasting with the Neyret-Gachet family of Chateau-Grillet, who allowed him to work two days' harvest, becoming the first of these producers to pick Viognier, and perhaps the first American in history to have picked Viognier ever. In exchange for his services, the Neyret-Gachet family gave him three bottles of wine. Jensen went on to work a stint at Domaine de la Romanée Conti, but the wines of Condrieu continued to haunt him.

They served only to confuse many with whom he shared them. In 1972 one of Jensen's friends and wine mentors, George Selleck, arranged for him to meet the legendary André Tchelistcheff over a long dinner.[5] That night, Jensen opened one of the bottles he had received as payment for his work at Grillet. According to Jensen, Tchelistcheff was impressed with the wine, saying it was a very good Riesling. Jensen politely corrected him. "'It's Viognier,' I told him. And he said 'Young man, I don't care what the label says, it's Riesling.'" Jensen thought it best to keep his mouth shut.

In 1973, as plans for his own winery and vineyards took shape, Jensen sought Viognier at local nurseries and research stations, to no avail. He formally petitioned the Foundation Plant Material Service (FPMS, known since 2003 as FPS), the importation and quarantine facility at the University of California, Davis, to import some—this started the process going.[6]

Jensen returned to Burgundy in 1974, just before founding his winery, to visit with friends and to taste wine. He intended to revisit the northern Rhône and see if he could procure some Viognier cuttings, but wasn't able to make the side trip. So he decided to contact Georges Vernay to inquire about some cuttings, requesting that Vernay send them to his hotel in Paris, where he could bundle them up just before his return to the states. To his surprise, Vernay complied. [7] Jensen left France with the vines nestled in the lining of his coat.

When Jensen returned, he turned the cuttings over to Golden State Vinegrowers, where the vines were grafted to propagate. There they thrived for two months on bench grafts, earning them the distinction of being the first Viognier planted on U.S. soil—but none survived. Less than two months later, the nursery informed Jensen that every one of the cuttings had died.

Viognier of a more permanent nature landed on American soil in 1976 and 1977 from three distinct entry points. The first known cuttings were registered at Geneva Station, New York, the home of Cornell's viticultural nursery program, imported in 1975 by a grape breeder and research technician named George Remaily.

Most of Remaily's career was devoted to the propagation and development of table grapes. He spent years in Bucks County, Pennsylvania, cultivating winter-hardy grapevines and developing hybrids. In 1960s he moved to Hammondsport, on Keuka Lake in the Finger Lakes wine region, where he assisted in the labs and vineyards at Geneva Station.[8] On occasion however he was known to pick up plant material that interested him or which might be of use the university's research staff. On a trip to France in 1975, Remaily obtained Viognier cuttings from the Pont de la Maye viticultural station in Bordeaux, and submitted it to Geneva Station, where it was evaluated and released for propagation in 1976.[9]

One year later, in 1977, FPMS was able to fulfill Jensen's petition with cuttings from Domaine de Vassal, the center for genetic and viticultural research in Montpellier, France.

That same year, Viognier cuttings came by back-channel means to the Napa Valley. One morning Stu Smith, winemaker and partner for Smith-Madrone Vineyards on Spring Mountain overlooking St. Helena in the Napa Valley, went to the St. Helena post office to retrieve a package. It had come from France, from his friend and colleague Jerry Luper, a Napa winemaker who did groundbreaking work for Freemark Abbey, Chateau Montelena, and Diamond Creek. When Smith opened the package, he found Viognier budwood, Chardonnay cuttings from Montrachet in Burgundy, and, he says, an especially fragrant wedge of Camembert cheese.[10]

Luper says that the cuttings were given to him by a reputable French nursery—but will not reveal which one. (He says they were tested there for disease and deemed to be pristine.) Inside the package Smith found a note that instructed him to graft the cuttings; upon his return to the states, Luper and his wife, who had been won over by the Condrieus they'd had in the Rhône Valley, were planning to make the country's first Viognier.

It wasn't meant to be. Luper returned to the United States to spend several memorable years at Chateau Montelena, and subsequently Bouchaine and Rutherford Hill, but he never started his own winery, and he never retrieved his Viognier vines.[11]

All the while, Smith faithfully sustained the cuttings. Though there were inquiries by interested producers like Joseph Phelps and Randall Grahm, Smith refused. After a few years however, it became evident that Luper was not going to retrieve his vines, and so when Pete Minor, Smith's neighbor and friend on Spring Mountain, asked about the Viognier, Smith relented.

Pete Minor was a dentist in Berkeley, California in the 1960s, and an avid home wine-maker, one whose hobby got the better of him. With each passing vintage Minor produced more and more wine, until there was too much to drink and too much to give away. "When you're getting up to 1,000 cases, suddenly you can't drink it all," he says. "Then we went up to 1,500, eventually I knew I couldn't do both." Minor didn't want to give up his dental practice but was more or less obliged to. "My parents were pretty upset," he admits.

In 1965 Minor purchased a small property on Spring Mountain just a stone's throw from Napa's border with Sonoma County. He named it Ritchie Creek, for the watershed that bordered his property, planting the hillsides to Cabernet and eventually Merlot. It was slow going: mountain vine growing was a treacherous business, and Minor encountered setbacks from birds, from powdery mildew, and from a scant water supply. It would be nine years before his first commercial vintage.

Like most home winemakers, Minor had an adventurous palate; he remembers his first Viognier, a bottle of Chateau-Grillet in the late sixties, in Berkeley. He pursued the grape as much as he could, and even arranged visits in the Condrieu area in 1977 when he made his first trip to the northern Rhône, where he visited a number of producers including Marcel Guigal. On the day of his Guigal visit, Minor remembers, Marcel was caring for his young son Philippe. Apparently Philippe was misbehaving so badly that morning that the elder Guigal apologized: "Perhaps this was not such a good day to visit," he told Minor.

The following year Minor learned that his neighbor Stu Smith possessed cuttings of the very vines that had captivated him, asked him for some, and Smith relented. So began, at Ritchie Creek Vineyard, the first commercial planting of Viognier in this country.[12]

It took Minor another four years to propagate enough cuttings to populate half an acre, on a parcel of land at about 1,700 feet in elevation, in 1982. Viognier, it turns out, was even less well-suited to the climatic conditions on Spring Mountain than Cabernet and Merlot. But while the Bordeaux varieties were eventually established, Minor's Viognier vineyard was plagued with problems almost annually. Croploads were notoriously uneven, and rarely ripened fully. Out of necessity, Ritchie Creek's wines ended up on the austere end of the spectrum, which lent the wines glorious aging potential, as evidenced by a tasting of the 1990 Viognier in 2009, still wonderfully fresh and vibrant as it entered its twentieth year. But by 1993 Minor had stopped production of Viognier altogether.

Meanwhile on the other side of the valley, Bill and Joan Smith had resurrected the nineteenth-century winery La Jota on Howell Mountain in Angwin, in 1974. Quite sensibly they planted Cabernet, as the winery's founder, Swiss immigrant Frederick Hess had done nearly a hundred years before.

In 1976 the Smiths were at the home of a collector named Frank Jason, when they tasted their first bottle of Chateau-Grillet. Transfixed, Smith scoured wine shops in Northern California for other Viognier-based wines to try, and found almost none.

The following year they traveled to the northern Rhône, staying at the Hotel Beau Rivage, where like Josh Jensen a decade before they sampled nearly every Condrieu then in production. They became friends with the maitre d' Yves Rigoni, who advised them on which producers to visit; over the next few days, Rigoni's wife, Anne, served as their tour guide and translator as they made visits to producers and conducted tastings.

The Smiths made several return trips to the Rhône, making appointments with the significant Condrieu producers of the day and taking meticulous notes on their wine-making and growing practices. They befriended several producers up and down the Rhône Valley, and were dismayed to learn, upon returning to the states, that many of these magnificent wines were unavailable. Having worked in the oil industry, Bill Smith had come to possess more than his share of stubborn self-reliance—and so rather than complain, he and his wife simply started a company, Rhône Wine Imports, in 1980, to import what he couldn't find. The company lasted just five years, but was responsible for introducing a number of important new-wave producers from the region to the California market, including Jean-Luc Colombo, Jean-Michel Gérin, and Yves Cuilleron.

In 1983, Smith learned about the Viognier cuttings at Geneva Station and immediately inquired. One week later, he received cuttings from New York. Written on the package was a name he'd never seen before: Josh Jensen, apparently the proprietor of another California winery, called Calera.

Meanwhile in Hollister, 150 miles to the south, Josh Jensen was opening an identical package and finding the name Bill Smith on the bundle of sticks in front of him. Incredulous, Jensen tracked Smith down and called him. "And he says 'Yeah, I'm looking at the same bundle, and it's got *your* name on it,'" says Jensen. Incredibly, both requests for the vine material at Geneva Station had come within days of each other. "We just decided," says Jensen, "to keep what we had, and that was that."

Both Smith and Jensen had poor luck in propagating their vines. Smith grafted his, with some success, but Jensen, who grafted his onto rootstock, got exceptionally poor take rates, which set back his production three years after Smith. "The initial efforts in trying to grow it," says Jensen, "had us all tearing our hair out. Half of the grafts would die, the others would perform so poorly that I didn't really get a commercial crop until my seventh leaf, in 1989." That was just an appalling rate of return, but Jensen learned that nearly everyone else had the same experience, even in France, a fact confirmed when Jensen met Marcel Guigal in Condrieu. "'That damn Viognier,' said Guigal, 'it wants to die if you look at it wrong.'"

Bill Smith propagated enough cuttings to plant two acres in 1983; Jensen's propagation efforts took longer, but by 1984 he had successfully planted two acres of Viognier on

Mt. Harlan. By the following year Minor, Smith, and Jensen had vines in the ground, and in 1985, when Pete Minor was able to pull off enough fruit to ferment about 80 gallons of wine, Ritchie Creek bottled its first Viognier release, 400 bottles, the first ever in California and the U.S. Most of it he gave away.[13]

The following year, 1986, both Ritchie Creek and La Jota produced miniscule amounts, while Calera's vine production proceeded at a snail's pace. In 1987 Jensen got the fruit equivalent of 54 bottles; the following year, the vines produced exactly double that amount, 108 bottles. In the meantime, Joseph Phelps Vineyards became the first to receive the Davis cuttings that Jensen had petitioned for twelve years earlier, which they planted at their home ranch off the Silverado Trail. By 1987 that plot was bearing; Phelps ordered an expansion, on a southward course, in keeping with what Craig Williams was learning about the climatic affinities of Syrah. Phelps produced all of 36 bottles in 1987, 14 cases in 1988, and a commercial crop the following year. By 1989, the four wineries had produced nearly 1,000 cases—commercial Viognier was out of the gate.

That same year, Jensen took a few of his 54 bottles to a comparative tasting held at a San Francisco restaurant called Pacific Heights Bar & Grill, organized by an innovative San Francisco retailer named Wilfred Wong, who had transformed his family's green-grocer's shop, the Ashbury Market, into a fine-wine destination in the Bay Area. Bill and Joan Smith brought wines, as did Bruce Neyers; Jensen brought a bottle of Chateau-Grillet, and Wong supplied some bottles of Condrieu. The tasting was conducted double blind. "Low and behold," says Jensen, "our wine came in first on seven of the eight ballots. And I remember it as one of those career-defining moments. 'Okay,' I thought to myself, 'Now I'm a Viognier producer; what have I gotten myself into?'"

On May 14, 1985, John Alban was in Fresno, preparing to celebrate his birthday with friend and fellow viticulture and enology student Dan Stromberg. One of their routine diversions was to present wines to each other that they'd never had before, partly for edification, partly for the pleasure of stumping each other. That evening Alban had brought a Pinot Blanc Reserve from Chalone. Stromberg brought a Condrieu from Chateau du Rozay.

John Alban knew early on that he was destined for an offbeat path. He'd studied wine informally for many years with the help and guidance of his father, Dr. Seymour Alban, an orthopedic surgeon in Southern California who had always appreciated wine, both as a beverage to enjoy with the meal and for the evident health benefits that came to light in the seventies with the so-called French paradox. Their shared enjoyment of wine inspired father and son to visit wineries and tasting rooms across California; even in Europe on backpacking trips, Alban visited wine regions and tasted wines that steered him toward winemaking as a profession.

From the outset he was amazed at how many different wines Europe produced, from so many different grape varieties. In California however, the entire state's production was largely limited to two grapes, Chardonnay and Cabernet Sauvignon. If Europe could produce hundreds of different wines, he reasoned, surely California could produce more than it did. And so when he enrolled in viticulture studies at Fresno State, alternatives were already on his mind.

Condrieu cemented that impression. Nothing had prepared him for a wine so rich, so powerful, so exotic and otherworldly. Not Bordeaux in its power, or Burgundy in its subtlety. The wine was rich, viscous, suggestive of apricots and lanolin, creamy smooth and powerful, rich and sensuous. It was entirely its own self. Even though Alban had had a few wines in his day, there was nothing in his memory to which he could compare.

A little over a year later, Alban was in Condrieu, seeking entry. He had received a little fellowship money and was determined to learn everything he could about Viognier. He started knocking on doors, asking to be introduced to the proprietor, to see if they'd let him volunteer.

By the early eighties the vineyards of Condrieu were still a long way from the revival they would enjoy just half a decade later. Wineries weren't yet getting the income they needed to improve their estates, and the wines of the area were being sold at far less than what was required to subsist, leaving producers in a depressed, protective state. And so when a brash young American began knocking on their doors asking to be taught everything they knew about Viognier, they were in no mood to be helpful.

It was, to Alban, like trying to get into Troy. At each doorstep, he was refused. One by one the producers turned him down flat, with classic Gallic obstinacy. As his frustration mounted, Alban became more determined and less polite, which didn't help matters. In at least one instance, he had to be physically removed. It put Alban in a desperate state. He had thrown most of his savings at this trip, maxed out his credit cards, and felt he had just this one shot to learn what he felt he needed, and was watching it slip away.

He knocked on one last door on Rue Cuvillière, at Domaine Pinchon, a domaine founded two generations earlier by Emile Pinchon, and now managed by his son Jean. The family's holdings in Condrieu were minimal, just 1.5 hectares—so little that Jean supplemented his income by selling cheese in a little cart in the village. Pinchon greeted Alban coolly. Alban took out a notebook and began asking questions about winemaking, to which Pinchon replied, simply, "non."

"And I pointed out," says Alban, "'Well, it wasn't really a yes or no question, it was kind of a 'what are you thinking and expand upon that?' question, and he said 'No, no questions.' So Alban closed his notebook, folded his hands and, as he describes it, went for broke.

"Look," he said, "I'm going to bet that I know your greatest fear. You think that I'll go back to California and plant a big vineyard exclusively to Viognier. Just to be up front with you, that *is* what I'm going to do, whether you answer my questions or not. I'm going to plant Viognier in California. I'm going to try to make Viognier in America. The irony is that that could be the best thing that happens to you. Because no one in the U.S. has ever heard of Condrieu, no one has heard of Viognier.

"So I figure, one of two things is going to happen. People are going to taste my wines and they're either going to like them or they won't. If they taste my wine and it's crummy, they won't ever bother with it again. But if they do like it, the only way to tell them about the wine they're drinking is to tell them about Condrieu. And if they like it, you know what they'll buy next? It's going to be Condrieu. Because that's what Americans do."

Pinchon was impassive, listening.

"I represent an opportunity," said Alban, pleading.

After a long moment, Pinchon moved to speak. "I knew you were coming," he said. "We all knew you were coming. We all know each other. We know whom you've seen, and we weren't supposed to talk to you. I know that no one has told you anything." Nevertheless, Pinchon was sufficiently moved by Alban's pleadings to let him stay, warning him not to ever tell anybody in the village what he was doing. And Alban stayed. He said little, he asked few questions, but gleaned as much as he could from a few weeks in the cellar of this willing producer.

In that month, Alban realized what these producers were up against. "They were right to be afraid," says Alban, "because they were on the brink of death." The region and its wines, hundreds of years of tradition and family heritage, all of it was on the brink of extinction. To be faced with an American just out of school demanding to be taught their secrets must have seemed preposterous and threatening. "They had no reason to think I merited their time." Alban saw that what he had said to Pinchon was more than a last-ditch effort. "I was making a promise to this man," he said, "and the promise wasn't just 'I'm going to keep you cloaked in anonymity, I'm going to do you proud.'"[14]

Alban was able to return from France with twelve Viognier cuttings.[15] He had not a cent to his name and a number of maxed-out credit cards. Upon his return he had arranged for a job with a small Central Coast winery, and just to firm things up before his return flight he called them to gain assurances that the job was still his. Somewhere between Orly and LAX, however, the winery changed its mind, and when he called them en route, they reneged on the offer.

Alban spent the next few weeks on the couch of a friend of his in Ventura named Paul Marinos, and together they charted a path of destruction through Marinos's wine cellar, in particular his collection of both French and American Rhône variety wines. It was here that Alban would first taste some of the leading lights of the day, including Phelps, Bonny Doon, Estrella River, and Qupé. He started calling around to see if these wineries needed help, but none could offer him work. Eventually he began calling anyone; "I could tell that after a while my buddy was really hoping I'd get a job soon," he says, "because we were depleting his wines and I was mooching off him."

Alban finally landed work at a small operation in nearby Oxnard called the Leeward Winery, which drew a fair amount of fruit from the Edna Valley, a small bucolic valley between San Luis Obispo and Arroyo Grande. This is where Alban started to look for a place to put down a vineyard. In the meantime, he started visiting wineries, tasting wines, assessing the early efforts, ultimately seeking validation for the audacious path he'd set for himself.

He was encouraged by the wines of Qupé and especially Calera, whose Viognier he sampled from a plastic carboy in the winery: "I remember being astonished by some of the elements of it," he says, "and thinking wow, this really can happen." Alban persuaded his employers to keep him on a loose leash, while he began the most ambitious Viognier project ever conducted.

He started with the hundreds of pages of meteorological data he had culled while in France going back forty years, calibrating the French data to correspond with the heat summation approach favored by the professors at the University of California, Davis. Then he began a painstaking search for places in California that might approximate these climate figures.

He propagated and propagated, until his dozen Viognier cuttings now numbered in the tens of thousands. Some of these he planted in small test plots up and down the Central Coast of California, from which he'd make wine in 5-gallon carboys, assessing the finished product for acid levels, sugars, potential alcohols, ascertaining to the best of his ability what sort of wine each region might produce.

Armed with this new data, he looked at dozens of properties across the state from Watsonville to the Santa Rita Hills, returning to the Edna Valley, where with the help of his family he purchased 250 acres.

Alban made five subsequent trips to the Rhône Valley in these early years, visiting producers, learning more about the varieties, and, presumably, acquiring plant material for Grenache, Roussanne, Syrah, and Counoise. All of these were propagated and planted on various sites throughout San Luis Obispo County.

Around the state, producers started hearing reports about an elusive figure planting Viognier at unheard of levels: 20, 30, 50 acres, the rumors went. Fellow winemakers thought he was mad. In the trade, sommeliers and retailers heard rumors about a weird type of Chardonnay going in the ground in San Luis Obispo, Paso Robles, and Monterey— a foreign grape with a funny name.

By the end of the decade, Viognier was on its way to becoming the "it" grape of white wines in California, making unprecedented increases in acreage and a modest explosion in bottlings. Both Pete Minor and Bill Smith were generous with their plant material, providing cuttings to those who wanted them at a nominal cost or even for free. In Rhône circles Smith became known as the Johnny Appleseed of Viognier; he gave away so many cuttings that when he realized how much time his vineyard crew was devoting to bundling budwood for other people, he reluctantly started to charge for the service.

Not surprisingly, the Syrah and other Rhône variety producers were paying very close attention to the new activity. Bob Lindquist contracted fruit in 1987, Steve Edmunds contracted a vineyard in Knights Valley in 1989, planted by Ward Noble, a friend of Pete Minor's. Plantings commenced at Bonny Doon, Kunde, McDowell, Frick, Cline, Babcock, Zaca Mesa, and Eberle; Dick Arrowood prevailed on Saralee Kunde to plant Viognier for him at her eponymous vineyard in Sonoma County. In an astonishing and little known fact, nearly all of these intrepid California producers were preceded by Steve

Smith of Grande River Vineyards in Palisade, Colorado, who planted Viognier there in 1987. In the two years that followed there were plantings in Virginia, Oregon, Washington, and Arizona.

Even Napa Valley Chardonnay fell victim to Viognier's ascendancy, when in 1990 Villa Helena grafted over a portion of its Chardonnay vines to Viognier; the following year, in the Sierra foothills, Lee Sobon did the same with existing Cabernet vines. Yes, you read that right—the commanding red variety in the state lost out to a virtually unknown white variety. By the end of 1993, Viognier was the second-most commonly ordered vine from California nurseries. In a little over a decade, it had gone from an unknown variety on the verge of oblivion to a grape with demand bordering on a craze.

Unlike the indifference with which Syrah's debut had been met a dozen years earlier, the reception for Viognier was immediate and positive. In the world of white wine in the late eighties, it was easy to stand out. White wine essentially came in two flavors, dry and sweet. The sweet consisted of Riesling and Riesling wannabes; in the dry category, Chardonnay ruled, followed by elaborately vinified Sauvignon Blanc bottlings, most of which were blowsy, overoaked Chardonnay imitators.

It's easy to see the appeal of a remarkable, not to say peculiar, new entry in the market. Like those who had been inspired to make it, the grape startled first-time tasters with its intensity of expression—it was like the antithesis of so many things in the market at that point, and whether you liked the flavors or not, you could hardly be neutral about something so in-your-face.

The initial releases of Ritchie Creek, La Jota, and Calera were given scores in a roundup of Rhône variety wines in the seminal article produced by the *Wine Spectator* in April 1989. "Fragrant, exotic, full-bodied and spicy," was the description of the 1987 La Jota Viognier, which received a less than exotic score of 86. Harvey Steiman preferred the Ritchie Creek bottling, whose "floral tones give it plenty of interest, making it more subtle than the others (89)." That Steiman should reward subtlety in his scoring suggests he still had a few things to learn about this flamboyant new variety.

The following year, Viognier was given special mention in an article by Steve Heimoff, who reported that both Californians and French producers, having embraced Syrah, were now "taking the Viognier plunge." Just two years later, it was deemed the next big thing. "Viognier may be the rarest noble white grape in the world," wrote the *Wine Spectator*'s Thomas Matthews in August of 1993, "but it looks like the next hot varietal."

John Alban's first release of Viognier in spring 1991 was 407 cases. As his wines matured in the bottle, he took some care with how he was going to try and sell such a large amount of wine. After all, Alban had devoted his entire winery and vineyard strategy to Rhône varieties, and had the most at stake.

He staked his claim with those whom he viewed as gatekeepers—sommeliers and important retail buyers—and tasted them on the wine, city by city, door to door. The wines startled first-time tasters with their exotic flavor profile and intensity of expression, in much the same way as Condrieu had for the winemakers who were early adherents. For Alban these customers became his messengers, and they were an influential lot: they included Larry Stone, then sommelier at Charlie Trotter in Chicago, Mike Bonaccorsi at the Cypress Club, and Peter Granoff at Square One in San Francisco, and especially an energetic restaurant owner named Manfred Krankl, a partner at an exciting new property in Los Angeles called Campanile.

Viognier epiphanies were hardly limited to the West Coast. In another corner of the country, a government contractor in Virginia was letting wine get the better of his obsessions, making the transition from dilettante to commercial winemaker. Rhône varieties, and Viognier in particular, figured prominently in his plans.

Dennis Horton spent the early eighties planting hybrid varieties, making a few barrels of Cabernet Franc which he enjoyed with his wife, Sharon, a former nurse, who grew to enjoy tending vines so much she became the winery's viticulturalist. They started making trips to California to explore the wine landscape there, including the nascent Paso Robles scene of the early eighties before Sharon put her foot down and announced her refusal to move to California.

So Horton set out to find varieties that he felt would work in Virginia.[16] This effort was largely pragmatic: he was interested in varieties that tasted good to him, to be sure, but he was mostly concerned with vinifera that could withstand the weirdness of the Virginia climate, with its cold winters but frequently cruel summers, characterized by excessive heat, punishing storms, and oppressive humidity. Presented with several options from the experimental station at Cornell, he planted test plots, and Viognier endured the region's climatic challenges with aplomb. It always sugared up nicely, says Horton, while reaching flavor and phenolic maturity, remaining relatively lean and vibrant when compared with the early efforts of Viognier in California. Best of all it seemed to be able to withstand the peripatetic weather in the Commonwealth. "If a grape burst or was compromised on a Viognier bunch, it *shriveled;* the rest of the cluster was left intact. If the same thing happened with Chardonnay, you had to pick that day, or you didn't pick it at all."

By 1989 Horton had planted 25 acres of Viognier in Orange County, within the Monticello AVA. The variety proved to be so well suited that he foisted cuttings upon fellow vintners, urged them to plant.[17] More than eighty producers now make Viognier in Virginia; and in 2011 the grape officially became Virginia's signature white variety, so deemed by the Virginia Wine Board; it remains the fourth-most planted variety in the state. The wines are quite different from the range of expression for the grape in California or Washington. They taste like continental wines, with impressive weight and depth of flavor—though they seem to retain more acidity than your typical California version.

Meanwhile, in Atlanta, Georgia, in 1981, a retail buyer named Mat Garretson had been given a birthday bottle of 1980 Condrieu Georges Vernay's Coteaux du Vernon, which he promptly stored away without giving it another thought. What happened to him, with that bottle, and the story of how it led to the most important Rhône wine festival in the world, is reserved for discussion in Chapter 20; but suffice it to say that while Syrah may have instigated the Rhône movement, Viognier was the most incendiary fuel for the period that resulted in its most rapid acceleration.

The fervor for Viognier has died considerably; just like most fads, the variety has settled into a comfortable middle age, with a little more than 3,000 acres planted, more or less holding steady, with another 400 or so in Washington State, and smatterings in every other western state with a legitimate wine program. It is certainly the centerpiece white wine of Virginia, as dozens of producers have followed in the footsteps of Dennis Horton. With just a few exceptions—Alban, Cold Heaven, Calera, aMaurice, and Gregory Graham—it is rare for Viognier to represent a significant stake in anyone's portfolio, and even the wineries mentioned above can no longer rely solely on Viognier sales for a living, and must "compensate" their love of Viognier with more prosaic offerings, like Syrah, Pinot Noir, and Rhône and Bordeaux blends. Even at its best, Viognier bottlings in California are dominated by fruit, typified by a fruit salad profile so assertive and overpowering that they can seem almost silly, lacking the subtle gravitas that so many French bottlings, from Condrieu and elsewhere, seem to pull off without much effort.

Viognier's runaway exoticism practically defined the alternative category for white wine in the early nineties, hitting its stride just as American consumers were becoming curious enough about wine in general to want something different. Viognier not only shocked the palate, it reminded those who tasted it that this world of white wine was far bigger than the parameters of Chardonnay and Sauvignon Blanc. Before Viognier, now commonplace catchphrases like "ABC," or "anything but Chardonnay," simply didn't exist. Viognier was not only one of the first real alternatives for white wine drinkers, it represented something even more powerful—a symbolic one. Viognier became a breakaway sensation because it was the only sensation; of course, once the gateway was opened plenty of other varieties pulled into view. Who's to say whether Gruner Veltliner, Pinot Gris, Albariño, would have received such enthusiastic reception without Viognier blazing a trail before them?

14

THE PURLOINED RHÔNE
How Suitcase Clones Shaped the Movement

There was no Rhône movement without vines in the ground, and for its first decade or so, from 1980 to 1990, that vine count was meager. Planting was limited by supply, and the material for these varieties was hard to come by.

Even if you had a source, questions abounded. Let's say you wanted to plant Grenache. There was plenty around, but most agree that until the mid-eighties the clonal selections were limited, even inferior. So you try and locate a plant that produced fruit of good color, snip a few sticks off such a vine, reproduce it a few thousand times (either by grafting and rooting it, or several parts of it) and voilà, vine stock enough to populate a vineyard.

But what do you know about your Grenache? What sort of Grenache was it? Sure, you found it in a Grenache vineyard, but the old vineyards of California were a notoriously mixed bag, with multiple varieties interplanted in an unholy mash up. Some you knew, some you thought you knew, and some, without a DNA test (not an available option for vinifera until the mid-nineties) probably remained mystery vines forever. So you might have a good idea, but there was plenty of room for doubt.

And how could you know the vine you chose was healthy? Plenty of potential pathogens could lie beneath the bark like time bombs ready to go off in your very expensive agricultural venture—structurally damaging bacteria, yield-crippling viruses, unseen harbingers of ill health or slow, inexorable death. And even if you could ascertain that the vine was healthy beyond a reasonable doubt, how would you ever know if it was the best selection for producing the best flavors on the site you were looking to plant? Wouldn't you want to consider alternatives?

In vines such alternatives are known as clonal selections, variations on a varietal theme. And in the U.S. in 1980, those variants among Rhône varieties were limited at best. This was typical of the day. Talk of clones among the trade, by journalists and even consumers these days is commonplace—among winemakers it's positively rampant—but in the early eighties, clones didn't yet matter, not even to researchers.

But they crept into consciousness through the attentions of the world's great viticultural research institutions, in Geisenheim, Germany, in the Veneto, Italy, in Catalonia, Spain, at Davis, and most critically (for our story, that is) in Montpellier, France, with ENTAV.

ENTAV was established in 1962 to collect, improve, and eventually disperse the stock of varietal selections in France, a herculean effort for a country so deep in viticultural assets. Its early work was very slow and painstaking as the staff gathered, cleaned up, archived. and assessed the genealogical treasures that thousands of years of French viticulture had bestowed. It would be decades before ENTAV turned to marketing and dispersing the material, and until such time, discussion of clonal selections was usually limited to the lab.

In California, one procured cuttings through licensed nurseries, which purchased and propagated stocks of disease-free vines from Foundation Plant Materials Service, or FPMS (now shortened to FPS). This agency, based in Davis and aligned to the university's viticulture and enology department, was tasked with maintaining the health and overall quality of the state's vineyards, preventing diseases, pests, and opportunistic organisms from entering the state's germplasm pool.

FPMS did not have the same historical or archival function in the United States that ENTAV did in France—at least not at first—but it was instrumental in dispensing clean vine material, and in cleaning up what was around. For a grower to circumvent this process could result in not only the propagation of compromised or inferior material, but in the perpetuation and spread of disease.

The mission of FPMS has been plain for nearly two decades, but in the years between 1980 and 1990, the execution of that mission was considerably more fluid and vague. Disease detection and elimination remained its principal function, but that function routinely endured a shift in emphasis, as the agency accommodated dual roles in the research of virology and plant pathology, and in the service of the industry and agricultural community. By the mid-eighties, as vineyard acreage expanded and demand for vine stock started to increase, verified plant service became an ever more urgent need.

For more than three decades, Dr. Austin Goheen administered the research facilities at FPMS. Goheen worked closely with other plant researchers, including William Hewitt and Harold Olmo, to clean up existing California plant material, and to import and process worthy vines from abroad, ensure their pristine status, and release them to nurseries for propagation and sale. Goheen held an import permit to do just this, and oversaw the indexing of new plant material, from existing plantings, and drawn from the tremendous foraging efforts of Harold Olmo, who had collected vine material from all over the world for their potential use in California vineyards, until his retirement in 1977.

Goheen himself retired in 1986, having made vast contributions to the advancement of California viticulture. But with his retirement came a difficult transition for his agency. The program temporarily lost the use of its import permit while Goheen's position remained unfilled. His successor, Deborah Golino, was hired in 1987. Her early protocol was dedicated to research above service commitments, leaving the system in an uncomfortable hiatus for five years, 1988–1993, in which no new vine material was indexed or released. This is a critical period with respect to Rhône varieties in America—even Tablas Creek, who would commit to the process of importing vines for each of the Rhône varieties, was obliged to seek another entry point for its earliest imports.

Golino was able to shore up the administration of her agency, strengthen its procedures, and reorganize and expand its facilities to respond to the resurgent interest in new varieties. FPS, as it's known now, was elevated to a full-fledged self-supporting department within the College of Agricultural and Environmental Science at University of California, Davis in 1994, and is one of the great repositories of healthy vine stocks in the world.

But even when the system is running at peak efficiency, the release and indexing of new plant material remains a slow, protracted process: imported vines are quarantined and observed for several growing seasons to reveal the pests, diseases, and other crippling debilitations they may have acquired. The wait for cleared material is as long as a half decade.

Half a decade, for someone in his twenties, just embarking on a career, is an immensely long time. Some, brash with youth, looking to seize the moment in the marketplace, and anxious to capitalize on a gathering wave of interest in the Rhône category, decided that the waiting interval was too onerous. Such were the circumstances that drove normally law-abiding winemakers to seek more expedient means.

"I was in a hurry," explains Bonny Doon's Randall Grahm, "and the stuff wasn't available. Some of these things I just imagined I would never be able to see again if I were to go through legal channels."[1]

The practice of self-importation is known as suitcasing (the cuttings are sometimes referred to as Samsonite clones). It is, in no uncertain terms, prohibited by law under the Plant Protection Act of 2000, designed to protect existing species from foreign pests. At present the practice, at least in viticulture, has slowed considerably, as the selection of vine material in the U.S. is currently quite robust. Twenty years ago however this was not the case.

Among the many accounts of suitcasing in California grapevine lore—most involving Pinot Noir, and the vineyards of Domaine de la Romanée Conti—there are about a half-dozen credible accounts of Rhône varietal cuttings brought into the country by illicit means in the 1980s and early 1990s. Owing to the clandestine nature of the acts it's to be assumed that these aren't the only incidents.

Additionally, there are many apocryphal accounts of purloined vines from repositories both in France and the U.S. Others circulated their own suitcase stories, like Gary Eberle, who claimed to have purloined cuttings from Chapoutier on Hermitage Hill—the source, he says, of the Estrella River clone. That origin is probably correct, but the story proved to be false—he was directed to the material in Davis, by one of his professors, Curtis "Doc" Alley, who had apparently stored the material, uncatalogued, in an underused vineyard where it awaited classification. Eberle says he invented the story to protect Alley and others who had known of the transaction.[2]

More stories: Josh Jensen, one of the first to work with Viognier in California, was so taken with Viognier that he phoned George Vernay in the northern Rhône and asked him if he'd be willing to part with some Viognier cuttings from his famed vineyards in Condrieu. Inconceivably, Vernay complied, mailing the sticks to Jensen's Paris hotel; from there they are said to have found their way into the lining of Jensen's overcoat. He conveyed them to a now defunct nursery, Golden State Vinegrowers, for propagation: none survived the grafting process.[3]

Three years later Stu Smith of Smith Madrone Vineyards on Spring Mountain in the Napa Valley retrieved a package sent by winemaker Jerry Luper, said to contain Viognier and Chardonnay cuttings from a French nursery.[4] Luper asked Smith to graft the vines, to sustain them. Smith bequeathed the Viognier vines to his neighbor Pete Minor, who ran a little winery called Ritchie Creek. The first American Viognier, then, had an illicit provenance.

In the late 1980s Michael Michaud, a winemaker at Chalone Winery in the Gavilan Mountains, befriended Jean-Louis Chave, scion of the great Hermitage winery Domaine Jean-Louis Chave; Jean-Louis is said to have sent Michaud Syrah cuttings from the home vineyard in 1992.[5]

Chave also is said to have exchanged cuttings with Bill Easton at Domaine de la Terre Rouge—Easton provided Zinfandel cuttings to Chave, who reciprocated with some Roussanne. There's no definitive word that clandestine Zinfandel is being grown on Hermitage Hill—or what sort of wines are made from it.[6]

But by far the most infamous winemakers to have allegedly brought vines into the U.S. directly from sources in the Rhône Valley and southern France were John Alban of Alban Vineyards, and Randall Grahm of Bonny Doon Vineyards. Their stories, their rationales and rationalizations, the recklessness and sheer audacity of their efforts are emblematic of the brashness of the age, of the maverick ethos, of ambition fanned to the point of desperation, and an uncomfortable but necessary chapter in the movement's history and in its lore.

In every conceivable way—in viticultural matters, in approach, methodology, and execution, in philosophy and temperament—John Alban and Randall Grahm diverge. Where Alban has remained faithful to Rhône variety wines, Grahm has dabbled in obscure Italian and Spanish varieties, Riesling, Malvasia, marc, fruit wine. Where Alban is focused,

Grahm is omnivorous. Where Alban is determined and calculating, Grahm is whimsical and improvisatory. Where Alban follows a single point of light, Grahm seems to follow so many he can appear to lack focus.

Throughout his career John Alban has possessed the steadfast resolve of a disciple. Randall Grahm, by contrast, seems driven largely by inquisitiveness. He is voracious in his intellectual appetites, interested in everything, willing to try anything. He's been known to take huge risks with his business and his energies, which are at times stretched thin. He sometimes has trouble sustaining his attention on a project, and to an extent his business has suffered from a lack of coherence; some have noted that Grahm's peripatetic nature is ill suited to winegrowing, since the practice requires a rote consistency that Grahm seems to find mundane.

And yet for all their differences, the careers of Alban and Grahm share remarkable parallels. Both devoted much of their career to planting and propagating the Rhône varieties well before they were popular. Both created successful, lasting brands indelibly linked to the Rhône, brands which remain among the most durable in the category. Both were instrumental in creating, then shaping, a market niche for their wines, and both were wildly successful (in wildly different ways) in promoting them to an unschooled public.

Both men are driven by tremendous personal ambition. Both are charismatic, possessing highly developed verbal gifts, charm, and skills of persuasion, skills which made them consummate marketers, attracting aspirants from all over the world.

As a result both became early members, and eventually leaders, of promotional organizations devoted to Rhône varietal wines, and while neither was responsible for founding these organizations, each emerged as a de facto spokesman, emissaries of the California chapter of the movement, poster boys for the attitude, vibe, and irreverence the movement projected.

And finally both men, as Grahm articulated so well, were in a hurry. Both came to the conclusion that to wait for plant material from official sources would be too laborious, too risky, and too untimely. And thus both men decided to circumvent normal channels in gathering cuttings, and in doing so, set off a series of events whose consequences are being felt to this day.

To judge from his conversion experience, you'd think that John Alban's embrace of Rhône varieties would have been anything but cautious. This was, after all, the same man whose single-sip thunderbolt conversion to Rhône varieties seemed to prevail over every last vestige of his prudence. So it is somewhat anomalous to picture Alban, gobsmacked as he was, approaching his wine project with a scheme so orderly and methodical it seemed like the antithesis of a thunderbolt. Nothing was left to chance. Alban was systematic in his study of the northern and southern Rhône icons, tasting the wines of the region's greatest producers and enduring routine epiphanies with each new bottling of Rayas, Chave, Chapoutier, Beaucastel, and others.

Alban tasted his way through the varietal bottlings available in California, and while impressed with a few of the wines, was unconvinced the vine material was optimal. For one thing, several were missing—Roussanne especially, a variety Alban had keen interest in. For another, he was skeptical that available clones of Syrah, Mourvèdre, Carignane, and Grenache, least of all his beloved Viognier, would serve his purposes.

"I decided, 'Let's step back,'" he explains, in a mock scenario. "'Why am I doing this? Well, I'm doing this because'—and this is hypothetical—'I've had a bottle of Chateau Rayas and that's supposedly all Grenache, and my heart started to take flight.' If you came to me and asked me to consult for you, and you said 'I'd like some Grenache,' I'd say 'You know what? Why take the chance? Why don't you get cuttings you know originate from that vineyard, because you were driven by Chateau Rayas you should plant whatever materials are used to make that specific wine.'"

"I was embarking on a winery that was going to make only Rhône varieties," he says, "so for me to wake up one day and discover that my Roussanne was Viognier, or that the Shiraz that I thought was the same thing as Syrah was actually some version of Durif or whatever, well, that would be terminal for me." Feeling he had no other choice, he went to France.

Between 1985 and 1988, Alban made five trips, to both the northern and southern Rhône, and in some instances extending his range to Provence, in search of the best vine material for his project. He returned with multiple selections of Viognier, Syrah, Grenache, Mourvèdre, Roussanne, and Counoise. Alban has never divulged the sources of the vines he ended up planting and propagating. But for a man whose systematic inclinations were meant to leave no doubt as to the quality and provenance of his material, it isn't difficult to make an educated guess on his sources.[7]

When asked in 2009 if he was in any way systematic about how he gathered his plant material, Randall Grahm replied, "Systematic? Am I systematic about anything?" But no one could doubt his urgency. With Le Cigare Volant's early success and his notoriety climbing, Grahm felt keenly the need to accelerate the process of making Bonny Doon a successful brand—and when it came to varietal planting, he concluded that the best way to do so was to take matters into his own hands.

Starting in 1984, Grahm started making trips to France, visiting important Rhône vignerons, tasting, asking questions, and often as not, asking permission to take cuttings. Grahm's principal interest was white varieties: he was seeking Marsanne, Roussanne, and Viognier—but he ended up purportedly obtaining only Viognier and Roussanne (Marsanne was obtained through FPMS).

He says he took what he could get. "I didn't have the chutzpah to ask for cuttings from specific vineyards," he explains. "In those days I was happy to get what [the producer] thought was interesting material. I hadn't yet developed the level of specificity to determine if, like, I needed Viognier from this vineyard. It was only later that I went looking for superior clones."

He noted the enthusiasm among his fellow winemakers for Viognier, but early interest had already made for a crowded field. "It was like a race," he says. "Everybody was obsessed with getting it into the ground, with being the first, because it seemed like it would be the next cool thing."[8]

In France, Grahm made visits in Condrieu and Chateau-Grillet, presumably departing with cuttings. His pursuit of Roussanne led him quite naturally to the door of Chateau de Beaucastel in Chateauneuf-du-Pape, the source of their Chateauneuf-du-Pape known as Vieilles Vignes, from Roussanne vines planted in and around 1909, and a sensation among collectors.

Grahm met with Pierre and Jean-Francois Perrin at the estate, and they expressed interest in helping him. But their vines, they told him, were probably not his most ideal source for propagation; they were too old, too disorganized, too riddled with unknown maladies. Instead, the Perrins directed him to another Chateauneuf-du-Pape winery. "They are a lot more organized than we are," Grahm recalls them saying.

Grahm says that this winery provided him with what they said were Roussanne cuttings, free of charge. He says it was the only material he procured from the vineyard, and he brought it, as well as Viognier cuttings from Condrieu and Chateau-Grillet, back to the states.

When John Alban returned to the U.S. from the northern Rhône he began to propagate his cuttings. Soon he had vines in the ground in Paso Robles, as well as in the Edna Valley. When his vineyard had been planted and his vines more or less established, he turned to marketing the better selections he'd acquired to other growers. It was in part a way to earn money. But in formative discussions with his father, he realized that not only was it incumbent upon him to earn back his investment, but that he stood in a unique position as the only solo Rhône proprietor: this gave him a marketing advantage.

"My father thought I was nuts to help other growers 'compete' with me. But I believed that in this instance, 'monopoly is death,'" he says. 'You don't want to be the only one making these wines; you don't even want to be the only good one.' I figured that for every ten growers who bought my vines, one was going to be really good. And when there were two or three, or even four good producers, well, that would be exceptional.

"Plus, it was a way to get information. We'd be able to see just how the material performed in different places, at different densities, different growing decisions and approaches. And if they succeeded, they would spread the message."

Alban became a trusted source for several Rhône varieties, especially his Grenache, which surpassed in quality much of what was planted at the time, and was known for its deep color and low yield. Producers loved its focus and intensity, loved the way it threw a much smaller crop than other Grenache vineyards in the state. But Alban was also the first to plant and to sell true Roussanne. Randall Grahm had also suitcased what appeared to be Roussanne, propagated it, planted a vineyard, replanted another, and gave away cuttings thinking it was what he says it was. But appearances, in vine stocks, go only so far.

From the time of its planting in 1983 alongside Marsanne cuttings at Bonny Doon Vineyard, until he was served papers for breach of contract by the Sonoma Grapevines Nursery in 2000, it had never occurred to Randall Grahm that the vines he transported, propagated, grew, and planted, transferred, the grapes he used, the cuttings he bartered with, and the wines he made, were anything but Roussanne. Grahm insists in hindsight that the vines were morphologically distinct from the Viognier and Marsanne vines he had planted in nearby blocks. The Marsanne had come from Davis; he had acquired four strains of Viognier in France. Each of these behaved alike in his vineyards and were, he felt, poor performers. They rarely ripened fully, and rendered lackluster wines.

The purported Roussanne, however, was another thing entirely. To Grahm it had a different morphology, a different appearance, different flavors. "From a ripening standpoint, the Roussanne ripened more completely, had higher acidity, and great ageability." He adds that the fruit from that vineyard showed the russeting quality of color that the grape is named for. It seemed, in other words, to fit the bill. "Then again," Grahm adds ruefully, "ampelography is not everyone's forte."

The Roussanne, with the Marsanne, went into a white Rhône-inspired blend from Bonny Doon called Le Sophiste in 1988 and 1989. The Sophiste blend was among the first white Rhône blends to hit the market and was generally very well-received. The vintages containing Roussanne and Marsanne from the original Bonny Doon planting were, according to Grahm, "responsible for some of the best, most distinctive white wines ever made at Bonny Doon."[9]

Grahm says that the wine even fooled Gerard Jaboulet, who tasted the 1992 Le Sophiste at the New York Wine Experience and pronounced it a great blend, never suspecting it wasn't what the label proclaimed.

Just a few years after it was established, this vineyard succumbed to Pierce's disease. Grahm was able to save a few cuttings of the Roussanne, which he planted at Chequera Vineyard in late 1991. According to Grahm, Rich Kunde approached him repeatedly asking for cuttings from his Rhône varietal stock, and Grahm relented in 1995, in what was probably a barter arrangement. Grahm insists that he did not accept payment for the vines, and also claims that, owing to his concern that these vines may carry Pierce's, he explicitly requested that the vines not be propagated or resold.

Kunde, who owned Sonoma Grapevines, states that the plant material he received was "bare canes," that is, a section of wood without any identifying markers. But he had no reason to doubt their authenticity, he says, because they'd come from none other than Randall Grahm, the father of the Rhône movement.[10]

Sonoma Grapevines propagated the cuttings and sold them as Roussanne to as many as ten wineries, including Zaca Mesa, St. Amant, and others. But the most ambitious planting attempted—indeed, it was one of the most ambitious white Rhône varietal planting to that point—was by Charlie Wagner of Caymus Vineyards, in a project situated in the Santa Lucia Highlands called Mer Soleil.

In the early nineties, Charlie Wagner had started in on a Central Coast operation to complement its well-established Napa brand, Caymus. By this time they had established a new Caymus white blend, composed partly of Central Coast fruit, called Conundrum, a name which may have reflected some of the whimsy that Randall Grahm had initiated in wine labeling and branding.

Wagner says he "had a little land in Monterey County to play around with" and planted several Rhône varieties, including Roussanne, Marsanne, Viognier, and Syrah.[11] Wagner had a limestone-inflected stretch of land that he felt would be a good spot for nervy whites, and decided to plant Roussanne there, a project which led him to plant an unprecedented quantity—30 acres—in 1995.

Like most Wagnerian efforts, the plan was ambitious. He intended to make one of the most expensive white Rhône wines to that point, retailing for $50, in an era where most Chardonnays were less than $35.

Four years later, in 1998, John Alban was walking the vineyard with Wagner. "We were walking up through the blocks, looking over the Roussanne, and John was sort of kicking around a little bit, being quiet. And he said to me 'You sure this is the Roussanne?' I told him that's what we planted. 'You know,' he said, 'I don't think this is Roussanne.' When I pressed him he said he thought it was Viognier. I thought it was similar to the Viognier, but it looked different—it was a different clone. So I had it checked out and it was [Viognier]."[12]

Wagner went to the nursery and said he'd received the wrong variety. "There was some back and forth," he says, "and they admitted they had given us the wrong vines. 'Well,' I said, 'what can we do about this?' We wanted to replant the vineyard, but they didn't have the wood to replace the vines." Then Wagner learned that the source of the cuttings wasn't from FMPS, that Sonoma Grapevines had received the wood from Randall Grahm.

Wagner was rankled by the fact that a commercial nursery would sell suitcased wood. "You just don't bring in contraband," he says. "That's the sort of practice that brought phylloxera to Europe." Wagner contacted Grahm, who was defiant: "He comes back to me and says 'I collected that wood from France, it's Roussanne, and that's that.'"

To this day Charlie Wagner has no love for Randall Grahm. "We are so polar opposites," says Wagner. "We don't see the world through the same eyes. When it gets to listening, he has a hard time if you don't agree with him." But it wasn't just the disagreement that troubled Wagner, it was that Grahm was dismissive of the entire affair. "He treated it all like it wasn't worthy of his time, that it was all ridiculous, frivolous. But it was my 30 acres."

Wagner says that while he tried to negotiate a solution with Sonoma Grapevines, the nursery stopped returning his phone calls. Wagner learned that they had sold the same material as Roussanne to several other producers and wanted to talk with them. Sonoma Grapevines refused to give him those names, a refusal which led to the first court action filed by Wagner. Eventually Wagner would sue Sonoma Grapevines for breach of contract, asking for millions of dollars in damages—the figure was reported to be $7 million, reflecting lost potential earnings of the $50 bottle of Roussanne that Mer Soleil never made.[13] Sonoma Grapevines in turn sued Bonny Doon and Randall Grahm in the same amount for its error.

The case received coverage in the press all over the world: Frank Prial wrote a column about it in the *New York Times,* as did Jancis Robinson in the *Financial Times.* Both sides aired their grievances in these reports, with Grahm insisting that he did not sell the cuttings to Kunde. "We think of it as giving them to him," said Grahm in a curious turn of phrase. "And they were supposed to be for the nursery's collection. He literally promised not to propagate or commercialize them."[14]

For his part, Rich Kunde placed the blame squarely on Grahm, "If you were looking for Rhône grapes in the early 1990's," Mr. Kunde said in an interview, "what better person to talk to than Randall?"[15]

After a brief tussle in the courts, the matter was settled privately. Sonoma Grapevines barely survived, long enough to face another far more serious crisis for its part in disseminating the so-called Black Goo fungus in its rootstock. The company was sold in early 2002.

As for Grahm, it remains one of the most painful periods in his professional career. He still feels aggrieved at his treatment and the financial and emotional burden it caused him, and is reluctant to speak of the matter years after it transpired.

Caymus retained much of the Viognier, which now comprises the bulk of its popular white blended wine, Conundrum. "When you're hard pressed to use something you don't want to need, you have to become creative," he says. "That's Conundrum. It's what we had on hand; it was the best way to deal with it."

And the other wineries? Zaca Mesa, who had won competition medals for its Roussanne, chose to simply relabel its wine the following year as Viognier. St. Amant, a small winery in the Lodi, came up with perhaps the most elegant solution. They renamed the remaining bottles, and all subsequent vintages, as Mystere.

In all the years since this chain of events took place, Grahm has never publicly divulged the source of the cuttings thought to be Roussanne. But after months of inquiry, and with the immeasurable assistance of John Livingstone-Learmonth, I can say with certainty that Grahm procured the purported Roussanne cuttings from Domaine de Nalys, in the village of Chateauneuf-du-Pape.

In 1983, John Livingstone-Learmonth published a revised and greatly expanded edition of *Wines of the Rhône,* one of the most definitive books on the category ever written in English about the Rhône Valley, and certainly a book that would have been on the shelf of every Rhône varietal producer in this country during that decade.[16] This book was the anecdotal source for the flying saucer decree that inspired Grahm's proprietary name for Le Cigare Volant, his Rhône varietal blend.

Livingstone-Learmonth subsequently made trips to the U.S. and met Grahm and other Rhône aficionados as he toured and tasted through California Rhône varietal producers. Stories about some of these visits populate his re-issued book in 2005. He was familiar, then, with the principal parties.

I met Livingstone-Learmonth in the Rhône Valley in 2009, at a buffet supper in Avignon, where he was busy entering a tasting note on a rather charmless Côtes du Rhône-Village Blanc in front of him. Soft spoken and thoughtful, Livingstone-Learmonth is so youthful-looking that the few producers in the region who haven't met him invariably say things like, "yes, hello, I've read your father's book."

We got to talking. I described what I knew about Randall Grahm's story about procuring cuttings in Chateauneuf-du-Pape from a place known for its extensive, well-organized stocks. Livingstone-Learmonth thought about this for a moment, and then suggested that I might want to seek out a fellow named Pierre Pelissier, at a winery called Domaine de Nalys. "He may have some answers to your questions," he said.

In the 1983 edition of Livingstone-Learmonth's book *Wines of the Rhône*, the author writes that the domaine flourished under Pelissier's predecessor, Dr. Philippe Dufays, who proudly grew all thirteen varieties on the property and who was "renowned for his studies in the Chateauneuf-du-Pape grape varieties, and for his wit in talking about them."[17] It certainly sounded like a likely place.

Three days later I paid a visit to Domaine de Nalys.[18] Entering the estate I saw, within sight of the famous ruin of the pope's castle, rows of show-vines on either side of the drive, each neatly staked with a placard that listed one of the thirteen sanctioned varieties of Chateauneuf-du-Pape. Pierre Pelissier met me in the tasting room, where with the help of a translator we tried to reconstruct a meeting that had occurred more than twenty years before.

Pelissier told me that he did remember receiving an American visitor, to whom he gave cuttings. He could not remember the man's name, but was able to describe the visitor as a man with long hair and tiny spectacles, a description that Randall Grahm would answer to even today.

Asked again if he could recall his name. Pelissier could not. Nor could he remember which varieties he might have given to this long-haired American. Just before leaving, I asked:

"Have you ever had Viognier on the property?" I asked.

"Non," said Pelissier emphatically, "jamais." Viognier, after all, is not one of the sanctioned vines for Chateauneuf-du-Pape.[19]

It's nearly impossible to trace the true source of the Viognier vines that Charlie Wagner ended up planting in the Santa Lucia highlands. They may have come from Randall Grahm, who in turn may have received them from a source in Chateauneuf-du-Pape, where Viognier is all but nonexistent. They may just as easily have come from some other cuttings which Rich Kunde had in his possession and mistook for the material given him by Randall Grahm, which he took to be Roussanne. It's entirely possible that Grahm gave Kunde Roussanne. It seems just as likely he gave Kunde Viognier. What's almost an impossibility is that this Viognier came from Chateauneuf-du-Pape, which is how the story gets told, usually.

We can say with certainty that when Randall Grahm left Chateauneuf-du-Pape with a bundle under his arm, that that bundle came from Domaine Nalys. But there are so many places for error along the pathway from the Rhône to the Mer Soleil vineyard, across so many years, that it's impossible to say who slipped up when. The line of transmission is at least five transactions long: France to Bonny Doon to Chequera to Sonoma Grapevines to Mer Soleil—longer still when you consider possible error sequences within each of these planting efforts. What if, for example, Chequera Vineyard grafts the vines given them by Bonny Doon at another site? What if propagation at Mer Soleil gets sullied? I can't say that the transmission from Grahm to Kunde to Wagner was flubbed at one handoff or another.

Here are some possibilities.

It seems most plausible that Randall Grahm left Nalys with Roussanne under his arm, and there seems to be plenty of anecdotal evidence that he planted Roussanne at the Bonny Doon vineyard, alongside or nearby Viognier, which Grahm insists was morphologically distinct, which resulted in ripe fruit possessing a russet color (the reason for Roussanne's name). Perhaps it's the next transfer where things go wrong.

As the Bonny Doon vineyard succumbed to Pierce's disease, cuttings from the dying vineyard were brought to Chequera Vineyard to salvage Grahm's suitcase efforts. This transfer is the most likely place for a mistake to have occurred. It's my belief that Roussanne was never planted at Chequera, that a switch occurred here that no one detected, and that Grahm unwittingly passed Viognier onto Sonoma Grapevines.

According to Grahm, Rich Kunde had never possessed Roussanne, and as he was receiving cuttings, wouldn't necessarily have had any experience with the variety or the plant once it budded. Grahm makes the second point: he insisted that Kunde not release the vines in keeping with his concern that these vines had just escaped certain death by Pierce's disease at Bonny Doon Vineyard, and it was still too early to be sure they would not succumb.

It isn't hard to imagine how every producer in California to that point who'd planted Roussanne, outside of John Alban, was having second thoughts about the authenticity of what they'd planted—and perhaps more than a few Viognier producers were having similar thoughts. Roussanne is still planted, and there is still an enthusiasm for the variety among Central Coast producers.

By the middle of the 1990s, much of this was resolved, as the clonal selections imported for the Tablas Creek project were being slowly released from quarantine, transferred to nurseries, and planted. For Roussanne, Grenache, and Mourvèdre, not to mention the supporting varieties like Rolle, Bourboulenc, Grenache Blanc, and Clairette, there could not have been a more reliable source; hence, most suitcase activity, for Rhône varieties at least, effectively ceased once these vines had come into production.

John Alban's vines are also still in circulation, still highly regarded for their flavors and their low yields. His vines in fact show a remarkable degree of success for plants that have circumvented the usual vetting process.

John Alban, however, is nothing if not careful—one need only go back to his initial rationale for this approach to be reminded of his conviction that he could not afford to fail, and that poor plant material would be catastrophic.

Alban's process of elimination was largely empirical. He made rigorous examinations of morphology and tissue analysis, but in the end, fruit quality remained the most important criterion for pursuing or maintaining a selection. "If a block was making superlative wine for more than a couple decades," he wrote recently, "it probably doesn't have anything terribly degenerative."[20] He added that his methods for testing reflected advances in the field as time went on; many selections, he said, didn't make the cut over time. Aside from shatter in his Grenache, a common problem for that variety, the selections associated with the Alban name are universally held in high regard.

Meanwhile the practice does continue, diminished but not unabated. In the summer of 2014, I toured a Central Coast vineyard whose proprietor proudly showed me plantings from cuttings procured in Cornas the year before, bundled, boxed, and flown across the ocean to California. When asked whether he'd quarantined the material, the owner said, "Nah, fuck that. Every vine in California has some virus. What's the point?"[21]

15

TABLAS CREEK, THE VALIDATOR

The American wine industry no longer needs an outside source to validate its existence, but for two decades, from 1970 to 1990, French investment played an enormous symbolic role in its legitimacy. For the French, the United States—and California in particular—was a land of opportunity. Wineries investing here could not only bust out of their appellation borders, they could plant what they wanted where they wanted, make growing decisions free of their country's stringent regulations. They could, if they liked, flaunt tradition, or transplant its best features.

In America, French investment was invariably interpreted as an endorsement. When the Rothschild family partnered with Robert Mondavi for Opus One in 1979, the eyes of the world shifted to the Napa Valley with newfound recognition and respect for its wine regions, though neither of these were the first to Napa—Domaine Chandon, with Moet Chandon as its parent, was founded in 1973. Mumm, Roederer, and Taittinger soon followed (as did the Spanish Cava producers Freixenet and Codorniu). California continued to attract Bordeaux producers, with the founding of Dominus in 1982 by Christian Moueix, while Oregon's wine industry was elevated considerably by the investment of the Burgundy négociant Domaine Drouhin in the heart of the Dundee Hills in 1988.

But no one changed the game quite like the Perrin family of Chateau de Beaucastel, when it decided in 1987 to bring its resources and its reputation to California, forming a partnership with the Haas family of Vineyard Brands called Tablas Creek.

In 1987, American Rhône efforts had been dogged and impressive, an upstart category that had captured the public's imagination and achieved modest success but relatively little traction. Plantings were small and strewn across the state. Further, what had been put in the ground to date had been a hodgepodge of suitcase clones, random old vine selections, and poorly documented nursery stock, selections that were more opportunistic than systematic.

To this chaos, the Perrin and Haas families brought order, a physical and philosophical grounding, an authoritative presence. But they did more than just validate and galvanize early efforts. Their efforts lent legitimacy to this ragtag collection of upstarts and mavericks, providing a reliable genetic material for their efforts, from a legitimate and respected Rhône Valley source, an unassailable foundation from which they could be taken seriously. It was a sign to the American wine industry that the category had global significance.

Tablas Creek is a partnership between two very successful wine dynasties, one quintessentially American, one irrepressibly French. Both grew out of the great boom in the wine business after Prohibition in the U.S. and the Second World War in Europe, taking advantage of American prosperity in the sixties and seventies.

In Chateauneuf-du-Pape the origins of Beaucastel trace back to the middle of the sixteenth century, when the "Noble Pierre of Beaucastel" purchased land in the southern Rhône in a place called Coudoulet. The family became important landowners in the area now known as Chateauneuf-du-Pape and produced wines beginning in the early nineteenth century. By 1870 the estate fell to the Perrin family, where its reputation flourished even through the 1960s and 1970s, when Jacques Perrin famously elevated the estate in a region laid low by war, deflation, and economic ruin. Perrin shored up vineyard practices and raised quality steadily until Beaucastel had become the premier estate in the southern Rhone.

By the time Robert M. Parker had begun fawning over Chateauneuf-du-Pape in 1987, his praise for the Perrins was unfailing, placing the family in the company of the Rhône royalty, Chave, Rayas, and Guigal: "Beaucastel represents more than just a great wine from Chateauneuf-du-Pape," he wrote, "They are the consummate craftsmen of their profession, committed to the preserving the tradition and grandeur of naturally made wine without any concession to the commercial wine world's demand for polished, ready to drink, zealously filtered wines incapable of any evolution and lacking the character of their place of origin."[1]

Beaucastel bestowed this sort of credibility on the Tablas Creek project, lending a confident French hand to an already steadfast, well-established American partner. Both families, already close, entered the partnership in part to expand and augment their relationship. While neither family had ancestral ties to California (the Haas family was from Vermont, by way of New York), they would go on to cement not just their own name in California soil, they changed the complexion of the Rhône movement irrevocably, lending expertise and much needed credibility that a loosely organized, rootin'-tootin' collection of producers had largely lacked.

Robert Haas was born in Brooklyn in 1927 and raised in Scarsdale, New York. He studied politics, history and economics at Yale, interrupted by a stint in the Navy, completing his studies in 1950. Upon leaving the service, Haas presumed he'd pursue a career in engineering. His father, though, steered him in a different direction.

Haas's father, Sidney, owned a retail wine shop in Manhattan called M. Lehmann, which became one of the first in New York to receive a liquor license after Prohibition. In 1963, they merged with Sherry Wine & Spirits Company to become Sherry-Lehmann, which remains one of the most successful wine and spirits retailers in New York.

In those days the business of importing wine was still fairly rudimentary—liquor stores mostly sold liquor; wine sales accounted for less than 20% of all sales at Lehmann shortly after Prohibition. Most good retailers employed brokers and liaisons based in Europe, who were well versed in working with négociants and vendors on the ground in the various regions. For many years Sidney Haas had contracted with Raymond Baudouin, founder of the *Revue du Vin de France* and envoy for several great Burgundy and Bordeaux producers, to help with selections for the store. Beaudouin died in 1953, however, and to reestablish ties with Beaudouin's enterprise, the elder Haas persuaded his son to make a trip to France the following year.

From his first steps on French soil, the younger Haas fell in love with the work. Because he possessed just a passing grasp of French, Robert toured French wine regions with Beaudouin's old secretary, traveling a nearly identical path as the late writer and consultant, paying commissions on relationships established by Beaudouin and making connections of his own.

At the time the production of most French wine was left to négociants, who served as great aggregators of fruit and finished wine from a given region (and often more than one), usually with a better eye for commerce than for quality. Indeed, most wines were blended with only passing regard for their sources: fruit from greater and lesser sites often went into the same vats, with the result that the standard was lowered for everything that was imported.[2] In the twenty years following Prohibition and the end of the Second World War, wine prices were horribly deflated, and it was a rare producer who could afford to keep up their property on the prices they were able to charge for their product.

That was certainly the case in Chateauneuf-du-Pape, when Robert Haas made his first trip to the region. Haas always had an interest in the Rhône Valley, but the market for these wines was so paltry that it was difficult for him to justify making the trip—rarely did his time spent there pay for itself. Nevertheless, in 1966 he journeyed to Chateauneuf-du-Pape, and had the good fortune of meeting Jacques Perrin.

At the time, Beaucastel was one of perhaps three wineries in the region that had risen above the devastation (the other two were Chateau Rayas and Mont Redon). Most of the rest were in terrible disrepair and their fruit was sold in bulk to négociants—it would be years before the domaines whose greatness we take for granted, like La Nerthe and Vieux Télégraphe, would shore up their properties.[3]

But Jacques Perrin always believed fervently in the region and in the role his property played in it. Years before his contemporaries, Perrin converted to organic practices and committed to levels of hygiene in the winery that the rest of the Vaucluse would be slow to imitate.

Haas and Jacques Perrin hit it off immediately. In Haas, Perrin saw a man deeply interested in the pursuit of wines of quality and character, the sort that he aspired to make and promote. In an early visit, Perrin took Haas on a kind of anti-tour of the region, to show him how far it had fallen. "He was disappointed with growers who'd settle for quantity rather than quality. Much of our getting to know each other, early on, amounted to me commiserating with him." Haas became the estate's third American importer. Within three years, they signed an exclusive pact. Haas would go on to make Beaucastel an enormous success in the U.S., and until he died in 1977, Jacques Perrin was a trusted friend and advisor to Haas.

After more than a decade of importing wine for his father and other companies—a busy decade indeed, which included several milestones, like being the first to sell Bordeaux futures and the first to exclusively import Chateau Petrus in this country—Robert Haas struck out on his own with Vineyard Brands in 1973. He became one of the most successful of the "new" import companies of this very fertile period in the wine import business, and for decades to come, and brought in dozens of other important Burgundy estates at this critical stage of development in the American market, which cemented the company's reputation, and its fortunes. Vineyard Brands was also responsible for developing American business for Dauvissat, Henri Gouges, Domaine Weinbach, and Marques de Caceres. Throughout, Haas's closest relationship remained with the Perrins.

During the early seventies, Vineyard Brands represented a number of California wineries in the East Coast market, including Freemark Abbey, Chappellet, Clos du Val, and Joseph Phelps. In 1973 Haas brought Jean-Pierre and Jacques Perrin to California. Haas remembers that Joe Phelps was just finishing construction on his winery, while other Napa Valley facilities were in the final stages of completion—there was a palpable excitement in the region that the Perrins certainly picked up on. "Jean-Pierre was particularly impressed," says Haas. "Even at that time he thought 'Boy, maybe we ought to be doing something over here.'"

Jean-Pierre remembers that first trip very well. "The first thing that struck me was the climate," says Perrin. "All these beautiful, modern wineries planting Cabernet Sauvignon and Chardonnay; I was astonished, because remember for me, I am from the south of France, and here were these warm sunny days just like where I come from. I couldn't understand why everyone was planting Cabernet instead of Syrah and Grenache. We spoke with Bob about it. And he said, 'Maybe one day.'"

Both companies devoted the next decade to developing their business. Haas had dropped most of his California representation, but by the mid-eighties had circled back around, lured by an appellation-specific Chardonnay project being developed by Brice Cutrer-Jones called Sonoma Cutrer (Haas was a founding partner and consultant in the venture). Meanwhile by the mid-eighties, the Perrins' next generation was in place, the families were prosperous and still close; the notion of starting a new project together was once again discussed in earnest.

In that period of time, according to Haas, the California wine industry had grown up. Consumer interest had grown dramatically, and the market expanded in kind, becoming, in effect, the first true global market, wherein all of the world's emergent wine regions competed.[4] Moreover, American wines had seen an impressive resurgence, thanks in part to the Judgment of Paris in 1976. And even though the victors in the Paris tasting were a Cabernet and a Chardonnay, it was no longer a Cabernet and Chardonnay world. Zinfandel had seen a mild resurgence, and Pinot Noir was gaining a modest foothold. Most surprisingly, Rhône varieties were in the market for the first time, and the market interest surely got the interest of the prospective partners.

Jean-Pierre and Francois Perrin made trips to California when time allowed in the early eighties, and Haas assembled the American Rhône bottlings of the time, as well as selections of well-made, well-regarded Zinfandels, because the variety seemed to thrive in Mediterranean climate zones.

Their exploration of the American Rhône wines was fairly systematic. Both parties were fans of the winemaking (and the personality) of Randall Grahm, but found his Mourvèdre-based wines a little short. They admired the wines of Steve Edmunds and Bob Lindquist—in tastings they seemed to fare quite well against other producers, and it helped to focus their interest on the Central Coast, where Rhône varieties seemed to thrive. But they were disappointed with the monovarietal wines to that point, and in touring vineyards from Monterey to Santa Ynez, it became clear to them that the available clonal material, for Grenache and Mourvèdre specifically—two varieties for which the Perrins had very high standards—left much to be desired. This was to be too big, too risky a project to settle for clones of middling quality. And so almost from the first, they decided that the only way to ensure quality plant material was to bring in selections themselves.

They made their first trip to look for property in 1985, a search that would last four years. The partners visited the Santa Cruz Mountains, the Santa Ynez and Santa Maria valleys, the Sierra foothills, Contra Costa County, even Ventura County, evaluating places where Zinfandel or Rhône varietals seemed ascendant. The partners established a small but important set of criteria they were looking for that the Perrins felt would be useful—proximity to water, high pH soils, and the heat required to ripen Mourvèdre and Roussanne fully. "If there were olive trees," says Jean-Pierre Perrin, "that was a good omen."

In the end, the high-pH soils of the Central Coast focused their search. "If we had done a little more homework," says Haas, "we'd have realized we didn't have so far to look." Calcareous soils are rare in California, but a narrow vein of limestone runs through of the Central Coast from Hollister in the north to the Arroyo Grande and Santa Ynez valleys to the south, including Paso Robles and the inland slopes that Chalone occupied. And there were few places where the evidence of chalk soils was more obvious, or inviting, than west of Paso Robles, especially the road cuts on the drive through Peachy Canyon: "It's just so striking," says Haas. "Nothing but chalk on either side."

They gave some very serious thought to Ballard Canyon in the Santa Ynez Valley—they toured what is now known as Purisima Mountain, which the Beckman family eventually planted to Rhône varieties, and nearly bid on the land now occupied by Stolpman Vineyard. But they found Santa Barbara Country building regulations restrictive.

At last in the summer of 1988, a piece of land west of Paso Robles became available about twelve miles from the ocean, well west of the 101 freeway near where most other growers had settled, a 120-acre, limestone-rich parcel of land which had never been planted, and had been used for pasture for the better part of a century.

"We probably should have done more geological studies," says Haas. "We more or less stumbled on Paso Robles, actually. We weren't aware of the kind of soils that were findable here until we'd brought the property. And even with the chalky soils, it wasn't clear what sort of wines they were going to yield."

Haas says that there were a few other lucky breaks for their particular site. "It's one of the coolest in the appellation," he explains. "There's a little dip where we are, between higher mountains. We probably get more frost than anyone else, but we have cooler nights, cooler than our neighbors next door even."

None of this, of course, was evident when Haas first laid eyes on the property. "I stood there," he says, "It was like 100 degrees and the wind was blowing 40 miles an hour." He was experiencing a phase of the nearly daily cycle of ocean breezes that would send the temperature plummeting in a matter of hours, a cycle that would do wonders for their white wines almost from the first vintage. They closed the deal in 1989.

The Tablas Creek project began with plant propagation; clones of Grenache Noir, Mourvèdre, Syrah, Roussanne, and Counoise were prepared in France for export.[5]

Their timing could not have been worse. The USDA office in Davis, directed for years by Austin Goheen, was set adrift by his retirement in 1989. For three years, from 1990 to 1993, the department lost its funding, at precisely the time that Tablas wished to bring in their new material. That left the plant processing center at Geneva Station in New York State, which was happy to take the material, but it meant that the time spent propagating the plants would be more protracted.

Vine quarantine is a straightforward but time-consuming process, in which plants are rooted and grafted in controlled growing conditions. Then the technicians wait and watch, looking for signs of virus or other problems. The waiting period is usually two seasons, but in Geneva Station, because it was so cold, and much of the work had to be done in greenhouses, it took an additional year. Tablas received its first cuttings in 1993. It was left to Haas and viticulturalist Dick Hoenisch to propagate.

In 1991 Hoenisch was a graduate student in plant pathology at the University of California, Davis when a colleague mentioned a posting on the job board in Paso Robles. Hoenisch said he was going to finish his French homework, and then he would check it out.

He sent in a résumé and Charles Falk, a Tablas partner living in San Rafael, contacted him, as did Robert Haas, by phone. Haas asked him to come to Vermont to talk further, and Hoenisch did so the following week; when he arrived at Haas's home in Chester, Haas greeted him at the door. Hoenisch says he squinted at Haas and asked him, "Don't I know you from TV?" In fact Haas had appeared in a national commercial for one of his brands, the New York winery Taylor Cellars. He wasn't exactly Orson Welles, but apparently Haas had more star power than he was aware of.

Shortly thereafter Hoenisch met with the Perrin family in Alsace, at the home of Colette Faller, proprietor of Domaine Weinbach, one of Vineyard Brands' revered properties and an eventual investor in the Tablas Creek venture. They discussed the project over several dinners and shortly thereafter Hoenisch was put to work in a trial in the Vaucluse at Gillibert Nursery, which prepared and cleared the Beaucastel plant material for export, as well as supplying virus-free ENTAV plant material.[6] Hoenisch was given a crash course in plant propagation, proving his mettle, evidently, since he was hired as vineyard manager, overseeing the vineyard planting and plant propagation for the Tablas Creek project.

Hoenisch divided his time between clearing the 120-acre property of boulders, vetch, and stands of poison oak, preparing the ground, and surveying the cleared land for planting. The rest of his time was devoted to setting up a grafting facility on a low-lying stretch of the property in front of where the winery now stands, where Haas and Hoenisch spent the next three years establishing mother plants, which generated graftable shoots to propagate. As the number of plants reached a reasonable level Hoenisch could be seen at viticulture conferences, standing behind a table of tiny vines in a crude display of the potential in these vines of such exceptional provenance.

News of the new plant material spread quickly among Rhône-ophiles, creating a demand well before there were enough vines in the pipeline. Propagation efforts took much longer than expected. The nursery location was one of its coolest on the property, and there were difficulties with grafting; fungus and disease also hampered their efforts initially.

In the course of the next eight years, Tablas Creek propagated 200,000 plants per year, with the State of California reaping immediate benefit: the acreage of Rhône varietals gained steadily in this period. The demand for sticks so exceeded supply that at times, Haas says, the company had trouble fulfilling its orders, leading to some fallow periods in the marketplace.[7] Eventually the Tablas clones became some of the most sought-after plant material in the history of the state.

In 1999, Tablas closed its own nursery operation and entered into a partnership with the nursery Novavine to manage and propagate their Rhône varietal program. By 2010 Tablas Creek had successfully imported fourteen varieties into California from the Beaucastel vineyard, all cleared of virus at Davis: Syrah, Grenache, Mourvèdre, Counoise, Roussanne, Marsanne, Grenache Blanc, Picpoul, Muscardin, Terret Noir, Picardan, Clairette, Vaccarèse, and Bourboulenc. One could make the argument that at present, Tablas Creek is the most successful Rhône varietal winery outside of the Rhône Valley. Its wines are critically acclaimed, as are its efforts in the promotion and marketing of the Rhône pantheon. Their marketing efforts remain generous and high minded, placing a high value on education, on familiarizing the public with the many varieties in the Rhône pantheon, serving the category at large, which in turn serves the brand it has so successfully built. It has taken a leadership role in the category's principal marketing entity, the Rhône Rangers, which is the last entity standing.

Both Hospice and Tablas Creek have contributed greatly to the legitimacy of Paso Robles as a haven for Rhône varietals. Tablas's commitment to the region has gone a great deal toward cementing the varieties with the regional character of the place, and it goes without saying that most of them used Tablas plant material in their Rhône plantings.

Robert Haas is now semiretired, dividing his time between Paso Robles and Chester, Vermont. Tablas Creek is ably managed by his son Jason, and they've enjoyed the service and experience of a single winemaker, Neil Collins, almost since the winery's inception.

Collins has benefited immensely from the practices of their venerable and more experienced partners, the Perrins—in viticulture and winemaking they've followed practices which were, for the region, groundbreaking, starting with the practice of organic farming, something the Perrin family had employed since the mid-sixties.

Vine spacing at Tablas Creek resembles that of Beaucastel—the configuration is different to accommodate different equipment, but the number of vines per acres, 1,900, is the same. And most recent plantings at Tablas are now head-trained and dry-farmed, something that is almost completely true for the plantings at Beaucastel.[8]

More than this, Collins has implemented less obtrusive barrel regimes and laissez faire winemaking years before such practices were reexamined by California winemakers. The use of wood tanks, *demi-muids* and puncheons, is more common now, but in the mid-nineties, few wines aged in wood employed anything other than a barrique, most new. The larger formats were employed in keeping with the Perrin's desire to minimize the impact of wood upon the wine.

Not much, however, could prepare the partners for how the varieties themselves would take to coastal California soils and climate. For starters, southern Rhône had nothing like the diurnal shift of 50 or more degrees that was a regular occurrence in western San Luis Obispo County. And many of the varieties, like Picpoul and Grenache Blanc, had had limited or no history in the United States.

No variety has been more surprising than Grenache Blanc, which has not only thrived in California but has a dramatically different flavor profile here. Most producers in the southern Rhône use Grenache Blanc in one form or another, but few have nice things to say about it; it is their workhorse variety, useful but uncomplex and uncompelling. But it has demonstrated considerably more character in American soil, an admirable level of acidity as well as serving as a blending grape for other Rhône white varieties like Viognier and Marsanne, for which it supplied a lean spine of acidity.

Tablas Creek's alliance with Beaucastel also tends to cast a favorable light on the varieties other than Syrah, especially those for which Beaucastel is most famous, namely, Grenache, Mourvèdre, and Roussanne. For each, there's consensus that the Tablas clones are the best, or among the best, available.

Not five miles as the crow flies from Tablas Creek, James Berry Smith had purchased a parcel of land originally cleared for barley and was thinking of planting wine grapes. James Berry Vineyard was planted in the early eighties, when the U.S. market was still being dictated by white wines; naturally Berry planted Chardonnay and Pinot Blanc in this cool corner of the Paso Robles area, less than ten miles from the ocean. Six years later John Alban approached the Smith family to try and persuade them to plant Viognier for him, which they did, along with Mourvèdre, in 1989—among the first Central Coast plantings of the variety.

Smith's son Justin, meanwhile, had gone to Cal Poly to study ecology, but the land and the lure of growing grapes on the family vineyard drew him back home. By this time he and his father had seen some of the early promise of Rhône varieties so they went that route in later plantings, sacrificing the Pinot Blanc and committing to Syrah, Mourvèdre, and Grenache with a small amount of Roussanne.

In 2000, Justin Smith founded Saxum Vineyards to draw on his family's growing prowess. Using just a tiny percentage of the vineyard for the project (most is still sold to area wineries like Linne Calodo and Villa Creek), Smith focused on mostly Syrah-dominant blends. The wines, from vines planted on impoverished soils overlaying shale and seabed deposits, were powerful and nervy all at once, a dramatic site for muscular Syrah and highly structured, mineral styles of Mourvèdre and Grenache, resulting in blends that would, by the middle of the first decade of new century, become iconic in the category, aided in no small part to the praise of Robert Parker and the distinction, in 2010, of producing the wine of the year for the *Wine Spectator*—a first for Paso Robles and a first for an American Rhône wine.

The validation of Paso Robles established the region as a Rhône powerhouse, and served as an anchor for an indisputable claim that if the movement had a center, it was the Central Coast of California. In countless ways, the region had been primed for this role. It was, after all, a kind of ancestral home for the movement, the locus of Estrella River's outsized Syrah vineyard and early source for cuttings and cajoling bestowed by Gary Eberle, with a tight-orbit diaspora for the variety in Santa Barbara, San Luis Obispo, and Monterey Counties.

It had some of the movement's greatest proselytizers, including Gary Eberle, Mat Garretson, Bob Lindquist, John Alban, and the Perrin/Haas team—and the latter two entities sold vines and cuttings statewide, though naturally their greatest influence was on the people and the places nearest to them.

The geography of the region represented an ideal proving ground for the half-dozen or so varieties that had taken hold, as producers explored ways to combine them in Côtes du Rhône-style blends; the climatic range found in these valleys even hinted at the climatic variations found in the Rhône Valley itself. Vineyards plantings crept further westward with each passing year, as producers tested the limits of ocean influence—a range that would be explored in blending trials for the next two decades.

Perhaps most importantly, it was easier and cheaper to break into the business here, in the wilds of the Central Coast, the state's last great blank canvas, a mostly underused patchwork of promising vineyard land with literally thousands of acres available to invest in, with some extraordinary sites, like Tepusquet, Bien Nacido, Sanford & Benedict, all pointing to its potential.

Such was the reasoning of Tom Stolpman, a Los Angeles lawyer who would establish one the earliest Rhône varietal plantings in the Santa Ynez Valley. Stolpman and his wife, Marilyn, were bitten by the vineyard bug in the mid-1980s when the couple attended the Napa Valley wine auction. Marilyn was so delighted with the experience that she dragged her husband on Napa Valley real estate tours that very weekend. Stolpman, however, didn't see the point of buying a pied-à-terre hundreds of miles away from their home in Palos Verdes, in the LA Basin. So they cast their eye on Santa Barbara County, just a few hours away by car.

They were helped along by Viognier producer Josh Jensen, who recommended that Stolpman look for limestone in his potential vineyard sites. Stolpman found some in Ballard Canyon, a valley composed of gentle hills just west of the 101 freeway and north of the Los Padres Mountains in the Santa Ynez Valley. The canyon had access to a rather mitigated ocean influence, rendering it cool but not too cool—ideal conditions for Syrah.

None of this was immediately evident to Stolpman, who planted nearly a dozen varieties including Chenin Blanc, Merlot, Cabernet Franc, Sangiovese, and Nebbiolo in addition to trial-sized vineyard plots of Syrah, Grenache, and Mourvèdre.

In 1993, Steve Beckmen and his father purchased most of these in trial quantities to see just what it is they wanted to make in their new winery in Los Olivos. They'd bought a vineyard and winery the year before, planted to Cabernet and Chardonnay, resulting in some rather disheartening first efforts. Beckmen sought out nearby growers for guidance and fruit. Stolpman—barely underway in his own venture—sold him what he had. Right away, says Beckman, the Rhône varieties excelled.

"Syrah was excellent right off," he says; "the Grenache wasn't as good but you could see its potential. And when you saw what guys like Bob Lindquist were doing in the area, it wasn't a difficult decision to move in this direction."

In an area still searching for its identity, this was a good sign. Soon others gravitated toward the area, drawn by the success of Beckmen and Bryan Babcock; winemakers like Craig Jaffurs, Chuck Carlson, and Andrew Murray formed an informal regional enclave of Santa Barbara Rhône aficionados, a Ranger satellite whose initial efforts were well received in the press.

All of these initial efforts were given a huge lift by the meteoric rise of Manfred Krankl, whose early vintages drew from Stolpman Vineyard fruit. Suddenly, with Rhône varieties, the Central Coast had an identity to which it could grab hold.

16

THE AMERICAN RHÔNE
IN WASHINGTON STATE

Like California, Washington State had a pioneer winegrowing industry prior to Prohibition, important and lasting, though not as extensive or as centralized.

West of the Cascade Mountains, only those vines that could survive the area's abundant rainfall were cultivated, and these were rarely vinifera. East of the Cascades, in a stark, dry, sprawling landscape defined by a rain shadow, serious viticulture developed, slowly. Around the beginning of the twentieth century systems of irrigation feeding off the Columbia and Yakima rivers opened up this high desert landscape to agriculture, and grapes were part of that growth. Even so, the region remained sparsely populated well into the twentieth century, with sporadic settlements conquering only tiny swaths of land—much of this devoted to orchards. Growth in the industry was halting and marked by setbacks: without proper care and preparation, early winemakers would lose entire plantings in brutal subzero winter freezes. Those that survived the harsh conditions were finished off by Prohibition. Even after Prohibition, shortsighted state policy and industry regulation handicapped the development of a serious wine industry in the state.

Nevertheless, a small and persistent viticultural effort has carved a niche in eastern Washington for more than a century and a half, and in fact at least one Rhône variety figures prominently in those efforts. When the state's potential was finally realized in the late seventies and early eighties, the Columbia Valley would prove to be one of the most enviable environments for grape growing in the country—and Rhône varieties would occupy a prominent place.

The first recorded vine plantings went into the ground in 1825 at Fort Vancouver, across the Columbia River from what would later become Portland, Oregon. By the middle of the 1850s, nurseries posted advertisements for vinifera and labrusca varieties in local trade papers, propagated largely by Frenchmen and French Canadians who had come to the Pacific Northwest as fur trappers.

Eventually grape-growing enclaves were initiated east of the Cascades in parts of Wenatchee, in and around Yakima, Walla Walla, and in the hills outside Clarkston and Lewiston, on what is now the Idaho-Washington border. These efforts were mostly limited to Labrusca varieties like Concord, Worden, and Niagara; in F. A. Huntley's *The Grapes of Washington*, published in 1908, the only vinifera grapes mentioned are Flame Tokay, Emperor, Black Cornichon, and Black Hamburg (Black Muscat)—not exactly a noble lineup.[1]

Less than a decade later a former lawyer named William Bridgman established Upland Winery on Snipes Mountain in what is now the Yakima Valley AVA. Between 1914 and 1917, Bridgman planted Carignane, Black Prince (Cinsaut), Muscat, Mataro, Zinfandel, and other varieties. His timing was impeccable: plantings commenced precisely when the state had begun to curtail the consumption of alcohol, two years before Prohibition became the law of the land.

And yet Bridgman would benefit from Prohibition, one of only a handful of producers in the state to take advantage of the loophole afforded givers of the sacrament and home winemakers. By 1934, Bridgman was farming nearly 170 acres of grapes.[2] But outside of a few individuals, vineyards died quickly in the harsh valley environment without proper tending and irrigation; by the time the Volstead Act was repealed in 1933, nearly all the vineyards in the state were gone.

Post-Prohibition, the wine-growing community remained small and largely tentative. Wine and liquor regulation fell to the state (which managed direct sales until 2012, through the Liquor Control Board). The board placed prohibitive tariffs on out-of-state wines in a shortsighted attempt to boost the local industry. But with a market excluding the rest of the world's wines, existing Washington wineries lacked the incentive to vinify a quality product, and most aimed low. The wines made were blends of multiple varieties, often combining hybrid and labrusca grapes with vinifera, covering flaws with excessive sweetness or madeirization; these were inferior efforts, cheaply produced and barely taxed. In the generation after Prohibition, mediocrity was rewarded.

In 1967, faced with the threat of a California embargo of Washington apples and other agricultural products, the Washington state legislature permitted the sale of wines from outside the state, thus ending the state's wineries' de facto monopoly on their citizens' wine-buying and drinking habits. That same year, thirty-four years after Prohibition, Ste. Michelle Vintners became the first winery to devote itself entirely to vinifera winemaking. Ste. Michelle was the outgrowth of a Seattle company called American Wine Growers (AWG), which was itself the merger of two wine companies, both founded in 1934, that had been primarily devoted to the production of fruit wines, Pommerelle and the National Wine Company (NAWICO).

Vinifera plantings were still minimal in Washington, though interest had grown to the point where AWG thought it worthwhile to explore the prospect, planting its first Riesling in 1965. According to Joel Klein, Ste. Michelle's winemaker through much of the seventies, it was AWG director Victor Allison's daughter Vicki who suggested the name Chateau Ste. Michelle; she announced at a Sunday dinner that the company name would benefit from a little French flair.

The wineries persuaded the state's agricultural research universities to undertake research on which varieties would work best in the state, and in the mid-1960s a wine research program was begun at Prosser Station, in what would become one of the region's viticultural centers.

There, a group of horticultural and food scientists from Washington State University began a systematic longevity study on grape and wine production. The team included Charles Nagel, George Carter, and Walter J. Clore. Of these men, Clore is generally regarded as the state's most important viticultural figure, Washington's "father of wine" and responsible for the elevation of vinifera grapes to the status they enjoy today, the man who devoted time and truck mileage to visits with farmers all over the Columbia Valley, spreading the word that grape growing in Washington State could be a successful and remunerative enterprise, recommending test plots and selections based on their efforts, and kick-starting the wine industry into a new, fruitful modern phase.

Born into a teetotaling family in Oklahoma in 1911, Clore came to Washington State with his newlywed wife in 1934 on a modest horticulture scholarship. He established himself in Pullman, Washington, near the Idaho border, where he undertook a host of horticultural studies, making important contributions to the cultivation of dozens of vegetable and fruit varieties, from asparagus to apples, from lima beans to chrysanthemums.[3] Eventually Clore moved his research efforts to an agricultural station in Prosser, nearer to nascent viticultural areas in the Yakima Valley and the Horse Heaven Hills. At Prosser a modest effort had begun to shore up the state's viticultural production with some careful study, and by the early sixties, Clore was heading up that effort.

Clore experimented with hybrid, labrusca, and vinifera varieties, evaluating their over-all wine quality and winter hardiness. He grew the grapes and monitored yields and fruit quality, noting the survivors in Washington's harsh winters. Nagel, a Napa Valley native from St. Helena (his father had been cellar master at Louis Martini Winery) was responsible for initial winemaking efforts, as well as the wines' evaluation, for which he assembled an informal network of faculty members and their wives to sample and evaluate the field efforts. Carter eventually succeeded Nagel as the winemaker for the team.

In multiple reports, published from the late 1960s through the 1970s, in bulletins from the Agricultural Station at Washington State University and reports in the *American Journal of Viticulture and Enology,* the team presented systematic findings on the tremendous potential for wine-grape growing in Washington State; its findings were resoundingly positive. While the group still expressed concerns about winter temperatures, they felt the climate was well suited to vines—the soils naturally kept many pests at bay, allowing for the grapevines to be planted on their own roots.

Among the dozen or so grape varieties they recommended for the Columbia Valley was a single Rhône variety: Grenache. "Very distinctive wines," they write of the varietal in their 1974 report, giving it a respectable mean taste score of 15.3 (of 20), higher than Pinot Noir, but lagging behind something called Buffalo.[4] In a report entitled "Ten Years of Grape Variety Responses and Winemaking Trials in Central Washington," a culmination of several such reports over a decade, published in April 1976, Grenache is again praised: "The variety is outstanding for the production of rosé wines," say the authors. "The bouquet is strong and distinctive, and the acidity is higher than that for the same variety in California."[5] They note, however, that Grenache is winter sensitive, and subsequent recommendations in the field tended to be for plantings near the Columbia River.

Professor Clore himself seems to have had a special fondness for Grenache. In *The Wine Project*, a history of Washington viticulture, Ronald Irvine relates an incident taken from a conversation with colleague Vere Brummond in 1966. Clore, whose upbringing had kept him abstinent much of his adult life, overcomes his aversion in a glass of Grenache Rosé. "Dr. Clore couldn't leave it alone," says Brummond. "I don't think he got tipsy, he was just delighted with that Grenache Rosé."[6]

The findings of Clore and his team lent tremendous credibility to viticultural efforts statewide. And yet in eastern Washington, whose appellation system would be another decade away, grape growing was still a hard sell. A ranch culture set the agents for change miles from one another, with farm communities few and far between, and opportunities for dialogue and influence minimal. Grapes had competition from other fruit crops like apples, pears, and cherries, whose orchards had proven to be more durable through the region's harsh winters.

So having convinced themselves of the viability of the Columbia Valley as a viticultural region, Clore now had to convince growers. He set out crisscrossing the valley, locating good vineyard sites, then knocking on ranch doors, and inveigling the inhabitants to consider grape growing for wine production on a parcel of their land. If there was water to grow grasses there was more than enough for grapevines and, he told them, it could be lucrative, too.

There remain a small number of nonagenarian farmers and ranchers in eastern Washington who in their youth answered the door when Walter Clore came knocking, and who were won over by his message about grape growing. Don Graves was one such recruit, a rancher in Dallesport, Washington, on the Columbia just across the river from The Dalles and west of Hood River, Oregon. Walter Clore invited himself in and persuaded Graves that he would do well to plant grapes on his land.

With Clore as his guide Graves planted a 1.5 acre test plot with twenty-four different varieties. George Carter made the wines, and of all the varieties sampled, Carter and Graves were most impressed with the Cabernet and the Grenache.

Grenache proved to be a good sell in 1970s America, mostly in the form of rosé, an easy, mildly sweet precursor to white Zinfandel. For decades, Graves sold grapes to Ste. Michelle for rosé production, and to Charles Henderson in nearby Salmon River, who owned the Bingen Winery and made a red Grenache from the grapes in the mid-seventies. As interest in rosé waned Graves became an important fruit source for Peter Brehm, whose Berkeley wine coop and home winemaking center, Wine and the People, had been so instrumental to Rhône wine aficionados in the Berkeley area. It seems plausible that some of California's early Rhône variety producers may have drawn from Grenache inspired by the passions of Walter Clore.

Concurrent with these efforts, Washington's potential for grape growing was being assessed, starting in the mid-1960s when Leon Adams, a wine journalist from the Bay Area, came to Washington to evaluate the region. Adams was researching his seminal publication *Wines in America,* its inaugural edition published in 1973, the most comprehensive look at American winemaking since Prohibition. A small number of local wines were assembled for him to taste.

Adams was by and large unimpressed. Most of what he tasted amounted to blends with vinifera grapes folded into labrusca and hybrid port-style wines. "I was amazed to find the wineries were wasting these costly grapes," writes Adams, "mixing them with Concord in nondescript port and burgundy blends."[7]

But a single wine, made by a group of nine wine-loving amateurs in the Seattle area gave Adams reason to hope. This collection of academics had started producing carefully made, 100% vinifera bottlings, mostly for their own enjoyment. The wines were made in the garage of Lloyd Woodburne, a professor of psychology and former dean of the College of Arts and Sciences at the University of Washington. In 1962 they took their hobby seriously enough to incorporate, as Associated Vintners.[8]

The only fine vinifera wine I tasted on that trip," Adams writes in *Wines of America,* "was a Grenache Rosé made by a home winemaker in Seattle."[9] It compelled Adams to suggest to Victor Allison, then manager of American Wine Growers, that he consider bringing in consultants from California. Allison asked for a few recommendations. "I mentioned a few good winemakers," says Adams, "including André Tchelistcheff, the great enologist of Beaulieu."

Within a year Allison had persuaded Tchelistcheff, one of the first masters of California wine, to come to Washington State to taste and consult. Like Adams, Tchelistcheff had to be won over; and like Adams, Tchelistcheff was impressed enough by his encounter with a single wine, a Gewürztraminer from AWV, to become convinced "that the potential existed to make great wine from Washington grapes."[10]

Tchelistcheff encouraged them to plant red varieties alongside white (already prodigious amounts of Riesling had been planted in the state), recommended that they slash their yields, to shore up their quality control, and above all, to focus on vinifera. His emphasis on quality changed the culture of Washington's oldest and most influential winery; in effect, Tchelistcheff taught the region for decades to come. Adams returned in 1969 to sample the wines Tchelistcheff had suggested, including two Grenache Rosés, and found them to be impressive.

"I have tasted subsequent vintages and found them equal to many premium-priced California and European wines," he wrote, reserving special praise for the Grenache. "Grenache rosé wines made from Yakima Valley grapes have had more intense Grenache varietal aromas than any wines of this variety I have sampled from California or from France. Andre Tchelistcheff predicts that a blend of Grenache, perhaps with Petite Sirah, in a full-bodied red (rather than pink) wine may become the most famous Yakima Valley vintage in years to come; he thinks it could excel the renowned red Rhône wines made from those grape varieties."[11]

The Washington wine industry grew at a breakneck pace throughout the 1970s and into the 1980s. For the most part, Grenache didn't hang on for the ride. Emphasis shifted to white varieties, as Washington State's Rieslings and Gewürztraminers, with their modicum of racy sweetness, appealed to the American public. In 1974, a *Los Angeles Times* blind tasting of Rieslings from all over the world picked a 1972 Riesling from Chateau Ste. Michelle as the finest. It was the first time a Washington wine had shone so well in international competition, and vaulted the state's viticultural efforts onto the national stage like never before.

Interest in red wines waned, as did the interest in Grenache Rosé. In fact as Rhône varieties were slowly taking root in California, they were being ignored in Washington State, that is, until Associated Vintners hired an ambitious young Master of Wine, whose global perspective changed the region's viticultural landscape forever.

Associated Vintners, almost from its inception, struggled financially. An audit of its resources and assets in the late seventies concluded that in order to survive, the winery would have to expand dramatically. To facilitate this, Lloyd Woodburne suggested that his board of directors hire outside of his fellow vintners' circle. In 1979, they hired a young Englishman named David Lake.

David Lake was born in Canada in 1943 to English parents. His father worked with the British intelligence service and was routinely stationed abroad, in Canada, Washington D.C., and in Britain. David attended McGill University in Toronto, and an interest in wine went with him to England after graduation. There Lake worked for the better part of a decade as an operations manager for a wine distributor, and embarked on a formal course of wine study that culminated in a Master of Wine certificate in 1975.

Soon after he moved to the states and took up winemaking studies at Davis. Upon completing his studies, Lake worked in Oregon's fledgling industry, at Eyrie and at Bethel Heights Vineyard in the Eola Hills, before Associated Vintners drew him northward.

It was a sensible move for a man with a keen intellect, a fascination with vineyard development, and a voracious palate. For Lake, Washington wine country presented an almost limitless set of possibilities, and he was uniquely positioned to explore its potential: few residents before him possessed quite like he did the imagination, the intellectual curiosity, and the breadth of knowledge to drive the industry in new directions.

In 1980, just a year in to his tenure at Associated, Lake met Mike Sauer. Sauer was about Lake's age, a grower and farmer who worked a vineyard in the westernmost reaches of the valley, just south and a bit west of the town of Yakima, on land that had been purchased from the indigenous Yakama Indian tribe by Sauer's wife's family a half-century earlier.

For generations, they raised cattle and farmed alfalfa, wheat, and potatoes. But in the early seventies, Sauer decided to experiment with grapes, planting about 30 acres of Concords. Inevitably, Walter Clore got involved, putting in a weather station and encouraging him to try vinifera varieties. Sauer obliged, planting an experimental plot of twenty-four varieties, four vines of each. The best, says Sauer, were the Cabernet Franc and Petit Verdot vines. Some years later a fellow rancher and compatriot in the National Guard offered him a truckload of Cabernet Sauvignon cuttings, and Sauer took them. "I didn't know what they were," says Sauer. "I didn't even know if it was a white or a red. I was just a young kid; I'd never drunk wine in my life, but I was mesmerized by those beautiful French names." Four years later Woodburne sent Sauer a contract for his Cabernet, sight unseen.

At a grape grower's meeting Sauer managed to hitch a ride with Lake back to his home in Wapato. As they talked in the truck, he was struck by the erudition and conviction of the man driving, a worldly wine-lover who knew more about wine than Sauer could ever hope to. "He was the only Master of Wine in the U.S. at the time," says Sauer. Lake would soon expand Sauer's vision dramatically. "You know that saying about standing on the shoulders of giants," says Sauer, "that's how I felt about him; that's what it was like for me."

And so the worldly, erudite Englishman began tutoring and inspiring a gifted farmer to become one of the most exceptional growers in Washington. Together they took the region to new heights, not only in the rigorous exploration of a unique terroir, but in the exploration of varieties outside the norm in Washington at the time. Sauer planted grapes to Lake's specifications, and Lake made some of the region's most classical bottlings to this point, showing the world what Washington could do, and rewarding his growing partner with the state's first vineyard designate wine, a Red Willow Vineyard Cabernet Sauvignon, in 1981.

Perhaps Lake's most lasting contribution was to get Sauer and other growers to overcome their reticence. In the Columbia Valley, planting decisions were often tentative; experience with harsh winters tended to stunt a grower's curiosity. "Everyone was pretty settled in with what we had," explains Sauer. "Winters were a lot colder then I think and kept people from doing too much experimentation. We just all knew the varieties that worked."

So Lake shared bottles of wine with Sauer from all over the world, brought him books and accounts of great tastings held in the nineteenth and early twentieth centuries. Sauer insists, however, that for him the scales were tipped not by Lake but by a Seattle-area restaurateur named Peter Dow, who approached Sauer in 1984 with an idea. Dow called on Sauer at his home. In his hands were two bottles of wine, a Barolo and a Barbaresco. Dow uncorked them to show Sauer the glories of Nebbiolo, the great varietal of the Piedmont, in a pitch to get Sauer to plant the grape at Red Willow.

"Peter is about as opposite to me as you can get," says Sauer, "He's quick-witted, he loves to talk, and wanted me to think about planting Nebbiolo. 'You know,' he says, 'Nebbiolo is the great grape variety the Piedmont, in Italy.' I'd never heard of Nebbiolo, I'd never heard of Barolo or Barbaresco; I'd never heard of Café Juanita—it sounded to me like some kind of taco stand. But we tasted some of the bottles and I said I'd think about it."

Within a week they had an agreement to go in on a small Nebbiolo planting, on a steep hill that Sauer had never developed, set at about the 1,300-foot elevation, above where the cataclysmic Missoula Floods had passed through, an Ice Age torrent that ravaged and reconstituted millions of acres in the Columbia Valley between 10,000 to 15,000 years before. Here, above the flood line, a completely different soil profile remained.

Indeed, it was a remarkable spot. To the west the Cascades loomed, from which descended cool sub-Alpine breezes. From that hill, looking west, the white dome of Mt. Adams feels so close that on some days it feels like you could reach out and touch it; suffice it to say, there was no other place like it in the Columbia Valley.

Lake politely dismissed Sauer's newfound interest in Nebbiolo, shifting the grower's attention toward another varietal Sauer had never heard of. "He told me, 'You know, one of the great great red wines of the world, and one of the great undiscovered red grapes, is Syrah, from the Rhône Valley, in France.'"

It seems likely that David Lake had been waiting for this moment all of his professional life. Syrah held a special place in his heart, and Washington seemed like the very place he might take the chance. "Coming here, I had a number of things that I felt would be really interesting to try,"[12] he said in an interview in 2004, toward the end of his life. "I wasn't quite sure how the climate would allow me to do this because at the time when I came to Washington there were a number of grape varieties that were already established here, but a number that were not." Lake, evidently, could be very convincing. "I very much moved him [Sauer] in that direction," he says. Sauer's curiosity was certainly kindled by Lake's. Sauer would become Lake's principal co-conspirator, the grower most willing to execute Lake's ambitions in the ground, a kindred spirit, certainly with respect to Syrah.

"He really did a sales job on me," says Sauer. "He told me it was one of the great red varieties of the world. He talked about nobility of the grape, how it found its way onto the tables of royalty in England and into other French bottles needing color. Sometimes, under cover of darkness, they'd slip it into Bordeaux to enhance the wines. And it was hardly discovered. He convinced me that Syrah was a better choice than Nebbiolo."

There was, perhaps, a level of destiny to this endeavor. Over the years, everyone close to David Lake felt that he connected with Syrah on some fundamental level. "He understood Syrah way before we understood the grape," says Sauer. "As far as I knew it was just another red wine variety, but with his pedigree and his education, he could see how special it was long before any of us could. As I look back on his life, I believe he hung his reputation and ultimately his legacy on this variety—probably more than any other wine he made."

Bob Betz, the state's second Master of Wine and Lake's former neighbor at Chateau Ste. Michelle, who now purchases Syrah from the original Red Willow planting, is even more emphatic: "I think that David's personal desire for structure and elegance was best interpreted in Syrah," says Betz. "David loved length, and spine; only Syrah could provide that natural grace, that fineness on the palate that he loved."[13]

The Columbia Winery procured cuttings from Joseph Phelps in 1984, propagated them for planting. On a spring day in 1985 Sauer gathered his crew for a celebration at the vineyard. The historical significance of this planting was not lost on David Lake. "He brought over his cellar crew from Woodinville and we all took turns planting different rows together," says Sauer. "We had a small barbecue where we enjoyed several bottles of northern Rhône Syrah. After lunch, we took several bottles and buried them in the vineyard, so the vines would know what they're supposed to be thinking about."

There is a picture of the group, posed in front of a small pit. Four bottles are in view: two bottles of Clape Cornas, a bottle of Jaboulet's famous Hermitage bottling La Chapelle, and possibly a bottle of Côte-Rôtie from Alain Paret. Sauer crouches down next the small pit, tousle-haired, a little flushed; David stands to the left, holding a glass of wine, looking in the direction of Mt. Adams, the pride in this achievement plain on his face.

Columbia's first Syrah bottling was released in 1988, and was an immediate success. And yet seven years would go by before more Syrah would find its way into the ground after Lake's initial planting. Such was the nature of "trends" in the Columbia Valley; with such efforts so far from one another, it was difficult to gather momentum.

Six years after the Syrah planting, Sauer took his first trip to the wine regions of Europe, a tour of Italy with Peter Dow. Sauer was struck by the ancient villages of Tuscany, in particular the stone churches which were invariably situated on the highest point of every hilltop village, Sauer began thinking about some such structure at Red Willow. When he returned he learned that his local priest, Monsignor Maurice Mulcahy—the man who had baptized all of his children, had passed away.

So in the fall of 1992, in memory of the Monsignor, partly in homage to La Chapelle on Hermitage Hill, and inspired by his vivid memories of Italian hilltop chapels, he started work on a similar structure at the apex of the hill where the Syrah had been planted at Red Willow. He was aided by an employee skilled in stone carving, Ezequiel Tzintzun. Sauer, his sons, and Tzintzun built the chapel from scratch, without a plan.

Three years later it was finished and dedicated, adding a focal point for one of the most dramatic and inspiring Syrah vineyards in the country.[14]

By the time Red Willow Syrah had hit the market, there were still hundreds of acres of Grenache in the Columbia Valley, most of it still going into cheap rosé or generic blends, just as it had in California. And just like California, those vines got older, dropped their tendency to throw enormous crop loads, accrued character, and went largely unappreciated for decades until the early nineties, when one newly minted winemaker saw it for its true potential, and accelerated Washington's Rhône movement.

Doug McCrea is a New Orleanian by birth, and that simple truth factors into several turns in his life. He's a man whose creative endeavors seem to derive from that city's burning passions, which instilled in him not only a love of wine but an abiding love of music, woodwinds in particular, a suite of instruments for which New Orleans is famous. Indeed, McCrea Cellars' flagship wine, Cuvee Orleans, pays homage to that city and you might say its flavors reflect a gumbo of Syrah elements: whether pepper and smoke, plum pudding and saddle leather, it is routinely complex and hard to categorize, like the city it pays homage to.

McCrea's father and mother were food lovers. His mother was from the wine region of Alsace; he remembers his grandfather pulling wine from great earthen casks and serving it with most evening meals, heady stuff that McCrea partook of at an early age.

McCrea studied music at San Jose State, where he became proficient in various woodwind instruments, starting with classical clarinet but including saxophone, oboe, flute, even recorders.

One day early in his studies he got a call from the music department at nearby Stanford University. A composer in the program, György Ligeti, wanted to meet with him. McCrea learned that Ligeti was a giant in the contemporary classical music scene, whose most visible triumph was the music he contributed to Stanley Kubrick's epic movie, *2001: A Space Odyssey.*

"He got me in his office," says McCrea, "and throws down this score and says 'I hear you are the only one who can maybe play this piece for me. Can you do it?'" Before him was the score for "Ten Pieces for Woodwind Quintet," a piece of music so complex and intricate it would consume McCrea for an entire year. The project took McCrea to Stanford, where he got an unparalleled musical education.

McCrea embarked upon a wide-ranging musical career that included teaching, arranging (for a college glee club, where he met his first wife and business partner, Susan), recording, and touring with some of the jazz legends of the era.[15] From Palo Alto he spent weekends traveling in wine country; a friend, Larry Sievert, had been hired as wine steward for the famous Napa Valley restaurant L'Auberge du Soleil; together they got stoned and polished off bottles of Bordeaux and Burgundy and received a crash course in French First Growths.

In 1980 he was able to secure a job with Hewlett Packard in Seattle (where Susan was employed). He started tasting wines from the region and was impressed, none more so than with Alex Golitzin's new winery, Quilceda Creek, which was made not far from the McCrea home was in Lake Stevens. McCrea asked if he could look over Golitzin's shoulder. Pretty soon he was making wine from purchased Columbia Valley fruit. This is how a McCrea Chardonnay ended up in the glass of Golitzin's uncle, André Tchelistcheff.

"He sniffed it and said 'you made this, huh?' I said yes. 'What do you do?' he asked me. I told him I worked at Hewlett-Packard. He went back to the wine, smelled it, looked back to me and said: 'I think you should maybe quit your day job.' I said ,'Huh? What are you trying to tell me? He says, 'This is the best Chardonnay I've tasted from Washington State—and I am including the wines I've made at Chateau Ste. Michelle.'"

Buoyed by this encouragement, McCrea added small lots of Merlot and Cabernet to his Chardonnay production. At a grower's meeting in Prosser in 1988 he met Don Graves, and learned about his three acres of Grenache. McCrea made him promise that if Peter Brehm couldn't pay off his bill, McCrea could take the fruit. McCrea's first vintage of Grenache was in 1989.

The following year, McCrea got Graves to expand. "I convinced [Graves] that if Grenache worked well here that Syrah was a shoe-in," says McCrea. They planted it in 1990, with cuttings from McDowell. By 1994 the vines were producing; the response, says McCrea, was "outrageous."

"It got incredible accolades," he says. "Bob Betz took the wine down to a Napa Valley tasting with twelve Syrahs from the U.S., and it won that competition—this was the second Syrah ever made in the state."

McCrea quickly lined up more growers to plant Syrah; the variety became his muse. "Something about the grape," he says, "the racy spicy headiness of that wine, it just drew me; and I liked working with something in uncharted territory. It was—I guess there's nothing really 'jazz' about Cabernet Sauvignon; it's as straightforward as it gets. I'm more free form than that."

McCrea's search for new sources came at a good time. A new breed of growers were devoting more acreage to vinifera grapes, managing difficult winter conditions, and showing a greater willingness to try new things. In 1994 McCrea was able to convince two growers, Dick Boushey and Jim Holmes, to plant Syrah for him. Their vineyards, Boushey and Ciel du Cheval, represent vastly different terroirs. Boushey is on the eastern end of the Yakima Valley appellation. Ciel du Cheval is thirty miles west on Red Mountain, a much warmer site, more given over to Bordeaux varieties.

Both growers have expanded varietal plantings of Rhône varieties in Washington State, including Picpoul, Grenache Blanc, and Mourvèdre, Counoise, and Cinsaut. Many of these became McCrea single-variety vineyard designates, most of them firsts for Washington State.

About seventy miles east, a parallel development was taking place in Walla Walla. Berle "Rusty" Figgins, Jr. was the youngest of eight children born into a Walla Walla farm family, of an Irish father, Berle Figgins, and an Italian mother, Virginia Leonetti. That farm family, according to Rusty's brother Gary, who would go on to found Leonetti Cellar, named for his mother's family, included Gary's two uncles on his mother's side, who never married and lived with them. There he says they grew "corn, onions, cows, and kids" as well as an acre of wine grapes meant for dinner consumption, planted to Black Prince (Cinsaut). "Most Italians around here grew it—Dago red—we called it that too," he says. Every Sunday the families would gather for a huge meal at Grandma Rose's farmhouse, "There was a smell of garlic coming out of the wallpaper," says Rusty Figgins.

As children Gary and Rusty were given wine with their meals, diluted with water, in proper Italian fashion. "We both came upon the sophistication after the fact," says Rusty. "We were raised with the appreciation of the combination of the flavor of food and wine." When Gary came of age he planted Cabernet Sauvignon and Riesling on family land, and before long Leonetti Cellar was off and running, the first bonded winery in Walla Walla.

An accomplished drummer, Figgins sat "on a three-way fence" while deciding which career to pursue: winemaker, musician, or electrician. But in 1986 he sat in on a tasting with his brother and the great Bordeaux négociant Peter Allen Sichel in Seattle. Sichel arranged for Figgins to work harvest at Chateau Haut-Brion in 1987, remembered as one of the coldest and wettest harvests in memory. "It rained every day of harvest," says Figgins. "We harvested all of the Merlot early; all the Cabernet rotted."

But the experience thrilled Figgins, turning him to winemaking once and for all. "I felt that pride, in making the wine, motorists driving by saying '*vive le vendangeurs!* [long live the harvesters].' Just the whole culture convinced me of what I wanted to do."

Figgins came back from France with brochures from various viticulture programs, and decided to learn the craft in Australia—Wagga Wagga, to be exact, tautonymous, like that of his hometown. It's where Figgins first encountered Shiraz, Australia's workhorse variety, and the way Rusty tells it, none of the students there really wanted to work with it. "I was absent the day the assignments were doled out," he says, "so I was given a block of Syrah to manage. No one spoke up for it: it wasn't the new and exciting thing for them—but it certainly was for me."

He came back from Australia with a strong desire to work with Syrah, which had not yet been planted in Walla Walla. Figgins managed vineyards at Pepper Bridge and Morrison Lane, and in both places he persuaded the owners—Dean Morrison and Norm McKibben—to plant Syrah, which he promised he would buy. The first Walla Walla vines went into the ground in 1992 at Pepper Bridge, followed one year later by a five-acre planting at Morrison Lane.

In 1995, Figgins founded Glen Fiona Winery. Having come from a winemaking, wine-loving family, Figgins also felt like he wanted to give a nod to the family in his brand—and yet, the desire to position himself outside his brother Gary's shadow was strong—"I needed to make my own path," he says.

Syrah offered him some separation. "With Syrah I could honor my family's winemaking heritage," he says, "but make wines in a different style, with different grape varieties.

I could take something I love with less recognition, something new and exciting and worth watching." He decided to call the brand Glen Fiona (the name, in Gaelic, means "Valley of the Vine"), to call attention to his family's Irish heritage.

Figgins had tremendous success with his early vintages, crafting beautifully savory, sensuous wines, richer and more voluptuous than most Washington efforts to this point, and far more approachable. They took the West Coast by storm in the mid-1990s.[16]

As McCrea and Figgins began to proselytize in the high desert on the wonders of Rhône varieties, as they spread the word on Syrah in its Washington digs, a young Frenchman driving in a pickup truck on the southern edge of the Walla Walla Valley, on a cold spring day, stared at a barren field strewn with river rocks, stopped the truck in its tracks, and had a game-changing epiphany.

Christophe Baron was born into a winemaking family from Charly-sur-Marne, a Champagne village roughly equidistant from Paris and Reims. His family had been in the region since 1633, making wine and growing wheat; their crops were sold in Les Halles in Paris, transported by barge on the Marne for centuries. To this day Baron's father sells his vin clair, mostly Pinot Meunier, to négociants.[17] As a boy Baron spent many vintages in the vineyard with his father and uncle; he learned how to prune vines when he was six years old.

Baron went to school in Beaune, spending weekends either in Lyons or in Vienne, in the northern Rhône (he preferred the latter city, he says: the nightlife was better). He and his friends would taste at local wineries and sometimes earn extra money working the vineyards of Côte-Rôtie and Cornas.

Upon completion of his studies Baron wanted to see the world, and learn English. The winemaking schools in France were buzzing about the newest French venture in America in the Dundee Hills of Oregon, where Burgundy négociant Domaine Drouhin had purchased land. For a year, Baron sought an internship in the Willamette Valley, and dreamed of one day putting down Pinot Noir vines of his own there.

He couldn't find work in Oregon. But a friend was working at Waterbrook winery in Washington State, in something called the Walla Walla Valley. "I decided, 'well, you know, it's pretty close to Oregon,' I may as well try it," he says. Baron spent nearly a year and half at Waterbrook, learning from the founders Eric and Janet Rindal and getting to know the terroir there. He used the spare bedroom of Janet's brother Scott Byerley, part of a large local clan of farmers who'd owned land and grown everything from wheat and alfalfa to apples and grapes for many years. They became friends, and Baron would show Byerley pictures of French vineyards, in his local Champagne, and especially in Chateauneuf-du-Pape, a place whose dramatic terrain Baron admired.

In 1994 Baron landed a job working crush in the Willamette Valley, at Adelsheim Winery, which cemented his desire to return there. He headed back to Europe, and in the course of the next year, Baron worked five harvests in four countries, doing *stages* in the Barossa Valley, Australia; the Marlborough Region on South Island, New Zealand;

Romania, and France. That winter his father asked him if he'd like to settle down, and Baron informed him that he planned to go to Oregon. "He gave me his blessing, and allowed me to take out my savings," he says, "to buy some land in the Willamette Valley, and to grow Pinot Noir."

On the way to Oregon he decided to stop in Walla Walla and visit his friends. Once again he stayed with Byerley. Byerley invited Baron to drive around the valley with him; Byerley's new truck had a great new feature, an outdoor temperature gauge, allowing him to take readings and note the variations, from one end of the valley to the other. Baron agreed to accompany him.

They set out before dawn, and traveling from Touchet east of town, then northeast into the Blue Mountain foothills, and finally down to the state line into Oregon, to Sunnyside Road, just north of the town of Milton-Freewater, a long straight-line road cutting between cherry, apple, and pear orchards. About a mile in, they passed a fallow 10-acre field.

Baron bolted upright in his seat and gripped Byerley by the shoulder. "I told him to pull over and I jumped out of the car." The field before him had once held a plum orchard, which had been ripped out a few years before. It was supposed to have been replanted, but the market for stone fruits was in decline, and so there had been a delay. "I bent over and grabbed a few rocks there and told him 'I'm not going to the Willamette Valley, I'm staying here in Walla Walla, and I'm going to plant Syrah.'" Byerley was speechless. "I asked Scott 'Are there vineyards planted in this area?' He looked at the rocks and said 'Are you kidding me?'"

What they were staring at was an ancient riverbed, where the Walla Walla River once flowed westward toward the Columbia and then receded, leaving huge fans of river cobble in a large but constrained area. Byerley had known about the area for years. "I've got a degree in geology," says Byerley, "so I tend to pay attention to stuff like that." But neither he nor anyone else had ever thought to plant grapes there, before Baron.

Baron reminded him of the pictures he'd shown him in a book on Chateauneuf-du-Pape. "You're going to break a lot of equipment," Byerley said. Baron quickly arranged a lease of the property and founded his brand, Cayuse, named for the native Americans of the region. The following year his father and mother came over to help him plant, using crowbars to work the vines into the meager soil, between cobbles. Cailloux Vineyard was planted with Estrella River Syrah, and the new Tablas clones which Baron collected in Paso Robles himself. Baron snatched up other parcels in the Rocks as they became available, most of it near or adjacent to his original parcel.

For three years area growers watched this crazy Frenchman plant grapevines in the most meager soils in the valley. They knew that poor soils could frequently yield very flavorful, unique fruit, but no one could even dream at what Baron had struck upon. Plus, Baron was brash, loud, a bit arrogant, with a penchant for partying and for attention getting: his behavior and his mad project among the Rocks certainly contributed to a reputation of being a little *fou*, a little unhinged.

But all of that changed when the first reviews started rolling in at the *Wine Spectator,* the *Wine Advocate,* and *Wine & Spirits.* The wines were by far the most exotic Rhône varietal wines that Washington had yet produced. Something about that basalt cobble provenance allowed wildly feral, unique wines, rich and exotic, bearing elements of fig pudding, anise, mocha, spice, blood, and pepper, all in a unique mélange that seemed to be held in suspension by a fine mineral texture. Even today, with vines in their early teens, Cayuse wines have a unique terroir imprint like few Syrahs in the country.

Back in 1996 when Baron was having his aha moment in the Rocks of northeastern Oregon, Charles Smith was actually managing rock bands in Copenhagen. He toured Europe with the Cardigans and the Raveonettes, two of Denmark's leading acts, grew his hair out—it's long and kinky, like a bush, really, more big than long—and partied like the rock stars he was working for. Along the way he developed a taste for good wine, the wines of Spain in particular, especially Priorat.

Three years later he was casting about on a road trip back in the states, wondering what was going to occupy him in the next phase of his life, when he ended up at a barbecue in Walla Walla, where he met Christophe Baron, and discovered that he shared with him a wine sensibility he had never really bothered to articulate to this point.

Sometime later, over what was described as "several bottles of '82 Bordeaux" (it was Smith's birthday), Baron suggested that he move here. Charles asked why. "Because," said Christophe, "everyone in Walla Walla thinks I'm an asshole."

"But you are an asshole," said Charles.

"Yes I know that," said Christophe, "but so are you. And if you move here, we can both be assholes together." Smith saw the opportunity right away: "We could be those guys," he says, "running behind the rest of them yelling 'Run! Run! Run!'"

Smith's wines resembled Baron's not least because he purchased fruit from Baron, as well as from Morrison Lane, an early source for Glen Fiona, and other distinctive Walla Walla sites. But it was his brash manner—Death Metal t-shirts and hot rod cars, a graphics identity system that wouldn't look out of place on a CBGB punk rock band poster—that set him apart, and Baron benefited by the association. Soon others followed in his footsteps, giving Walla Walla a reputation as rockers among the Rocks, cementing the region's standing in Syrah production.

Smith has since become a kind of crass force of nature in the Washington wine community, outsized, loud, instinctual, whose antics make Christophe Baron seem positively priestly in comparison. He has proven to be an incredibly gifted marketer, with a knack for exploiting ideas that on their face seem too simple to succeed, like calling his Syrah brand K (as in *que sera sera*—only fewer letters) and his mass market brand House (these wines he bottled under a second label, humbly titled The Magnificent Wine Company).

In 2005 Smith stepped out of the Walla Walla Valley in pursuit of some warmer sites, particularly in a lesser known viticultural area called the Royal Slope. Smith put together three new *cépages* from a single vineyard on the Royal Slope called Stoneridge, near

Othello. Since their debut vintage in 2005, they each have routinely garnered near perfect scores in the *Wine Advocate* and the *Wine Spectator*—bringing them into a very elite group among Syrah producers in the United States.

Other producers edged into the forefront of Washington Rhône production. After a brilliant twenty-eight-year career at Chateau Ste. Michelle, Bob Betz and his wife, Cathy, made their first wines in 1997. During that time he'd traveled the globe visiting barrel rooms and cellars on every winemaking continent, benefiting from Ste. Michelle's international strategies (making wine with multiple international partners). In 1998, after years of study with his mentor and friend David Lake, Bob Betz became the second Master of Wine in Washington State after Lake himself. Soon he and his wife would be throwing themselves into their brand, Betz Family. Syrah was always at the heart of their plans. "We're hedonists at heart," he explains. "In terms of the absolute pleasure it delivers, Syrah is a hedonist's wine."

For Betz, Syrah had always represented the broad stylistic range that the vast Columbia Valley had to offer. Betz has typically employed three and sometimes four different Syrah sites, "It's the chameleon of Washington reds," he says. "It completely changes its character based on where it grows. You see that in France, of course, so it's no surprise that the same thing is true in Washington." Currently he bottles three Syrahs: single vineyard bottlings from Boushey Vineyard (La Serenne) and Red Willow (La Côte Patriarche). A third, La Côte Rousse, blends two Red Mountain sources, Ciel du Cheval and Kiona's Ranch at the End of the Road. All three of these wines became benchmark Syrahs for Washington State in the mid-2000s.

Back in the Walla Walla Valley, the Rocks became a planting hotbed: producers laid down Syrah, Grenache, Tempranillo, Mourvèdre, and many other Rhône varieties including Viognier, as well as Cabernet Sauvignon, Petit Verdot, and Merlot.

Syrah had been planted elsewhere in the Walla Walla Valley too—since Rusty Figgins's plantings at Seven Hills and Pepper Bridge vineyards, it had been a presence there. But now the emphasis shifted slightly toward higher elevation sites where producers discovered a more attenuated, cool-climate fruit expression—something wines from the Rocks could not claim.[18] The most expressive planting of this type would have come from Les Collines Vineyard, a relatively high-elevation site with a wild and distinctive flavor profile. Les Collines was developed by the Amavi estate, established in 2001 and owned by the same partnership that had established Pepper Bridge Winery three years before.

Amavi and Pepper Bridge shared the same winemaker, Jean-Francois Pellet, who came from a Swiss winemaking family and, in both his Cabernets and Syrahs, favored a more elegant European style.

Wines such as these drew the attention of wine-sellers across the country, including a young sommelier named Greg Harrington from the B. R. Guest restaurant group in

New York City, who was introduced to Walla Walla Syrah through Glen Fiona when he was studying for his M.S. degree in San Francisco and Las Vegas. The Rock Stars drew attention there yet again less than ten years later.

In the spring of 2004, Greg Harrington and his wife, Pam, found themselves at a rooftop picnic in Brooklyn sponsored by the Washington Wine Commission, where he tasted some wines. Harrington had had his share of wine epiphanies over the years, but this one was different: for the first time he looked into the glass and imagined his future. He and his wife were impressed enough to undertake an exhaustive tasting tour of the region later that year, and just a short time later make the unlikely move west from Manhattan to Seattle, to get closer to the action in the Walla Walla Valley, and to make wine.

In these wines Harrington saw enough of a potential for elegance he'd not seen in California. "Every wine I've ever loved has had great acid structure," says Harrington, "so all of my decisions had to involve preserving acids."

When he got to Walla Walla, he discovered kindred spirits. "There was this cool underground network doing the sort of things I liked in wine," mentioning Jean-Francois Pellet of Pepper Bridge and Amavi, Jamie Waters of Powers Winery, and Caleb Foster of Buty Winery. Harrington founded Gramercy Cellars in 2005.

Harrington's success has rekindled interest in more elegant styles. Eventually two stylistic poles emerged in the Walla Walla Valley, one represented by Gramercy Cellars, Amavi, and other lean-and-mean stylists, and one represented by the Rock Stars, K, Cayuse, and others. A growing number of producers are exploring both styles. Matt Reynvaan, one of the most talked-about new talents in the valley, is one of those whose vineyards straddle the two styles. The Reynvaans have one vineyard called In the Rocks Vineyard, and another high elevation site called Foothills in the Sun, which is showing similar character to its neighbor, Les Collines. It's my sense that he won't be alone in exploring multiple Syrah terroirs, and in the coming years another subregion, located in the steep slopes and canyons formed by the North Fork of the Walla Walla River, will take root, established by a radical Baron planting that resembles Côte-Rôtie in its steep aspect and dense planting.

But it is the Rocks that give the region its Rhône identity. Despite a century of history with Rhône varieties, and despite more than a decade of active exploration of these wine grapes, the whole notion of Washington as a Rhône-varietal producing region does not really begin until Christophe Baron's bold decision to plant here. Finally, the state could claim a terroir that was not only spectacular for its unique expression, Syrah's natural place, but so ideally suited to the variety that its very identity was enhanced by the association, the way the Napa Valley elevates Cabernet Sauvignon, the way the Russian River and Willamette valleys augment the reputation of American Pinot Noir.

Baron's story dramatizes, in effect, one of Syrah's first terroir triumphs, not only in Washington, but in the whole U.S.—a bona fide, wildly expressive, site-specific boon to the category. Of course Syrah had been planted in good places before this, it had thrived in Ballard Canyon and west Paso Robles, in the Edna Valley, even the Yakima Valley, but these places, lost among the thousands of acres planted in the nineties, still hadn't emerged as unique. The Rocks gave Syrah a place upon which it could build an identity; it became *the* place where Americans first start to care about Syrah terroir.

Not only that, but the Rocks fell effortlessly in the slipstream of American Rhône tropes. With its visually dramatic connection to Chateauneuf-du-Pape, the Rocks linked the U.S. to the Rhône Valley in a thoroughly new way. Not only this, but once journalists started to connect the Rocks with the flamboyant personalities tending them, the "Rock Star" motif was born, a potent image that heightened the reputation of the wines and the place, an identity that circled back to all of the maverick, radical tropes that had given the category its early momentum—all you had to do was swap out your Rangers for Rock Stars. It was a marketer's dream.

Cayuse's success leads to a kind of gold rush in the Rocks; in February 2015, The Rocks of Milton-Freewater became the region's newest viticultural area. Several other Walla Walla Syrah stylists make names for themselves in and out of the Rocks, including Buty, Reininger, Dunham, Reynvaan, Three Rivers, Dusted Valley, Amavi, Abeja, Waters, Va Piano, aMaurice, Maison Bleue, Rôtie, and L'Ecole No 41. There is, in short, a quorum with which to build this terroir-driven regional identity.

The revival of Syrah in the Walla Walla Valley rekindled interest in Rhône varieties elsewhere in the state. Grenache and Mourvèdre have found homes in the Horse Heaven Hills and on Red Mountain, where both can achieve a heady level of ripeness without threat of autumn frosts. Also Syrah's northern Rhône counterpart, Viognier, has come into its own in the cooler reaches of the Yakima and Walla Walla valleys. The variety seems to thrive in the warm days and cool nights of this cooler-than-average region, and manages to retain a great deal of acidity even as it reaches full flavor maturity. The result? The wines are fresher and more lively than many California counterparts.

By the middle of the 2000s, contracts on some high quality Rhône-varietal vineyard blocks had opened up in the Yakima Valley, contributing still more to the sense that the varieties had a natural affinity for the terroirs of Washington State. Both Dick Boushey and Jim Holmes, owners of Boushey Vineyard and Ciel du Cheval, had expanded their Rhône variety plantings and freed up some blocks from long-term contracts, so that more people were getting the fruit and making great wine from it. The excellent quality found in these vineyards earned many single-vineyard-designate bottlings.

In 2006 David Lake eased into retirement, and the Columbia Winery decided to relinquish some of its vineyard commitments, including that of the Syrah vines at Red Willow. It was a chance for Mike Sauer to open up his coveted Syrah plantings to multiple interpretations, and producers lined up for the chance.

Red Willow Syrah from the older blocks and from a fine ancillary lower-elevation site, Marcoux Vineyard, became available for the first time. Those in pursuit of the fruit there amounted to an early betting line for quality Syrah producers in the Northwest; they included Owen Roe, Gramercy Cellars, Betz Family, Mark Ryan, Andrew Rich, and Efeste, and that number would grow to nine producers, most of whom produced a vineyard designate.

PART V

BOOMTIME

17

THE BIRTH OF THE RHÔNE RANGERS, 1987–1990

We refer to the Rhône movement as a movement, which implies coordination and organized effort. Prior to 1988 however, this was hardly the case. In 1987 there were less than two dozen Rhône-varietal producers in California. There were vineyards, newly planted, rediscovered, accidental, residing on the slopes of Mt. Veeder and in Oakley's delta flats, on Napa Valley mountaintops, dotting the hills of the transverse valleys of the Central Coast; there were old vines in Mendocino and young vines in Paso Robles; everything was new, and none of it proximal.

In fact it would be hard to imagine a more far-flung collection of California winemakers. Like a dozen tops spinning on a vast tabletop, there was exceptional momentum, lots of kinetic energy, little of it impactful. Aside from fruit sources, plant material, and the occasional phone call, the players were connected by novelty and little else.

To this point, few practitioners had met each other except in passing; most remained ignorant of each other's efforts. Collective knowledge and experience was meager. "We were all pretty much operating alone, very remote from one another," says John Buechsenstein, whose outpost in the McDowell Valley was among the most isolated.

Imagine being Pete Minor, Bill Smith, and Josh Jensen in 1985, about to embark on making Viognier for the first time in this country. Imagine facing your first commercial crop from the stunningly remote outposts of Spring Mountain, Howell Mountain, and Mt. Harlan respectively. What did Viognier want in California? What was its ideal crop load and yield? How was it supposed to taste when it was ripe? Was it susceptible to oxidation? What were the best yeasts to employ? How long should it age, and in what?

Would it be necessary or desirable to induce a malolactic fermentation? Should one occur at all?

There was, in short, an almost limitless number of mistakes to make, and virtually no one to ask for guidance. Vintages occurred just once a year, almost not often enough to learn enough from. Connections to the Rhône Valley and Australia, the remote growing regions where some of the varieties had a tradition, were limited. "The wines were still fairly rustic and coarse," says Buechsenstein. "I remember thinking that by the time we figure out how to make these wines there won't be anyone left interested in trying them."

And yet by 1987 a modest network had begun to emerge. "We phoned each other sometimes with questions during harvest or tips," says Buechsenstein, "'What about that? What do you do when you come across this?' and, of course, 'Do you know anyone who has any extra fruit?'" Now that this style of wine was a category, there came a restless need to improve it. This is what motivated Buechsenstein and his colleague Steve Edmunds, who came into each other's orbit in Mendocino County in 1986. Buechsenstein was just one year into his stint at McDowell; Edmunds had just completed his second vintage for his own label, Edmunds St. John.

Greenwood Ridge Winery sponsored an annual competition called the California Wine Tasting Championship at its winery in the Anderson Valley. Amateurs and professionals squared off to taste wine flights; points were scored for guessing the correct variety, with extra points for vintage, region, and winery. Edmunds and Buechsenstein faced off in the "Professional Singles" category, and at the end of the competition they were tied for first place. "There was a taste off," says Edmunds, "and he won."

They kept in contact. Before the year was out Edmunds had paid a visit to Buechsenstein in the McDowell Valley, where they discussed for the first time an event to gather together all of the Rhône variety producers. "We thought it would be great to taste each other's wines side by side," says Edmunds, "and talk about some of the issues we all faced trying to do this. So we started pulling together names and putting our heads together to try and pull something off."

They identified twenty-one wineries across the state with some semblance of a Rhône program, and started planning a get-together in the Bay Area, a reasonable gathering point. As a venue, Edmunds suggested Lalime's, a Mediterranean-inspired restaurant then in Albany, not far from many of the places that Rhône producers frequented, including Kermit Lynch, Trumpetvine, and Solano Cellars.

Lalime's was owned by two couples: two Armenian friends, Vahe Keushguerian and Haig Krikorian, had become brothers-in-law by marrying two sisters, Cindy and Andrea Lalime. Haig was a talented chef, while Vahe ran the front of the house and managed the wine list. Vahe agreed to open the doors of the restaurant on a Monday, usually a dark night.[1]

Buechsenstein drafted a letter, proposing a tasting and dinner on Monday, December 7, 1987, with just producers and guests. Of 21 producers, 19 responded yes; with spouses and winemakers, a total of 37 people attended. Wines were assembled, uncorked, and placed on unset tables. A good deal of the first hour was spent getting acquainted, tasting each other's wines, soliciting comments and opinions. Then everyone sat down for a meal. Krikorian prepared pizzette, a goat cheese salad, grilled pheasant, rack of lamb, heaping plates of French cheeses.

Business was discussed. Some producers, like John McCready, were eager to form a formal organization to promote and market the category. Others, like Bob Lindquist, preferred to keep things loose. "The best thing about the organization," he said of the early years, "is that there was no organization."[2] The matter was discussed at length but no formal agreement was reached. Also discussed was the prospect of giving the group a name. "A few very lame suggestions were thrown out there," says Edmunds, "and basically the subject was dropped."

There were many, many bottles of wine opened and tasted that evening. To Edmunds, it was fairly clear that much of the wine bore the mark of their makers' isolation. The best possessed a rustic charm and faint resemblance to counterparts in France, while less successful bottlings made it plain that there was still much to learn. For the category to improve, lines of communication would have to be established.

The following day Edmunds wrote a press release giving a brief account of the proceedings, which was sent to most of the prominent journalists of the day. "Producers gathered to dine, taste one another's wines, and discuss common concerns," he wrote, cataloguing the varieties and blends tasted, and the wines presented. He laid out the menu highlights and proposed future endeavors: "Participants engaged in a lively discussion regarding future meetings, the possible formation of an informal association of California Rhône variety producers, and the likelihood of public events to acquaint consumers with these unusual wines."[3]

One wrote back: "I received a press release regarding your tasting on December 7 of wines made from Rhône Valley grape varieties that have been planted in California," wrote Robert M. Parker, Jr. on February 16, 1988. "I am the author of a book on the Rhône Valley and Provence and have always been interested in the potential for top quality wines made from the viognier, syrah, mourvedre, as well as roussanne, marsanne and grenache in California."[4] He requested that each participating winery send him sample bottles for review, and offered to pay for their transport. Within a week Edmunds and Buechsenstein had alerted Lalime's attendees, urging participants to submit wines for review. The underdogs had found their crusader.

Robert Parker came to his role predisposed to the Rhône Valley and its varieties. His first visit to the Rhône Valley was in 1970, on the way to the French Riviera. He was struck with the sunny warmth of the place and taken with the wines, simple and delicious, which to him seemed to reflect the sights and smells of its neighbor, Provence.

When he returned he sought out what he could about the region, and found there was little to go on—Alexis Lichine, André Simon, and Frank Schoonmaker had all written about the region sparingly and without much depth or enthusiasm. "There wasn't a lot of information, which struck me as odd, given how good the wines were."[5]

On a return trip to France in 1973 Parker and his wife splurged on a meal at the famed three-star restaurant Taillevent in Paris. There he perused the wine list and found many things he would have liked to drink, from Bordeaux and Burgundy especially, all of them too dear for the young lawyer to afford.

So he settled on something he could afford, a well-priced 1955 Chateauneuf-du-Pape from Chateau Mont-Redon, a wine that added to the luster of a memorable evening. It was so good in fact that on subsequent visits to Taillevent he sampled more of the '55 and of the '61 ("I did my duty," he wrote in the second edition of *Wines of the Rhône Valley,* "in nearly exhausting their stock").[6] Those memorable wines, he said later, ignited his passion for the region past the point of no return.

In 1978, Parker made his first trip to the region as a wine critic, a ritual that would be repeated more than thirty times over the next three decades. Early on he remained surprised by how little known these wines were; it became his duty, as advocate of the underdog, to tell the world about them. To Parker Rhône wines embodied the essence not only of an entire country, but of his entire enterprise, a world yet undiscovered which he could help reveal. Parker decided to be the man to bring these treasures to light, "wines that transcend normal wine vocabulary and establish new tasting parameters for even the most advanced wine enthusiast."[7]

He loved the wines of Guigal, Chapoutier, and Chave, of Rayas, of Henri Bonneau and August Clape, and bestowed high scores on these wines, adding to their already august reputations. He visited their properties and tasted from barrel in their cellars; the wines, he wrote, were "the very heart and soul of France," adding "despite the grandeur many of them may possess there is nothing pretentious about their prices or their proprietors. They represent France's and the world's most underrated great wines."[8]

Parker published *Wines of the Rhône Valley and Provence* in 1987. It was not the first book on the region, but it was perhaps the most visible in this country to date, benefiting from his wine buyer's guides and his hugely influential 1985 tome on Bordeaux.

It is an impressive book to read now—Parker loves to flaunt his critical authority, and when speaking of the wines of Bordeaux and California he rarely misses an opportunity. But in both editions of his Rhône books, there is an added fervor in his prose, an uptick in hyperbole, an enthusiasm he does little to muffle with critical distance or reserve. Asked whether he felt that these were his most passionate books to date, he agreed completely: "I always thought of it [the Rhône] as a sort of viticultural underdog that deserved more attention."[9]

These young California upstarts represented another cadre of underdogs to the critic. They fit seamlessly not only into the zeitgeist of the Rhône as he perceived it, but with his enduring motivation to champion the overlooked and undiscovered. Parker came to the project of tasting these wines predisposed to liking them, and in his wine buyer's guide no. 57, he aired his enthusiasm.

The results of the *Wine Advocate's* first focused tasting of American Rhône-variety wines were published on June 30, 1988. "I recently tasted through the impressive offerings of eighteen (18) California wineries which are making wines from syrah, mourvedre, grenache, viogneir, roussanne and marsanne,"[10] writes Parker in the lead-in to the section, titled "California Syrah, Mourvedre, Grenache and Viognier (Great Promise!)."

"These are the major grape varieties of the Rhône Valley and have been planted in California with remarkable results." Not without a bit of self-congratulation, he continues: "I immediately asked myself why no one in the wine media seems to be paying any attention to some extraordinary and historic winemaking efforts. Certainly the quality of a number of wines was exceptionally promising."

This was an era that preceded the heated, grade-inflated 2000s by more than a decade; the scores then were more evenly weighted between 50 and 100, which is to say Parker was routinely scoring wines in the seventies and low eighties, even as he praised them. He gave his highest score, 91, to Bonny Doon's barrel-fermented Roussanne (a wine we would later learn was probably Viognier) which he described as "awesome," a wine "with the flavor, depth and dimension and depth of Ramonet Montrachet."[11]

He praised other Bonny Doon wines, Le Cigare Volant and the Old Telegram, and was equally taken with the Edmunds St. John Mourvèdre, Sean Thackrey's Orion, Kendall Jackson's Durell Vineyard Syrah, Domaine de la Terre Rouge's Rhône blend, and the first release Viognier from Joseph Phelps (90 points), "a fabulously scented, rich dry, full bodied wine that explodes on the palate," he wrote. "When can we see more?"[12]

In all thirty-five wines were tasted, of which twenty-six scored 85 and above—analogous, probably, to scores of 90 and above today. Parker's followers, who tended to express their enthusiasms with their pocketbook, responded with a flurry of purchases. "The phone started ringing," says Edmunds. "People started calling from all over the country, consumers, distributors. It seemed like a great splash at the time."

One month after the Lalime's tasting, the movement was given another incalculable boost—they adopted a name.

Steve Edmunds is credited with putting the name Rhône Rangers into play, but he gives credit for the name itself to a retailer named Mike Higgins. Higgins owned an Oakland wine shop called Vino! which Edmunds frequented, and to whom he sold wine occasionally. Higgins says that in one of the many idle midafternoon hours in the store, he came up with the notion of bottling a proprietary blended wine and calling it The Rhône Ranger. When the wine didn't take flight, he mentioned it to Edmunds the next time Edmunds was in the store.

"Mike had some of my wine in his shop," says Edmunds, "and while I was visiting he said that he'd had this idea that I should change the name of my blend Les Côtes Sauvage to The Rhône Ranger." Edmunds thought about this for a moment, and said "That's just about the dumbest thing I've ever heard," but as he drove away it occurred to him that the name could serve another purpose: "Almost immediately I realized that this would be the perfect name for this group."

In 1988, the group finally captured the attention of the most influential sectors of the press. Soon every major newspaper and magazine that reported on wine heralded the existence of a new category, with an irresistible moniker: The Rhône Rangers.

Almost from the first, the praise was extreme. The wines were embraced as historic, heretical, innovative, their producers subversive, contrarian, nonconformist—all this well before the category had proven it was worthy of the distinction: "In a very real sense," wrote Eleanor and Ray Heald in the April 1989 edition of *Wine & Spirits* magazine, "Rhône varieties like syrah, grenache and mourvedre have been rescued from extinction in California by Randall Grahm and the Rhône Rangers."[13] "They will be remembered as visionaries," wrote Harvey Steiman in the *Wine Spectator* in 1989, "not just as an obscure group fooling around with unfamiliar grape varieties."[14]

In July of 1988, Buechsenstein and Edmunds planned a follow-up event, this one held at Oliveto Restaurant in Oakland, to which the press was invited. It was well represented—*Bon Appetit*'s Anthony Dias Blue attended, as did Gerald Boyd (*San Francisco Chronicle*), Dan Berger (*Los Angeles Times*), and Larry Walker, then of the trade journal *Wines & Vines*. Meanwhile, Edmunds composed a letter to his fellow producers announcing plans for the Oliveto event, leading with the salutation "Greetings, fellow Rhône Ranger."

A freelance writer named Bill O'Brien, who attended the Oliveto event, was the first to use the Rhône Ranger caption in print, in an East Bay free paper called *The Monthly*, published in October of 1988. It was adorned with a clever illustration by Pablo Haz of five Rangers, each astride a spigoted barrel and armed with bottles and corkscrews, each engaged, to one degree or another, in rootin' and tootin'.' Haz's illustration would embellish much of the Rangers' early literature (and the cover of this book), and O'Brien's article helped establish an element of whimsy in the movement's efforts.

In March 1989, Frank Prial devoted his *New York Times* Wine Talk column to the new Rhône varieties inhabiting California soil, and followed up with a much longer story in the *New York Times (Sunday) Magazine* in October of the same year. Articles in the *Los Angeles Times, San Francisco Chronicle,* and the *Chicago Tribune* quickly followed on the heels of Prial's first articles.

All wrote breathlessly about this new trend, brimming with enthusiasm and expressions of gratitude, as if, finally, there was something new to write about on the American wine scene: "The trend towards these Rhône-style wines is a wonderful breakthrough," wrote Frank Prial in his March 15, 1989 column in the *New York Times*, "not just for the consumer but for the producers, who have been concentrating all their efforts on trying to come up with yet another style of cabernet or chardonnay, many of which taste the same."

But none of these efforts had the impact of a single cover story appearing in the *Wine Spectator* on April Fool's Day, 1989. There, the movement acquired its poster boy: Randall Grahm.

In 1989 the *Wine Spectator* was still a fairly colloquial effort, some years away from the authoritative voice it would earn in the industry. Its coverage was still a bit loose and informal as it actively sought to avoid the snobbishness inherent in most wine writing. This was a quintessentially American wine publication; it lacked airs and was proud of that fact, and its calculated irreverence closely matched that of the Ranger ethos.

Only one year before the *Spectator* had changed its format to roughly that of its current form, from an unfolded tabloid to an oversized staple-bound edition. It was still evolving into its glossier countenance, and still possessed an irreverent spirit, as evidenced by the design of the April Fool's edition in 1989, which bore two covers: the joke back cover featured a comely young woman in a lycra bikini propped alongside a signed magnum of Mouton Rothschild, and leaden headlines that read "First Annual Swimsuit Issue," "Geraldo Rivera: Favorite Wines of Serial Killers," and "Pre-Phylloxera Nouveau Beaujolais: Do They Age?" On the front cover of the non-mock edition was Grahm.

Harvey Steiman, one of two *Spectator* critics covering California at the time, wrote the cover article. The other, James Laube, covered the state's Cabernet, Chardonnay, and Merlot; Steiman took on less conventional bottlings, from Zinfandels and other heritage varieties to the emergent Italian varietals just getting a foothold in the market. He was about to get very busy.

Steiman had been tracking Rhône varietal wines in California. Many were already being sent to the offices of the magazine, but for this article he sought out all he could find. In the mid-eighties he had become conversant with most of Phelps's Rhône bottlings, as well as the wines of Estrella River and Steve Edmunds. But he was most taken with both the wines of Bonny Doon, quite independent of Randall Grahm's irresistible energy.

Of course once he met Grahm, Steiman learned the winemaker was just as colorful as his wines. He was taken with Grahm's intellect as much as his panache with marketing. "He's a very smart guy," says Steiman, "more commercial than he owned up to. He was very persuasive, and knew how to make wines people wanted to buy. Part of the reason we wanted to do the Rhône story was because there weren't a lot of people in the business as charismatic as him."[15]

According to Grahm, it was the *Spectator*'s idea to dress him up as the Rhône Ranger. "I get a call out of the blue," says Grahm, "with them saying 'We want to take your picture, would you mind?'" Grahm said sure. He was less amused at having to supply his own outfit, though he had no trouble finding one: "Santa Cruz is very theatrical," he says, "you can always get a costume if you need one.

"Then they ask me, 'And can you, just like, bring a *horse* to the photo shoot?'" says Grahm. "I was like 'What? You want a horse?' 'A *white* horse.' I figured if they wanted a horse, I'd get them a horse. I said, 'Yeah, I'll see what I can do.'" He borrowed a white mare from one of his neighbors (his vineyards were surrounded by horse farms). It had a black diamond on his forehead, so they applied white shoe polish to cover it.

"In a world obsessed with Cabernet and Chardonnay," wrote Steiman, "the 35-year-old owner and winemaker of Bonny Doon Vineyards has staked his future on Syrah, Grenache, Mourvèdre, Marsanne, Roussanne, and Viognier, the primary grapes of the

Rhône region of France. His future is by no means certain, but so far he has put together an amazing string of brilliant wines that have made him the man of the hour in California."[16]

In the picture Grahm stands next to the horse, wearing a powder blue polyester cowboy suit, red scarf, a harlequin's diamond; his long curls spill out from under a white Stetson. Around his waist is a holster, which holds a pair of Muscat bottles. He's beaming—even the horse wears a bemused expression that suggests he too is in on the joke. The headline reads: "Randall Grahm, California's Rhône Ranger." In that single indelible, iconic image, the course of the movement's next several years was established: Grahm became the Rhône Ranger—he was typecast. "He took the ball," said Steve Edmunds, "and he ran with it."

Tucked behind a feature article about Grahm was perhaps the most comprehensive critical assessment of American Rhône wines to date, with the first formal evaluations of the wines. Steiman cannily interviewed a select group of French vignerons, including Daniel Brunier of Domaine du Vieux Télégraphe, Michel Bettane of *Revue du Vins du France,* and Francois Perrin of Chateau de Beaucastel, who by this time was looking to stake his claim in California soil. "I think California has more of a future in the Rhône grapes than with Cabernet or Chardonnay," said Perrin. "The climate is more suitable. Twenty years ago, when California was making its way, Bordeaux was considered the model."[17] Phelps, McDowell, Edmunds St. John, Cline, and others are favorably mentioned, and Steiman wrote forty tasting notes.

As a marketing entity, "The Rhône Ranger" became one of the most potent tools ever employed in the American wine industry, an indelible, irresistible icon, a caricature that the public could readily embrace, even if the category of wines it represented hadn't yet been fully defined. With Grahm as its principal spokesman and *agent provocateur,* the Rangers would go on to dominate the imagery of Rhône variety wines for the next two decades. You could hardly have a tasting of these wines without someone donning a cowboy hat, wielding a six-shooter, vest, or a sheriff's badge—and the dominant color a brilliant red.

With the help of Grahm and other seditious elements, they successfully cast their wines as maverick, rebellious, subversive. Cabernet and Chardonnay were decried as "establishment" varieties, the vinous equivalent of the dominant paradigm, while Rhône varieties, with their exotic flavor profiles and relatively ignoble stature outside of the heralded realms of Burgundy, Champagne, and Bordeaux, were thought of as countercultural and cool. These were wines of the people, and the message resonated deeply in northern California, especially in its cultural center the Bay Area, which remained proud of its history of subversion, a place where the contrarian and the unconventional were still privileged.

No one used these rhetorical devices with more flourish than Grahm, who employed his considerable verbal gifts in a fiercely productive period of creative marketing—like a songwriter cranking out hit after hit, Grahm went through a period of promotion that seemed boundlessly fertile. None of it was particularly well-aimed, or for that matter targeted for broad appeal. On the contrary, Grahm's skills lay in parodying a pantheon of utterly esoteric literary texts if you had a Ph.D. in English you might stand a chance at getting all the jokes—but in most instances his so-called promotions flew over the head of nearly every target.

But what he lacked in literary populism he made up for in excess. He wrote huge tracts: "Don Quijones, the Man for Garnacha" and "A Clockwork Orange Muscat" and "The Rimeshot of the Ancient Marsanner" and not least, the rock opera "Born to Rhône" (with apologies to Bruce Springsteen).

Grahm wrote light verse, haiku, limericks, iambic pentameter, musicals, epics, and operas, composing newsletters that extended into the thousands of words. He approached the marketing newsletter with the skills of a comp lit professor, with an almost defiantly esoteric approach and execution so high-falutin' as to be almost off-putting. As the promotions grew more baroque, it almost seemed as if he was playing a game of one-upmanship with himself.

And somehow, all of it worked. An entire generation of American wine drinkers tuned in to his antics to see what he'd come up with next. Grahm's literary shenanigans came to exemplify the seditious nature of the Rhône message. Whether or not you bought into the message (and many producers chafed at its frivolity, fearing they and their wines wouldn't be taken seriously), there was no question that, just as Steiman had proclaimed, the Rhône Rangers had gone from unknowns to visionaries, almost overnight. With Grahm striking a nerve, the entire industry lurched into motion, powered by Rhône varieties, liberated by the winemakers who made them. Tastings, wine dinners, wine pairings, and events became more and more common, and more welcome, and the Rhône messaging crept into the lexicon of American wine appreciation.

18

THE ACADEMIC BACKUP FOR
THE AMERICAN RHÔNE MOVEMENT

Robert M. Parker, Jr.'s report in July of 1988 cast a glowing light upon Rhône Ranger efforts, but it didn't solve the collective problem of a lack of experience. Rhône varietal wines would have no traction in the market without quality wines to back up the rhetorical claims, and while communication lines opened after 1988, there was still much to learn. "We were just a bunch of guys throwing wines down on a table and getting people to come taste them," says Steve Edmunds, "I mean how much of a group *was* this group?"[1]

There remained persistent questions for many of the American practitioners of Rhône varietal wines, about winemaking, blending, about vine growing for the rapidly growing pantheon of varieties, about ways to tease out a variety's ideal expression. How did the *élevage* for Syrah, for Grenache, for Mourvèdre and Viognier differ from other French varieties in California soil? What was the proper handling of these wines in the fermenting tank? In the cellar? Most of the winemakers now taking the lead in this new category were still woefully inexperienced, relying on intuition, good sense, and plenty of luck for their successes to date but very little practical knowledge of the genre they were creating.

Fortunately for them, a scholar came into their midst with just the sort of practical knowledge all of them lacked. A journalist and author named Robert Mayberry had been quietly toiling in the vineyards of southern France, gathering winemaking information from old vignerons from Vienne to Vaucluse, and had published this collection of secrets in a book called *The Wines of the Rhône Valley: A Guide to Origins*, which described in an almost inscrutable shorthand the secrets of dealing with the varieties in the Rhône pantheon.

When he published his book he knew almost nothing of the winemakers who were toiling in California to make similar wines, but they quickly found him. It changed the prospects of the willing almost overnight. "All of a sudden," says John Buechsenstein, "we had something to work with."

Robert Mayberry was born in 1938 on the heels of Prohibition to an all but teetotaling household in Morristown, New Jersey. From an early age he excelled in writing and literature, majoring in English and philosophy at Swarthmore College; he went on to earn a master's degree in English at Cornell, with an emphasis on creative writing. At Cornell two things interested him; first, the Pragmatists, an important philosophical movement of the nineteenth and early twentieth century whose most visible figure was William James. James's guiding principle involved the employment of practical application in theoretical pursuit. "He believed that to really learn something," says Mayberry, "you had to learn to *do* something"—a thing that extended to teaching, too.[2]

Mayberry's other great interest was wine and food, a passion he shared with his future wife, Rozelyn, who was herself raised in a family loving wine. Just across the street from Mayberry's dormitory was a wine shop whose proprietor Mayberry befriended, and he started to take a great interest in it. He and Roz spent their courtship preparing meals out of Julia Child's cookbooks and trying out new wines from France. "That was our social life," says Mayberry, "We didn't party. We ate and drank wine."

For their honeymoon in the summer of 1966 they took a trip to France, touring the country's wine regions, testing the limits of their language skills in the Loire Valley, in Paris, in the villages of Beaujolais. They got as far south as Tain l'Hermitage and tasted the wines of Jaboulet in that village; that is where Mayberry first got the notion to focus on the Rhône Valley, which hadn't yet been written about in any significant detail, compared with Burgundy, Bordeaux, and Champagne.

In 1971 Mayberry received his first academic appointment, as a founding faculty member of William James College, in what was then known as the Grand Valley State Colleges in Allendale, Michigan, on the shores of the lake. In keeping with James's Pragmatist tenets, Mayberry was instructed to pick a course of study which would be the medium for his journalistic enterprise as he taught, a course of study which would define his professional life. Without hesitation, Mayberry chose Rhône Valley wine as his subject.

For the next twenty years, Mayberry and his wife spent every summer break, and most sabbaticals, in southern France. They used a rental property in the village of Vaison la Romaine, near Chateauneuf-du-Pape, eventually renting a small suite of rooms from the curé of Vacqueyras, a rotund priest named Père Michel, whose vow of poverty made him especially appreciative of the open bottles of wine his renters made available to him each evening.

In those years, Mayberry estimates he visited 300 Rhône producers multiple times, tasting wines from barrel and from multiple vintages (usually the wines in bottle he would taste over the course of at least two days).

This was not easily done. The winegrowers of southern France were a difficult group to get close to, says Roz, who had studied music in France and not only knew French fluently, but a bit of Provencale as well, a bonus that eventually endeared her to several producers.

"French peasants are insular, tough-minded, close-mouthed," she says; "they didn't talk to each other, didn't taste each other's wines. They were peasants, *paysans* in the French sense of the word, as someone tied to the earth. So a huge part of what Robert did initially was to get these people to trust him, to open up to him and talk about how they made their wines, what they did and why they did it. He worked enormously hard at that."

And he was admired for his determination. "Growers frequently appreciated and commented on the fact that Robert came, stayed, paid attention, asked questions, listened, tasted over and over, visited and revisited their wines over a period of years," says Roz, "unlike most Americans, who breezed in for a cursory glance, a swish and a spit. I often heard Rhône growers make the distinction that he was *sérieux,* unlike most American critics." Mayberry gained access to and befriended hundreds of producers; indeed, no one in the English-speaking world outside of perhaps John Livingstone-Learmonth was better connected, especially with respect to the southern Rhône. "They loved and respected him tremendously," says Roz; eventually, he was given perhaps the most lofty compliment of all, when they stopped referring to him as 'the American;' instead, they started calling him *le Prof.*"

Eventually, Mayberry compiled a selection of his vast collection of tasting notes and profiles into one volume, *Wines of the Rhône Valley,* published in 1987. Mayberry had amassed so much information that the manuscript overwhelmed his publisher, Rowman & Littlefield, who asked him to trim the volume to a manageable size. But rather than cut material, Mayberry decided to abbreviate huge tracts of winemaking data to conform to the publisher's page counts. The result is a book written virtually in an encrypted language, a tangle of abbreviations, concatenations, elisions, and codes. Whole sections are indecipherable to any but the most dedicated reader. Mayberry abbreviates varieties, villages, soil types, and winemaking methods, as in this excerpt on Domaine de la Serriere:

> 75 ha, one group of parcels in qrt St.-Jean and Pied Redun (E), the rest S and NW. About ¼ of the vines are more than 50 years old. Red cepages, eastern portion: 80% GR, 10–12% SY, around 5% MV. Remainder: 70% GR, 10% CS, 10% SY, 10% diverse, 5 ha of white: BR, CT, CR, with RS and PL. 12 ha of CDV at Caromb (Vaucluse), 90% GR, plus CR (was to plant SY 1985).[3]

His method, however, was systematic and impeccable, and many of his overarching remarks on each domaine were limpid, precise, and insightful, as here, on Vieux Télégraphe:

> It becomes ever clearer that Vieux Télégraphe is one of the great masterpieces of the aesthetic tension definitive of Chateauneuf du Pape—that between alcoholic warmth and

richness and an ensemble of alcohol-volatilized fragrances that are fresh and cool, leafy, resinous, even mentholated. To this add flowers, essential oils, truffles, and hints of stones and seawater from the terroir.[4]

Despite almost routine flashes of descriptive brilliance, this was not the sort of book that would appeal to a general reader seeking more information on the Rhône Valley. No, this was an instructional manual, a set of crib notes for geeks. And John Buechsenstein was precisely the sort of geek to whom this peculiar book would appeal.

In California, no one quite remembers how Robert Mayberry came onto the radar. Steve Edmunds says that someone from Michigan, he doesn't remember who, visited his winery and mentioned a professor in Michigan who was writing about Rhône wines, a fact that Edmunds privately held to be preposterous. Edmunds asked Kermit Lynch, who told him that there *was* someone, an American, working in the Rhône and known as *le Prof,* but Lynch had never met him. Finally Edmunds tracked him down through an article he was able to find on Tavel in *Practical Winery and Vineyard Management,* an article so incisive that Edmunds says "it basically taught me how to make rosé wine." Then Mayberry's book appeared, and Mayberry was no longer spectral.

Edmunds and Buechsenstein devoured its contents. "This book had the detail I felt I needed to know," says Buechsenstein. "Robert went into production methodology, he picked the brains of everybody, why they did what they did, why their grandfathers did. The little things we couldn't know anything about. He captured the traditions of the region, he recognized them as important details, and we ate them up."[5]

Mayberry's book put both men leagues ahead of where they'd been one vintage earlier. It unlocked secrets from French producers that were simple in practice, if you knew to practice them. It gave winemakers a glimpse into a multigenerational methodology, practices unique to the Rhône that no one had recorded yet in English; it was a treasure trove of winemaking insight hiding in plain sight.

Less than a year after its publication, Buechsenstein was able to persuade Mayberry to teach a class on southern Rhône winemaking at the Davis extension in 1988. They were taken with each other. "He was such an articulate guy," says Edmunds, "so thoughtful, presenting things in a manner that I had never imagined thinking about them before. He helped us understand the things that made the Rhône Valley unique vis-à-vis the other winegrowing regions in France."

The first of these classes was held on December 3, 1988, in which Mayberry covered an extraordinary range, from Côte-Rôtie to the southern Côtes du Rhône villages. He described the complex geographical systems which delineated these subregions and their climates, sunlight, rainfall, and winemaking for each variety grown there.

Mayberry's lectures were careful, thorough, pragmatic. He had become one of the Rhône Valley's most accomplished students of typicity—he developed, for his book, a kind of template of flavors and textures to expect from the Grenache of Sablet, as opposed to the Grenache from Gigondas. Few could delineate a given variety in greater detail, with greater nuance: Côte-Rôtie Syrah, for him, exhibited violets, pine resin, tobacco, and black raspberry; Saint-Joseph Syrah more meat, fat, and cinnamon, while Hermitage's aromatics fell more to sorrel, truffle, cassis, and flint; the Marsanne from Hermitage displayed sour grass and green apples, more so than the Marsanne from Saint-Joseph, which showed an aromatic profile more like clover honey.

Eventually his instruction turned to winemaking practices in the Rhône, with methodologies about barrel use, stem use, maceration periods, the intricacies of *élevage*. He explored in great detail the topic of blends—American producers of course knew that Côtes du Rhône wines were often blends, but were inexperienced in how to interpret them, how to parse the flavors of one variety from another. They knew even less about the rationale for them, and how the varieties fit together, the role of each component, and how they came together in an intricate matrix for a wine to achieve a state of balance. Mayberry guided them.

Mayberry's organizing principles proved to be vital to the new winemakers. He had analyzed every winemaking step in the southern Rhône, had codified hundreds of years of tradition into fairly practical rationales and methodologies.

In Bordeaux the major factor in the character of wine was tannin; in Burgundy it was acid; Mayberry argued compellingly that in the southern Rhône, the character-defining trait was alcohol. Alcohol was the given, and could detract from a wine at times; the trick was to make a harmonious wine using alcohol as one of the elements.

He detailed the things that set the Rhône apart, the clay-and-limestone soils, the Mistral, the incredible heat of the summer. With respect to Chateauneuf-du-Pape, Mayberry insisted that the best of these wines were successful for the way they managed their Grenache component, and by extension, their alcohols. "He taught us that, in the south, the way in which Grenache oxidizes organizes the winemaking effort," explained Edmunds, "that most winemaking was designed to ameliorate that tendency, by using Mourvèdre and Syrah as reductive 'counterweights,' to bind the stuff that makes Grenache oxidative."

Over that next decade Mayberry and Buechsenstein assembled a number of Rhône-inspired classes, on winemaking, on the valley itself, on California counterparts, with topics like "Rhône Varietal Production in California," "Rhône Reds in California and France," "Syrah and Viognier in the Northern Rhône and California," and "Marsanne, Roussanne, and Syrah." Buechsenstein was able to draw funds from the university that allowed him to bring in an all-star selection of winemakers from the Rhône to supplement Mayberry's instruction, including Daniel Brunier of Domaine du Vieux Télégraphe, Jean-Pierre Perrin of Chateau de Beaucastel, Alain Graillot of Domaine Graillot, Alain Dugas of Chateau La Nerthe, as well as dignitaries from the AOC agencies of Côtes du Rhône and InterRhône.

Star power like this drew an astonishing cross section of the young and ambitious in California winemaking, including Heidi Barrett, Sonoma grower John Clendenen,

Preston winemaker Kevin Hamel, Hess Collection winemaker Robert Craig, Lou Preston, Folie a Deux winemaker Scott Harvey, Cain winemaker Christopher Howell, Sierra Vista winemaker John McCready, Zelma Long, Kathryn Kennedy, Charles Ortman, David Ready, Clark Smith, Fred Schroeder, Andrew Rich, Douglas Nalle, Ward Noble, Philip Staley, Bob Steinhauer, Rudy von Strasser, Hugh Chapelle, Ken Brown, Paul Hobbs, William Jekel, Steven MacRostie, Ed Sbragia, Delia Viader, Don and Margo Van Staaveren, Rich Kunde, Nick Goldschmidt, David Gates, Jim Moore, Eli Parker, David Ramey, Craig Williams, Andrew Murray, Leon Sobon, Robert Brittan, Robert Blue, Dennis Fife, Karen McNeil, Larry Hyde, Derek Trowbridge, and Anthony Truchard.

Not only did Mayberry dispense information through his books and lectures, he became a vital conduit between newly established import companies and worthy Côtes du Rhône producers, who were themselves coming into their own, and waiting to be discovered. Mayberry helped them with that process.

The Côtes du Rhônes in the American market just prior to this period were still fairly rustic, even ponderous wines, subdued by long periods of *élevage* on oak foudres, whose full expression was sometimes held in check by reduction, brettanomyces, and other bacteriological impediments, which cut into their freshness.

But in the late seventies and early eighties the zeitgeist was shifting even in the Côtes du Rhône. Small producers from Valréas to Vaucluse were tossing out dirty barrels, applying fresh coats of epoxy on their concrete vats, buying stainless steel tanks or purchasing clean used foudres. They were scalding the dank corners of their cellars with hot water jets. They were making better fruit selections. They were using stems to bring out new exotic flavors in lieu of oak aging. Most importantly they were bottling wine; from the end of the Second World War until the mid-seventies, the wines of southern Rhône villages had found their way into négociant tanks or cooperative stores, where producers could be spared the expense of bottling their wines, much less marketing and selling them. When your product was selling for $40 a case and less, even bottles (and bottling lines) seemed out of reach.

At the time a few producers had pierced through the veil of rusticity to make wines that managed to exhibit the exotic, *sauvage* flavors that Americans associated with the Rhône, but with an additional element—freshness—captured in a bottle with bright fruit and exceptional charm.

In his annual sojourns across the southern Rhône, Robert Mayberry was making note of these changes and paying attention to the producers of little wines that were heeding the lessons from more progressive producers in Chateauneuf-du-Pape and Gigondas. Mayberry was among the first to recognize the effortless charm found in Côtes du Rhône Villages wines as they modernized, emerging from the region's cultural and economic torpor. And as he opened doors, smart suppliers followed him through.

One such entrepreneur was Stephen Grant, a Chicago importer with an abiding interest in the Rhône and in wines of authentic regional expression. Grant met Mayberry in a Michigan wine shop, the two hit it off, and Mayberry assisted Grant in introducing him to several producers, most completely unknown. "These were utterly uncommercial wines," says Grant. "Nobody knew about them; they weren't even under the radar—there was no radar."[6] Grant eventually imported several of these producers; through Mayberry he was introduced to Jean Steinmaier of Domaine Sainte-Anne (Saint-Gervais), Romain Bouchard (Valréas), Paul Joyet of Domaine des Girasols (Rasteau), Remy Klein of Domaine Remejeanne (Cadignac), and the Alary brothers, Frederick and Francois, of Domaine de l'Oratoire St. Martin (Cairanne).

Grant and Mayberry both had a special fondness for these traditional village wines, wines from lesser appellations that required less time in oak casks, making up for their relative lack of complexity with their freshness and charm. "This was a group that wasn't pushing things," says Grant, "who believed in ripe clean fruit, who were careful not to pick too ripe or too early either—that was common, because they were afraid of rot at harvest."

After harvest in 1989 Mayberry and Grant put together a tasting of wines that represented this new breed of producers from the Côtes du Rhône, and presented them to Buechsenstein and Edmunds, who flew out in November. They met at Grant's father-in-law's house in Evanston, Illinois, set up a folding card-table in the basement, surrounded by unpacked moving boxes, and uncorked thirty wines, young vintages, from younger vintages and older ones, too, which Grant was keen on displaying. "We really wanted to look at wines with bottle age," he says, "to find out how this stuff evolved."

The wines were a revelation to Buechsenstein and Edmunds alike. "The whole day blew us away," says Buechsenstein, "we'd never seen wines like this before. I kept coming back to the Grenache, to the power of the Grenache, again and again I kept smelling these wines and coming to grips with the fact that this was one of the great varieties of the world, particularly when it was older, when it could show those deep, intense resinous flavors after the jam was gone." And it was a variety which existed only nominally, comprised of poor clonal selections, in California—to Buechsenstein, if they could get it right, Grenache felt like the future.

For Edmunds, the wines almost instantly caused him to doubt everything he knew about his craft. "My understanding of winemaking was pretty undeveloped in a lot of respects," he says of that time. "I had it in my mind that since everyone ages wine in barrels, that barrels made a wine better. But these people weren't making wines where the barrel was important; it was the raw material that mattered."

What he discovered in these wines, by contrast, was freshness. "I had never tasted such a young Rhône wine from bottle," he says. "I was astounded by how fresh and pretty these wines were, so much more energetic than when they've been sitting around in barrels for a long time, not primary, not simple or grapey, more a reflection of the origins of the fruit." Even more than this, Edmunds realized he *was familiar* with wines like these; he had encountered them in his own cellar. "I could recognize in the smell of these wines some things I'd noticed in what I was making in California, in the early stages of its development." Edmunds realized in a flash that he could replicate the feel of these wines. "When I got back from Chicago," he says, "I had a whole new sense of what I was going to do in the cellar."

During the course of his time at Davis, Mayberry visited several California wineries interested in developing their Rhône programs, tasting wines, offering advice on methods and flavors. He was tremendously encouraging to those starting out, all the while corroborating his belief that California's climate virtually mirrored that of the southern Rhône.

By the time Mayberry was wrapping up his final classes, he started to have trouble walking; by the late nineties he was diagnosed with multiple sclerosis, a disease which cut short his career and his research. In a room above where he convalesces are several boxes full of papers that would constitute a second edition of a book he never got to complete.

Mayberry is assisted with nearly all of his physical activities. His mind, though, is as sharp as ever, as is his memory. He remains one of the unsung heroes of the American Rhône movement—well, perhaps not altogether unsung.

In January 1998, on the recommendation of the French minister of agriculture, Robert Mayberry was declared a Chevalier d'Honeur de l'Ordre du Merit Agricole, or Order of Honorary Knight, for his contributions to French culture, joining the ranks of Jacques Pepin, Roland Passot, Bernard Loiseau, Elizabeth David, and Kermit Lynch. This honor was bestowed for his book, but it took a French sensibility to recognize how important it was to Mayberry to capture the traditions of this place. His exact sentiments are found within the short talk he gave upon accepting the Order of Knight at the French Consulate in Chicago in September 1998:

"There is a harmony among all things and the places in which they are found." Mayberry began his remarks with this concise quote from Waverly Root's *The Food of France*, and went on to suggest that that harmony was threatened by the encroachment of the mass market, and by technology, and it was our responsibility to watch over and preserve this harmony.

His goal, he says, was simple, "to make sure that the arrival on our shores of Rhône wines and Rhône grape varieties with them came some expression of their meaning, that is, their origins, the processes which produce them, and the social and cultural relations implicated in their production and consumption."[7]

These are the very things he instilled upon his American colleagues. "Until Mayberry's gift of scholarship," says John Buechsenstein, "we'd lacked the detailed frame of reference for how these wines were made. Through his meticulous work we gained sensitivity to their cultural context, viticultural environment, vinification, *élevage*, and flavor outcome. It was like getting the Rosetta Stone; it was what we needed to inform and inspire our work in the New World."[8]

19

THE BRIDGE
FROM CALIFORNIA TO FRANCE
A Colloquium to Bring the Rhônes Together

At the end of the volume of transcripts chronicling the events of the International Colloquium on Rhône Varietals, held in the Napa Valley at the Meadowood Resort, in mid-May 1990, there are two photographs.

In the first, nine winemakers, "The American Contingent," are assembled in two uneven rows trailing up a sloping path. It is a calm, almost moody group shot, as if each person has just emerged from a powerful reverie. They look earnest—more than earnest, they look tremendously serious. Most are wearing the winemaker's equivalent of Sunday best: pressed white shirts, pleated trousers, hair smoothed. Some wear sport coats, some have their sport coats slung over their shoulders. In what is perhaps the most startling detail, nearly all of them are wearing ties. Only the loud floral pattern on Randall Grahm's necktie betrays anything that might be construed as levity.

The second photograph, "The French Contingent," shows a larger group trailing up the same shaded path, crowded into three rows, outnumbering the Americans and looking slightly more bespoke, but also more relaxed: there are fewer ties, at any rate. They look calm and self-assured, and all gaze confidently into the camera, all except for Gerard Pierrefeu, whose gaze has wandered away. Rather unlike the American contingent, many of the French are smiling outright—and the young Michel Chapoutier, looking bookish in bow tie and spectacles, is positively beaming.

We're left to interpret the mood in each photograph. The French seem pleased with themselves, having described the inherent features of the subregions with precision and aplomb (the "physiognomy," as one presenter called it), with Rousseauistic certitude.

They have fulfilled their obligation, have shared without revealing much; to the American audience, the region's mysteries are still mysterious. While they have been impressed with the zeal and the energy of their American counterparts, they do not feel as if these nascent efforts can, nor ever will, measure up to the nearly 2,000-year history of viticulture and winemaking in the Rhône Valley.

The Americans' reverie may come from having butted up against the mildly obfuscatory stance the French have placed before them; or they may be facing, for the very first time, the magnitude of their lack of experience in relation to their guests, and the realization that they, as a generation of producers, will never have the benefit of history to guide them. They have no foundation yet, little to stand on; they have only the present to work with. Indeed, they *are* the foundation of the American Rhône tradition—and the stunned look on their faces may be the apprehension that they have a long, long way to go.

Tucked behind the heads and shoulders of the French producers and participants is Robert Haas, smiling. Haas is not yet an American producer, and not a French one, so he's modestly miscast in the French camp—and yet if anyone has a foot in both, it's him. Without Haas, these two parties would not have come together at all.

In 1989, Robert Haas and his future Tablas Creek partners, the Perrin family, were touring the California countryside in search of suitable vineyard land. As they visited with producers across California, Haas noted just how important these meetings and tastings were for the American producers, many of whom hadn't yet traveled in France, or met a French winemaker, much less one from the Rhône. They were full of questions, and meetings invariably went long past their allotted time. It became clear to Haas that a more formal meeting would be useful.

Few people were better equipped to bring this off than Haas. He was intimately involved in the affairs and the markets of both countries; he had worked with producers on both continents and sold wine in the states from both countries. Furthermore, it was not his first foray into such meetings. In 1986, Haas helped to create an International Symposium on Chardonnay at Sonoma-Cutrer, one of the first-ever gatherings on California soil between French and American producers.

In the mid-1980s Brice Cutrer-Jones came to Haas with the idea to elevate his brand by drawing French and American producers together for a conference. Haas was only too happy to help; he brought over an impressive collection of white Burgundy masters, including Bernard Morey, Gerard Boudrot of Etienne Sauzet, Jean-Marc Boillot, Thierry Matrot. They were joined by Californians Steve Kistler, David Ramey, Mike Grgich, and others. The conference was such a success that the meeting was repeated in some form every four years for the next two decades, alternating between France and California. Haas had this model to draw from as he planned his next joint venture.

For the Rhône colloquium, Haas recruited Bruce Neyers and Richard Keehn to assist with planning and organization. In France, he persuaded Jacques Puisais, president of the Union

National des Oenologues, France's professional organization of winemakers, to organize a French group. Puisais was an old friend of Haas's, and since they had worked together for the Chardonnay symposium, was an old hand at such efforts. Committees were formed to help recruit participants and organize the content of the meeting. Sopexa, a wine-marketing arm of the French government, was involved in logistics and recruiting, and supplemented the travel costs of the French contingent. John Buechsenstein was tasked with coordinating more than a dozen technical presentations, from French and American presenters, which, with dinners and tastings, would form the bulk of the proceedings.

The committees gathered very different groups. The American winemakers included Steve Doerner from Calera, Fred and Matt Cline from Cline Cellars, Bill Easton, Bob Lindquist, Steve Edmunds, Randall Grahm, David Lake, John McCready, Bill Smith, Lou Preston and his winemaker Kevin Hamel, Craig Williams and his assistant Gary Brookman, Pete Minor, Adam Tolmach, and Jed Steele.

The French team included some of the region's most successful winemakers: Marcel Guigal, Michel Chapoutier, and the Perrins were invited; but so too were representatives from the Institut National des Appellations d'Origine, emissaries from the Côtes du Rhône Syndicate, from Comite Interprofessionel de Vins d'AOC des Côtes du Rhône et de la Vallée du Rhône (C.I.C.D.R.) and not least, the renowned ampelographer Pierre Galet, the world's leading expert on vine morphology and identification, who was in the U.S. conducting seminars and making site visits.

Thus the French contingent constituted the region's bureaucratic powers, the veritable keepers of the Rhône Valley, arbiters of appellations and general directors of large wine cooperatives. The disparities between the two groups could not have been more stark: on the one hand, a group of mavericks eager for information, and on the other, a largely august body of authorities, custodians of tradition, responsible not for growing and producing, but for evaluation and assessment.

They came together in May of 1990 at Meadowood, in St. Helena, a picturesque resort set among vineyards and forest at the base of Howell Mountain in the Napa Valley, a property renowned for hosting the Napa Valley Wine Auction, and a setting which certainly wowed the visitors with its bucolic charm.

The organizers—Keehn, Neyers, Haas, Gerard Pierrefeu (president of C.I.C.D.R.), and Jacques Puisais—each delivered opening remarks expressing their hopes for the meeting; Gerard Pierrefeu captured these sentiments best: "Wine is responsible for the best encounters," he said.[1] "I believe that in these moments of coming together, it is wine that helps us get to know each other, share our experiences, and develop friendships. In our evenings here, I am sure we will all take full advantage of it."

Pierrefeu's remarks and indeed every word of the proceedings were recorded, subsequently transcribed and translated into French and English, and distributed to the participants; in addition to the fifteen presentations, the transcript included a full rendering of the question-and-answer sessions following each paper, which were often more informative, and always more lively, than the papers themselves.

More than this, Haas supplied equipment and personnel for on-the-spot translations of each presentation. The audience wore headphones and the speeches were translated by professionals from the Monterey Language Institute, one of the country's best language resources, whom Haas hired at great expense.

The fifteen presentations (the French presented eight papers, the Americans seven) took the form of a detailed introduction to each other's regions. The French laid out the history of the valley, its appellations, its twenty-two varieties; they drew out distinctions between northern and southern Rhône terroirs, explored rosé, red, and white wines in each broad locale.

The Americans reciprocated, inasmuch as they could. After all they had far less to go on, and a limited history from which to draw. But their efforts here represented the first assessment the movement had made of itself.

The differences in approach, however, betrayed an inherent tension: the French rarely questioned their appellation restrictions, while the Americans were still laboring with such distinctions. For the French, *typicité* was a foundation; for the Americans, typicity was still a fuzzy concept; there hadn't been enough time, or enough wines, to make any but the broadest conclusions. And so from their first words, the French contingent and the American contingent were speaking different languages. This may in the end explain the disparities in the photographs: the French rest on their august history, while the Americans, in having met the French, are confronted with, and daunted by, how much they didn't know.

Henry Bouachon and Pierre Galet shared the first presentation, a kind of Rhône 101 seminar that laid out distinctions between northern and southern Rhône practices. Galet introduced thirteen grape varieties, described their ampelography, their habits, their ideal environments, their strengths and weaknesses, focusing on those common to the southern Rhône. Outside of the work of Robert Mayberry, it may have been the most comprehensive introduction to blending practices in the Rhône to date for many of the American team.

The French were followed by Craig Williams, of Joseph Phelps Vineyards, who compiled an excellent historical overview of Rhône varieties in California, rendering a comprehensive history of the category as well as a crash course on Prohibition. The Californians examined Syrah in warm-climate settings and cool (Bob Lindquist delivered harvest data for Paso Robles and the Santa Maria Valley); the Cline brothers reported on the performance of Mourvèdre in the San Joaquin Delta. John McCready made comparative studies of California and Rhône climate data. And Randall Grahm reported on the progress of American Rhône varietal white and rosé wines. Most presentations had a tentative quality, as if each presenter was a little self-conscious of the paucity of their experience.

The French presentations, by contrast, drew on data literally compiled since the birth of Christ, passed from generation to generation, codified during the organization of the appellations, and maintained by governing bodies, sustaining a tradition built upon propriety and time. As such, the French could not be blamed for feeling a little superior. Their diffidence may have been derived in part from their confidence. They never failed to be cordial and polite, but kept their secrets close to their chest.

To this end, the bureaucrats employed jargon; the scholars evoked the canon; the syndicate directors draped themselves in the spirit and letter of terroir, which they defined somewhat opaquely and used as a sweeping rhetorical device to gloss over things which couldn't be explained or which they'd prefer to leave mysterious.

To describe the Americans as eager, by contrast, doesn't fully capture the depth of their zeal. "I have several questions," said Randall Grahm after the conclusion of the first French presentation. "I've been waiting a long time to ask you questions I've been collecting."[2] It was for many their first opportunity to plumb the secrets of the Rhône from its winemakers, and they seemed determined to reap every scrap of knowledge from their guests. They crammed the Q & A with their eager curiosity—on at least two occasions Robert Haas had to intervene, if only to suggest that the topics could be addressed again at dinner.

Whatever reticence may have been present during the daytime discussions melted away during the evening tastings and meals. Each contingent provided a chef for an evening meal. Cindy Pawlcyn was one of Northern California's best known woman chefs and owner of the Napa Valley restaurant Mustard's. The French chef, Franck Gomez, was her equal in reputation. Gomez and his wife, Josiane, ran a Michelin one-star restaurant in the southern Rhône village of Séguret, called La Table du Comtat. Dinners ran late, fueled by bottles from both countries, and much goodwill was forged at each meal.

There is no doubt that the international Colloquium on Rhône Varietals was a useful endeavor, but its lasting effect is somewhat hard to quantify. The American contingent was clearly starstruck, thrilled that their efforts had attracted the attention of their progenitors. Lasting relationships were established during this event, and more than a few trips abroad were planned in these days. The French made overtures to the Americans, suggesting that they would host the next colloquium. Neyers and Haas were keen on continuing the dialogue, and as the years passed the French were reminded of their commitment to host a follow-up, but the meeting never materialized. "My guess is that they felt there was nothing to gain," says Haas, "or perhaps they thought they might have something to fear."

The colloquium is a grand footnote in the Rhône movement narrative, one of the first great acknowledgements that this was a global effort and, potentially, a collaborative worldwide enterprise. But in a few short years an annual celebration with a similar mission would cement that objective and put a public face on the Rhône as a global cause.

20

HOSPICE DU RHÔNE
The Festival to Bring the Rhône World Home

Celebrations abound in the American wine industry, each one of them taking on the personality of the place that serves as its host. In Napa it's the annual wine auction, held at the Meadowood country club in St. Helena in early June, where the very definition of wine as lifestyle has been nurtured for more than thirty years, fueled on canapés from Wolfgang Puck and Thomas Keller, washed down with oceans of ripe Chardonnay and Cabernet, where fat cats swathed in linen and seersucker overspend on large-format bottles of Cabernet Sauvignon, beneath a vast circus tent.

In Oregon it's IPNC, the International Pinot Noir Celebration, reveling in all things Pinot and celebrating the Oregon vine and vibe, with a laid-back mien, a genteel, convivial, slightly quirky cool. In California there's WOPN, the World of Pinot Noir Celebration, a Central Coast carbon copy of IPNC but with a whiff of surf culture, tri-tip barbecue, a mellow white-jean and huarache chic.

For Rhône varieties, for twenty years, the destination has been Hospice du Rhône, in Paso Robles, in the bucolic mid-state region. Paso is to Napa what the southern Rhône is to Bordeaux. The style is laid back, provincial: the preferred garb is bowling shirt and Hawaiian print gabardine, flip flops and unpleated shorts, a cheerful thumb-to-the-nose toward the tonier aspects of wine lifestyle posturing.

Hospice is held at Paso Robles's Mid-State Fairgrounds, a locale so cowtown that it might as well be the anti-Meadowood. The wine seminars are held in cavernous corrugated warehouses that serve as horse paddocks and roller rinks in other months. Meals are served family-style on picnic tables lining a mock western town square that carries endorsements from such pioneering industries as Food 4 Less and Budweiser. There is, in short, no pretense, and in this, the vibe is easy and forward, corresponding seamlessly with the wines it celebrates. "Rhône wines are not stuck up," says Gigondas producer Louis Barruol of Chateau de St. Cosme, a frequent attendee. "They are friendly; in the glass they come to you and jump on your nose."

In 2012 Hospice du Rhône celebrated its twentieth year. It was the oldest, and probably the grandest, celebration of Rhône wines in the world. If you were dedicated in any way to Rhône varieties, if you produced them in Chile, Italy, Australia, or France, Paso Robles was a place to see and be seen, where discoveries were made and stars were born.

And just as Napa Valley Cabernet lovers would not feel complete without attending the auction, most lovers of Rhône varieties haven't really consummated their fandom without attending at least one Hospice du Rhône in their lifetime. "We think it's reached a point," says John Alban, one of the event's founders, "where you can't separate Hospice du Rhône from the Rhône movement in this country."[1] Hospice remains a synonym of the Rhône movement, an emblem of its strengths and weaknesses, its attitudes and aspirations, a celebratory mirror held to the face of the movement itself.

Hospice begins improbably in 1981, in the suburbs of Atlanta, Georgia. There Mat Garretson, a wine buyer at a local supermarket, had been given a birthday bottle of 1980 Condrieu, Georges Vernay's Coteaux du Vernon. Garretson had stored it away without giving it much thought. "I was one of those guys who believed that you only drink white wine after you'd run out of red," he says.[2]

Then one evening he was cooking, and the recipe called for white wine. Garretson remembered the bottle and got it out, uncorked it, and walked back to the stove. He was standing five feet away when its aroma found its way to him. "I thought, 'what the hell is that?'" he says. He smelled honeysuckle and peach, camellia flowers. "And I put it in a glass and tasted it, and said again 'what the hell is that?'" As he tasted the wine, it was as if he was struck by a thunderbolt. "It still haunts me," says Garretson, "textures I thought impossible from a 'mere' white wine. It was my one-bottle epiphany."

Soon after Garretson took a sojourn from the wine business, accepting a rather soul-crushing position with his father's company, an aerosol manufacturing plant responsible for filling cans with everything from Barbasol to WD-40. By night, he sought redemption in the life-changing properties of Viognier. He learned everything he could about the variety, tried every bottle he could get his hands on—a very small number.

By this time California Viogniers were trickling into the market, and Garretson snatched them up, taking trips west when time permitted and visiting the variety's earliest boosters, like Qupé, Joseph Phelps, and Calera. He printed bumper stickers emblazoned with the directive "Drink Viognier!" which may as well have been written in Urdu for its utter lack of familiarity.

He won a few converts along the way, however, and before long Garretson began to think that the variety required the propulsion of a marketing entity—and that he should be the one to run it. In 1992, he established the Viognier Guild. He reached out to the California producers, like Bill Smith at La Jota and Pete Minor at Ritchie Creek, to Josh Jensen at Calera, and Joseph Phelps; he tracked down a kindred Quixote in Virginia named Dennis Horton, who had become the first in the eastern states to produce a commercial Viognier.

To each of them he broached the subject of an event to gather producers and wines around which consumers and the trade could rally. It would be held in Georgia—an idea that was met mostly with derision. "I remember Josh Jensen hearing me out on my proposal," says Garretson, "and saying 'Viognier in Georgia? How the hell does that make any sense?'"

Meanwhile in California, Garretson started to hear rumors about a producer somewhere in the Central Coast planting epic numbers of Viognier vines. That man's name, he learned, was John Alban. Garretson tracked down a phone number for Alban Vineyards and called, got no answer. He tried the next day, and no one picked up, nor the day after that. For weeks he called, and for weeks, he got no answer. "It got to be a joke," he says. "I made calls for three months straight, at all hours, at three in the morning, two in the afternoon, in the middle of the night, letting the phone ring and ring; never once was there an answer."

Then one day just as he was about to hang up, he heard someone say "Hello?"

"Is this Alban Vineyards?" asked Garretson.

There was a short pause before the voice on the other line answered "Yes."

"Is this John Alban?"

"Yes," said the voice on the other end. Garretson could hardly believe it.

"I'm surprised you were able to reach me here," said Alban.

"I'm not," said Garretson. "I've been trying to reach you for the last three months at this number."

"No, it's not that," said Alban.

"This is the number of your winery, isn't it?" said Garretson.

"Not exactly," said Alban.

It turns out that Alban was still a long way from building a winery. The phone number was connected to a modem line on Alban's vineyard property, fifteen miles away, which linked to an Edna Valley weather station; on rare occasions, Alban plugged into it with a device that allowed him to make outgoing calls. On that day he had just happened to be out in the vineyard, had made a call, and was about to unplug the receiver when the phone rang.

Garretson told Alban about his plans to form a Viognier marketing group. When Alban heard this, he says, he told Garretson "that is positively the most preposterous thing I think I've heard all year, and can I be member number one?" Months later, when Garretson invited him to attend an event he'd decided to throw, Alban agreed to send wine but wasn't interested in attending. Garretson persisted, sending him the list of wines being poured and the other attendees. Alban realized that no one, not even he, had tasted so many Viogniers at one sitting. How could he refuse?

Garretson held his first event, which he called "Viognier: A View from the Vineyards," on May 8, 1993, one week before his first marriage, at Mossy Creek Vineyards in Clermont, Georgia, a small agricultural town about seventy-five miles northeast of Atlanta, and at the center of what was then a very modest Georgia wine region.[3]

The wines (25) outnumbered the attendees (22)—both were listed in the program. They included two producers (Alban and Horton) and two members of the press, Patrick Fegan and Barbara Ensrud, who did not fail to note the historic nature of the day, nor the weirdness of embracing something this obscure. "I recall a lot of hilarity there," says Ensrud, "just a lot of merriment attached to the idea of starting up something called the Viognier Guild. So it had the feel of a joke at first—but then it sort of got serious."[4]

The wines were tasted blind, in five flights of five, from four countries (Australia, Italy, France, and the U.S.), and five states (California, Virginia, Oregon, Utah, and Colorado), constituting the most comprehensive tasting of the world's offerings of Viognier ever held.

"Viognier is a variety that has arrived," wrote Garretson in the opening pages of his program:

> Your presence here today attests to an ever-increasing interest in this noble yet overlooked grape. This seminar reflects the toil of a handful of growers and producers who—in a Chardonnay world—were determined to pursue something better; something, in my opinion, decidedly better. Every producer we have encountered in preparation for this event displayed an almost religious zeal for Viognier. Against impossible odds and improbable success, they have nurtured a "forgotten child" into a thing of beauty. We owe these modern-day Quixotes our full support.

He closed with the words "In Viognier Veritas," words that would become a trademark for him and his organization.

On the following page was an encouraging note from "Mr. Viognier" himself, Georges Vernay, who congratulated the participants for their interest, pulling together the briefest of histories of the variety and describing the sad news of its postwar demise when, he says, "the war and other more profitable crops limited its production to a mere 15 acres, spread out amongst a few winemakers." From that low point the Condrieu region started to expand, in part because of technological advancement in the cellar and on the vineyard terraces; Vernay announced that the appellation, in ensuing years, had gone from 200 hectoliters of production to ten times that figure, "produced," he wrote, "by about forty different winemakers, who are confident of the future of this."

He closed with the words "This is the rebirth of an appellation"—as much a hope as a prediction, but it would prove prophetic: these were the first steps in the Viognier revival, witnessed by almost no one, just a tiny coterie of Quixotes who refused to admit defeat.

On this rare occasion for Viognier aficionados to taste wines side by side, a remarkable thing was revealed: the wines were wildly different from one another. There were lean wines and buxom wines, wines with a range of exotic fruit tones, wines cloaked in oak flavors, wines devoid of them, wines with viscous textures, and wines that displayed more mineral contours. Even longtime lovers of the grape marveled at the range, a range no one really knew existed until then, not even Garretson, who may have tasted more variations than anyone alive. "I think most of us walked away with a sense of how tremendous the grape was," he says, "but I don't think anyone was any closer to defining it, since the examples were so wildly different."

As a wine lover, Garretson was thrilled; as a marketer, he was worried. He knew that acreage in California was starting to rise dramatically; soon there would be hundreds of tons of fruit in production, and bottles rolling into the market. If producers didn't start adopting a more concerted approach to selling it, all of this early enthusiasm would end up languishing on shelves. When the day ended Garretson and Alban debriefed. Garretson voiced his concerns, arguing the need for making this some kind of annual event.

Alban agreed, but insisted that any subsequent celebrations should take place in California, where they'd find a more sympathetic crowd. Within a year, Garretson had moved there, landing a job at Eberle Winery, which gave him an opportunity to travel the state and proselytize in between sales calls. Where Bill Smith played the role of Viognier's Johnny Appleseed, Garretson played his proselyte, spreading the gospel. He was soon recruiting for a second Viognier summit, this one held in 1994 at Alban Vineyards and marketed solely to the trade and media; it was the first held in sight of a Viognier vineyard.

In one year, the number of California producers had doubled from fourteen to twenty-eight. Additional plantings were reported on in Arizona, Colorado, Georgia, Louisiana, Maryland, Michigan, Missouri, New Mexico, New York, North Carolina, Ohio, Oregon, Texas, Utah, West Virginia, and Virginia. More than 200 attended, including prominent journalists Karen MacNeil, Dan Berger, Dennis Schaeffer, Steve Pitcher, and Larry Walker.

Manfred Krankl was recruited to cater the event; he brought a talented young chef from his kitchen named Suzanne Goin.[5] Krankl also presided over the panel of that day, entitled "Why We Need Viognier," inspired by an article by a skeptical wine writer who had dared to beg the question. The panel included many of the producers making Viognier at the time, including Alban, Lindquist, Matt Cline of Cline Cellars, Bill Caldwell from MacDowell, Craig Williams, and Bill Smith.

The program opened with a letter from Marcel Guigal, who with Vernay had done so much to revive Viognier's ancestral home. "We all share the same passion for this vine and its winemakers, and would like to be able today to share with you this wine of such originality, delicacy, and finesse, which makes for such a marvelous tasting experience."[6]

The panel was followed—upstaged, you might say—by a putative Frenchman who interrupted the proceedings to have a say in the matter. This was Bill Craig, a friend of Garretson's and a California wine educator who performed, in a preposterous French accent, a send-up of Guigal, complete with black beret and ponderous syntactical ellipses. "I shrugged my shoulders a lot," says Craig, "and more or less punctuated each sentence with that 'oe' sound that French men make that sounds sort of like 'boeuf.'"[7]

It fit the vibe they wanted exactly. "The world was chock-a-block with stuffy, pretentious wine events," says Garretson. "We wanted to try and make it a good time, and we hoped that attendees and the media would pick up the not so subliminal message that these wines were really a lot of fun."

In 1995 the event moved to Sonoma County, to Saralee's Vineyard, where Rich and Saralee Kunde had planted Viognier for Dick Arrowood. The event's 160-page program was comprehensive, to say the least—in fact the text itself represented most of the available information on the variety, including fables, histories, an ampelography primer from Pierre Galet, discussions of typicity, an essay devoted to its expense, reports from France, Australia, and the U.S., and an index of all the vine's producers, including a state-by-state survey from California to Virginia.

The following year the event was held at MacDowell Winery in Mendocino County, on a hot day in July that coincided with the anniversary of the first lunar landing. There were viticultural and trade seminars, and it was the first year that Garretson and Alban invited guests of honor—including the "Person of the Year"—in this case, Monsieur Viognier himself, Georges Vernay, accompanied by his son, Daniel.

Following the celebration at McDowell in 1996, Alban and Garretson started to rethink their statewide, "roving" approach—it was expensive, and the dates tended to change from year to year, the sort of inconsistency that riled fans of the event. So Garretson struck a deal with the Mid-State Fairgrounds in Paso Robles, a venue roughly equidistant from San Francisco and Los Angeles, and close to Garretson's and Alban's homes.

There were several important consequences to this decision. The first was the effective irritation of John McCready, whose winery Sierra Vista was slated to host the event the following year in the Sierra foothills. The event's shift in venue prompted him to formally relaunch the Rhône Rangers as a nonprofit professional organization. Second, it became the impetus needed for the organizers to move beyond Viognier and embrace the rest of the Rhône pantheon. They called the celebration "Raisin' Rhônes" in 1997, before settling on the organization's current title, Hospice du Rhône, in 1998.

Thirdly, and perhaps most importantly, the first Paso event included a tasting for the general public. Until this point, the organizers' focus was on the movers and shakers of the business, tastemakers in the press and the trade, sommeliers, and retailers. Those targets had done their job; now it was time to directly engage a wider audience. To this end an auction was introduced, to raise funds and to reflect the activities of the venue from which they'd borrowed their name, the famed Hospice du Beaune.

From its inception, Hospice du Rhône was an international celebration, in part because of the paucity of Viognier itself: for there to be a quorum, Alban and Garretson would have to be inclusive. A global reach became one of the hallmarks of the enterprise, and it attracted star international participants.

Hospice du Rhône assembled some of the most comprehensive, thoughtful, and far-reaching seminars ever held for a regional or varietal category. These were tastings of wines that had never before been seen in this country, verticals of rare bottlings, comparisons of, say, Roussannes from around the world, or Syrahs from three corners of it; the greatest living French and Australian producers agreed to participate, lured to a place that none had ever heard of.

There were Mourvèdre master classes, comprehensive tastings of Gigondas, Vacqueyras, and Chateauneuf-du-Pape; there were in-depth explorations of the great Australian Shiraz brands Torbreck, Penfolds, Henschke, and Clarendon Hills; epic verticals of Domaine Tempier, Chateau de Beaucastel, Chateau la Nerthe, Chapoutier, and E. Guigal, led by their winemakers; and first-ever retrospectives for some of the pioneers of the American Rhône movement, like Steve Edmunds, Randall Grahm, Christophe Baron, and Manfred Krankl. There were groundbreaking tastings of Languedoc, Roussillon, Priorat and Provence, as well as varietal examinations from Spain, Italy, Argentina, and South Africa. Alban, who took the lead on curating the seminars, had a knack for assembling producers that carried the zeitgeist of the day, getting in front of trends with uncanny prescience.

Hospice's emphasis on international guests and wines was vital in establishing the category as something more than just a provincial effort, but like the best intentions exemplified at the International Colloquium, the two sides had more than just rivers and oceans to cross. Many of the early participants were polite and solicitous, but they also treated the weekend with an air of diffidence, as if they'd prefer to put some distance between them and the proceedings. This occasionally led to extreme acts on the part of the Americans. In one famous story Alban, who had been rebuffed by the Guigal family many times, slipped into an Ampuis elevator with Phillippe Guigal, scion of that great chateau in the northern Rhône Valley, and hit the Stop button, telling him that neither of them were going to leave the elevator until Guigal agreed to host a seminar.[8]

On another such trip Alban and Garretson met Yves Cuilleron, the young winemaker for a well-established northern Rhône producer who was busy reviving the family's estate. They hit it off, and Alban and Garretson invited Cuilleron to Hospice, with Cuilleron demanding invitations for two of his friends, Francois Villard and Yves Gangloff.

That is how three of the Four Amigos made their first trip to Paso Robles in 1998. Alban picked them up at the airport, meeting Villard and Gangloff for the first time.[9] They made a late dinner at the Alban home and started opening bottles. Around three A.M., says Alban, his wife, Lorraine, came downstairs to shut them down; she'd heard Jimmy Buffett's "Wasted Away in Margaritaville" on the CD player one too many times.

Of these three young producers, only Cuilleron had a winemaking background; he'd recently taken over his family's eighty-year-old estate. (Villard learned winemaking in Cuilleron's cellars.) Gangloff, by contrast, had never made wine before a half-decade earlier. He was (and is) a talented guitarist who traveled to Vienne on occasion in part because of the robust jazz scene there, and stayed in part because he met his future wife, Mathilde, there, eventually working harvests at Delas for seven vintages before they purchased their first hectare in Condrieu. The Fourth Amigo, Pierre Gaillard, was the oldest, a producer who had been working a little more than a decade on his own wines and who was trained in the cellars of Guigal.[10]

They slipped effortlessly into the Hospice milieu as an inseparable group of Frenchmen, with an antic, sunny, thoroughly accessible demeanor, always moving, always partying, always game for trying a new wine or a new avenue of winemaking. They bowled for the first time. "At the beginning I was bad," explains Villard, "after three glasses of wine I felt very good—but after two bottles it became more complicated."[11] Bowlers took to touching Villard on his bald pate for luck, and were invariably met with a luminous smile that more than made up for the fact that he didn't know a word of English. "We went to Villa Creek," says Villard (the preferred postevent watering hole), "and didn't pay for a drink. We were the Frenchies; we were taken care of."

The Frenchies attended for the next twelve years. They gave seminars and poured from their ever-growing, but always rare portfolios, making new friends, even collaborating on joint projects, some based in California soil, some in French soil, some bottlings literally a combination of the two. And their business in the U.S. was unparalleled after making such important connections. "We spoke the same language," says Gangloff. "I remember thinking 'I feel like I'm at home!' That feeling never quit me."[12]

Mat Garretson and John Alban seem an odd pair to carry off any organized event together. John is short and wiry, pencil thin, all acute angles and sharp elbows. Mat towers above John at 6'3", with a substantial girth. John is famously droll, with an exceptional facility with language, speaking his mind with great deliberation and forethought, as if you can see him weighing his words as he says them.

Garretson tends to blurt what he has to say, as if his thoughts are hurtling past his mouth before he has a chance to think them. He is a kind of malaprop master, a skill he uses to great comic effect, and which complements an overall sense of hucksterism. And he has no threshold for silliness when it comes to the message, whether he's playing a ballerina in pink tights and tutu, or a pink-leathered motorcycle gang member; he has been known to commit some of the movement's most unforgivable puns, like portraying the rapper "Mo-Vedre" at a Hospice luncheon. His effusive, frequently undirected energy and creativity defined Hospice proceedings, a seat-of-the-pants quality that went to the very heart of the event.

The shenanigans, all of the events, venues, international guests, meals, lodging, seminars, tastings, and logistics—all required exceptional organization and communication skills, which was ironic, since both Alban and Garretson were capable of almost epic disorganization. There were late lunches, lost wines, long lines, deficient service, ugly t-shirts, ice shortages, logistical fires in constant need of dousing. For years it seemed that Garretson and Alban would have to commit every logistical mistake at least once in order for it not to be repeated.

Perhaps the worst occurred in 1997 in their first year at the fairgrounds, when at the end of the first day they stood in a room where there had been an earlier tasting, gazing on rows of tables filled with thousands of dirty glasses. "And I said to Mat," says Alban, 'so which part of the fairgrounds has the dishwasher?'"

Slowly it dawned on them that there was none, and that neither of them had given it the slightest thought. They called in favors of all the town's restaurateurs to use their dishwashers after service, worked through the night, finishing just hours before the next day's first seminar.

Perhaps Hospice's most famous annual event is the bowling tournament, probably the only major wine festival in the world that features one. But that's not to say it's not serious. In between the glasses of Côte-Rôtie and Pic St. Loup and Barossa old-vine Grenache, or the local Syrahs and Viogniers, or the Coronas and the occasional shots of tequila, it's extremely competitive. Participating teams bring in hotshot bowlers to work harvest just so they can gain an upper hand the following spring. The bowling trophy is as coveted as it is garish (the winning team gets to add its own touches to the existing pastiche); a recent iteration sported beer-top pasties on its bowling pin bust line.

Garretson, not surprisingly, is responsible for the tournament. While still living in Georgia he was invited to attend an early International Pinot Noir Celebration, held annually in McMinnville, Oregon. That event concludes with a traditional salmon bake, a meal Garretson shared with Lynn Penner Ash, then the winemaker for Rex Hill Winery in Newberg. Penner Ash was saying to Mat, "God, how do you top this?" she said.

"Well you go bowling," said Mat, surprised at his own suggestion.

A light went on above Lynn's head. "You know," she said, "I've got a friend who owns a bowling alley in McMinnville; I bet she'd stay open if we took her some wine." So they headed over to the alley and bowled into the wee hours.

Garretson remembered this evening when he and Alban were casting about for ways to make the event feel informal and unpretentious. The bowling tourney is the first event to sell out every year.

Enthusiasm for such bacchanalian revelry can prove hard to sustain; in this case, Hospice's fate was tied to that of its flagship variety, Syrah, whose own fortunes in the marketplace have been somewhat peripatetic. After suspending formal operations for three years, it was revived in Paso Robles in the spring of 2016.

Whatever its fate, no celebration has been more important in drawing together the world's Rhône-varietal producing regions, linking these wines with an overall feeling of immediacy, pleasure, and ingenuousness. Such achievements have not gone unnoticed or unrewarded.

In March 2005, the Four Amigos invited John Alban, Mat Garretson, and Vicki Carroll (who had been hired in 2000 as director of the Hospice event) to the northern Rhône for tours and tastings. What they did not tell them is that they'd conspired with local producers to bestow upon Alban and Garretson the order of Decurion by the Confrerie of Côte-Rôtie, to celebrate what they've done to advance the northern Rhône appellations.

Garretson, Carroll, and Alban were instructed to go to an antiquities museum in Vienne, the Musée Gallo-Romain Saint-Romain-en-Gal. Alban was told to bring a magnum of wine. The Four Amigos stood before them. Inside the hall were ancient mosaics of Roman life, which had inspired Alban's label, a mosaicked grapevine. Above them on a mezzanine stood the families of the producers whom Alban had long ago tried to hector into working with him—and who had rejected him. Now they applauded him and Garretson for their efforts at Hospice du Rhône, and announced that they were hereby deemed "Decurions" of the region, members of the Brotherhood of Côte-Rôtie.[13] "Every year," explains Gangloff, the principal mover behind this effort, "wine people are enthroned, like chefs, sommeliers, and other wine professionals. John and Mat were enthroned because they created Hospice du Rhône and contributed to the promotion of Rhône wines and especially Condrieu and Côte-Rôtie."

To the assembled, Gangloff presented them thus: "At Hospice many growers from the Rhône as well as fanatics from all over the world taste, discuss, and share opinions regarding Syrah and Viognier, whether from Napa or the Edna Valley, or even Australia. But all remember that it was Côte-Rôtie and Condrieu with which they first fell in love. We are very happy to distinguish John and Mat, to say officially to them Thank you! Thank you for what you did for our area!"

No one was more moved than Alban, who could say at last that he had delivered on his promise to Condrieu producers so long ago: he'd made them proud, he'd helped to bring them back, and all of them faced a healthy, vibrant future. And Hospice du Rhône had served as an improbable, preposterous, outlandish conduit to their revival.

PART VI

IRRATIONAL EXUBERANCE

21

THE RISE AND FALL OF AMERICAN SYRAH

Rhône varietal wines fell into the slipstream of the American market just as consumer interest in wine increased from essentially naught in the late eighties to something virtually boundless as the twentieth century came to a close.

In retail settings, on-premise (restaurants and bars), and off (everywhere else), wine suddenly found a home in venues it had never before occupied, or which had never really existed. The nation's restaurant industry grew at a geometric rate, and wine programs expanded with them, accommodating the surge in consumer interest. A new position with a new name, borrowed from the French—*sommelier*—was adopted to describe this emergent class of wine-slingers, and gatekeepers like Kathy King, Larry Stone, Michael Bonaccorsi, Peter Granoff, Debbie Zachareas, Evan Goldstein, Joe Bastianich, and others established their reputations at the nation's wine-centered restaurants, including the French Laundry in Yountville, Campanile and Spago in Los Angeles, Rubicon, Square One, Boulevard, and Stars in San Francisco, Daniel, Chanterelle, and Gramercy Tavern in Manhattan, Charlie Trotter in Chicago. In turn these powerhouse restaurants grew competitive with each other, as establishments vied for bragging rights on the largest, most comprehensive, or most innovative wine programs. To be innovative meant embracing wines from the Rhône Valley and the American Rhône.

The retail landscape had changed with comparable speed. Wine overtook liquor in the aisles, occupying shelves at grocery stores and supermarkets, a retail space they'd not inhabited much before 1990. A new phenomenon called the wine bar took hold in revitalized urban enclaves, featuring all of the convivial comforts and social value of a bar or tavern, now given a vital added element—wine education. These were places where wine could be enjoyed while it was being demystified, where snobbery and highbrow notions withered and died.

Before long wine-growing regions became more than just distant lands from which issued these exotic liquid products—they became destinations, places to weekend or to visit as part of a longer vacation strategy, one with some built-in, controlled inebriation. Americans came home from road trips with trunks full of wine from California, Oregon, Washington or Colorado, New Mexico, and Idaho. By the end of the millennium, every state in the country could boast of being a wine producer.

It was Robert Mondavi, of course, who orchestrated this transformation in the Napa Valley, a California tourist destination second only to Disneyland in popularity. Before long, wine tourism extended to all corners of California hospitable to the grapevine, from Mendocino to Murphys, Petaluma to Paso Robles, from Los Olivos to Temecula. Tasting weekends became part of the ethos of the leisure economy, and soon restaurants and wine bars were joined by another concept, the tasting room, as an avenue of education, marketing, and wine appreciation, an activity immortalized in 2004 in the Central Coast road/buddy/wine country film, *Sideways*.

Wineries formed at a breakneck pace to meet demand and fill the shelves. Brands which are now household names like Kendall-Jackson, Fetzer, Geyser Peak, Columbia Crest, Hogue, J. Lohr, R. H. Phillips, Meridian, and Firestone were all established in this period. Storied properties in the Napa Valley like Beaulieu Vineyards, Beringer, Benziger, Sterling, and Robert Mondavi, spurred on in part by international investment, began producing wines outside of their home region, supermarket lines with California appellations that, for better or worse, traded on their regional importance to become household names.

Not only this, but new labels were popping up in every conceivable arable region, as newly wealthy inhabitants of the Golden State, doctors, lawyers, and dot-com millionaires purchased vineyard land, invested in garage wineries, and dreamed of second careers as gentlemen farmers. Indeed, it was as if Robert Mondavi's prophecy of wine "raising the art of living well" was coming to pass among U.S. consumers, whose own aspirational vision of the good life included a glass of wine in the frame. Just one decade later, in 2010, the United States would overtake France as the largest wine market in the world.

Between 1990 and 2000, the popularity of Rhône varietal wines reflected this breakneck pace, starting with an almost mind-boggling surge in planting. It's easy to sound hyperbolic when describing the growth: in 1990, plantings statewide in California for Syrah, still the flagship Rhône variety, amounted to 200 acres. Ten years later, that figure had grown to 13,000. Viognier, Syrah's counterpart in white varieties, experienced an equivalent meteoric rise, from 80 acres in 1990 to nearly 1,800 a decade later.[1] Viognier emerged as the great Chardonnay alternative among white varieties, headlining an increasingly common niche on the nation's wine lists and retail sections, for the anything-but-Chardonnay cohort.

Surely the Rhône Rangers' caricature appeal contributed to this frenzy of interest. If there was a wine category that symbolized the death of wine snobbery it was the rootin'-tootin' Rangers, whose adherents, dressed in mildly cheesy cowboy chic, could be seen mingling with the crowds at public tastings with a garish regularity.

The category's flagship remained Syrah, loved for its exoticism, for its wildness, its power and suppleness, its versatility in the vineyard and diversity in the bottle. It fell between the tannic rigor of Cabernet Sauvignon and the more attenuated mysteries of Pinot Noir, gaining a foothold among middle-register wine varieties like Zinfandel and Petite Sirah. For those already producing these varieties, Syrah was an attractive complement; Ridge, for example, one of the state's most venerable Zinfandel houses, started producing a varietal Syrah in 1996, cofermented with Viognier and drawing in part from a small patch of ancient Syrah vines at Lytton Estate.[2] Several other Zin specialists soon followed, including Ravenswood, Renwood, Rabbit Ridge, Trentadue, and Parducci.

In Napa, some well-established upmarket brands like Lewis, Pride, and Araujo debuted Syrah bottlings, the latter employing an established parcel planted by Milt Eisele on behalf of Joseph Phelps. Other Napa properties like Clos Pegase and Hess Collection jumped in as well (though both of these brands hedged their bets with Cabernet-Syrah blends). Pinot Noir producers, too, explored Syrah's iterations in cooler California regions, from the Russian River to Santa Maria and Carneros; these included Dehlinger, Arrowood, Truchard, Talley, Foxen, and Babcock. Even a Sangiovese specialist, Atlas Peak, an early flagbearer for the Cal-Ital phenomenon, could not resist introducing a short-lived Syrah program in 1999.

Ask any critic or pundit or market soothsayer, and there was hardly any doubt: Syrah was destined to be the next great American red wine. With so much acclaim for the Rhône movement in the press, and for Syrah in particular, it seemed inevitable that consumer interest would follow along. Producers threw themselves upon this hope: when phylloxera reappeared in California vineyards, many growers took this opportunity to plant the hot new variety, Syrah.

It all seems so headlong in hindsight, growers eagerly putting down ambitious plantings seemingly without ever once wondering if the public would have the appetite for all this new wine. But that is how the market worked in the early nineties; the *Wine Spectator* and the *Wine Advocate* were on the leading edge of every market trend; Robert Parker, James Laube, and Harvey Steiman became the de facto arbiters of American wine taste, with journals like the *Wine Enthusiast* and *Wine & Spirits* not far behind in interest and influence.[3]

In September 2003 *Wine Spectator* columnist Matt Kramer, author of several influential books on wine, wrote a column called "The Next Really Big Red," in which he made a bold prediction: "The most exciting wine in America today," he claimed, "is Syrah. I'd love to say that it's Pinot Noir, but I cannot tell a lie. It's Syrah that's slated for stardom."[4]

It was, he said, more than just a question of its being popular. "Really Big," he wrote, "is when golf courses and bed-and-breakfasts use the name. When it becomes a lipstick shade or a paint color. This is precisely what's going to happen to Syrah."

In the next 700 words Kramer laid out a litany of reasons on why Syrah was to be The Next Big Thing. They were, in this order:

Really Big Rule #1: "There has to be a lot of it," he wrote. "For a grape to become Really Big it has to be commodified."

Really Big Rule #2: "The variety has to have a pinnacle wine." Cabernet had the First Growths, Chardonnay had Montrachet, Merlot had Petrus. Syrah could claim Côte-Rôtie and Hermitage, as well as the Shirazes of Penfolds Grange and Henschke's Hill of Grace. California, said Kramer, had Syrah stars, "soon to shine."

Really Big Rule #3: "The variety has to grow successfully in multiple climates and soils. And it has to deliver commercial yields," which Kramer defined as yields of at least 3 tons per acre.[5]

Finally, Kramer made what in hindsight would prove to be a profound miscalculation, in Really Big Rule #4: The wine, he said, had to be "obvious." He cleverly quoted H. L. Mencken's immortal observation, that "Nobody ever went broke underestimating the taste of the American public." "Subtle wines," he added, "don't sell." The wines which did sell, Chardonnay, Cabernet, and Merlot, were "full of flavor, color, and fruitiness," and Syrah had all of these in spades.

"Not even Syrah's most ardent defenders," said Kramer, "would suggest that it's subtle. Syrah is always, at minimum, a lush gush of fabulous fruit. You can't miss it."

Clearly, Syrah's minutes of fame were upon it. Was it ready?

Looking back we can say with some certainty that the answer was, emphatically, no. In the end, demand never sustained the 13,000-acre vote of confidence the producers bestowed upon it. Syrah held a niche, but wine drinkers never took up the variety with the sort of gusto and constancy they bestowed upon Cabernet Sauvignon and, eventually, Pinot Noir. Despite outsized expectations, Syrah remained a stubbornly marginal interest. It took a stab at a lead role in the mainstream, but as it hit its mark on center stage, the spotlight shifted. You may not have been able to miss its lush gush of fabulous fruit, but you could, in the end, tire of it. The story of its fall may be every bit as compelling as the story of its rise.

The mainstreaming of American Syrah set in motion a series of complex factors which, taken together, cut into its character and distinctiveness in the American marketplace. Grown in more places, it became less distinctive, softer, smoother, more benign. It strayed from the complex wildness that had drawn people to it in the first place. It is hard to believe, but Syrah was wending its way to being boring.

Until 1990 the style of American Syrah was unfailingly linked to the Rhône Valley itself, given to feral accents, to spice and meat and game, a rasher of bacon fat and wood smoke, tense and savory. Those bringing the variety in to the mainstream, however, steered their efforts toward smoother waters, privileging texture over aromatics, plushness over spice. For this, they had a built-in model from the opposite end of the earth, just breaking into the market.

The road to the mainstream for American Syrah passes directly through Australia and its singular interpretation of that country's flagship wine, which they called Shiraz.

Shiraz, of course, had been in the ground in Australia long before it had found its way to the U.S. Most attributed its introduction in the down under country to James Busby, an early viticulturalist and botanist who was the principal source for the more important vinifera plantings in Australia in the nineteenth century. Busby was born in Scotland in 1801 and emigrated to New South Wales in 1824, embarking in 1828 on a viticultural expedition through the wine regions of Europe. He returned from his second European tour in 1833 with hundreds of cuttings from Spain and France, vines which included Syrah, calling the vine alternately "scyras" and "ciras."[6] These blunders (there were dozens in his manifest) morphed into "Shiraz" soon thereafter—leaving one to wonder whether all subsequent conjecture about the grape's origin (that it had come from Syracuse in Sicily, or Shiraz in Iran) were simply the end product of Busby's atrocious spelling.

Less than a decade later Shiraz was being planted enthusiastically in South Australia and New South Wales, where its affinity with the country's mesoclimates and its propensity for good solid yields put it in favor with the country's emergent winemakers. It quickly became the most important, most widely planted red grape in the country, a distinction it holds to this day.

In the U.S., Australian wines had little in the way of visibility until the early 1980s, and even then imports remained a trickle. But by 1990 they were finding their way onto retail shelves; the most successful Australian wine in the U.S. market was a Chardonnay from Rosemount, the Diamond Label, a brisk, golden-fruited white which sold for as little as $3.50 a bottle, and hugely overdelivered for that price.

On Chardonnay's coattails Shiraz made inroads; the country's wines earned a brand identity for drinkability and an attractive price point. Those discovering and importing these wines in the early 1980s, like John Gay, who would go on to run Southcorp in the U.S., could not believe their good fortune: they were "dazzled" by the wines' attractiveness and quality for price. Nothing in California, says Gay, could compare with what he was seeing from Australia. As the market for these wines took shape they became known, for better or worse, as the "cheap and cheerful," wines of almost effortless charm and fullness of fruit, requiring neither sophistication nor tremendous wine knowledge, simply a few bucks and a few working taste buds. When the *Wine Spectator*'s Harvey Steiman bestowed a 91-point score on a 1989 Hunter Valley Shiraz, the American consumer engaged in a long love affair with Australian wine.

Australia had another thing that California Syrah producers couldn't offer: volume. By 2000, revenues for Southcorp brands in the U.S. alone were in excess of $150 million, with Shiraz accounting for a significant portion of this; of course, sales of American Rhône wines would claim no more than a tiny fraction of this revenue figure. Brands like Rosemount, Wolf Blass, and Penfolds became household names.

Australians quickly developed acumen in the global market. Some of this was practical, as the population on the continent (17 million in 1990) couldn't possibly consume what the country was capable of producing. In 1996 the Winemakers Federation debuted a document called Strategy 2025, in which the industry stated its intention to become the world's preeminent supplier of wine. It seemed wildly ambitious and almost foolhardy— and for all intents and purposes, it was accomplished in less than ten years.

Australian wine firms didn't merely want to be export kings; they also began exploring the possibilities of becoming producers in California, as French, Italian, and Spanish wine companies had before them.

In 1989 Penfolds's parent company, Adelaide Steamship Group, partnered with the Trione family of Geyserville, in Sonoma County, to jointly own Geyser Peak, an underperforming winery in the Alexander Valley. It was the first such investment in the California wine industry by an Australian company, and was heralded in the Australian press as "a situation of virtually unlimited potential for both parties."[7]

Geyser Peak was already nearly a century old, but its reputation as a premium brand had been tarnished by an ownership stint by the Schlitz Brewing Company, which steered the brand toward cheap Chablis- and Burgundy-style blends, some of which, in the late seventies, weren't bottled, but rather canned, in six-packs.

Penfolds signaled its commitment by exporting one of their most promising winemakers, Daryl Groom of Adelaide, who in 1984, at the age of twenty-six, crafted the first of six consecutive vintages of Grange. Groom chose to focus the winery's efforts in two categories where Australians excelled, and which would be distinctive in the American market. The first was in Sauvignon Blanc, produced in a crisp, light, herbaceous Southern Hemisphere style.

The second was Syrah. Groom planned to enter the market with an Australian-styled wine—a Shiraz in name and form—a style American consumers would find irresistible. "At the time in California," says Groom, "the Syrah wines were more Rhône-like to us, with more white and black pepper, more meaty, more earthy. We were looking to produce the style we knew, darker and more purple, more vibrant and silky."[8]

Geyser Peak produced its first Syrah in 1991, sourced from multiple sites, blending in a bit of Petite Sirah for color and ballast, since purchasable Syrah in California was still limited. They were obliged, their first vintage, to label said bottling as a Syrah, since the Bureau of Alcohol, Tobacco and Firearms was disinclined to allow "Shiraz" for a domestically produced wine (they relented the following year). Soon thereafter Geyser Peak was producing from its own fruit sources.

Groom was encouraged by the early results. The fruit was fairly effortless to grow in this warm northern valley, and its potential ripeness lent itself to Australian interpretation. He used a couple of Grange-type tricks, modulating press cuts to control the tannic payload, bleeding off some of the free run to concentrate the wine, fermenting it in American oak barrels expressly brought over from Magill for the purpose, with a Penfolds signature of toast and seasoning. They expanded the program dramatically every year: within a decade they were making five Shiraz bottlings, an entry-level wine (called Canyon Road) and some appellation, single-vineyard, and reserve bottlings—even a sparkling Shiraz, a first for California.

By 2002 the winery was one of the top ten producers of Syrah in the country, even though Penfolds, obliged to free up cash for its parent company, had since backed out of the partnership, the first fit of many fits and starts that would typify Australian involvement here. The winery changed hands a half-dozen times in the ensuing years, but Groom and his winemaking partner, New Zealander Mick Shroeter, stuck with the brand until 2006, maintaining and promoting "Shiraz" in name and form for many years.

Groom and Shroeter became not only the winemakers at Geyser Peak for many years, they were the de facto ambassadors in this country for Australian Shiraz in both style and attitude.[9] Cool, easygoing, always smiling, they became two of Australia's most visible and amenable emissaries, two easy-to-embrace personalities propelling Syrah into the mainstream on an easy-to-embrace style.

"Daryl changed the winemaking philosophy in California," says John Gay. "He understood flavor and balance like few others did—he still does—and channeled an archetypal Australian style."[10] Dan Berger, a journalist closely covering that period agrees. "Daryl was a modern day pioneer," he says. "What he did was brought the theory and practice of Australian winemaking into practical use in California."[11] Not surprisingly, American producers took notice.

By 2000 several Shiraz bottlings could be found on wine shelves in supermarkets and wine shops alike, most of them Australian, some of them American, as California wineries went in pursuit of the cheap and cheerful. The varietal names may have been interchangeable, but within the trade the words *Shiraz* and *Syrah* were used to delineate the difference in style between a good drink and a more French-inspired, aromatically driven style. Trying to enforce the difference, even while insisting that the two names were synonymous, was the first of many seeds of confusion planted that would last for a decade or more, as Syrah sought a foothold in the marketplace. Many consumers remained either baffled or altogether ignorant of the distinction.

Meanwhile, the rapid growth of the market in the mid-1990s inspired a flurry of acquisitive activity worldwide in the beverage industry, fomenting a period of investment and consolidation never before seen in the history of adult beverages. It was an era of global companies and partnerships, where brands like Gallo, Pernod-Ricard, Allied Domecq, Diageo, Brown Forman, and Constellation Brands solidified their stake in the global marketplace. And no sector of the market was more volatile, or more bewildering, than Australia.

For much of the twentieth century Australian wine firms competed largely within the country's borders, articulating the wine style that would come to charm the world in relative isolation, before the wave of "flying winemakers"—Southern Hemisphere practitioners traveling north for a second harvest in a year—became a common occurrence.

But the continent was soon producing vast amounts of wine, and export markets became an urgent necessity. To compete globally required a company with the scale and reach to establish efficient distribution systems—size suddenly mattered.

The result was a kind of amalga-mania: a half-dozen companies, like lumbering ships, began to collide and merge and grow larger with each year; one company comprised of a half-dozen historic wineries swallowed another, also composed of a half-dozen historic wineries, each of these seeking to drive their wines into multiple price tiers and extend their brands into every nook the market exposed to them.

In two of the earliest merger deals Penfolds, in 1985, acquired Wynns and two other wineries. Six years later Wolf Blass and Mildara merged to form Mildara Blass, which was itself acquired by the brewery giant Fosters in 1996. The Penfolds Group, meanwhile, having changed its name to Southcorp in 1994, continued to troll the waters for deals. In 2000 Fosters acquired Beringer Wine Estates, one of the more successful vertically integrated California brands, for the then-staggering sum of $1.5 billion, forming a wine-centric division of the company the following year called Beringer Blass. Next, Southcorp—consisting of Penfolds, Wynns, Seaview, Lindemans, and a handful of other smaller brands—purchased Rosemount for $1.5 billion, becoming the world's largest premium-brand wine company—for a time. Constellation Brands, an American conglomerate based in upstate New York, responded by purchasing BRL Hardys for $1.1 billion, making it, in 2003, the world's largest wine company. Two years later Southcorp and Foster's merged.

It is hard to calculate with certainty how the mergers, the acquisitions, the fluid management strategies and shifting sales team priorities affected the fate of Shiraz. But it's not hard to imagine how the messaging for this singular variety, the flagship export of "Brand Australia," would be forced to take a backseat to more pressing concerns about brand extension, market share, internecine wrangling, and ultimately global domination, when there is abundant evidence that in practice, a single brand was routinely subjugated to serve the interests and ambitions of the company at large. No doubt these are still legitimate concerns of multitier, multiregional conglomerate wine companies—as is the bottom line, of course. But these issues arose at a particularly difficult stage in Shiraz's stake in the market, just as American consumers were becoming acquainted with its virtues.

If there's any reason to doubt this effect on Shiraz's fortunes, one need only look at the meteoric rise of a single brand, Yellow Tail, which threw all other merger and acquisition strategies into a deep tailspin (if you'll pardon the pun) it's still climbing out of.

Yellow Tail is the creation of Filippo Casella and his son John.[12] Casella was an Australian of Sicilian ancestry who developed a large vineyard in a district of New South Wales called Riverina. Casella had been a supplier for decades and wanted to try his hand at making a wine of his own. Formerly sellers, he and his son became buyers, just as a surfeit of juice came onto the market cheaply. To sell it, they came up with a plan.

The Casellas found an import partner in the U.S., William Deutsch, whose partnership with Georges Duboeuf of Beaujolais in France had been a tremendous success, particularly owing to the huge market for Beaujolais Nouveau in the states, a wine which, it might be said, was the original cheap and cheerful red wine in the American market.

The Casellas debuted a wine in 1999 called Carramar Estates, looking and sounding much like the many estate brands that had gone before it, from Rosemount to Lindemans, which traded on tradition and family bearing. The brand was indistinguishable from the other legacy brands from Down Under, and it was an utter bust.

So Casella and his marketing man John Soutter came up with a radically different approach, eschewing legacy altogether in deference to a much more visually arresting label—of a more marsupial nature.

The design came from an Adelaide graphics house, and an artist, Barbara Harkness, who specialized in wine labels. She produced for them a wallaby; a kangaroo-like creature the likes of which most Americans had never seen before. Upon the creature's clumpy long tail Soutter splashed a drop of yellow ink and some modest aboriginal adornment; the ensuing brand was called Yellow Tail. Of course it didn't matter that no one knew what a wallaby was; it mattered only that the wallaby was cute. The "critter wine" was born in this moment, a brand that did away with tradition in the wine business, replacing it with cartoon immediacy and a pop-culture superficiality. Australian wine imports would never be the same.

Yellow Tail debuted with a Chardonnay and a Shiraz in 2000. The wines were cheaper and sweeter than most of their competitors in the entry level, and at $4 a bottle, irresistible to American consumers.

According to an account by Frank Prial in the *New York Times*, William Deutsch initially agreed to take 25,000 cases, but his son convinced him to increase the order to 60,000 on the strength of the label alone.[13] The first shipment arrived in June 2001. By year's end, Deutsch had sold 225,000 cases. Four years later, the brand was selling 7.5 million a year. By 2006 the brand accounted for 40% of the Australian market in the U.S.; by 2009, it was over half.

Not surprisingly, their success bred imitators, many of these employing other cute animals on their labels, mass-produced brands made from mechanically harvested, over-cropped vines, sweet simple juice with all off-flavors corrected, simplified, smoothed over with flavor additives, oak dust, color fixatives, and sugar. The storied history of Australia's traditional family brands was practically meaningless set against the critter wines, which took more of the market share with each vintage.

Overnight, Australian wine wasn't a category, with a range and a host of players—it was a type, monochromatic and unrefined. With a single swipe the market was stripped of the serious, and a country's image devolved into one of almost mawkish simplicity. "Fine wine?" wrote the great Australian wine market analyst Campbell Mattinson, "Regional wine? Greatness? Luxury? Single Vineyard? Old vines? New oak? French oak? Famous winemakers of famous brands? Bugger that. Let's give 'em a cartoon kangaroo on a bottle, and let's give it to 'em sweet, simple and cheap!"[14]

In the end, wrote Michael Steinberger in 2009 on slate.com, "consumers came to equate Australia with wines that were flavorful but also cheap and frivolous, a perception that became a major liability when those same consumers got interested in more serious stuff; rather than looking to Oz, they turned to Spain, Italy, and France"—leaving Australian Shiraz behind altogether.[15]

In 1996 Penfolds, now bearing the name Southcorp, reentered the American wine industry in a partnership with another established wine family, the Nivens of Arroyo Grande, growers in the Central Coast's Edna Valley—where they produced mostly white wines. They were keen on having a red grape source when Southcorp came knocking; the new brand was called Seven Peaks. The Australians brought a team of their own to research and plant the new project, with a very clear idea of what they wanted to accomplish. Simon Graves led the planting efforts.

"Our research was extensive," says Graves, who still runs the project, now known as Camatta Hills Vineyard. "We wanted to emulate the climate and soils of many of our top-performing vineyards in the Barossa Valley. Specifically we had one place in mind, Kalimna Vineyard."[16] Kalimna was traditionally the source of some on the best fruit in Penfolds' possession, and a top contributor to Grange.

They settled on a site in Paso Robles—not far from Tablas Creek. Thus two winemaking teams from opposite sides of the earth, seeking to replicate a set of terroir parameters found in their home regions, located those very conditions in the same California appellation, not twenty miles from each other.

The Australians, naturally, had picked the warmer inland site. The Camatta Hills were warmer than Tablas Creek by a couple of degrees by day, but they were also cooler by night and in the winter months. Both were situated around 1,500 feet, both contained significant amounts of limestone, though sand and clay depositions—similar to the soil makeup of Kalimna—were more common in the Camatta Hills. By the end of the decade Graves had planted nearly 400 acres, half of which was devoted to Shiraz.

As with the Shiraz plantings at Geyser Peak in the Alexander Valley, the team at the Paso Robles Seven Peaks site sought to establish a Shiraz style in the U.S. "When we came over," explains Ian Shepherd, "we felt we wanted to emulate the styles we knew in the Barossa and the McLaren Vale, full-bodied, dark-fruited plummy characteristics. We weren't really after a red berry, peppery spicy style. We were there to do an Australian style wine. So the fruit we initially sought tended to be warmer climate, similar to South

Australia." Shepherd described the results as a hybrid. "You could see elements of South Australian style in there, but the nights were cooler, so you'd get a cool-climate feel to the wines, slightly more red-fruited than what I was used to."[17]

The brand ramped up production, approaching 100,000 cases in 2000 and was projected to reach 200,000 by 2005. But in 2001, Southcorp and Rosemount, another of Australian wine giants and another Shiraz powerhouse, merged. In an unusual move, the management team from the smaller Rosemount was tasked with running the entire company, and there were obvious tensions and confusion from both parties as they tried to create a working managerial environment. Once again, priorities shifted, and once again, Shiraz's fortunes hung in the balance.

Early efforts on red wines and on Syrah in particular from the Camatta Hills were exceedingly promising. Shepherd made wines of exceptional quality, for less than $20; the brand was in every way poised for success.

However, in a recurring irony practiced by publicly traded wine companies, Southcorp could not exhibit the patience necessary to let their vineyard and their wine project grow. By 2002, facing years of development for the fledgling brand, Southcorp was already looking to sell its interest in Seven Peaks; the partnership with the Niven family dissolved in 2003, and Seven Peaks was sold to the Boisset family in 2004. By 2005, says John Niven, what remained of Southcorp's second abortive entry into the U.S. market was being offloaded to Trader Joe's, a California grocery chain, who sold it for $2.99 a bottle. "To see where we ended up, from where we started with the Rosemount people," says Niven, "was tough to swallow."

Southcorp was not altogether out of the game however. Grandfathered into the merger with Rosemount was a partnership that the Oatley family, owners of Rosemount, had established with Robert Mondavi. This arrangement took a rather complicated form, establishing two Shiraz-based brands: Talomas, made in California, and Kirralaa, made in Australia. Both lines were to be sold in both countries, headlined by two *tête de cuvée* Syrahs, one from each country, sold at $80 (for the Barossa Shiraz, Kirralaa) and $50 (for the Central Coast Syrah, Talomas)—launching them, from inception, into the top price tier for Syrah in the world. Ian Shepherd was retained to make both wines; both reflected an opulent Australian style.

The scheme exemplified the global ambitions of Robert Mondavi and his family, who had pioneered such international partnerships starting with the stunningly successful Opus One, established in Napa in 1978 with the Rothschild family of Bordeaux. The Mondavis pursued equivalent partnerships in Chile with the Chadwick family of Errazuriz, and in Italy with the Marchese di Frescobaldi. A high profile partnership with the Oatleys, an esteemed Australian family winery, seemed like an inevitable next step. Its success might have meant a significant boost to Shiraz's place in California, an Opus One of Rhône varieties, and a boost to Australian wine as well.

But there was a rather significant hitch in these plans: the Mondavi family had almost no significant winemaking experience with Syrah of any sort, from any region, with just one exception, sprung from the rib of a recent acquisition and conducted with relative stealth under their nose. The brand was called Io, and it represents an odd subchapter in Syrah's decline.

This detour in the Mondavi family fortunes begins in the late 1980s as the family explored new opportunities for expansion and embellishment of their line.[18] It purchased Byron winery in the Santa Maria Valley, straddling the San Luis Obispo and Santa Barbara counties, a cool benchland property not far from the valley's most famous tenant, Bien Nacido Vineyard. The Mondavis retained Byron's founder, Ken Brown, as winemaker and brand emissary, and seeded their new acquisition with investment in vineyards, winery infrastructure, and promotion, giving Brown *carte blanche* on winemaking and vineyard development. "They encouraged me to experiment," says Brown.[19]

Experimentation may have been the rationale for Brown's under-the-radar plantings of Syrah not long after the sale. Brown's interest in Syrah had remained on a slow burn since the days he'd dabbled with the variety alongside colleagues Bob Lindquist, Adam Tolmach, and Jim Clendenen at Zaca Mesa winery in the early eighties. He had not worked with the variety since, but its runaway success in nearby Bien Nacido Vineyard, from whose fruit both Lindquist and Randall Grahm had been producing some of the state's best Syrahs, seemed to justify a planting at Byron. Brown grafted over 2.5 acres of underperforming vines, adding some Grenache and Mourvèdre.

Brown put together a Syrah-dominant blend, employing estate fruit and fruit from the newly planted Stolpman Vineyards in Ballard Canyon. From 1994 to 1996, Brown bottled a Santa Maria Syrah without Mondavi's express knowledge. Finally in 1998, with the '96 ready for release, he presented his boss with a sample of his side project, taking his bottled wine in unmarked, unlabeled bottles to Rutherford, to try and sell the concept.

The reaction, says Brown, could be characterized as cautiously optimistic. "Their marketing and sales teams were always looking for new niches to explore," explains Brown. "They could see taking this on a ride, to see where it went."

To the Mondavi empire, this gift Syrah was like being dealt a hand in a poker game that you didn't intend to play, but the rising value of the pot obliged you to stay in the game. Of course by this time the family was used to placing well-calculated bets in vineyard regions all over the world; their involvement with Syrah seemed as inevitable as a ballooning pot. That the company had almost zero experience and not much interest in a category all but thrust upon them, was beside the point: with unprecedented leverage with the distributor tier of the business, they felt they had nothing to lose.

Rather than divert the Burgundian aspirations at Byron, the marketing team instead came up with a separate brand for Rhône-oriented bottlings, going with a mythic, two-letter, two-syllable puzzle of a name, Io. In Greek mythology, Io was a nymph seduced by Zeus, who shape-changed her into a cow to keep her from being discovered by his very jealous wife, Hera.

In 1999, the company released their first Syrah, a brooding, slightly meaty red with brickish colors and dark earth notes. For all that, it retained a spicy aromatic profile; in its cool-climate demeanor and whiff of barnyard, it was clearly taking France as its inspiration. It was one of the most expensive Rhône-variety bottlings in California: in this sense, at least, it resembled Opus One.

With Southcorp edging away from the Seven Peaks investment, the company transferred Ian Shepherd to Santa Maria to Byron/Io for three fruitful years. There Ken Brown, his assistant Jonathan Nagy, and Shepherd set out to reconcile their different approaches.

While Ian Shepherd was appreciative of Byron's French leanings, his team managed to persuade Brown to broaden the portfolio with an Australian iteration, which they called Ryan Road—the address of Camatta Hills. Ryan Road debuted in 2001, and with it, Io became one of the first wineries in the U.S. to present a Shiraz-style and Syrah-style red under the same winery umbrella. Such paradoxes seemed easy to justify in a large publicly traded company like Mondavi, who were always eyeing ways to expand its markets. But consumers still had trouble grasping the difference, or the need for one.

Moreover, according to Lee Nordlund, the Mondavi executive tasked with marketing these wines, the family decided to increase production. "We started to raise the volume," he explains, "without realizing that this needed to be small. It wasn't a concept that you could grow quickly."[20] Despite making more than a thousand cases a year, Nordlund admits it was very difficult to sell more than a couple hundred. "It should have been easy to get customers on board," he says, "because Syrah is such a good wine in California, so versatile. But we never really clarified what the wine was supposed to be."

If a single brand, making wine in two different styles, could get lost in the stylistic expression of their own wines, what chance did consumers have? "Connoisseurs wanted wines with more restraint and more structure," says Nordlund. "But the big fat market was into big fat wines. Already the grape was going through an identity crisis. No one knew what it stood for."

Even "natural-born" Shiraz producers ran aground trying to steer American consumers past their own confusion. "Our biggest problem," says Daryl Groom, "wasn't quality, and it wasn't sourcing, and it certainly wasn't the winemaking. Our biggest problem was consumers not understanding the difference between Shiraz and Syrah. We were constantly being asked if Syrah and Shiraz were the same thing. We got bogged down trying to answer the question; even retailers didn't know where to put it."

Mick Shroeter, Groom's winemaking partner at Geyser Peak, agreed. "In California you loosely held to the distinction that if you called it Shiraz it was made in an Australian style, and if you called it Syrah it was more French-like. But even within those categories the styles were all over the place. So on the one side, it's neat to have a diversity of styles, but on the flip side, no one knew exactly what to expect."

This was a continual refrain—that Syrah, no matter what you called it, was never going to be the sort of mass-market driver that everyone assumed it would be. That place had been reserved for other red wines, like Cabernet, which would always surpass Shiraz in sales and popularity. "As much as Shiraz was in my heart," says Daryl Groom, "and as much as we loved it and wanted to be the kings of Syrah, you could see the reasoning that in the Alexander Valley, Cabernet was what we should be focusing on."

Of course if a wine was critically successful, it sold no matter what it was called, where it came from, and what was in it.

As the wine world entered and embraced the era of the Emperor of Wine, Robert Parker's abiding interest in the Rhône Valley and Rhône varieties contributed immeasurably to the category's early success in the market. His praise seemed at once omnivorous and agnostic: his was an equal-opportunity enthusiasm, whether for French Rhône wines, for Barossa bush vine cuvees, or for the myriad wines emerging from California's coastal appellations. "I always thought," wrote Parker in a recent interview, "that the Rhône Valley, and to a lesser extent, California's Central Coast and Australia's wine regions, have been under-valued, under-exploited, and under-covered by other wine writers. The quality of the wines certainly merited more attention than they had received, and I was in a position to give them that attention."[21] In California, it could be said that without his support, the movement might have faltered before it ever emerged from the gate.

But that influence was not without consequence. It was difficult, if not impossible, to wean oneself from Parker's advocacy. The 100-point scale remained one of the most potent marketing tools ever invented, and in an ever-more crowded field of competition, Parker's imprimatur had a considerable impact on the bottom line for many wineries. In fact, Parker's approval, scored at 90 points and above, meant much more than just sales; it meant that countless startup wineries could leapfrog over the cumbersome process of building a brand, clearing the rails before ever establishing a track record—a convenience for those worthy of his praise, and a formula for enduring dependency.

Most American wineries were more than willing to pay the price. As Elin McCoy wrote in her volume on Parker, *The Emperor of Wine,* many felt they "didn't have decades to build reputations, they needed to do it fast, and the media was the best marketing machine they could get in a country where 12 percent of the population drank 88 percent of the wine."[22]

As Parker's power in the wine community grew, it became more and more difficult to resist his preferences, which, as the decade wore on, grew more vociferous, constrictive, and doctrinaire. It was one thing to make a wine he liked—increasingly, you also had to concern yourself with *not* making a wine he *didn't* like.

By 1994 he had started to publish lengthy, potent manifestoes laying out his likes and dislikes in no uncertain terms. The practice reached fever pitch in a December 1996 essay titled "California: The Big Time (An Historic Period)."[23] He proclaimed the vintages of 1990–1996 the greatest the state had ever experienced, marveling at a level of consistency that Europe's regions could only dream of. "History in the making," he proclaimed, "six consecutive vintages of largely dazzling quality." In this California trumped even his beloved France, since threats of bad weather in the harvest season were virtually nonexistent in California.

Having established what the state was capable of, Parker then condemned those whose wines did not deliver "exhilarating levels of fruit, intensity and richness." The subheading—"The Changing Mind-Set (from insipid food wines to savory, real wines)"— laid out the battle lines clearly.

Of the wines he finds deficient, Parker equates perceived faults to be "sins," describing the winemaking as "appalling," "bankrupt," "fabricated," "self-destructive," calling their flavors "harsh," "hollow," "sterile," "undrinkable," "neutral," "monolithic," "simplistic," the textures "shrill" and "eviscerating." He reserves a special dose of contempt for what he called food wines, describing them as "pathetically neutral and uninteresting, designed for masochists rather than anyone in search of pleasure." He calls out the professors of enology at Davis for allegedly teaching the techniques that led to such "appallingly ridiculous" winemaking, accusing them of "destroying the joy of wine in the name of progress."[24] Finally, he sets upon the existing community of "wine writers" for perpetuating "a philosophy of industrial winemaking," and "advocating an anti-wine philosophy."[25]

These rhetorical flourishes seemed designed to secure the critical high ground, but as the critic's own tastes lurched toward wines of excess ripeness, the rhetoric shifted toward sophistry, his descriptive language became more equivocal and tendentious. Contradictions abounded, supported by an uneasy scaffolding of metonymic constructs, all designed to uphold the basic premise that oversteeped tea was better than tea. Thus the term "intensity" was used to justify extraction; "flavor" was best applied thickly; elements like oak and residual sugar enhanced it. "Richness" was privileged over energy, "opulence" and "extravagance" the measures of character, and quality was measured in units of "hedonism."

While Parker made the reputations of countless producers—John Alban, Manfred Krankl, Justin Smith, Christophe Baron, Charles Smith, and many others—yet others he ignored, or worse, singled out for not making wines in a style he found appealing, or even for openly defying his preferences. Randall Grahm was reprimanded several times for "selling out"; of Bob Lindquist's *tête de cuvées* he tsked, in 2007, "I expected the wines to be more interesting." And in 2008 he went out of his way to express disenchantment with the wines of Edmunds St. John: "A stemmy, vegetal, spicy, cinnamon-scented nose," he wrote of one Edmunds wine, "at odds with previous experiences. Given the talent and the track record here, this is a disappointment."

Of course language could only go so far in this context: it was the point score that mattered, the point score that had lasting impact, and the point score which would be seen as Parker's most enduring legacy. Syrah comes of age in the Age of Parker, which means that the years of exploration and attention paid to site and where to grow a grape was obscured by the shorthand of the numeric score. Put another way, a great Syrah in this country was rarely associated with where it came from, the way Napa is linked with great Cabernet, and the Russian River is with Pinot; rather, it's associated with a style. "One hundred points," says winemaker Pax Mahle of Wind Gap Vineyards. "That's the reference point by which Syrah's identity is based in the U.S."

What Parker liked, of course, was a bigger wine. The problem was that in the case of Syrah, "bigger" almost always meant less distinctive. "As Parker and the *Wine Spectator* rewarded riper wines with higher scores," explains Bob Lindquist, "people started making it in riper styles. For a while consumers tried them out because Parker told them to, but they realized they weren't getting much."

Parker had a similar impact on Australian Rhône varietal wines. Certainly the prevailing style of wine found there played into Mr. Parker's predilections, but as the years passed that style seemed to become distended. Parker's highest scores went to the fiercely rich wines of the Barossa Valley and environs in South Australia, wines with levels of concentration that few bottlings elsewhere in the world could match.

There is a telling story about the transition by Campbell Mattinson in his chronicle of the Australian wine industry, *Why the French Hate Us,* published in 2007. Mattinson describes how then-unknown Barossa Shiraz producer Chris Ringland was awakened by the fax machine in his home office in the wee hours one morning in 1998. Bleary eyed, he went to the fax and pulled off a document—it was a request for his Shiraz, from an American consumer. As he read it he thought some poor inebriate had drunk-faxed him with a meaningless order. But then the fax machine beeped to life again, and a second order was transmitted, then a third, and fourth. By first light the orders were coming in by the dozen. Weeks before, unbeknownst to Ringland, someone had put a bottle of his wine under the nose of Parker, who wrote this combustible review: "Viscous, full-bodied, extremely thick and heavy (no finesse to be found in this monster)," he wrote, "this wine represents the maximum, or some would say the extreme expression of its terroir and varietal composition."

The score? 99 out of 100 points. In just a few sentences, the standards for Australian Shiraz, once diverse, were locked into a new paradigm, one where "extreme expression" was to be strived for. Parker's rave set pace for the entire industry, with Barossa leading the way.

For the rest of the country's Shiraz producers, two problems emerged. The first is that all of the other styles of Australian Shiraz were devalued in deference to the style Parker preferred. The Parker style, such as it was, became more and more contorted with each new vintage, reaching an apex perhaps in 2005, with the debut of the Mollydooker brand of wines from South Australia, thick, syrupy concoctions unsuited for consumption with any meal other than perhaps a plate of crullers.[26] Collectors soon learned that there was little difference between one wine and the next. Overnight, premium Australian Shiraz became monochromatic. In a country full of iconoclasts, everything had begun to taste the same.

Again, consumers responded by staying away. San Francisco retailer Chuck Hayward, one of the foremost experts on Australian wine in the U.S., called it a case of "fruit-bomb fatigue." And Michael Steinberger, in slate.com, wrote this: "People ultimately found the wines to be overbearing and tiresome."[27]

This became Syrah's milieu in a developing, volatile market, a confusing synergy of corporate ambition, drives for leverage and market share, and an inescapable sense that style was to be the reigning paradigm in discussions of this variety: not place, not region, not terroir. Syrah's versatility and range was lauded by winemakers, but it was a variety upon which winemakers could execute their will. They could let the fruit hang and ripen, let the acids recede and the grip of tannins soften, let the terpines and polyphenols and tension leach out of the fruit. Forget Syrah's inherent wildness—wildness was in effect a contrivance because growers could control just how wild their Syrah was going to be.

Syrah was amenable; it had an uncanny ability to produce a decent wine almost anywhere. It thrived on sunbaked hillsides normally reserved for Cabernet Sauvignon, and did just fine in relatively frosty sites the next block over from Pinot Noir. Like a gifted center fielder, it practically ran the gamut of climatic territory for red wine grapes. "Syrah," wrote Andrew Jefford in a paper on the subject delivered in Rome in 2004,

> is the most Protean of all red grape varieties. It contains multitudes. No other single red variety is capable of such a range of so many different expressions. And, like a great actor, that Protean quality is based not on a desire to display but rather on a profound sympathy with circumstances and predicament—which for a grapevine means its physical location. No other red grape variety, I believe, is capable of responding so sympathetically and so articulately to different terroirs.[28]

Predictably, this led to a range of results, contributing to the uncertainty suffered by the average red wine consumer. In a given bottle, which of the many faces of Syrah would be revealed? Animal or mineral? Spice box or jam pot? Power or nuance? A grape so peripatetic in style would inevitably show many shades, but no one could have predicted how its fate, in the end, was tied to its mutability.

"There was so much confusion over what you were actually going to get," says Justin Smith of Saxum Vineyards in Paso Robles. "Unless you'd done your research, it was sort of a minefield out there."

In the end the power of the critic, the primacy of style, and the ascendancy of a variety with a narrower bandwidth, Pinot Noir—a variety whose own wan stylings would frequently get bolstered by the addition of a dollop of Syrah—condemned Syrah to a decade in the doldrums.

Three years after Syrah plantings had crested at 13,000 acres, a movie came out that shifted the gaze of American consumers away from the Rhône pantheon altogether, toward another maverick. *Sideways*, directed by Alexander Payne and starring Paul Giamatti, Thomas Haden Church, Virginia Madsen, and Sandra Oh, based on a novel by Rex Pickett, debuted in theatres in October of 2004.

The film centered on a wine-country road trip with Miles Raymond (played by Giamatti) and his longtime friend Jack Cole (played by Church). Jack is about to be married, and so he and Miles decide to have one last bachelor weekend together in the wine-country of the Santa Ynez Valley. There they tour, taste wine, golf, and hit on a couple of women, Maya and Stephanie in the wine and restaurant trade (played by Madsen and Oh). The characters are comically small-minded, and yet throughout the movie small eruptions of wisdom and grace leak out of their mouths as if by accident, in particular from Miles, the most tragicomic of all. What he has to say about wine ends up being remarkably and unintentionally impactful. To the surprise of everyone who buys, sells, and drinks the stuff, a few well-turned lines in the film altered the course of the wine market with uncanny swiftness and force.

The first involved a single profanity-laced ultimatum in a Buellton back alley, wherein Miles condemns Merlot to its own special circle of hell with a vituperative outburst just before he and Jack enter a restaurant to meet their dates. "If any one orders Merlot I'm leaving," says Miles, "I am *not* drinking any *fucking* Merlot!" The line deals a body blow to a grape variety already on its heels in the American market.

Hours later he and Maya are left alone in a candlelit living room and Maya asks him what he loves so much about Pinot Noir. His response is tender and honest, describing the grape and, in no uncertain terms, his own fragile state:

> It's thin-skinned, temperamental, ripens early. It's, you know, it's not a survivor like Cabernet, which can just grow anywhere and thrive even when it's neglected. No, Pinot needs constant care and attention, you know? And in fact it can grow only in these really specific, tucked away corners of the world. And only the most patient and nurturing of growers can do it, really. Only somebody who really takes the time to understand Pinot's potential can then coax it into its fullest expression.

This paean to the virtues of Pinot Noir sent its fortunes skyrocketing. Interest in the variety exploded in the wake of the movie, creating a tidal wave of momentum that has hardly abated to this day.[29]

Though Syrah had the numbers, though it was poised to enter the market in force, Pinot Noir stole its fire, ignited by a hapless fictional character's single noble utterance. The movie came and went, but the impact of those two scenes still reverberate for the American consumer.

22

WHAT WE TALK ABOUT
WHEN WE TALK ABOUT AMERICAN SYRAH

By 2005, Syrah was a variety frequently rewarded for its lack of varietal character, possessing two names and multiple styles, with prodigious growing ability and few if any models from which to draw. It lacked, for the time being, a regional association which might bolster its standing in a state whose growers had embraced it without committing to the style they intended to pursue. The net effect was to render Syrah indistinct.

Syrah's inherent wildness—the exotic scent of wood smoke and violets, the hint of wild herbs and white pepper, the light-bending core of dark fruit, the weirdly thrilling flavors of blood and meat and olive and earth, its *sauvage* quality—receded, literally and figuratively. The wines became tamer: sweeter, fatter, more buxom, more monochromatic, akin to a pot of jam or a glass of port. The sensuality that had made the category irresistible had been baked, ripened, or oaked out of them. The wine became, as one winemaker put it, "amenable, but dull." Damning words for any wine, of course, but for Syrah, unthinkable. Just a few years before, similar language had been used to condemn Merlot. The category, suddenly, was in steep decline.

At first the signs were hard to read: Rhône Ranger membership rolls kept climbing, vines were still being put in the ground. Each year, Hospice du Rhône, the category's preeminent celebration, sold out. Each year its producers returned to pour and to participate in seminars and parties, to bowl together and taste together in a global celebration.

The category still received plenty of critical notice from the *Wine Spectator,* the *Wine Advocate,* the *Wine Enthusiast, Wine & Spirits,* and other industry publications, not to mention ink in the nation's newspapers. Most American wine magazines now had a section of tasting notes devoted to the American Rhône, and while the wines never quite reached the heights of critical perfection that Napa "'cult" Cabs had achieved in the mid- to late nineties, critics were more than happy to extol their virtues, to round up newcomers, and fan the flames of the maverick myth, long after the category had lost its claim to any gonzo sensibility.

Paso Robles, the spiritual and geographic epicenter of the movement, was booming, with new vineyards and wineries popping up all over, especially in the Templeton Gap, west of the 101 Freeway where the climate was cooled by ocean breezes. New varieties from the Tablas Creek portfolio of germplasm were arriving, being planted, and thriving—varieties that had not been in American soil since the nineteenth century like Picpoul, Clairette, and especially Grenache Blanc. This last variety almost seemed more of a natural fit in California than in its native France, achieving mature flavors at higher levels of acidity, providing bracing lemony notes, and serving as a much-needed blending component for the more dour Marsanne and Roussanne.

Meanwhile the hoopla surrounding the white varieties like Viognier had started to ebb. Like Syrah, Viognier suffered from multiple personalities despite having a much narrower stylistic range. The grape proved to be so difficult to grow, and the bandwidth of proper climate so narrow, that consumers seemed to experience a Viognier fatigue far more quickly than they did with the Rhône reds, preferring a brief intense dalliance to a long-term relationship. Besides, the Anything-but-Chardonnay cohort now included an ever greater range of alternatives, Albariños from Spain, Gruner Veltliners from Austria, not to mention Pinot Grigio, whose neutral stylings would in the end make it vastly more appealing to the general public than the quirky Rhône whites.

Red wines got bigger and more unwieldy with each vintage, spurred on by the lavish praises of Robert Parker and James Laube. The trend was hardly limited to Rhône varieties, but amplitude wasn't helpful in the case of Syrah, whose distinct character could be lost in a surfeit of ripeness. Nevertheless wines were generally rewarded for trending this way, even as they proved to be poor agers, even as consumers and winemakers alike started to articulate an ambivalence to the category. Most telling of all, producers quietly admitted to wine journalists that they no longer drank their own wines, or those of their peers.

"I've stopped drinking my own wines," said Adam Tolmach of Ojai Vineyard to the *Los Angeles Times* in 2008. "We lost our rudder when we went for even bolder, riper flavors," admitted Tolmach, who'd been making Syrah since 1983. His stunning admission was a bombshell that backfired upon his fans and customers, made worse by his clumsy attempt to save face by recanting what he'd been quoted saying. But he wasn't the only one.

Such was the case in 2010 with two Rhône stars from Sonoma County, Pax Mahle and Wells Guthrie, of the brands Pax and Copain. Each was part of a group of Rhône producers whom Robert Parker referred to as the young Turks; each had made critically acclaimed, collector-coveted Syrahs for the better part of a decade. They shared vineyards, winemaking techniques, and workspaces with each other—as well as many cases of wine. But in 2010 Mahle went into his cellar and realized that he had about forty cases of Copain on hand—all of them, he says, with just a bottle or two missing out of each case. Guthrie reported similar numbers in his stash of Pax. They had stopped drinking each other's wines.[1]

Mahle founded his eponymous winery in 2000, devoting nearly all of its energies to the expression of Sonoma County Syrah, which he explored through the county's diverse sites, making as many as a dozen vineyard designates of Syrah in a given vintage, more than anyone else in the county, and probably the state. While Mahle takes pains to point out that there was always a range of styles in the portfolio, most of the critical attention was reserved for wines of a certain magnitude—for which alcohols occasionally crept above 16%.

Indeed, only a handful of wines in California could compare with the Pax wines for their amplitude and power. Despite this, Mahle held to the belief that his wines still reflected much of what he loved from Cornas and Hermitage—only as the years progressed, he realized his wines weren't behaving like Rhône wines at all. "I'd tricked myself into believing I was the Thierry Allemand of Sonoma County," says Mahle. "But Allemand's wines were still young with five years of bottle age, and mine were falling apart."

Like Mahle, Wells Guthrie felt he had been making Syrah with a European pedigree. "I worked for Chapoutier for two years," says Guthrie. "I assumed that most of my sensibility was European." But it was hard to admit to himself that adding water and acid to his fermenters probably wasn't very European.

If anyone should have possessed a working knowledge of what the critics wanted in American Syrah it was Guthrie, who in the late nineties worked as a tasting coordinator in the offices of the *Wine Spectator,* side by side with Harvey Steiman and James Laube. Not surprisingly his early work was critically acclaimed by that magazine, and by Robert Parker.

Copain became known for some of the more muscular Syrahs in California (and a few from Washington—Cayuse's Christophe Baron sold Guthrie fruit from Cailloux Vineyard for several vintages). He drew from vineyards known for their brawny fruit profile, like Thompson, James Berry, and Garys' in the Central Coast; his wines were described by Parker as "full-bodied, multilayered, and enormously well-endowed." Guthrie admits it was difficult not to be swayed by this sort of attention. But a side project with a San Francisco sommelier pushed him in a different direction entirely.

In 2001 Guthrie met James Atwood at Rose Pistola, a bastion of Ligurian cooking in San Francisco's North Beach, where Atwood was running the wine program. Guthrie was taken with Atwood's intensity and enthusiasm, a trait which certainly helped him to sell case upon case of Guthrie's wines at the restaurant.

Guthrie was sufficiently inspired to collaborate with Atwood on a wine in 2003, a Pinot Noir from Cerise Vineyard in the Anderson Valley. Atwood insisted that the wine be made in a lighter, more transparent style. "He kept saying 'you need that nerve and tension in the wine,' and I'd say 'Yeah, that sounds good,' but I wasn't really committed," says Guthrie. He picked in the vicinity of 22.8° Brix, instead of the usual 25-plus, for a potential alcohol of about 13.6%. As he monitored the wine's progress over the winter, he was not optimistic. "It made me nervous," he says. "For a while there I was not digging it, but I figured that if it didn't work out I could just walk"—that is, leave Atwood to sell it on his own.

Post-harvest Guthrie spent part of the winter in Burgundy and immersed himself in French Pinot Noir. When he returned he learned that Atwood, distraught over a failed personal relationship, had taken his own life. Guthrie was stuck with an unfinished wine, a wine that wasn't altogether his, made to another's specifications. He decided to leave it in barrel sixteen months, longer than usual for him; when he tasted it again, it had been transformed. "Maybe I had come back with a Burgundy palate," he says, "but it felt like it was picking up weight; it still was a delicate wine but it had a lot of tension to it."

Guthrie bottled the wine, calling it "l'Esprit de James Atwood," in February 2005. Rajat Parr was so impressed he bought about fifty cases for Michael Mina's new flagship restaurant in San Francisco; the rest Guthrie donated to Atwood's high school in Maine, where a scholarship was established in his honor.

Guthrie was left to ponder not just the legacy of the man whose passions inspired the wine, but the wine itself. For most of the ensuing vintage he struggled to come to terms with his extended flirtation with ripe fruit. Reining in his Pinot bottlings wasn't too onerous, but then he wasn't known for Pinot Noir. His Syrahs had made his reputation; they were lauded for the very style he was thinking about abandoning. "We were all-in with the Pinots, but with the Syrahs we hadn't gone there yet," says Guthrie. "I didn't know if I could take my entire production down that road; I kept worrying the wines would be too lean."

Two years later Paul Roberts, then the sommelier at Napa Valley's French Laundry, proposed a joint project for Syrah along the lines of l'Esprit de James Atwood. Roberts wanted to use fruit from Hawk's Butte, in the Yorkville Highlands of Mendocino County, Guthrie's coolest source by a wide margin. He and Roberts made a wine together, the fruit coming in at 22.3° Brix.

Guthrie was so taken with the results that within two vintages he had dropped all of his warmer Syrah sites, and placed all of his focus on the cool highland reaches of Mendocino County. "They were all the wines I'd gotten high points for," says Guthrie. "Everyone thought I'd lost my mind; maybe I had." The wines, in their transparency, their focus, their "crunchiness" (an apt word coined by Rajat Parr to describe a particularly bracing texture), made it clear that he had not: savory and dark, spicy and lean, they possess a gripping, lasting minerality that reminds one that Syrah's place begins with the soil.

In the Petaluma Gap, Pax Mahle had gotten to a similar point with his Syrahs. It would be a few more years, however, for him to work up the nerve. He realized he'd have to harvest grapes less ripe, pick before the flavors he was seeking emerged—and ripe flavors, to this point, had been too seductive to ignore. "Obviously the sweeter a grape is," says Mahle, "the better it's going to taste. If you give a kid a choice between caviar and candy bar he's going to take the candy bar every time." However much Mahle wanted to pick at 22.5° Brix, things typically ended up north of 25°.

In 2004, Mahle and his then-assistant Duncan Meyers pulled in the fruit at a small vineyard in the Petaluma Gap owned by Mary Ann and Jim Kerschner, called Majik. Conditions were such that the fruit was fully mature at 22° Brix, exactly the sort of balanced numbers he'd been seeking the last several years. As they monitored the wine during its *élevage,* it seemed to get better and better: savory, smoky, dynamic, and lithe with each passing month.

Taken in the context of the Pax portfolio, there were a lot of things the wine didn't have: extract, power, intensity, forward fruit, heat. It presented Mahle with one of the more interesting dilemmas in his young career. "This was what I'd said I'd always wanted," he says. "What do I do now?"

In ensuing vintages, Mahle started to explore growing techniques that brought him closer to the flavors he achieved at Majik. Mahle shaded the afternoon side of the vine row to slow sugar development, but he also trimmed primary leaf growth in favor of secondary shoots, which produced young leaves later in the season. "I think that young leaves were just more efficient at turning sunlight in to ripening factors," he says. When the plant got to veraison, he reasoned, the younger leaves accelerated phenolic development. "You ended up ripe at 22°, and not 25°," he says.

A few years later Mahle gained access to Syrah fruit from Clary Ranch, which proved to him once and for all that this was the right path. Clary Ranch is set on a southwest-facing hill not ten miles from Bodega Bay, where it fully bears the brunt of Pacific winds that the Petaluma Gap is famous for. Wind Gap and Arnot-Roberts share the fruit on the site, by far the coolest for both. As they tasted it over the winter of 2006 and 2007, it was clear that this wine was different. "It was the watershed wine, for Pax and myself," says Meyers. "The energy was so apparent, and it got better and better in the barrel."

"It was pretty inspiring," says Mahle. "It had more freshness than anything we'd made before, and had those olive and black pepper aromas that are unique to Syrah."

It reminded him so much of the northern Rhône that he invited Wells Guthrie over to try it. "I told him 'I really needed to know,' says Mahle, 'is this cool or is it just me thinking it's cool?'"

Guthrie put his nose into the glass and said, "What is this, Trollat?" He was referring to the Saint-Joseph producer in the northern Rhône, whose wines they both admired.

Mahle smiled and said, "That's all you needed to say."

Through this entire period, Duncan Meyers has been at Mahle's side, either making wine with him or looking over his shoulder, and with his winemaking partner Nathan Lee Roberts, he had taken the conversion to heart as well.

Duncan Arnot Meyers and Nathan Roberts had known each other since the third grade. Both grew up in Napa, were Cub Scouts in the same troop and graduates of Vintage High. Their upbringing offered close ties to the Napa wine industry; Nathan's father, Keith, ran one of California's first local cooperages (Nathan eventually learned barrel-making), and Duncan's father was a local lawyer. They decided to make some wine together in 2001, though neither was able to commit to something full-time. Roberts continued to make barrels; Meyers, after apprenticeships at Caymus and with John Kongsgaard, had joined Pax Mahle as assistant winemaker.

By mid-decade they had a few contracts, checking their ambition by not overreaching, reining in their use of new oak barrels (presumably to the consternation of Nathan's father), managing small lots and looking for cooler sites to draw from. Those sites were out there—planted by eager would-be family growers out of passion, or convenience, or defiance, or naïveté, typically overlooked or undervalued, as winemakers sought out vineyards that could deliver wines that befitted the Age of Parker. Both Meyers and Roberts found themselves edging away from that aesthetic. Meyers and Roberts embraced these out-of-the-way places. In doing so they'd become part of a modest group of producers who were unwittingly forging a movement: they were reintroducing the importance of place in determining a wine of quality—a distinction that Syrah desperately needed.

It's not that place had had no place in the discussion of American Syrah—certainly among growers, among certain producers, the discussion was vital and engaged. And certain sites had proven to be almost effortlessly full of character and expression, places where Syrah could reach physiological ripeness without becoming too sweet. But for the first time wine writers and critics saw how cooler climates, or warm sites in cool places, were vital to retaining an arresting aromatic profile.

Arnot-Roberts' best-known fruit source had been Hudson Vineyard in the Carneros, a windswept, clay-loam-infused place devoted to Chardonnay, Merlot, Cabernet Franc, and Syrah, established in 1981 by oil scion Lee Hudson. Hudson had become one of the premier Carneros vineyard sites, and one of the region's finest for Syrah. Meyers and Roberts got access in 2003 through Meyers's old mentor, John Kongsgaard.

"We were taking our cues from him," explains Meyers, "when to pick and what to look for; allowing the tension in the skins to relax a little bit, just as they began their downward trajectory. It's almost like desiccation, but not quite. And of course we made burly wines, and we thought that's what we needed to do, make impact-driven wines."

But in 2005, a notably cool vintage, the Hudson fruit had an especially ethereal quality. "We realized that we had better flavor and higher phenolic maturity at lower sugar, and that it tasted good. So we pulled the trigger at a potential alcohol of 13.5%." It was as if someone had shone a high beam on the wines' aromatics and flavors—everything was in high relief. "In the fermenter it was stunning," says Meyers, "in its aromatics and detail." It became clear to them that the style of the wine was in their hands, that they could take their wines down this leaner, more aromatically driven pathway.

Meyers and Roberts started to actively seek more tension and a lower pH in ensuing vintages. By 2008, they picked Hudson at 22° Brix, for a potential alcohol of 13.2%. That year, when Meyers called Hudson and asked him to pull the trigger, "I expected him to call me crazy," says Meyers, "or say he wouldn't let me. Instead he's like 'Well goddamn, I'm glad someone's got some balls around here, let's do it!'"

One year later, at a gathering of Hudson Syrah producers, attended by heavy hitters like Kongsgaard, Andy Erickson, and Randy Lewis, winemakers who hardly shy away from alcohol and extract, Meyers and Roberts presented their wine. "We went into it like 'Okay, here we are, all our clothes are off,' says Meyers, 'but we thought we'd give it a shot.' We expected to get beat up, but we got a lot of good comments."

Eventually they dropped their allocation at Hudson for Syrah, shifting their focus toward the coast. "I really love that vineyard," he says, "and I loved working with Lee. But our aesthetic was moving in another direction."

If you'd been raised on a diet of California Syrah during, say, the past decade, tasting wines like these was disorienting. The first time I tasted the Pax Mahle's Sonoma Coast Syrah, a blend of the five coolest Petaluma Gap sites, I spent a couple of days pacing the room, offering sips to my wife, to friends, to get their take. With its dirty martini aromas and prickly, discordant energy, the wine was disconcerting, a feeling I found hard to disguise when I ran into Pax on a couple of occasions in the following months. Plainly, I didn't get what he was up to, though I didn't want to let on.

But six months after my first tasting I got my hands on another bottle: the wine had lost its jitters. The cluster spice had blossomed and expanded (to build out the middle palate and temper some of the fruit's acidity—and, because it's done in Tain and Ampuis, all of these producers use significant amounts of whole clusters in their fermentations). There was newfound harmony in the flavors.

Clearly these wines demand cellar time to integrate, the way the wines of Cornas and Barolo do. As Guthrie says, "No one drinking a current release of Barolo thinks it's at the pinnacle of where it should be." And like those wines, "fruit," the hallmark of modern California Syrah, is not what they lead with. On the contrary, they're almost fiercely savory.

There was another marker for wines of this type, this one involving semantics. These winemakers had more or less abandoned the usual lexicon when it came to describing their wines—none of them spoke of fruit flavors, juice, textural markers of ripeness. Instead, they spoke of their wines in terms of energy, tension, nerve, movement, play on the palate. Their vocabulary, like their wines, had become weirdly kinetic and alive.

"I used to wait for the perfect tasting grape," Mahle told me in a recent conversation. "Now more and more I don't care what a grape tastes like. Now when I pick I want to know what it looks like, how healthy is it, when I pull it off how easily does it come off the stem, if I squeeze it does color come off the skin, is the pulp pushing off the skin of my fingers?"

Such calculations, I point out, have more to do with tension than flavor. "Well, sure," says Mahle. "If I was marketing grapes I would pick them on flavor alone. But I'm not selling grapes, I'm making wine."

This seems to be the direction that will save Syrah. The class of well-made, powerful, rich, extract-laden Syrahs will always have its adherents, as long as wines like Alban and Sine Qua Non and Saxum are there to collect and covet.

But the future of Syrah, I am convinced, lies in the class of wines that allow place to shine in the bottle. And it's increasingly clear that such places exist only where the accumulation of sugar and the physical maturity of the grape—the point at which the grape's full flavors are expressed without being overwhelmed, masked, or muted by sugar ripeness—occur at roughly the same time.

No winemaker in California has been a more conscientious student of this physiological *pas de deux* than Ehren Jordan, who has stewarded ripening grapes in more than eighty California vineyards and dozens more in France, who has worked not only with Syrah but with Chardonnay, Pinot Noir, white Rhône varieties, and also Zinfandel which, when it comes to ripening, is arguably the most confounding red grape to grow in California.

Ehren Jordan was born in Sewickley, a suburb of Pittsburgh, Pennsylvania, in 1967. He studied art history at George Washington University, taking side jobs stacking boxes in wine retail shops in Washington D.C. After working briefly in wine sales in Aspen (and doing plenty of skiing on the side), he drifted to Napa where, in 1991, he met Bruce Neyers, then vice president at Joseph Phelps Vineyards.

Neyers hired him on the spot as an administrative assistant; his first assignment was helping to coordinate the International Colloquium of Rhône Varieties in 1990. Jordan traveled up and down the North Coast collecting wine and meeting with early Rhône Rangers, including Pete Minor, John Buechsenstein, Bill Smith, Randall Grahm, and others. With this firsthand look at American and French style winemaking, Jordan was presented with a dichotomy that he'd take to heart, long before turning to thoughts of winemaking.

One year later Jordan joined Neyers and the Phelps team on an American contingent to Vinexpo, the annual international wine exposition held in Bordeaux. Jordan had made plans to travel in France after the show, but on his first night met up with a couple of French Rhône producers, Jean-Luc Colombo and Michel Chapoutier, who took Jordan under their wing for the next week. They dined and drank their way through Vinexpo, and when the show ended they insisted that Jordan cancel his appointments elsewhere and come with them back to the Rhône.

Jordan kept one appointment—at Domaine de la Romanée Conti—but soon joined them in Tain, visiting cellars, tasting deep into the collection of Chapoutier, including some pre-phylloxera Hermitage, creating an indelible impression as to the wonders of Syrah in the Rhône. He returned from France with a fundamental understanding of how wrong the Phelps program was.

"I was going to Kermit Lynch's shop and drinking Saint-Josephs that were perfumed and elegant and delicate," says Jordan, "and then I'm back up in Napa drinking the Phelps wines, and they're clunky and monolithic and they lack varietal character. And then I'm meeting Bruce and Joe, who are super passionate about Syrah and about what they're doing and yet—and yet, I'm thinking, 'You drink these wines? well, then why are you making *these* wines?'"

It was a year of frustration, but it taught him some valuable lessons on how not to make Syrah in California. The Phelps team after all was a Cabernet house, and Jordan was rapidly coming to the conclusion that Syrah could not be handled like Cabernet.

"Cabernet needs to be worked over a little bit," says Jordan, "not just worked, beaten into submission. Syrah is much more like Pinot Noir. You have to be gentle, you have to leave it alone. You know how they used to say that making great Pinot was such a holy grail of a wine? I say it's the easiest thing in the world to make: you just find a great site and get out of the way. That's what you do with Syrah, too."

When Bruce Neyers was wooed away from Phelps by Kermit Lynch, Jordan weighed his options, and decided it was time to return to France. He faxed applications for harvest employment to George Lorentz in Alsace, to Jean-Marc Roulot in Burgundy, and to his old friend Colombo. He received some tacit assurances from Roulot, and set out by car to the East Coast—he intended to ship his car to France—and stopped at his parents' home outside of Pittsburgh to say good-bye.

When he got there, Jordan's mother had two pertinent bits of information. The first was that someone with a thick French accent had left a message—that turned out to be Colombo. And an old friend from high school, Anne-Marie Failla, was in town—she urged him to pay her a visit. He did, learning that she was going to be in Europe at the same time he was; they exchanged some contact information. Meanwhile Jordan called Colombo, who informed him that he had just lost the *stagier* tasked with running his harvest—would he help with harvest? Of course, said Jordan. He would live in the northern Rhône, marginally employed, for the next two years.

In Cornas Jordan continued his apprenticeship on the intricacies of French Syrah. Since Colombo was a négociant, he introduced Jordan to dozens of producers up and down the Rhône Valley, and exposed him to many other Rhône varieties, *cépages,* and techniques. Jordan learned how Syrah was grown in other parts of France, how it behaved in different sites and aspects; he learned Syrah *in situ* the way few Americans had ever done.

Moreover, since Jordan could not legally draw a French salary, Colombo fed him, gave him lodging, slipped him cash now and again when he needed it. In perhaps the best arrangement of all, Colombo paid Jordan in wine from his own cellar and those of his contemporaries. Jordan rapidly accumulated an enviable collection of wines from the region.

Not only this but over the next year Jordan became Colombo's travel and dining companion, accompanying him on journeys to Paris and Lyon, visiting the many friends Colombo had in the business of making, growing, and serving food in France.

When Bruce Neyers came to France on a buying trip that first winter abroad, he asked Jordan to be his translator. And so this young winemaker not only got to visit the cellars of Kermit Lynch's legendary stable of winemakers, but to convey, in English, their wine-making practices, methods and secrets. He was being paid to translate the how-to of French technique.

Well, not exactly paid. When the time came to settle on a fee, Jordan asked, instead, that Kermit Lynch Wine Merchant incur the cost of transporting all of the wines he'd accumulated in his time in France; in subsequent years, payment usually took the form of setting up interesting meetings with producers all over the country at Jordan's beck.

Six years later, in 1998, Jordan had married Anne-Marie Failla and founded Failla-Jordan Winery, where he could put into practice all of the French techniques he'd learned while abroad.[2] He made wines for Neyers's eponymous winery as well as the successful Zinfandel producer Turley, whose founder, Larry, had benefited immensely from the success of his sister Helen.[3]

Until the mid-2000s, Jordan was best known for his long winemaking tenure at Turley Cellars, a winery famous for its Zinfandels, as well as being a Parker darling. Jordan's long stint at Turley amounted to an ongoing study of ripeness in California fruit; Zinfandel has long been considered one of the trickiest.

"I made my share of really big wines at Turley," he says, "and there were older wines that we opened and weren't that excited about and would want to know why. So we'd go back and deconstruct the wines, and we realize that in nearly every case we'd picked the vineyard too late. We'd started to believe our own bullshit, telling ourselves we were waiting for the flavors to get ripe. But what we really had to do was change our farming."

Over the years Jordan learned how to manage his vineyards so that the grapes retained their vitality at the end of the season. He also had to train himself not to pick for flavor. "This business of picking for flavor drives me insane," he says. "You're nuts if you think that's what you're waiting for. When people say they're waiting for flavors they're actually looking at the Brix. Twenty-eight Brix grapes taste really good, they're awesome; what they don't do is make really good wine."

Alcohol levels in older California wines didn't creep into the mid-teens, he reasoned; why was it necessary in the modern era? Jordan started to suspect that at least part of the problem with modern winegrowing was that the plants had been trained to be too efficient, they grew better than ever, and that was throwing off the balance in the fruit.

"In the modern era," he says, "growers would call bullshit, they'd be like 'how could an older wine possibly be 12.8% alcohol and not smell like green beans and bell peppers?' In today's vineyards that's often true. But back then a cluster could get physiologically ripe at 23° Brix because it was grown on a relatively inefficient trellis. Modern viticulture has maximized the efficiency of the trellis, and California heat, what you get at 25° Brix is the wine smells like green beans and bell peppers. So then you're obliged pick at 30° Brix, and that has a whole host of issues that go along with it.

"I think we've taken viticultural efficiency to its logical extreme," he says. "The vines accumulate sugar too rapidly, well before they're physiologically ripe, to the point that they truly don't taste good, and yet they're 15% potential alcohol." This has proved especially disastrous for Syrah, whose character disappears as the sugars and alcohols rise.

The Failla wines are as demonstrative as Syrah can be in California, with wildly exotic scents of mostly an herbal tinge, owing to Jordan's proclivity for harvesting when the fruit is still tense and vibrant, and because he practices whole-cluster fermentation, wherein the fruit is not destemmed but macerates and is pressed off with stems in the must. This lends an inimitable tealike spice to the flavors and aromas. These are also exceedingly nervy wines, built to age, and can seem a bit backward in their youth, but that, to Jordan, is the nature of wine itself. "It has to have a life," he says, "if it doesn't, I don't see the point."

In June 2010, less than seven years after Matt Kramer's paean to the "Next Really Big Red" in the *Wine Spectator*, *New York Times* wine columnist Eric Asimov wrote a story titled "Is There Still Hope for Syrah?" The story opened with a riddle: "What's the difference," asked the author, "between a case of Syrah and a case of pneumonia?" And the punch line? "You can get rid of the pneumonia."[4]

"In the last few years," Asimov wrote, "sales of American Syrah have essentially dropped off a cliff." He cited winemakers like Randall Grahm ("It's crashed and burned in this country"), Ehren Jordan ("a collective running into a brick wall"), and others to add to the mix of metaphors, but the message was the same: this was a category on life support, and those who loved it and made it were desperate to find a pulse.

Asimov described a wine that had lost its way, hamstrung by moribund sales figures, a crippling distribution bottleneck, and a complex, deep-seated, unrelenting consumer malaise. These conditions persisted, Asimov wrote, despite the presence of dozens of captivating wines in the marketplace, and he went on to laud many of the brands named in this chapter, including Copain, Wind Gap, Arnot-Roberts, and Failla, as well as Peay, Bonny Doon, Qupé, and Edmunds St. John, all of whom, said Asimov, were making wines as dramatic and inspired as any in California; they just happened to be made with Syrah.

Asimov voiced hope that the variety could find its legs, and championed in particular the wines made in cool-climate locales, where alluring, savory aromatics prevailed over excessive fruitiness. To Bob Lindquist, he gave the last word: "It's a great grape, obviously," says Lindquist, "and great grapes always rise to the top."

Over the next year several articles, by Jordan Mackay, Talia Baiocchi, Jon Bonné, and myself, expended thousands of words trying to get to the bottom of Syrah's sclerotic market presence, most expressing sheer bafflement that such a noble variety, capable of producing some of the world's most haunting wines, could be perceived with such enmity and indifference.

Some three months after Asimov's article, in what seemed like a desperate attempt to "own the message," the Rhône Rangers teamed up with GAVI (Global Alliance for Vaccines and Immunization) for a charitable program they called "Pneumonia's Last Syrah," hoping, one supposes, to subvert the unflattering imagery with which Eric Asimov had saddled the variety. The collected funds were paltry—the effort, mostly symbolic—but the campaign succeeded in forever linking Syrah to a deadly respiratory ailment.[5] It was hard to imagine how much further the category could fall.

A Los Angeles wine professional named Amy Christine wrote her Master of Wines thesis on just this topic in 2012, and provided some cold statistics to answer this question. Syrah sales, she reported, fell by one third between 2008 and 2012, from nearly 22 million bottles sold to just under 15 million; and Australian Shiraz bottle sales fell in similarly precipitous numbers. In addition, writes Christine, "All other red varieties listed a higher average bottle price compared to Syrah," which was "the only major red variety long on supply in bulk-wine positions."[6]

Having played such a pivotal role in establishing an alternative universe in the American wine market, Syrah and other Rhône bottlings now stood at a precipice. A combination of seemingly disparate elements—overzealous and injudicious planting; rapid vineyard expansion; the perils of mainstreaming; the deleterious effect of *surmaturité* upon Syrah's essential character; the failure of Australia's voracious global wine companies to anchor the position of its flagbearer; the Parker effect; the *Sideways* deflection; Pinot Noir's meteoric overnight success—all of these elements, coalescing in the span of half a decade, had created a perfect storm of misfortune for Syrah, squandering its standing in the market and tarnishing its reputation among consumers new and old.

Some producers felt obliged to take matters into their own hands. In the spring of 2010, just before the annual Rhône Rangers tasting, Bob Lindquist and importer Patrick Will organized a panel tasting and discussion of Syrah's cool-climate virtues, called "A Question of Balance," in which they sought to prove that Syrah was a wine still to be reckoned with.[7]

Even though this seminar was designed to accentuate the positive, coordinator Lindquist, considered one of the more even-keeled winemakers in the business, could not help but vent his frustration at the outset: "If I meet one more salesperson who says 'I can't sell Syrah,'" he said, "I'm going to fucking kill them."

Things were considerably more upbeat from this point, starting with the lineup of wines and winemakers: joining Lindquist was Stephen Singer of Baker Lane, Rajat Parr, then of Parr Selections, Jason Drew of Drew Cellars, Duncan Meyers and Nathan Roberts of Arnot-Roberts; the wines of Steve Edmunds were also represented. Nearly every journalist present wrote a story extolling these efforts and describing with particular urgency the necessity for this line in the sand.[8]

Less than two years later, on the heels of a wildly successful twentieth anniversary celebration, the organizers of Hospice du Rhône announced that its annual event in Paso Robles would cease. They cited several reasons for this: despite routinely selling out, ticket sales had been sluggish and trending downward for some time, especially since the economic downturn of 2008. There was some feeling that the reason for the celebration itself—to draw attention to the category—was no longer necessary, since the category no longer had to struggle for attention. "We've always wanted to move forward," says John Alban about the decision, "but we reached a point where we felt that the same event in the same format wasn't progress," adding, "I believe (wine critic) Bob Parker once referred to the event as an 'orgy.' I think some of us are ready for a monogamous relationship."[9]

Hospice itself, of course, had not been the same celebration it once was for some time. It ran smoothly, without drama or incident, which is to say it didn't feel as scruffy or alternative. Indeed, the proceedings, while still occasionally irreverent, were no longer perceived as particularly nonconformist. The category's maverick status, that much-vaunted trope that seemed to capture Hospice's general air of intransigence, was difficult to sustain. "To be 'successful' and a 'maverick' is oxymoronic," John Alban pointed out, adding "If you were to market Rhône varieties now as something new and innovative or Bohemian or whatever, you'd really have to find someone living in a closet."

But rather than generating interest, the mainstreaming of the category had led to a flood of brands virtually indistinguishable from one another. Hospice's genial nature remained intact, but its messaging was neutralized when American Rhône wines could no longer be positioned as countercultural. This lack of distinction seemed insurmountable. "People don't have a clear picture of what Syrah is," says Carole Meredith, the esteemed University of California, Davis vine researcher and founder of Lagier-Meredith winery. "It still has no history for Americans; it hasn't had a Judgment of Paris, it hasn't had a movie. What it has is a lot of schlocky wines that have really worked against it."

Nor did it help that there was little turnover among the Hospice faithful. Winemakers expressed a mixture of delight and frustration at seeing the same faces every year; new fans were increasingly hard to find. There was a pervasive sense that Hospice had become hermetic, a chance to preach to the converted and nothing more. "It's hard to keep up that initial spark of energy and enthusiasm," says Steve Edmunds of Edmunds St. John Winery, who stopped attending in 2008. "It must be what Burning Man is like now."

At Hospice du Rhône in 2009 I took a walk through the cavernous Grand Tasting room with the event's founder, John Alban. This was in the opening few minutes, before the crowds descended upon the winery tables and the room succumbed to its usual high-decibel, purple-tongued pandemonium.

John was hoping to taste a few wines before being called upon to pour at his own booth. We decided to pay a visit to Pax Mahle, who was then exhibiting the wines from his new label, Wind Gap, dramatic cool-weather iterations of the variety that reflected how radically his direction had shifted.

Alban by this time had hit upon a new direction of his own. After many years of flirting with a more muted "French" style of Syrah, Alban had altered his winemaking and his winegrowing to produce wines of an incredible richness, with animal scents and opulent textures, wildly exotic and powerfully, stratospherically ripe. Rather than draw you in, these wines seemed crafted to blow you back.

Here, in the personages of two Syrah superstars, stood the two stylistic poles which defined American Syrah, one ethereal, aromatic and savory, one sumptuous, heady and powerful. Syrah's prodigious range had allowed them to manage these huge shifts in direction and style. Not only this, but their respective evolutions had taken each to where the other had started. In effect, they had crossed paths. And now, for the first time, post-conversion Alban was saying hello to postconversion Mahle. This may account for the peculiar tension I sensed between them, which I could not immediately interpret.

Alban and I politely took a small sample from Mahle and sniffed it. Mahle smiled nervously. Probably he had a sense of how Alban would feel about the wine, but he seemed apprehensive all the same. Alban, ever gracious, commented on the new direction and said something diplomatic, along the lines of "well, that's different." Since both men were in the presence of a journalist, they kept their opinions close to the cuff.

When we left the table I remarked to Alban about how wild these wines seemed. "That's one word for it," Alban said, but let on little more. It was clear that the wines from postconversion Mahle were a kind of affront to postconversion Alban. These two gifted winemakers would remain friends, but in matters of Syrah, would have little to agree on going forward.

Tensions aside, it's likely that American Syrah will live along this continuum for some time. It is a wine that can be coaxed toward a level of excess that seems obscene on its face, more voluptuous and sensual than any wine made in California. It can be so exotic, so hedonic, and so over the top it's as if the wine is breaking some laws of oenological decency. If you are prudish or patrician in your aesthetics, that can seem like an outrage. If you're not, you may be moved to a special, purple-tinged state of euphoria, one which few grape varieties can offer.

The rules of decorum for wine in general seem not to apply to American Syrah. Its most collectible wines are arguably its most wanton and tumescent, a thing which cannot be said for nearly every other great grape variety on earth.[10] It is a red wine capable of producing some of the world's most unforgettable wines, and yet it's also capable of an almost astonishing degree of insipidity, wines so generic and innocuous they almost don't register as wine at all, but as a thick purple liquid spiked with alcohol and sugar. Considering how great it can be, when it underperforms like this the end result comes off as not just disappointing, it's reprehensible, even cynical. That letdown may be the single greatest explanation for the consumer indifference with which Syrah was met in the mass market. Syrah's greatest sin, to date, has been in being boring, and in the marketplace it has paid dearly for that sin.

In this regard it is like another noble variety which also struggles to find a foothold in a swiftly moving market: Riesling. Like Riesling, Syrah is capable of a multitude of styles, must weights, levels of ripeness (comparisons end, hopefully, at levels of residual sugar). At its best it is among the most ethereal of white wines, but its reputation has been severely tarnished by mass market missteps, in particular by a group of white wines popular in the seventies, Liebfraumilch blends called variously Blue Nun, Black Tower, Zeller Schwarz Katz. These were sweet, blended, Riesling-heavy German wines that rightfully earned a reputation as some of the most insipid on earth. In the American market at least they sullied the reception of German wines, and Riesling specifically, for decades. With its rise and fall and prospective rise, Syrah may be the Riesling of red wines, a wine whose ethereal pleasures are rare enough that your average consumer has yet to experience it. What they have experienced, however, is mediocrity in its many forms—and that mediocrity has left a lasting impression.

In the last decade, Syrah's market recession has cleared the way for many other Rhône varieties to come to the fore, notably Grenache, Mourvèdre, and even Cinsaut which, for its ability to retain acidity in warm vintages, may be the red variety in the Rhône pantheon best equipped to withstand the rising temperatures brought on by global warming.[11] Perhaps the biggest surprise among red grape varieties has been the modest renaissance of American Carignane, especially those sourced from the old vineyards that had been underappreciated for decades from Mendocino and Sonoma counties, and even Lodi. A small number of new producers (and an old one, Randall Grahm), are making simple, delicious reds from venerable sources that are at once affordable and delightful.

Grenache, meanwhile, continues to improve as growers figure out how to make it and winemakers get to the heart of its mysteries in California. Old vines too are being preserved where once they'd been uprooted; those that remain represent a heritage, and others have planted the variety in places which actively challenge its natural tendency toward vigor and overcropping. Jon Bonné, in a story written in 2013 for the *San Francisco Chronicle,* firmly believes that Grenache is capable of taking up the mantle of Rhône varieties where Syrah could not. "It stands to become a great hope for West Coast wine," he writes, "stepping in where Syrah boldly tried to go."[12]

There are certainly some laudable examples of Grenache in California soil, and Bonné lists several, from producers like Birichino, Broc, and A Tribute to Grace. Indeed some of the powerhouse Syrah producers of California—Saxum, Sine Qua Non, Alban, and others—make bold versions of the grape, proving that Grenache is well suited to their over-the-top styles. I myself have yet to be convinced that Grenache is capable of the profundity that Bonné seems to locate here—it seems to lack the gravitas found elsewhere in the world—but I'd never say it wasn't something that could happen in the future.

Grenache is routinely employed in the new regime of blended wines that are legion in the American market in 2014. Indeed there has been a kind of blend renaissance since the mid-2000s, which is at once exciting and opportunistic, taking advantage of plentiful

Syrah in the bulk market, while carefully eschewing the use of that varietal name on the label.

Of course blends have been part of the Rhône repertoire for decades; some of its most famous wines, from Le Cigare Volant to Pleiades and Esprit de Beaucastel, have been blends. Marketing the blend has always been a kind of ontological playground for the Rhône movement, a wine that says as much about the personality of the winery and the winemaker as it does about the contents of the bottle. Most draw inspiration from the Côtes du Rhône, aiming for agreeability and simple pleasures. (They're generally less expensive than monovarietal bottlings even though, arguably, their *cépage* requires a bit more skill.) Artistic license runs rampant in the naming of these wines, which go by monikers like Rock n Rhône, High on the Hog, *%#&@!, Pape Star, Troublemaker, and Idiot du Village, to name a few.[13]

Until recently blends have had had mixed success in the American market, where consumers have tended to balk at a wine that isn't forthcoming about its varietal identity. But there have been exceptions, suggesting that blends represent a kind of barometer for American consumers' seesawing sense of confidence. The most successful blend in recent years has not been a Rhône blend exactly, but Rhône varieties do contribute a quarter or more of its contents.

It's called The Prisoner, and it's a blend developed by a young winemaker named Davis Phinney, who in 2000 corrected a stuck fermentation of Zinfandel with Cabernet, Syrah, Grenache, Petite Sirah, and whatever else he found to pull it into balance. The end result was a juicy mouthfilling red, to which he applied a label that reproduced a dark and splendid etching by Goya of the same name.

It is an arresting image: a man in shackles, his head buried in shadow and heavy beard, in a blood red room—and it lends its share of gravitas even if the image is more serious than the contents of the bottle. The wine is simple, smooth, and relatively expensive ($35 and up) for what it is, a concession perhaps to the 80% or so Napa Valley fruit inside.[14]

Viognier continues to occupy a niche in the market that is dogged and admirable, despite the backlash that had sent its fortunes plummeting in the early 2000s. It's worth noting that Viognier seems to have found a place in Washington State, where more temperate growing conditions—the grapes have higher levels of acidity at peak maturity—have resulted in wines that have more natural balance than many of its counterparts in California. It remains an outlier, but is easier to grow and make up there.

Marsanne and especially Roussanne remain beloved by winemakers even if these wines not as wholeheartedly embraced by the general public. The great Roussannes and Marsannes of California—from Qupé, Alban, Sine Qua Non, Peay, Domaine de la Terre Rouge, Truchard, Beckmen, Stolpman, DeLille, Clos Solene, Tablas Creek, and others— are mostly underground sensations, sold in wine clubs and tasting rooms and occasionally admired for their outsider standing, but their flavors and general reticence afford them a kind of curio status. These three remain the most widely planted in the whites pantheon, though Grenache Blanc, Picpoul, and Clairette are all in the California soil, and are being explored.

All of these varieties work seamlessly in white blends, which, while not as popular as red blends, have their niche, and are perhaps the most compelling whites in the entire Rhône pantheon. They serve to leaven the exuberance of Viognier, to elevate the neutral vibe of Marsanne, to tame Roussanne's Janus-faced mysteries, to make something companionable, balanced, and delicious with the other, more acid-driven components in Picpoul, Clairette, and Grenache Blanc. Viognier is also still employed as a blending component to Syrah bottlings in some instances, just as it's done in the northern Rhône and, increasingly, in Australia.

Meanwhile I keep coming back to Steve Edmunds's comment in 2012 about Hospice du Rhône. "It's hard to keep up that initial spark of energy and enthusiasm," he told me; "It must be what Burning Man is like now." It's a statement that can be easily extrapolated to describe the entire American Rhône pantheon.

Burning Man, of course, is a long way from dead. It's one of the most successful countercultural celebrations in the western states, and though its "outsider" credibility erodes with each passing year, it still represents a life-changing event for those who attend.[15] I have never been to Burning Man, but as a California resident for the last twenty years, I have scores of friends and acquaintances for whom this Labor Day weekend celebration is an annual rite.

Burning Man got its start in San Francisco in 1986, when Larry Harvey, Jerry James, and a small group of friends burned a nine-foot effigy on Baker Beach, near the churning waters of the Golden Gate. In 1990 the celebration was moved to the Black Rock Desert in northwest Nevada, and crowds followed in droves: in 2013 more than 50,000 scantily clad revelers attended. "Black Rock City," as the encampment is known, is by far the most populous environment in northwest Nevada, dwarfing the small towns that support it.

The demographic of Black Rock City has changed with the years, of course. Initially the tribe was composed largely of outliers and mavericks: artists, theatre actors, musicians, puppeteers, vaudevillians, along with designers, welders, and carpenters to help construct the sets and spectacles. Of course these groups continue to attend, but they're joined now by computer scientists and CFOs, Silicon Valley accountants and computer programmers, dot-com denizens of Google and Autodesk and Intuit and Facebook who, for the right price, can be "alt" for the week and get out of the cubicle, physically, mentally, spiritually.

One man I know takes his entire family, two rambunctious boys and a wife who is a visual artist. He himself is a real estate developer in the Bay Area, and has a net worth of tens of millions of dollars. Except for perhaps travel, he does nothing to excess. He is in fact one of the more buttoned up people I know, and that makes him as unlikely a person to attend this sort of event as I can imagine. But that is exactly what Burning Man is like now.

I'm sure there are still hundreds of hippies and artists and hippie artists who have attended Burning Man for many years, even since its inception. I'm sure that many disdain what it has become, lament the co-opting of its anarchic spirit by newcomers, dilettantes, posers. But what else can it do but endure? The celebration remains vital and largely self-sustaining, it has survived its own assimilation into the larger cultural framework by adapting, by broadening its appeal. It still moves hearts and minds, though the net it casts to reach them is wider and more inclusive than it's ever been.

It has survived the way countless other countercultural institutions have survived, whether Peet's Coffee or the Gap, Apple Computer or Ben & Jerry's, Whole Foods or Planned Parenthood or Chez Panisse, or the University of California, Berkeley. To paraphrase John Alban, to be "successful" and "anarchic" is oxymoronic; you can't be both at the same time.

So too with the Rhône movement. Rhône varieties are grown all over the country and enjoyed by millions of American consumers annually. The wines may no longer be considered maverick, but perhaps they are as maverick as late-stage capitalism may allow, and must ride the wave of markets and trends just like all of the other companies whose founders were inspired by sixties values, and who have had to evolve in the postindustrial era. Few of them, I would suggest, have entered the new millennium with their countercultural credibility wholly intact.

Meanwhile two of California's great music festivals, Coachella, in the desert outside of Palm Springs, and Outside Lands, in San Francisco's Golden Gate Park, are now as well known for their food and drink offerings as their vast musical program. And this being California, the wine offerings show tremendous allegiance to nearby producers.

It's worth noting that those festivals aren't serving Cabernet and Chardonnay. The attendees want a wine they can enjoy with simple food and throw back without fear of tannic overload, a wine that's not too complicated, that captures note for note the vibe of a music festival, which is to say not vanilla, not conventional, not mainstream. The wines which best meet these needs are Rhône varieties, and they are consumed with gusto and abandon at such venues because they seem to be made just for this sort of experience.

Last year's Outside Lands featured thirty-six wine booths; twenty-six offered Rhône varietal wines or had Rhône affiliations.[16] The American Rhône wine category may play a diminished role in the culture, its reputation may have tarnished over the years, it may have been subsumed in an ever-expanding global melting pot of wines, but it is not dead. In the U.S., the Rhône pantheon still functions much as it did when it began, when Randall Grahm and Sean Thackrey and Manfred Krankl were seeing it as not only a medium for their vinous ambitions, but as an outlet for their creativity, a means to break through the stigmas that American wine suffered from. That is still the case today.

The American Rhône is the one of the wine categories through which innovations have flowed most freely, where abandon and humor, ease of use, and more immediate pleasures got their vinous foothold in the American culture, a place where wines could be enjoyed without concern for tradition or an advanced degree in wine education. The American Rhône is a category, in the end, where one might encounter wine in a state of play, and it is also the river this country's wine lovers traveled to get there.

NOTES

CHAPTER 1. THE SIXTIES, HEADWATERS OF THE AMERICAN RHÔNE

1. The details for this account come from David Kamp's *United States of Arugula* (New York: Broadway Books, 2006) and Thomas McNamee's *Alice Waters and Chez Panisse* (New York: Penguin Books, 2007).
2. Kamp, p. 130.
3. Ruth Reichl, *Tender at the Bone* (New York: Random House, 1998), p. 257.
4. Forward by Alice Waters, in Richard Olney, *Lulu's Provencal Table* (New York: HarperCollins, 1994), p. xi.
5. Kermit Lynch, *Adventures on the Wine Route* (New York: Farrar Strauss & Giroux, 1986), p. 26.
6. In conversation with Kermit Lynch, 1/5/2009.
7. Lynch, p. x.
8. Ibid., p. 100.
9. From a Trumpetvine newsletter: Stan Hock, "The Grape Who Knew Too Much," vol. 7, no. 1, January 1985.
10. Olney, p. xi.
11. In conversation with Steve Edmunds, 1/5/2009.

CHAPTER 2. A PLACE AND ITS PROGENY

1. The ecologically themed mural is called Aquarius and depicts a child pouring water from a shell, a disturbingly tranquil image for the cooling tower of a nuclear reactor.

2. In Côte-Rôtie, of course, the Syrah is often supplemented by a small percentage of Viognier—and in Hermitage a similar blend is made with Marsanne or Roussanne.

3. Waverly Root, *The Food of France* (New York: Vintage Books, 1992), p. 322.

4. Robert W. Mayberry, *Wines of the Rhône Valley: A Guide to Origins* (Totowa, NJ: Rowman & Littlefield, 1987), p. 2.

5. Ibid., p. 15.

6. Ibid., p. 2.

7. Ibid., p. 34.

8. George Saintsbury, *Notes on a Cellar-book* (London: MacMillan & Company, 1921), pp. 6–7.

9. In conversation with John Alban, 7/8/2009.

10. This explanation, that Mourvèdre earned the nickname "dog-strangler" for its harsh tannins, is common, and plausible, but is almost certainly erroneous. Most likely Mourvèdre received the name for the huge, low-hanging canes it would produce in the spring; any but the smallest dog running through the vineyard then was doomed.

11. The passage goes on to acknowledge that passably good reds can be made from older plantings but concludes, "Let some interesting old Carignan vines be treasured but let it not be planted." Jancis Robinson and Julia Harding, *The Oxford Companion to Wine*, 4th ed. (Oxford: Oxford University Press, 2015), p. 143.

12. Jancis Robinson, Julia Harding, and José Vouillamoz, *Wine Grapes* (New York: HarperCollins, 2012), p. 617.

13. [Louis Paparelli and Eugene W. Hilgard], *Report of the Viticultural Work, During the Seasons 1887–1893, with data regarding the vintages of 1894–95. Part I. a. Red Wine Grapes. b. White Wine Grapes. c. Table and Raisin Grapes. Part II. Notes on Various Subjects* (Sacramento: State Printing Office, 1896), p. 112.

14. Robinson and Harding, *Oxford Companion to Wine*, p. 143.

15. This makes Nebbiolo Viognier's cousin.

16. These difficulties suggest that in its decline a bit of natural selection might have been at work.

17. According to Carole Meredith, retired plant geneticist at University of California, Davis, the two varieties are almost certainly related, but the nature of that relationship (whether parent/offspring or siblings) has yet to be determined.

18. See www.drinkrhone.com, Livingstone-Learmonth's excellent web site for all things Rhône Valley.

19. *Pacific Wine and Spirit Review*, March 28, 1885.

20. In fact this may have been the source of Alban's material as well, though clonally they are distinct—as one would expect if one's source is an old vineyard propagated by massal selection.

21. Chateau de Beaucastel does employ the variety in their Coudelet de Beaucastel Côtes du Rhône blend, a stone's throw from their Chateauneuf-du-Pape properties.

22. Jancis Robinson, *The Oxford Companion to Wine*, 3rd ed. (New York: Oxford University Press, 2007), p. 334.

CHAPTER 3. HOW RHÔNE VARIETIES GOT TO AMERICAN SOIL

1. Michael Pollan, *The Botany of Desire* (New York: Random House, 2001), p. xviii.

2. Jancis Robinson, Julia Harding, and José Vouillamoz, *Wine Grapes* (New York: Harper-Collins, 2012), pp. 550–551.

3. Charles A. Wetmore, *Ampelography of California: A Discussion of Vines now known in the state, together with comments on their adaptability to certain locations and uses* (New York: Merchant Publishing Company, 1884), p. 3. Also found in the *San Francisco Merchant,* vol. 8, no. 2 (November 7, 1884).

4. Charles Sullivan, *Like Modern Edens* (Cupertino: California History Center, 1982), p. 13.

5. LeFranc's heirs dropped the "New" from New Almaden Vineyards and created a brand that survives to the present day.

6. The account here is derived from multiple sources, including Haraszthy's own story, *Grape Culture, Wines and Wine-making* (Harper & Brothers, 1862); David Darlington's *Angels' Visits: An Inquiry into the Mystery of Zinfandel* (New York: Henry Holt & Co., 1992), Thomas Pinney's majestic two-volume *A History of Wine in America* (Berkeley: University of California Press, 1989), and Brian McGinty's *Strong Wine: The Life and Legend of Agoston Haraszthy* (Stanford: Stanford University Press, 1998).

7. From *The Journals of the Senate and Assembly of the Twenty-Fourth Session of the Legislature of the State of California,* vol. 2 (Sacramento: State Printing Office, 1881).

8. Pinney, *A History of Wine in America,* vol. 1, p. 262.

9. *San Francisco Merchant,* vol. 15, no. 6 (January 1, 1886), p. 83.

10. Derived from various sources, including the *San Francisco Merchant, Reports of the Viticultural Work,* George Husmann's *Grape Culture and Wine-Making in California* (San Francisco: Payot, Upham and Co., 1888) and Charles Sullivan, *A Companion to California Wine* (Berkeley: University of California Press, 1998).

11. Taken from Pinney, *A History of Wine in America,* vol. 1, p. 327.

12. Bioletti served at Hilgard's side throughout the 1890s, after which he headed up the University's Agriculture Experiment Stations; he became professor of viticulture at Berkeley, where he served until 1935.

13. Eugene W. Hilgard, *Report of the Viticultural Work, During the Seasons 1883–4 and 1884–5, being Appendix No. IV to the Report for the year 1884* (Sacramento: State Printing Office, 1886), p. 101.

14. Hilgard, *Report of the Viticultural Work, During the Seasons 1885 and 1886, being Appendix No. VI to the Report for the year 1886* (Sacramento: State Printing Office, 1886), p. 83.

15. Little has changed here, except that those sugars are converted to alcohol in the present day.

16. Louis Paparelli and Eugene W. Hilgard, *Report of the Viticultural Work, During the Seasons 1887–1889, with data regarding the vintage of 1890. Part I. Red Wine Grapes* (Sacramento: State Printing Office, 1892), p. 177.

17. Ibid., p. 184.

18. Wetmore, p. 15.

19. Ibid.

20. *San Francisco Merchant,* March 27, 1885, p. 180.

21. Paparelli and Hilgard, *Report of the Viticultural Work, During the Seasons 1887–1889.*

22. Ibid.

23. Wetmore, p. 17.

24. Ibid., p. 12. See note 10 in chap. 2 for an alternative explanation of the metaphor *chien-entrangler.*

25. Ibid., p. 12.

26. Ibid., p. 12.

27. Frederic T. Bioletti, "The Best Wine Grapes for California," *The Bulletin of the University of California Experiment Station,* no. 193 (1907), p. 145.

28. Paparelli and Hilgard, *Report of the Viticultural Work, During the Seasons 1887–1889,* p. 192.

29. [Louis Paparelli and Eugene W. Hilgard], *Report of the Viticultural Work, During the Seasons 1887–1893, with data regarding the vintages of 1894–95. Part I. a. Red Wine Grapes. b. White Wine Grapes. c. Table and Raisin Grapes. Part II. Notes on Various Subjects* (Sacramento: State Printing Office, 1896), p. 112.

30. Husmann, p. 154.

31. Ibid., p. 156.

32. [Paparelli and Hilgard], *Report of the Viticultural Work, During the Seasons 1887–1893,* p. 171.

33. *San Francisco Merchant,* March 27, 1885, p. 181.

34. Wetmore, pp. 16–17.

35. *San Francisco Merchant,* March 27, 1885, p. 180.

36. Hilgard, *Report of the Viticultural Work, During the Seasons 1883–4 and 1884–5,* p. 127.

37. Ibid., p. 128.

38. Ibid., p. 126.

CHAPTER 4. THE CURIOUS CASE OF AMERICAN PETITE SIRAH

1. For decades, historian Charles Sullivan has tried to cleave the names, the reputations, and the provenance of these two varieties from one other. For the most part, I will adhere to his treatment in various published reports and one important unpublished report, as most of my research dovetails with his findings. I can vouch for his assertion that Petite Sirah "is a variety with a confused history, but it is not a mysterious history."

2. Peloursin itself is an obscure Rhône variety once employed in the Isère region of the valley, near the Alps.

3. Claude Valat, "Syrah N, Grosse Syrah, Petite Syrah et Durif," *Le Progrès agricole et viticole,* 113 (1996), pp. 204–205.

4. Ibid., p. 205. Translation by Sylvie Sullivan.

5. *Pacific Wine and Spirit Review,* April 20, 1892, p. 29.

6. In some senses, it is a curious list; he is plainly marketing some vines for which he has good supply. But he leaves off the most highly regarded varieties in the Napa Valley to this point, Zinfandel, Mataro, and Carignane; Cabernet Sauvignon, he concludes, "does not bear enough to be profitable."

7. *Pacific Wine and Spirit Review,* January 26, 1891, p. 16.

8. *St. Helena Star,* April 8, 1892.

9. *Pacific Wine and Spirit Review,* April 20, 1892, p. 29.

10. Unfortunately McIver's opinions on the topic were never recorded; he was never quoted in print. Crabb, on the other hand, is voluminous.

11. *Pacific Wine and Spirit Review,* January 8, 1897.

12. Frederic T. Bioletti, "The Best Wine Grapes for California," in California Agricultural Experiment Station Bulletin no. 193, 1907.

13. Charles L. Sullivan, "The Petite Sirah in California: A History" (unpublished article, Los Gatos, 1998), p. 14.

14. Ibid., p. 10.

15. Followed just weeks later by Lee Stewart and Souverain Winery.

16. Gerald Asher, "California Syrah: Getting to the Bottom of the Warm-Hearted Reds, *Gourmet,* March 1997.

17. Charles Sullivan, *Napa Wine: A History from Mission Days to Present* (San Francisco: The Wine Appreciation Guild, 1994), p. 194.

18. Frederic Bioletti and F. C. H. Flossfeder, *Phylloxera-Resistant Rootstocks,* in California Agricultural Experiment Station Bulletin no. 331, p. 126.

19. Leon Bonnet, "The Petite Sirah," *California Grape Grower,* June 1924, p. 4.

20. M. A. Amerine and A. J. Winkler, *Grape Varieties for Wine Production* (Berkeley: University of California, Department of Agriculture, Agricultural Experiment Station, Circular 356, August 1943), p. 10.

21. Although the current estate managers of these respective wineries could corroborate the short-lived bottlings, neither could explain why their forebears had decided to do such a thing.

22. H. P. Olmo, "Our Principal Wine Grape Varieties, Present and Future," *American Journal of Enology,* vol. 5, no. 1 (1954), p. 19.

23. Frank Schoonmaker and Tom Marvel, *American Wines* (New York: Duell, Sloan and Peabody, 1941), pp. 136–7.

24. Frank Schoonmaker, *Dictionary of Wines,* ed. Tom Marvel (New York, Hastings House, 1951), p. 58. Interesting to note that he writes "see also Duriff" in the entry—but there is no entry for Duriff—the wild goose chase continues.

25. Frank Schoonmaker, *Encyclopedia of Wine,* 6th ed. (New York: Hastings House, 1977), p. 119–120.

26. Maynard A. Amerine and Vernon L. Singleton, *Wine: An Introduction for Americans* (Berkeley: University of California Press, 1965), p. 34.

27. Robert Balzer, *California Wine* (New York: Harry Abrams, 1978), p. 70.

28. Doris Muscatine, Maynard Amerine, and Bob Thompson, *The University of California Sotheby Book of California Wine* (Berkeley: University of California Press, 1984), p. 239.

29. Paul Draper, *History and Philosophy of Winemaking at Ridge Vineyards, 1970s-1990s* (Berkeley: University of California, The Bancroft Library, Regional Oral History Office, 1994), p. 73.

30. Foppiano Vineyards, *Grape Tidings,* vol. 11, no. 2 (Fall/Winter 1992).

31. Dennis Fife, "Petite Sirah: The Mystery Uncovered," *Wines & Vines,* vol. 81, no. 9 (September 2000), p.52,

32. In conversation with Carole Meredith, 6/12/2008.

33. Carole Meredith, "What is Petite Sirah?" *Practical Winery & Vineyard* (March/April, 1996), p. 23.

34. www.psiloveyou.org.

35. The TTB did recently streamline the spelling of the Sirah part of Petite Sirah, proclaiming that the term Petite Syrah was no longer a sanctioned variant.

CHAPTER 5. RHÔNE VARIETIES THROUGH PROHIBITION AND AFTER

1. Sweeping national legislation was passed with the 18th Amendment, over Woodrow Wilson's veto, on October 29, 1919.

2. Ruth Teiser and Catharine Harroun, "The Volstead Act, Rebirth, and Reboom," from The University of California/Sotheby's *Book of California Wine* (Berkeley: University of California Press, 1984), p. 55.

3. Ibid.

4. Thomas Pinney, *A History of Wine in America,* vol. 2 (Berkeley: University of California Press, 2007), p. 15.

5. Teiser and Harroun, pp. 50–51.

6. Pinney, p. 19.

7. Ibid., p. 27.

8. Charles Sullivan, *Napa Wine: A History from Mission Days to Present* (San Francisco: The Wine Appreciation Guild, 1994), p. 193.

9. M. A. Amerine and A. J. Winkler, "Composition and Quality of Musts and Wines of California Grapes," *Hilgardia,* vol. 15, no. 6 (February 1944).

10. Much of this account is derived from the University of California's Bancroft Library Oral History Center. Harold P. Olmo was interviewed in 1973 by Ruth Teiser; https://archive.org/details/plantgenetics000olmorich.

11. Ibid., p. 2.

12. Two of his more successful hybrids—Symphony, a cross between Grenache Gris and Muscat of Alexandria, and Ruby Cabernet, a cross between Carignane and Cabernet Sauvignon, are staples in Central Valley wine production.

13. Olmo, The Bancroft Library Oral History Center, p. v.

14. In conversation with Darrell Corti, 11/6/2008, and from *Patterson's Beverage Journal,* 1950s and 1960s.

15. In conversation with Darrell Corti, 11/6/2008.

16. None of these importers focused on Rhône variety wines the way Kermit Lynch would less than a decade later.

CHAPTER 6. THE PATH TO THE FIRST AMERICAN RHÔNE

1. In conversation with David Bruce, 1/2009.

2. In conversation with Joseph Phelps, 6/12/2008.

3. In conversation with Walter Schug, 11/11/2008.

4. In conversation with Bruce Neyers, 4/17/2009.

5. They also persuaded Milt Eisele, of Eisele Vineyard in Calistoga, to plant the grape for them, providing budwood from the same sources, establishing a Syrah program there that its current owners, Bart and Daphne Araujo, have maintained.

6. Unpublished manuscript by John Kongsgaard and W. M. Hin.

7. Joseph Phelps, The Bancroft Library Oral History Center.

8. In conversation with Charlie Wagner, 6/29/2009.

9. When Gary Eberle's selection at Estrella River and the strain found at McDowell became available, the Phelps team employed them, too.

10. In conversation with Craig Williams, 4/17/2009.

11. Around 1990, the team made a concerted effort to document their plantings and clonal sources, led by Williams and Markus Bokisch. Bokisch authored many of the reports that resulted in 1991; he was able not only to trace the original plantings of most Rhône varieties (Grenache, Carignane, Mataro, and Syrah), he isolated the four clones in use on the Phelps Ranch and explored a fifth, from a nursery called Pont de la Maye in Bordeaux, a vine that was never released due to its multiple weaknesses. For a brief time the team was under the impression that what Gary Eberle had planted in Paso Robles, at Estrella River, was in fact the same strain, Pont de la Maye. This has never been corroborated, however.

12. In conversation with Markus Bokisch, 5/17/2013.

13. Text courtesy Joseph Phelps Vineyards.

14. In conversation with Bruce Neyers, 4/17/2009.

CHAPTER 7. SYRAH'S PROUD FATHER

1. In conversation with Gary Eberle, 5/4/2008.

2. In conversation with Brian Croser, 5/23/2008.

3. On Darrell Corti's office wall is a Zinfandel label signed by Brian Croser in which Croser has written "Fucking good red!"

4. Tain l'Hermitage is the town at the base of Hermitage Hill, in the northern Rhône.

5. Eberle delivered a eulogy at Harold Olmo's funeral in 2006.

6. Corti recalls that after his first vintage at Estrella River, Gary Eberle called and said "I have to thank you very much; the only grapes I've been able to sell, this harvest, is the Muscat you told me to plant."

7. The name means "restful place" in the native Chumash language.

8. Lindquist wins the prize, hands down, for most devoted Dodger fan in the California wine community. His wine is served at Dodger Stadium, where it sells briskly.

9. Ethan, who went on to become a winemaker himself, making Syrahs under his own eponymous label.

10. In conversation with Bob Lindquist, 7/22/2008.

CHAPTER 8. OTHER PIONEERS

1. Karen Keehn was raised in nearby Ukiah and had never heard of McDowell Valley before their first visit.

2. In conversation with George Bursick, 4/23/2009.

3. Attempts were made at a red Grenache, but the old vine selection on the property proved to be less than satisfactory for red wine.

4. In conversation with Karen Keehn, 4/18/2009.

5. Well before its time for any place but Berkeley.

6. In conversation with John Buechsenstein, 4/23/2009.

7. In conversation with Lou Preston, 3/25/2010.

8. The blend has mostly been Syrah dominant—hence the name "Syrah Sirah." But there have been a few vintages where Petite Sirah is the lead wine, and in such cases Preston changed the name to "Sirah Syrah." The lords of labeling, the TTB, were never the wiser.

9. Into this milieu Mick Unti, with his father, has developed a 60-acre biodynamic estate, of which about 35 acres are planted to Rhône varieties, which are purchased by several Rhône practitioners statewide. Unti Vineyard may be the largest bastion of Rhône varieties that remains in the Dry Creek Valley.

10. In conversation with Bill Easton, 5/31/2009.

11. Mark Miller's restaurants included Fourth Street Grill and Santa Fe Café in Berkeley, and Coyote Café in Santa Fe.

12. Easton's Roussanne is said to have come from a hallowed site, Hermitage, spirited to him by none other than Davis enology student Jean-Louis Chave (who may or may not have planted Zinfandel on Hermitage Hill).

CHAPTER 9. RANDALL GRAHM

1. Indeed auctions, fundraisers, and special dinners were themselves new phenomena.

2. Randall Grahm, *Been Doon So Long: A Randall Grahm Vinthology* (Berkeley: University of California Press, 2009), p. 2.

3. In conversation with Randall Grahm, 1/07/2010.

4. In conversation with Ruth Grahm, 12/11/2009.

5. Though a '49 Comte de Vogüé Musigny in magnum came close.

6. Grahm, p. 53.

7. Then as now, there are no grades bestowed on the students at University of California, Santa Cruz, though students can request them for their transcripts.

8. The winery has been in the town of Santa Cruz since the late 1980s.

9. Grahm has always preferred the term "meridional" to describe the varieties he likes, a mildly archaic word used to describe the south, and especially the south of France.

10. As Grahm says in his anthology, finding nearly ten-year-old wines still on the shelf might have clued him to the dubious economic viability of his enterprise.

11. To this point, only one winery had produced multiple Rhône-style bottlings—McDowell Winery had started producing a Grenache Rosé, to supplement their Syrah, in 1980.

12. Old Telegram debuted as a 100% Mourvèdre in 1986.

13. John Livingstone-Learmonth and Melvyn C. H. Master, *Wines of the Rhône* (London: Faber & Faber Books, 1983), p. 178.

There is a kind of Flying Saucer theme running through the journalistic career of John Livingstone-Learmonth. His first published article, in 1969, appeared in a journal called the *Flying Saucer Review,* wherein he reported on the mysterious appearance of a field of giant mushrooms in the pampas of Argentina. Apparently in this mushroom patch authorities found scorch marks and evidence of some sort of tripod-legged craft, which may have landed nearby.

You could say he was predisposed to such information when in his initial research on the Rhône Valley he came upon a single line referencing the Flying Saucer decree in an account by Peter Hallgarten, an English importer of Rhône wines who had put together a small pamphlet on the region.

Grahm, meanwhile, claims that there have been documented UFO sightings in Bonny Doon well before his time.

14. "I've often thought I should get a royalty for that wine," says Livingstone-Learmonth.

15. While it's impossible to canvas all of the world's wine labels until 1985, this assumption is made with a strong working knowledge of the American wine scene to that point. However Frogs Leap Winery, whose label was also designed by Chuck House, had the word "Ribbit" printed on their corks as early as 1981.

16. Ironically Grahm's first efforts at labeling, his Vin Rouge and Vin Blanc labels, inspired by Gallimard editions of French novels, were dour and humorless.

17. On its label, Le Cigare Volant has always been billed as a "Red Wine," with a California appellation designation.

18. Via email with John Livingstone-Learmonth, 12/22/2009.

19. Grahm's collection of such writings, called *Been Doon So Long,* won a James Beard Foundation Award in 2010 in the Best Beverage Book category.

20. The following section was originally published in Patrick Comiskey, "A Vertical Dooniverse," Zesterdaily.com, Los Angeles, April 26, 2010.

21. In conversation with Edward Bowell, 6/26/2013.

22. To date, Bowell has identified nearly 600 planetary objects—objects held in the sun's gravitational pull—including more than 500 asteroids.

23. From Bowell's July 17, 1992 press release.

24. In conversation with Ruth and Randall Grahm, 6/27/2013.

25. Bowell gave several of his celestial objects names of artists he admired, invoking Geoffrey Chaucer, William Shakespeare, Anton Webern, Arnold Schoenberg, Aaron Copland, and Charles Dickens. As for vinous holdings, there were a few of these too: Barbaresco (#11473), Roero (#8075), and Barolo (#6590).

CHAPTER 10. STEVE EDMUNDS

1. From multiple conversations with Steve Edmunds, especially 6/12/2008 and 1/5/2009.

2. Just a few years later, an Edmunds wine provided a similar catalyst for Jean-Pierre Perrin of Chateau de Beaucastel. Perrin was still weighing the prospect of establishing Tablas Creek Winery, his partnership with Robert Haas that was devoted to Rhône varieties, and asked to meet with Edmunds so he could taste the '86 Brandlin Ranch Mourvèdre, which he had heard of. They met and tasted, and Perrin was so impressed with the wine he cites it as a tipping point for him, too.

CHAPTER 11. SEAN THACKREY

1. Allan Bree, "Do You Know the Way to Bolinas? An Afternoon with Sean Thackrey," July 2001, blogs.gangofpour.com (Detroit).
2. His first commercial success, in fact, was a Carneros Merlot, produced long before Merlot became a household word. It's plausible that if Merlot's popularity hadn't skyrocketed in the mid-eighties, he'd still be making it.
3. In conversation with Sean Thackrey, 10/15/2008. Patterson is the creative force behind a number of restaurants, past and present, in the Bay Area, including Elisabeth Daniel, Coi, Plum, and Il Cane Rosso.
4. In conversation with Sean Thackrey, 10/17/2008.
5. Bree.
6. Thackrey claims that the vineyard's makeup defied identification even by plant geneticist Carole Meredith, who politely refutes this claim. With her French colleague Jean-Michel Boursiquot, an expert on plant morphology, Meredith was able to identify ten different varieties, most of which were Petite Sirah, but at least a few were Syrah.

CHAPTER 12. MANFRED KRANKL

1. In conversation with Manfred Krankl, 1/20/2009.
2. Elin McCoy, *The Emperor of Wine: The Rise of Robert M. Parker Jr., and the Reign of American Taste* (New York: Ecco Press, 2005), p. 226.
3. The waiting list to get on the list to receive wine is now nine years.
4. Several of Krankl's assistants and serving staff who assisted in the wine program have gone on play important roles in the LA wine scene, including George Cossette, Randy Clement, David Rosoff, Jay Perrin, Claudio Blotta, and Matthias Pippig.
5. With its ever-changing labels, Sine Qua Non certainly reflected this spirit.
6. In conversation with Manfred Krankl, 9/20/2010.
7. Dujac and Jayer are two very important Burgundy domaines.
8. *The Wine Advocate*, no. 190, August 2010.
9. McCoy, p. 227.

CHAPTER 13. VIOGNIER

1. Via email with John Alban, 10/22/2009.
2. Josh Jensen, in conversation, says that when he put forward his initial petition for Foundation Plant Material Services (FPMS) to introduce Viognier into the country, he was told that Viognier had been introduced to the California Agricultural Experiment Station in 1910, but no record of this planting exists.
3. Kermit Lynch, *Inspiring Thirst* (Berkeley: Ten Speed Press, 2004), p. 5.
4. This perception caused Bonny Doon's Randall Grahm, notably, to avoid this competitive corner of the market in deference to Roussanne—a fateful decision.
5. The centerpiece of that dinner was two bottles in Selleck's collection of older Beaulieu Vineyard Pinot Noir, which Tchelistcheff had often referred to as the best Pinots he had ever made.

6. The Foundation Plant Material Service name was changed in 2003 to Foundation Plant Services (FPS) to reflect an expansion of services offered by the agency.

7. Jensen went to the Paris food emporium Fauchon and bought Vernay some foie gras and Cognac in thanks.

8. Two of these, the Remaily Seedless and the Marquis, are grown in the eastern United States to this day, where they're appreciated for their winter hardiness.

9. Viognier was evaluated for New York's vineyard regions by Bruce Reisch, a plant scientist who still works at Geneva Station, who quickly determined that the vine would have a difficult time with East Coast winters.

10. Luper's version of the story includes neither the Montrachet cuttings nor the Camembert.

11. He is now a winemaker in the Douro, Portugal.

12. Did Smith ever consider making Viognier himself? "I was already making four varieties at Smith-Madrone," he says—these included Cabernet Sauvignon, Chardonnay, Merlot, and Riesling—"I needed a fifth like a hole in my head." He and his brother thought that if Luper didn't make his claim that they might make a small amount for the Napa Valley auction, but this never happened.

13. The production was so tiny that Minor himself doesn't consider the wine a commercial release, even if, technically, it was the first in the country.

14. Alban kept Pinchon's identity a secret until well after his death in 1990, long after most of what he'd predicted had come to pass, and most were at peace with the outcome of events.

15. Alban has declined to identify the sources for what were several cuttings from the Rhône Valley.

16. The better, too, to maintain his contracting business, where he was responsible for tens of thousands of supply items for the U.S. government. He boasts that he sold nearly two million paper shredders to the government, including the one in use on Air Force One.

17. With the possible exception of Petit Manseng, the Jurançon-based variety which is being planted in minute quantities currently.

CHAPTER 14. THE PURLOINED RHÔNE

1. In conversation with Randall Grahm, 1/7/2009.

2. In conversation with Gary Eberle, 4/29/2010.

3. In conversation with Josh Jensen, 9/10/2008. Nursery employees referred to the project's vines as "voyager" since Viognier was too difficult to pronounce.

4. Via email with Jerry Luper, 9/29/2009; in conversation with Stu Smith, 10/3/2009.

5. In conversation with Michael Michaud, 7/12/2012.

6. Via email with Bill Easton, 8/6/2012.

7. If we are to believe that Alban would settle for nothing less than the finest material the Rhône Valley and Provence had to offer, then the following vineyards would have been the ones whose plant material he'd have tried to acquire. For Syrah: Domaine Jean-Louis

Chave, M. Chapoutier, possibly a Côte-Rôtie source like Guigal. For Grenache: Chateau Rayas, perhaps Chateau de Beaucastel. For Viognier: Chateau-Grillet, Coteaux du Chery, perhaps Domaine Niero-Pinchon. For Roussanne: Chateau de Beaucastel, perhaps Domaine Jean-Louis Chave.

8. In conversation with Randall Grahm, 9/9/2008.
9. In conversation with Randall Grahm, 6/15/2008.
10. Lynn Alley, "Vine Mix-Up Lands California Winemaker and Grower in Court," *Wine Spectator*, October 31, 2000. Kunde, who is retired and in ill health, has refused to speak with me, and has not cooperated with this account.
11. In conversation with Charlie Wagner, 6/26/2009.
12. Phone conversation with Charlie Wagner, 6/26/2009.
13. Frank Prial, "Wine Talk: A Tangle of Vines and Lawsuits," *New York Times*, November 1, 2000.
14. Ibid.
15. Ibid.
16. In 2005 University of California Press published John Livingstone-Learmonth's *The Wines of the Northern Rhône*, a thorough rewrite of his 1983 material covering the northern regions.
17. John Livingstone-Learmouth, *The Wines of the Rhône*, 2nd ed. (London: Faber & Faber, 1983), p. 208.
18. This conversation with Pierre Pelissier occurred on 3/8/2009.
19. Pelissier knew of only one Chateauneuf producer who had Viognier: Mont Redon. At the time only a small number of southern Rhône producers had planted Viognier, including one discussed on that day's visit in 2009, Domaine Sainte-Anne, in Saint-Gervais.
20. Via email with John Alban, 6/23/14.
21. Unnamed Central Coast source.

CHAPTER 15. TABLAS CREEK

1. Robert M. Parker, Jr., *The Wines of the Rhône Valley and Provence* (New York: Simon & Schuster, 1987), p. 232.
2. In fact it was Raymond Baudouin, with the assistance of Frank Schoonmaker, who was able to convince producers with exceptional terroirs to bottle their wines separately. But the practice was still undeveloped at the time.
3. Beaucastel sold as much as 80% of its fruit to négociants in certain vintages.
4. This remains more true here than any other market on earth, especially in the world's wine-producing regions, which tend to be understandably chauvinistic about their wines but which results in a fairly provincial selection. Only in the U.S. is the selection of wines for consumers truly global.
5. Leaving nothing to chance, Beaucastel also imported its own rootstock.
6. It has long been assumed that Chateau de Beaucastel is the source of the plant material now known as the Tablas clones. That is not entirely the case: among the clones imported through Beaucastel for the Tablas Creek project is material that did not come

from Beaucastel at all, but from ENTAV. ENTAV is responsible for releasing plant material from French vineyards, and typically assigns an index number to a clone, once it passes quarantine and disease treatments. At the time of the Beaucastel importation, however, the selected clones had not yet received their index number. It is difficult, then, to verify which clones are from Beaucastel and which are from another source culled from ENTAV.

7. Eventually the entire operation would be assumed by Novavine Nurseries in Sonoma, in a leasing arrangement with the Tablas partners—after this, the material was donated to FPS where it will be a permanent part of the material stocks the service offers to nurseries.

8. Only Syrah is trained on a lyre in Chateauneuf-du-Pape, because its shoots tend to project horizontally and not vertically.

CHAPTER 16. THE AMERICAN RHÔNE IN WASHINGTON STATE

1. This account is taken from Ronald Irvine with Walter J. Clore, *The Wine Project: Washington State's Winemaking History* (Vashon, WA: Sketch Publications, 1997), p. 407.

2. Paul Gregutt describes a visit to a hillside planting on Snipes Mountain in the Yakima Valley where, he says, he encountered Muscat vines the size of trees, believed to have been planted in 1917, presumably a remnant of this original Bridgman planting. Paul Gregutt, *Washington Wines and Wineries: The Essential Guide,* 2nd ed. (Berkeley: University of California Press, 2010), p. 37.

3. Clore was in fact crowned "Mr. Asparagus" by the Washington State Asparagus Association for his contributions to the industry.

4. "A Summary of Experimental Testing of Grape Varieties for Wine in Washington," *American Journal of Viticulture and Enology,* vol. 25, no. 2 (1974), p. 94.

5. W.J. Clore, C.H. Nagel, V.P. Brummond, and G.H. Carter, "Ten Years of Grape Variety Responses and Winemaking Trials in Central Washington," Washington Agricultural Research Station Circular no. 823. (Pullman: Washington State University, 1976), p. 23.

6. Irvine, p. 221.

7. Leon D. Adams, *The Wines of America* (San Francisco: San Francisco Book Company/ Houghton Mifflin, 1973), p. 335.

8. Now Columbia Winery—they changed their name in 1983.

9. Adams, p. 335.

10. Gregutt, p. 6.

11. Leon D. Adams, "The Wines of Washington," a promotional brochure commissioned by Chateau Ste. Michelle (undated, mid-1970s), p. 4.

12. Interview of David Lake by Julie Kerssen (Seattle: Museum of History and Industry, January 2004), drawn from seattlehistory.org, p. 19.

13. In conversation with Bob Betz, 4/1/2012.

14. It's been given two names, the Chapel of the Monsignor, and the Chapel of the Vines.

15. McCrea has played with many jazz greats, including Joe Henderson, Eddie Gale, and Weather Report, which included Joe Zawinul and Wayne Shorter. His band, Noema, was often referred to as the Weather Report of the West Coast.

16. Glen Fiona's 1998 vintage was marred by some hygiene issues, causing a drop in interest; Figgins fought to reestablish the reputation of his brand, but by 2000 was no longer directly involved. Figgins would go on to have an especially peripatetic decade working on various winery projects until turning to spirits, founding Ellensberg Distillery in 2008.

17. The estate currently has eighty-five-year-old Pinot Meunier vines.

18. The pH of fruit coming from the Rocks is usually quite high, resulting in a richer wine.

CHAPTER 17. THE BIRTH OF THE RHÔNE RANGERS

1. Though it has moved from its original location, Lalime's is still a popular East Bay venue. Cindy Lalime and Haig Krikorian have owned five other area restaurants, whose wine lists still reflect a devotion to the Rhône Valley, and to its American adherents.

2. In conversation with John McCready, 12/11/2008.

3. Press release, East Bay Wine Works, December 1987.

4. Unpublished letter, 2/16/1988.

5. In correspondence with Robert Parker, 10/21/2010.

6. Robert A. Parker, Jr., *The Wines of the Rhône Valley*, revised and expanded edition (New York: Simon & Schuster, 1997), p. 438.

7. Robert A. Parker, Jr., *The Wines of the Rhône Valley and Provence* (New York: Simon & Schuster, 1987), p. 13.

8. Ibid., pp. 14–15.

9. In correspondence with Robert Parker, 10/21/2010.

10. *The Wine Advocate*, no. 57 (June 30, 1988), p. 12.

11. Ibid., p. 12.

12. Ibid., p. 13.

13. Eleanor and Ray Heald, "The Rhône Rangers: An Adventurous Band of California Winemakers Dare to Be Different," *Wine & Spirits Magazine*, vol. 8, no. 2 (April 1989), p. 6.

14. Harvey Steiman, "How the Rhône Rangers' Wines Rate," *Wine Spectator*, vol. 45, no. 1 (April 1989), p. 27.

15. In conversation with Harvey Steiman, 12/1/2009.

16. *Wine Spectator*, vol. 45, no. 1 (April 1989), p. 20.

17. Ibid., p. 27.

CHAPTER 18. THE ACADEMIC BACKUP

1. In conversation with Steve Edmunds, 1/5/2009.

2. In conversation with Robert Mayberry, 8/3/2009.

3. Robert W. Mayberry, *Wines of the Rhône Valley: A Guide to Origins* (Totowa, NJ: Rowman & Littlefield, 1987), p. 87.

4. Ibid.

5. In conversation with John Buechsenstein, 8/3/2009.

6. In conversation with Stephen Grant, 5/12/2011.

7. Taken from "Place and World," Mayberry's address in acceptance of the Ordre du Merit Agricole, given in 1998; published in *Grand Valley Review,* vol. 19, no. 1 (1999), p. 16.
8. In conversation with John Buechsenstein, 10/23/2014.

CHAPTER 19. THE BRIDGE FROM CALIFORNIA TO FRANCE

1. Pierrefeu was quoting a colleague, one Professor Tremoliere, from Paris.
2. From unpublished colloquium transcripts. p. 13.

CHAPTER 20. HOSPICE DU RHÔNE

1. In conversation with John Alban, 5/12/2005.
2. In conversation with Mat Garretson, 12/11/2008.
3. He singled out his bride-to-be in the program, thus: "Mat would like to especially thank his soon-to-be wife, Anita, whom he will marry May 15th [1993]. Why he decided to host a Viognier seminar and get married in one week attests to his obsession with Viognier . . . Anita's patience and understanding in him doing so attests to how lucky he is." They divorced in 1994.
4. In conversation with Barbara Ensrud, 10/25/2009.
5. Goin is now chef/owner of several Los Angeles restaurants, including Lucques, A.O.C., and Tavern.
6. Reprinted in *Viognier: A View from the Vineyards,* Viognier Guild pamphlet, 1994.
7. In conversation with Bill Craig, 6/8/2012.
8. Guigal finally relented in 2008.
9. It was Gangloff and Villard's first trip to the United States; Villard had never been on an airplane before.
10. Partly from the camaraderie forged here in California, Villard, Gaillard, and Cuilleron have a négociant business in the northern Rhône, which they call Vins de Vienne.
11. Via email with Francois Villard, 11/15/2015.
12. Via email with Yves Gangloff, 11/23/2015.
13. A decurion was a member of the Roman colonial senate.

CHAPTER 21. THE RISE AND FALL OF AMERICAN SYRAH

1. From 2000 to 2005 each grew further still: Syrah plantings increased by 25%, from 13,000 to 17,500 acres, while Viognier grew from 1,750 to 2,325 acres, a comparable percentage increase.
2. Ridge's early adoption of other lesser varieties occurred even sooner than with Syrah: Petite Sirah, Carignane, and Mataro bottlings preceded a varietal Syrah production by a half-decade.
3. And to a lesser extent Jancis Robinson and Steven Tanzer.
4. Matt Kramer, "The Next Really Big Red," *Wine Spectator,* September 30, 2003, p. 36.
5. On this basis, Kramer wrote, Pinot Noir "will be popular, but it will never be Really Big."

6. According to James Halliday, Busby wanted nothing less than to supply Australia with the entire catalog of the vines on hand at the Montpellier Botanical Garden, some 570 varieties in all. He managed to collect more than 400; 363 survived, many labeled with creative spellings or altogether unrecognizable monikers, like "sevent noir to l'Herault," and "passadoule Bougie."

7. *The Age* (Melbourne), July 18, 1989, p. 27.

8. In conversation with Daryl Groom, 2/9/2014.

9. Shroeter was frequently mistaken for Australian at such times.

10. In conversation with John Gay, 2/6/2014.

11. In conversation with Dan Berger, 3/14/2014

12. Yellow Tail's official name is set in all lowercased letters and enclosed in brackets, as [yellow tail].

13. Frank Prial, "The Wallaby that Roared Across the Australian Wine Industry," in his Wine Talk column, *New York Times*, April 23, 2006.

14. Campbell Mattinson, *Why the French Hate Us* (Prahran, Victoria, Australia: The Wine Front, a division of Hardie Grant Books, 2007), p. 59.

15. Michael Steinberger, "Not Such a G'Day: How Yellow Tail Crushed the Australian Wine Industry," slate.com, April 8, 2009.

16. In conversation with Simon Graves, 12/18/2013.

17. In conversation with Ian Shepherd, 1/24/2014.

18. They would take their company public in 1993, so expansion was no doubt part of their plans.

19. In conversation with Ken Brown, 11/14/2013.

20. In conversation with Lee Nordlund, 12/5/13.

21. Via email with Robert Parker, 10/21/2010.

22. Elin McCoy, *The Emperor of Wine: The Rise of Robert M. Parker Jr., and the Reign of American Taste* (New York: Ecco Press, 2005), p. 204.

23. *The Wine Advocate*, no. 108, December 1996.

24. University of California, Davis is a perennial nemesis in the Parker gallery of enemies, but just who among its faculty is guilty of these offenses is never clear.

25. It isn't at all clear whom Parker is referring to here, other than his competition.

26. One critic I know described their texture as "glue mixed with jam."

27. Steinberger, slate.com, April 8, 2009.

28. Andrew Jefford, "Syrah Worldwide," delivered at the Syrah Worldwide conference and tasting held in Rome, April 2004.

29. In annual interviews with sommeliers for the *Wine & Spirits* restaurant poll, dozens of sommeliers continue to cite the movie *Sideways* as a recurring theme in Pinot Noir orders in restaurants.

CHAPTER 22. WHAT WE TALK ABOUT WHEN WE TALK ABOUT AMERICAN SYRAH

1. The following section was originally published in *Wines & Spirits Magazine*, 2011.

2. The winery's name was shortened to Failla after a legal skirmish with Jordan Winery.

3. Jordan's brief stint with Helen Turley and her partner at Marcassin, John Wetlaufer, had led to the gig at Turley.

4. Eric Asimov, "Is There Still Hope for Syrah?" *New York Times,* June 1, 2010. I am also quoted in this article, laying out some of the issues covered in this chapter.

5. The campaign committed some egregious punmanship (e.g., "pneumonia's last hurrah") in the process.

6. Amy Christine, "The Decline of Varietally Labeled U.S. Syrah: A Comparative Approach for Determining the Perceptions and Preferences of American Consumers for U.S. Syrah" (Unpublished thesis, The Institute of Masters of Wine, 2013), pp. 4–5.

7. "In Pursuit of Balance," a much more enduring marketing effort in the service of Chardonnay and Pinot Noir, has persisted to this day, inspired by this original seminar on Syrah.

8. This was the unfortunate occasion for Lindquist's profane utterance about recalcitrant Syrah sales representatives.

9. "Rhône Wines at a Crossroads," *San Francisco Chronicle,* July 23, 2012.

10. Arguably, this is true for Grenache as well.

11. Among whites, Picpoul and Vermentino (Rolle) may also play this role.

12. Jon Bonné, "Grenache Displays its Stunning Side," *San Francisco Chronicle,* March 29, 2013.

13. Perhaps the worst of the groaners, however, comes from South Africa, in the blend known as "Goats do Roam."

14. The brand was purchased by the Agustin Huneeus family in 2009.

15. It is also no longer an occasion to "rough it"; there are excursion packages worth tens of thousands of dollars that allow participants to live in relative luxury and air-conditioned comfort in RV spas.

16. Two wine booths served Cabernet.

INDEX

Photographs and illustrations are gathered after page 138. They are indexed using figure numbers.

San Francisco Bay Area food and wine scene, xi–xiii, 5–12, 99; American Rhône producers' early ties to, 10–11; Bay Area wine retailers other than Lynch, 10–11, 98–99, 118, 124; Lynch and his wine shop, 6–7, 8–10, 11, 12. *See also specific restaurants and wine retailers*

San Francisco Merchant, 39, 40, 43, *fig3*. *See also Pacific Wine and Spirit Review*

Sangiovese, 176

Santa Clara Valley: Bonny Doon's Cigare Volant and, 112; Carignane and, 24; David Bruce Grenaches, 71–72; early viticulture in, 19, 35, 38, 40, 44, 49, 50, 52; Grenache in, 19, 44, 71–72; Mourvèdre in, 22; Petite Sirah in, 52

Santa Cruz and the Santa Cruz Mountains, 107. *See also* Bonny Doon Vineyard

Santa Maria, 18. *See also* Bien Nacido Vineyard

Santa Ynez Valley, 85, 171. *See also* Ballard Canyon; Zaca Mesa

Saralee's Vineyard, 150

Sauer, Mike, 183–85, 194–95, *fig19*. *See also* Red Willow Vineyard

Sauvignon Blanc, 151, 153, 238

Saxum Vineyards, 20, 175, 258, 265. *See also* Smith, Justin

Schaeffer, Dennis, 225

Schlitz Brewing Company, 238

Schmidt, Arthur, xiii, 124, 125, 126

Schmidt Vineyard, xii–xiii, 124–25, 126

Schneider, Anna, 28

Schoonmaker, Frank, 6, 55–56, 75, 201, 275n24, 282n3

Schug, Walter, 54, 73–74, 77, *fig7*

screw caps, 104, 105

self-importation, 156. *See also* clonal selections; *specific grape varieties*

Selfridge, Tom, 80

Selleck, George, 143, 280n5(ch13)

Seppelt Winery, 75

Serene, Crabb on, 50–51. *See also* Syrah

Serine, 53, 126

Seven Hills, 192

Seven Peaks, 242–43, 245

Shenandoah Vineyards, 98. *See also* Sobon, Leon

Shepherd, Ian, 243, 245

Sherry-Lehmann, 169, 170

Shiraz, 56, 237; Australian-influenced California Syrahs, 238–39, 240, 242–43, 245–46; Australian Shiraz wines, 81, 227, 237–38, 240–42; California Shiraz wines, 238, 239, 240–45; Figgins and, 188; FPMS Shiraz clone, 75, 83; Shiraz/Syrah grape in Australia, 16, 75, 81, 237

Shorb, J. DeBarth, *fig3*

Shroeter, Mick, 239, 245, 286n9

Sichel, Peter Allen, 188

Sideways (film), 234, 249–50, 286n29

Sierra Foothills, Rhône varieties in, 97–99, 121. *See also* Domaine de la Terre Rouge; Edmunds St. JOhn; Sierra Vista

Sierra Vista Vineyards and Winery, 13, 97–98, 226. *See also* McCready, John

Sievert, Larry, 186

Silver Oak, 73

Silverton, Gail, 129

Silverton, Nancy, 129

Simi Winery, 87, 92

Simon, André, 201

Simple French Food (Olney), 7, 8

Sine Qua Non, 128, 132, 133–36, 247, 258, 280n5(ch12); as cult winery, 127–28, 136, 137, 280n3(ch12); current/recent wines, 265, 266; fruit sources, 132, 136, 176; Grenaches, 20; Syrahs, 127–28, 135, 136, 265; white wines, 136, 266; wine names and label designs, 134–35, 280n5(ch12). *See also* Krankl, Manfred

Singer, Stephen, 124, 262

Singer and Foy, 124

Singleton, Vernon, 56, 63

Sirac, 42

Sirac Noir, 39

Sirah, 42. *See also* Syrah

Sirah Syrah/Sirah Syrah (Preston), 96, 278n8(ch8)

Smith, Bill, 78, 142, 145–47, 150, 218, 225. *See also* La Jota

Smith, Charles, 191–92, 193, 247

Smith, James Berry, 20, 175

Smith, Joan, 145–46, 147. *See also* La Jota

Smith, Justin, 20, 175, 247, 249

Smith, Steve, 150–51

Smith, Stu, 144, 145, 157, 281n12